# THE IMMUNE SYSTEM
a course on the
molecular and cellular basis
of immunity

# THE IMMUNE SYSTEM
## a course on the
## molecular and cellular basis
## of immunity

M.J.HOBART

MA, PhD, VetMB
Lecturer in
Immunology

IAN McCONNELL

MA, PhD, BVMS
Senior Lecturer in
Immunology

Royal Postgraduate Medical School, London

THIRD PRINTING

BLACKWELL SCIENTIFIC PUBLICATIONS

OXFORD LONDON EDINBURGH MELBOURNE

© 1975 Blackwell Scientific Publications
Osney Mead, Oxford OX2 OEL
8 John Street, London WC1N 2HY
9 Forrest Road, Edinburgh EH1 2QH
P.O. Box 9, North Balwyn, Victoria, Australia

ISBN 0 632 00157 7

First published 1975
Revised reprint 1976
Reprinted 1978

Distributed in the United States of America by
J. B. Lippincott Company, Philadelphia
and in Canada by
J. B. Lippincott Company of Canada Ltd., Toronto.

Printed in Great Britain at
the Alden Press, Oxford
and bound by
Kemp Hall Bindery, Oxford

# Contributors

**Peter Alexander** Chester Beatty Research Institute, Sutton, Surrey

**Susan Bright** Department of Pathology, University of Cambridge

**David Brown** Royal Postgraduate Medical School, University of London

**Max Cooper** University of Alabama Medical Center, Birmingham, Alabama

**Peter Démant** Institute of Experimental Biology and Genetics, Czechoslovak Academy of Science

**Arnold Feinstein** A.R.C. Institute of Animal Physiology, Babraham, Cambridge

**Hilliard Festenstein** Tissue Immunology Unit, London Hospital Medical School

**Rodney Harris** Department of Human Genetics, University of Manchester Medical School

**Mike Hobart** Royal Postgraduate Medical School, University of London

**Peter Lachmann** Royal Postgraduate Medical School, University of London

**Ian McConnell** Royal Postgraduate Medical School, University of London

**Alan Munro** Department of Pathology, University of Cambridge

**Christopher Spry** Royal Postgraduate Medical School, University of London

**Colin Stern** Royal Postgraduate Medical School, University of London

**Michael Taussig** Department of Pathology, University of Cambridge

**Helgi Valdimarsson** Royal Postgraduate Medical School, University of London

v

# Contents

EDITORS' PREFACE, xix

ADVICE TO READERS, xxiii


I       **IMMUNOCHEMISTRY**
        Preamble to Section I, 1


1       IMMUNOGLOBULINS AS PROTEINS, 2
        M. J. HOBART

1.1     Introduction, 2
1.1.1   Basic anatomy, 2

1.2     Heterogeneity of immunoglobulins, 3
1.2.1   Light chain types, 3
1.2.2   Heavy chain classes, 6
1.2.3   Subclasses of chains, 6
1.2.4   Allotypes, 6
1.2.5   Idiotypes, 8
1.2.6   Other polypeptide components of immunoglobulins, 9

1.3     The variable region, 9
1.3.1   V-region subgroups, 9
1.3.2   Hypervariable regions, 11

1.4     Biological activities, 11
1.4.1   Complement fixation, 11
1.4.2   Transfer across membranes, 12
1.4.3   Cell-binding immunoglobulins, 13

1.5     Integration and biosynthesis, 13
1.5.1   Allelic exclusion, isotypic and idiotypic selection, 14
1.5.2   Integration, 14
1.5.3.  Synthesis, assembly and secretion, 14


2       GENETICS OF IMMUNOGLOBULIN DIVERSITY, 16
        A. J. MUNRO

2.1     Introduction, 16

2.2     Alleles, tandem genes and linkage, 16
2.2.1   The distinction between alleles and tandem genes, 16
2.2.2   Linkage, 16

2.3     Arrangement of immunoglobulin genes, 17

2.4     The number of variable region genes: arguments from proteins, 19
2.4.1   How many 'genes' do we 'need'?, 19
2.4.2   How many proteins do we make?, 19

2.5     Germ line versus somatic mutation, 20

2.6     The number of germ-line genes: annealing studies with
        nucleic acids, 21


3       THE THREE-DIMENSIONAL STRUCTURE
        OF IMMUNOGLOBULINS, 24
        A. FEINSTEIN

3.1     Introduction, 24

3.2     Electron microscopy, 24

3.3     X-ray crystallographic studies of immunoglobulins, 31

3.4     A stochastic approach, 32
3.4.1   Sequence data, 34
3.4.2   Carbohydrate, 34
3.4.3   Dissociation of IgM, 34

3.5     Rules for immunoglobulin model building, 35

3.6     A model for IgM, 36

3.7     Discussion, 37


4       THE ANTIBODY COMBINING SITE, 42
        M. J. TAUSSIG

4.1     Introduction, 42

4.2     Antibody affinity, 42
4.2.1   Measurement of affinity, 44
4.2.2   Avidity, 47

4.3     Size and specificity of the combining site, 43
4.3.1   Size, 48
4.3.2   Specificity, 49

4.4     The structure of the combining site, 51
4.4.1   Sequence information, 51
4.4.2   Affinity labelling, 51
4.4.3   X-ray diffraction data, 54


5       THE IMMUNOCHEMISTRY OF COMPLEMENT, 56
        P. J. LACHMANN

5.1     Introduction, 56
5.1.1   History, 56
5.1.2   Glossary of complement terminology, 56
5.1.3   The complement components, 57
5.1.4   The activation of the complement system, 57

5.2     The generation of C3 converting enzymes, 59
5.2.1   The 'classical' C3 convertase, 59
5.2.2   The 'alternative pathway', 59
5.2.3   The C3b feedback cycle, 64
5.2.4   The cobra venom factor, 65

5.3     The C3 step, 67
5.3.1   Activation, 67
5.3.2   Inactivation, 67
5.3.3   Control of C3 biosynthesis, 68

5.4     The terminal complement sequence, 70
5.4.1   Reactive lysis, 70
5.4.2   Generation of the lytic lesion, 70

5.5     The complement lesion on membranes, 71
5.5.1   The lytic event, 73

5.6     Kinetics, 73

5.7     Summary, 74

6     THE EVOLUTION AND GENETICS
       OF ANTIBODY AND COMPLEMENT, 76
       M. J. HOBART

6.1     Introduction, 76
6.1.1   Evolutionary origins, 76

6.2     Gene duplication, 77
6.2.1   Polyploid duplication, 77
6.2.2   Tandem duplication, 78

6.3     The evolution of immunoglobulins, 79
6.3.1   Evolution of heavy-chain classes, 81
6.3.2   Evolution of heavy chain subclasses, 81

6.4     Allotypes and sporadic events, 81
6.4.1   Human heavy chain allotypes, 81
6.4.2   'Lepore' heavy chains, 86
6.4.3   Heavy chain disease proteins, 86

6.5     Complement, 87
6.5.1   Complement deficiencies, 87
6.5.2   Complement allotypes (polymorphisms), 87
6.5.3   Complement evolution: a wild speculation, 89


II       IMMUNOBIOLOGY
        Preamble to Section II, 91

II.1     Introduction, 91

II.2     Antigens, 91
II.2.1   Rigidity, 91
II.2.2   Valency, 91
II.2.3   Hapten-carriers, 92

II.3     Antigen recognition and the allergic response, 93
II.3.1   Initial phase, 94
II.3.2   Central phase, 94
II.3.3   Effector phase, 94

II.4     Homeostatic control of the allergic response, 96

II.5     Lymphoid tissues, 96
II.5.1   Primary lymphoid organs, 97
II.5.2   Secondary lymphoid organs, 97


7      T AND B LYMPHOCYTES, 98
      I. MCCONNELL

7.1     Introduction, 98

7.2.     Lymphocyte markers, 98
7.2.1   Alloantigens and heteroantigens, 98
7.2.2   Lymphocyte surface receptors, 99
7.2.3   Surface immunoglobulin, 103
7.2.4   Mitogen responsiveness, 105
7.2.5   Analysis of lymphocyte populations, 105

7.3     Expression of surface markers during
       lymphocyte differentiation, 107

7.4     Recognition of antigen by lymphocytes, 108
7.4.1   Techniques for identifying individual antigen-binding cells, 108
7.4.2   Techniques for analyzing antigen-specific cell populations, 109

7.5     Characterization of the B lymphocyte antigen receptor, 109
7.5.1   Immunoglobulin nature, 109
7.5.2   Class, subclass and allelic exclusion of
       surface immunoglobulin, 111
7.5.3   Distribution of cell surface immunoglobulin, 112

*Contents*

7.6     Characterization of the T lymphocyte antigen receptor, 114
7.6.1   Surface immunoglobulin, 114
7.6.2   Characterization of soluble specific factors from T cells, 115
7.6.3   Specificity of antigen recognition by T cells, 116
7.6.4   Immune response (Ir) genes and T cells, 116

8       THEORIES OF ANTIBODY FORMATION, 120
        P. J. LACHMANN

8.1     Introduction, 120

8.2     Selective versus instructive theories, 120
8.2.1   Ehrlich's selective hypothesis, 120
8.2.2.  Instructive or template hypothesis, 120
8.2.3   Clonal selection hypothesis, 122
8.2.4   Accurate sample hypothesis, 122

8.3     The accurate sample hypothesis, 122
8.3.1–8.3.6 Tenets of the hypothesis, 122–124

8.4     The problem of antibody diversity, 124
8.4.1   The generator of diversity (GOD), 124
8.4.2   The epitopic universe, 125
8.4.3   The antibody repertoire, 125
8.4.4   One or two generators of diversity, 125

8.5     The origin of GOD, 126
8.5.1   Somatic or germ line, 126
8.5.2   Histocompatibility antigens as the driving stimulus to antibody diversity, 127
8.5.3   The idiotype paradox and the network theory, 127

9       CELL INTERACTIONS IN THE ALLERGIC RESPONSE, 130
        I. McCONNELL

9.1     Introduction, 130

9.2     Experimental models, 130
9.2.1   The adoptive transfer system, 130
9.2.2   Graft versus host reactions (GVH), 130

9.3     Cell populations, 131
9.3.1   T lymphocyte populations, 132
9.3.2   T lymphocyte enriched populations, 133
9.3.3   B lymphocyte populations, 133
9.3.4   B mice, 133

9.4     *In vitro* systems for antibody formation, 134
9.4.1   Mishell and Dutton culture, 135
9.4.2   Marbrook culture, 135
9.4.3   Jerne plaque assay, 135

9.5     Lymphocyte cooperation, 136
9.5.1   Restoration of response to SRBC in immunologically unresponsive mice, 136
9.5.2   Analysis of the response to hapten-carrier conjugates, 139

9.6     Possible mechanisms of lymphocyte cooperation: I—specific cooperation, 141
9.6.1   Hypothesis, 141
9.6.2   Experimental evidence, 142

9.7     Mechanisms of lymphocyte cooperation: II—non-specific cooperation, 143
9.7.1   Hypothesis, 143
9.7.2   *In vitro* experimental evidence, 145
9.7.3   *In vivo* studies, 146

9.8     *In vivo* significance of cell cooperation, 147

*Contents*

9.9    Other levels of cell interaction, 148

9.9.1   T cell suppression, 148
9.9.2   T–T cell interactions, 148
9.9.3   Macrophage–T cell interaction, 148

9.10   Cell membrane requirements in cell interactions, 149


10     IMMUNOLOGICAL TOLERANCE
       AND UNRESPONSIVENESS, 152
       P. J. LACHMANN

10.1    Introduction, 152
10.1.1  Historical, 152

10.2    Factors promoting tolerance induction, 153
10.2.1  State of the lymphon, 153
10.2.2  Properties of antigen, 153

10.3    Tolerance at the cellular level, 155
10.3.1  Tolerance induction in T and B cells, 155

10.4    T cell mediated suppression and regulation, 157
10.4.1  Suppression via the B cell receptor, 157
10.4.2  Suppression via antigen, 158
10.4.3  Summary, 159

10.5    Tolerogenic interactions between B cell receptor and antigen, 159
10.5.1  Blocking of B cell receptors by antigen, 159
10.5.2  Influence of epitope density, 159

10.6    Blocking factors, 161
10.6.1  Immune complex blocking factors, 161

10.7    Blocking factors in vivo, 161

10.8    Conclusion and prejudices, 162


11     ANTIGENIC COMPETITION, 165
       M. J. TAUSSIG

11.1    Introduction, 165

11.2    Mechanisms of antigenic competition, 165
11.2.1  Sequential competition, 167
11.2.2  Intra- and intermolecular competition, 169

11.3    Models for intramolecular and intermolecular competition, 173
11.3.1  Intramolecular competition, 173
11.3.2  Intermolecular competition, 175

11.4    Conclusion, 177


12     EFFECTOR MECHANISMS
       IN CELLULAR IMMUNITY, 179
       H. VALDIMARSSON

12.1    Introduction, 179
       The effector cells of cell-mediated immunity, 179

12.2    Mononuclear phagocytes, 180
12.2.1  Origin and maturation, 180
12.2.2  Lysosomal enzymes, 181
12.2.3  Macrophage activation, 181
12.2.4  Microbicidal mechanisms, 181

12.3    K cells, 182
       Lymphocyte activation and its consequences, 183

12.4    Lymphokines, 185
12.4.1  Classification and characterization of lymphokines, 185
12.4.2  Production of lymphokines, 188

xi                                                      *Contents*

12.5    Cytotoxicity, 189
12.5.1  Direct cytotoxic activity of lymphoid cells, 189
12.5.2  Allograft cytotoxicity (type 1), 189
12.5.3  Tumour antigen-induced cytotoxicity (type 2), 189
12.5.4  Mitogen-induced cytotoxicity (type 3), 191
12.5.5  Antibody-induced K cell mediated cytotoxicity (type 4), 191
12.5.6  The requirement for effector–target cell contact, 191

12.6    Attempts to relate *in vitro* phenomena to manifestation of cell-mediated immunity *in vivo*, 192
12.6.1  Effects *in vitro* of factors produced *in vivo*, 192
12.6.2  Effects *in vivo* of factors produced *in vitro*, 192
12.6.3  Clinical observations, 193
12.6.4  Histological studies of CMI reactions, 193

12.7    Schematic translation of the *in vitro* activities into unified model for CMI mechanisms, 193

12.8    Concluding remarks, 193


13      B LYMPHOCYTE DIFFERENTIATION, 197
        M. COOPER

13.1    Introduction, 197

13.2    Clonal development, 198
13.2.1  Primary site of B lymphopoiesis in chickens, 198
13.2.2  Primary site of B lymphopoiesis in mammals, 199
13.2.3  B lymphocyte differentiation in human fetal liver, 199

13.3    Mechanism for generation of Ig class heterogeneity among mammalian B lymphocytes, 200

13.4    Antigen-induced B lymphocyte differentiation, 201
13.4.1  Role of antigen, 201
13.4.2  Role of T cells, 202

13.5    Defects of B lymphocyte differentiation in man, 202

13.6    Summary, 204


14      STRUCTURE AND FUNCTION
        OF LYMPHOID TISSUE, 206
        I. McCONNELL

14.1    Introduction, 206

14.2    The lymphon, 206
14.2.1  Experimental models for analyzing lymphocyte traffic, 206
14.2.2  Lymphocyte life-span, 207

14.3    Cell content and cytoarchitecture of lymphoid tissues, 207
14.3.1  Cell content, 207
14.3.2  Thymus and Bursa of Fabricius, 208
14.3.3  Lymph nodes, 209
14.3.4  Spleen, 211
14.3.5  Gut associated lymphoid tissue (GALT), 212
        Lymphocyte circulation, 212

14.4    Lymphocyte migration from primary lymphoid organs, 213
14.4.1  Bone marrow—blood, 213
14.4.2  Thymus—blood, 214

14.5    Lymphocyte recirculation between secondary lymphoid organs, 214
14.5.1  Blood→lymph node→lymph→blood, 214
14.5.2  Blood→tissues→lymph node→blood, 216
14.5.3  Blood→spleen→blood, 216

14.6    Lymphocyte migration within spleen and lymph nodes, 216

14.6.1   Lymph nodes, 216
14.6.2   Spleen, 216

14.7     Uptake of antigen by lymphoid tissue, 217
14.7.1   Access to lymphoid tissue, 217
14.7.2   Localization in lymphoid tissue, 217

14.8     Non-specific effects of antigen on lymphocyte traffic, 218
14.8.1   Cell 'shutdown', 218
14.8.2   Lymphocyte recruitment, 219

14.9     Specific effects of antigen on lymphocyte traffic, 219
14.9.1   Specific lymphocyte recruitment, 219
14.9.2   Antigen-specific effects within lymphoid tissue, 220
14.9.3   T–B cell cooperation *in vivo*, 220

14.10    Circulation of virgin, primed and activated lymphocytes, 221


III      **IMMUNOGENETICS**
         Preamble to Section III, 225

III.1    Introduction, 225

III.2    Alloantisera to cell-surface determinants, 225

III.3    Graft rejection and its *in vitro* 'correlates', 226
III.3.1  Mixed lymphocyte reaction (MLR), 226
III.3.2  Cell-mediated lympholysis (CML), 226
III.3.3  The distinction between SD and LD antigens, 227

15       THE MAJOR HISTOCOMPATIBILITY SYSTEM, 228
         A. MUNRO AND S. BRIGHT

15.1     Introduction, 228

15.2     The *H-2* complex, 228
15.2.1   The *H-2* map, 229

15.3     K and D regions, 229

15.4     The I region, 232
15.4.1   The Ia antigens, 232
15.4.2   Immune response genes, 233

15.5     The Ss-S1p region, 233

15.6     The TLA region, 233

15.7     The human major histocompatibility system, 233

15.8     HL-A system, 233
15.8.1   HL-A antigens, 235

15.9     Special features of HL-A genetics, 235
15.9.1   Extent of polymorphism, 235
15.9.2   Linkage disequilibrium, 236

15.10    The MHS gene products, 236
15.10.1  The biochemistry of the *H-2* and HL-A gene products, 236
15.10.2  The biochemistry of the Ia gene product, 237
15.10.3  Arrangement of the MHS products on the cell surface, 237

16       THE GENETIC CONTROL OF
         IMMUNE RESPONSES, 239
         A. J. MUNRO

16.1     Introduction, 239

16.2     Genes controlling the overall level of antibody responses, 239

16.3     Immunoglobulin-linked immune response genes, 240

16.4     The histocompatibility-linked immune response genes, 241

16.4.1   Antigens to which the response is controlled, 241
16.4.2   Inheritance and arrangement of *Ir* genes, 241
16.4.3   The number of *Ir* genes, 243

16.5     The significance of H-linked *Ir* genes, 244

16.6     The cellular level of expression of *Ir* genes, 244
16.6.1   The response to PLL in guinea-pigs: evidence for expression of *Ir* genes by T-cells, 244
16.6.2   The response to (T,G)-A- -L: evidence for expression of *Ir* by T-cells, 245
16.6.3   The response to (T,G)-A- -L: evidence for expression of *Ir* by B cells, 246

16.7     Conclusion, 247


17       THE GENETIC BASIS OF
          CELL-MEDIATED REACTIONS, 249
          H. FESTENSTEIN AND P. DEMANT

17.1     Introduction, 249

17.2     Genes controlling lymphocyte activating determinants (Lads), 249
17.2.1   Lads in man, 249
17.2.2   Lads in mice, 249

17.3     Relationship of the Lads antigens to other products of the *H-2* region of mice, 250
17.3.1   Molecular identity of the Lads gene products, 251

17.4     The M locus, 251
17.4.1   Comparison of M-locus with MHS Lads, 251

17.5     Genetic determinants involved in CML, 253
17.5.1   The effector cell stimulating locus (ECS), 253
17.5.2   One way situations, 253

17.6     *In vivo* significance of Lads, 255
17.6.1   Experimental, 255
17.6.2   Clinical, 256

17.7     Genetic control of magnitude of reaction, 256
17.7.1   Mixed lymphocyte reactions, 256
17.7.2   CML reactions and rejection of grafts, 257

17.8     Tissue typing and graft survival, 257
17.8.1   The role of linkage, 258
17.8.2   The role of linkage disequilibrium, 259
17.8.3   The role of summative effects and 'controlling' loci, 259
17.8.4   The role of multi-locus typing, 259


18       HL-A AND DISEASE, 261
          R. HARRIS

18.1     Introduction, 261
18.1.1   Linkage disequilibrium, 261
18.1.2   Disease associations, 261

18.2     Ankylosing spondylitis, 262
18.2.1   Inheritance of ankylosing spondylitis, 263

18.3     Ragweed hay fever and HL-A, 264

18.4     Coeliac disease and HL-A 1,8, 264

18.5     Multiple sclerosis (MS) and HL-A, 265

18.6     Possible explanations for HL-A associations, 266
18.6.1   *Ir* genes and hypersensitivity, 266
18.6.2   Direct participation of the HL-A macromolecules in disease, 267
18.6.3   Which of these explanations most plausibly explains the associations between HL-A antigens and various diseases?, 267

18.7    Practical applications of HL-A disease associations, 269
18.7.1  At risk individuals, 269
18.7.2  Diagnosis, 269
18.7.3  Prognosis, 269
18.7.4  Epidemiology, 270
18.7.5  Genetics, 270


IV      IMMUNOPATHOLOGY
        Preamble to section IV, 273


19      BIOLOGICAL ACTIVITIES OF COMPLEMENT, 274
        D. L. BROWN

19.1    Introduction, 274

19.2    Adherence reactions, 274
19.2.1  Adherence reactions *in vivo*, 275

19.3    Peptide fragments, 276
19.3.1  Anaphylatoxins, 276
19.3.2  Chemotactic factors, 276

19.3.3  Neutrophil mobilizing factor, 276

19.4    Lytic reactions, 277
19.4.1  Complement deficiencies, 277
19.4.2  Bystander lysis, 277

19.5    Complement components as auto-antigens, 277

19.6    Role of complement in destruction of microorganisms, 279
19.6.1  Bacteria, 279
19.6.2  Virus neutralization, 279

19.7    Interrelationships between the complement and coagulation
        systems, 280
19.7.1  Platelet reactions, 280
19.7.2  Hageman factor activation and hereditary
        angio-oedema (HAE), 281

Complement and allergic inflammation, 282

19.8    Type II allergic reactions, 283
19.8.1  Forssman shock, 283
19.8.2  Antibody-glomerular basement membrane (GBM) antibody, 284

19.9    Type III allergic reactions, 284
19.9.1  The Arthus reaction, 284
19.9.2  Serum sickness, 284
19.9.3  Aggregate anaphylaxis and acute endotoxaemia, 285


20      AUTOALLERGIC DISEASES, 287
        C. J. SPRY

20.1    Introduction, 287

20.2    Concepts of autoallergic disease, 287
20.2.1  T-lymphocyte unresponsiveness to autoantigens, 287
20.2.2  The role of suppressor T lymphocytes, 288

20.3    Autoallergic disease in man, 289
20.3.1  Types of autoallergic diseases in man, 290
20.3.2  Autoantibodies in man, 290
20.3.3  Antibody to lymphocytes, 290
20.3.4  Type IV reactions to autoantigens, 290

20.4    Experimental models of autoallergic diseases, 292
20.4.1  NZB/NZW mice and SLE, 292
20.4.2  Thyroiditis in obese chickens, 293

20.5    Genetic aspects of autoallergic diseases, 293

21     TUMOUR IMMUNOLOGY, 296
P. ALEXANDER

21.1    Introduction, 296

21.2    The nature of tumour-specific transplantation antigens (TSTAs), 296
21.2.1  Detection of TSTAs, 297
21.2.2  Classification of TSTAs, 297

21.3    Immune surveillance, 298

21.4    Resistance to tumours, 298
21.4.1  Tumour escape from allergic destruction, 299

21.5    Immunotherapy of cancer, 301
21.5.1  Passive immunotherapy, 301
21.5.2  Active immunotherapy, 302

21.6    Attempts to establish the role of immunotherapy in the management of malignant disease, 303
21.6.1  Conduct of trials, 304
21.6.2  Trials of non-specific immunotherapy, 304
21.6.3  Trials of specific immunotherapy, 305

21.7    Conclusion, 305


22     FETO-MATERNAL RELATIONSHIPS, 308
C. M. STERN

22.1    Introduction, 308

22.2    Mutual exposure to antigen, 308
22.2.1  Maternal exposure to antigen, 308
22.2.2  Fetal exposure to antigen, 309

22.3    Maternal responses to fetal antigen, 309
22.3.1  Humoral responses, 309
22.3.2  Cell-mediated responses, 310

22.4    Fetal responses to antigen, 311
22.4.1  Fetal immunocompetence, 311
22.4.2  Humoral responses, 312
22.4.3  Cell-mediated responses, 313

22.5    Factors which may suppress allergic reactivity, 313

22.6    Effects of histo-incompatibility, 314

22.7    Conclusion, 315


23     IMMUNITY AND IMMUNITY DEFICIENCY, 317
H. VALDIMARSSON

23.1    Introduction, 317

23.2    Protective mechanisms, 317
23.2.1  Evolution of protective mechanisms, 318
23.2.2  Non-specific surface factors, 318
23.2.3  Non-specific humoral (tissue) factors, 320
23.2.4  Non-specific cellular mechanisms, 320
23.2.5  Phagocytosis and intracellular killing mechanisms, 322

23.3    Specific defence mechanisms, 323
23.3.1  The functional dichotomy of specific immunity, 323

23.4    Anergy, 325
23.4.1  Cellular anergy, 325
23.4.2  Humoral anergy, 326

23.5    Immunity deficiency syndromes, 328
23.5.1  General haemopoetic deficiency, 328

23.5.2   Combined phagocytic defects in patients with normal lymphocyte function, 328
23.5.3   Selective defects of PMN leucocytes, 329
23.5.4   Combined deficiency of B and T lymphocytes, 330
23.5.5   Failure of B lymphopoesis, 330
23.5.6   Antibody deficiency (B lymphocyte maturation defects), 330
23.5.7   Isolated failure of T-lymphocyte differentiation, 331
23.5.8   Lymphokine deficiency (T lymphocyte maturation defects), 331
23.5.9   Combined T and B lymphocyte dysfunction due to putative macrophage defect, 331

APPENDICES

A.   Classification of Allergic reactions (Gell and Coombs, 1963), 334

B.   Gentle Genetics, 336

C.   W.H.O. Nomenclature for the HLA System, July 1975, 340

GLOSSARY, 342

INDEX, 351

# Editors' preface

This book arose from the lectures given at the Advanced Course sponsored by the Department of Immunology at the Royal Postgraduate Medical School, University of London.

Multiauthor books often suffer from lack of uniformity of style and overlap of content between chapters. We have attempted to avoid this by extending the role of editor to convert some recorded lectures into 'ghosted' chapters and to rewrite, in some cases quite extensively, the manuscripts submitted by the authors. These versions were then worked up into the chapters in consultation and collaboration with the authors. We accept much of the responsibility for the style and choice of content of the book. We are especially grateful to Alan Munro, Rodney Harris, Mike Taussig and Sue Bright for the provision of material not in the original lecture course and to Peter Alexander and Hilliard Festenstein for greatly expanding the subject material of their chapters over and above their lectures. Several authors have permitted us to publish recent findings, notably Hilliard Festenstein, and Arnold Feinstein who has done us the great honour of allowing us to publish one of the first accounts of his recent work on the structure of IgM.

References to published work are idiosyncratic, at best, in this book. We have attempted to restrict references to papers of major historical importance, specifically exemplary experiments and recent experiments not referred to in the reviews recommended for further reading. Many of our colleagues will find their results mentioned without reference: we apologize, but you may be glad that your work has reached canonical status!

We are grateful to our publisher who waited and did not complain, and even more to our wives.

REVISED REPRINT

We have taken the opportunity of the second impression to correct errors which we have noticed or which have been brought to our attention. We have also changed small parts of the text to conform with the new HLA nomenclature and updated it where recent findings have been especially pertinent to the understanding of the immune system.

# Acknowledgements

The Editors and Publisher are grateful to the following for permission to reproduce copyright material:

Academic Press:
  *Advances in Cancer Research*, Fig. 16.2; *Advances in Immunology*, Fig. 1.4; *Cellular Immunology*, Fig. 11.5.
The American Association for the Advancement of Science:
  *Science*, Fig. 4.6, Fig. 4.7, Fig. 11.1.
The American Association of Pathologists and Bacteriologists:
  *American Journal of Pathology*, Fig. 13.2.
The American Chemical Society:
  *Biochemistry*, Fig. 3.8; *Journal of the American Chemical Society*, Fig. 4.1a.
American Society for Clinical Investigation:
  *Journal of Clinical Investigation*, Fig. 5.7.
Blackwell Scientific Publications:
  *Handbook of Experimental Immunology*, Fig. 14.2; *Clinical & Experimental Immunology*, Fig. 10.3, Fig. 14.4a; *Immunology*, Fig. 9.10, Fig. 10.2, Fig. 14.4.
Cambridge University Press:
  *Journal of Physiology*, Fig. 3.11, Fig. 3.13, Fig. 5.5.
Cold Spring Harbor Laboratory of Quantitative Biology:
  Fig. 8.2.
McMillan Journals Ltd.:
  *Nature*, Fig. 14.8.
MTP-Butterworth:
  *Defence and Recognition*, Fig. 2.1, Fig. 2.2, Fig. 16.3.
National Academy of Sciences of the U.S.A. (Proceedings):
  Fig. 3.7, Fig. 4.4.
New York Academy of Sciences (Annals):
  Fig. 3.3, Fig. 3.4, Fig. 3.5, Fig. 4.2, Fig. 4.3.
North-Holland Publishing Company:
  *Progress in Immunology II*, Fig. 3.12, Fig. 3.13b, Fig. 17.1, Fig. 17.2; *The Principles of Human Biochemical Genetics*, Fig. 6.2b.
Pergamon Press:
  *Progress in Biophysics and Molecular Biology*, Fig. 1.2.

Plenum Publishing Corp.:
  *Microenvironmental Aspects of Immunity*, Fig. 13.3.
Prentice Hall Inc.:
  *The Cells and Tissues of the Immune System*, Fig. 14.3, Fig. 14.5.
The Rockefeller University Press:
  *Journal of Experimental Medicine*, Fig. 1.5, Fig. 7.7, Fig. 9.12,
  Fig. 16.1, Fig. 16.5.
The Royal Society of London (Proceedings):
  Fig. 8.1.
Springer-Verlag:
  *Current Topics in Microbiology and Immunology*, Fig. 11.3,
  Fig. 11.6, Table 11.2, Table 11.3.
The Williams and Wilkins Company:
  *Journal of Immunology*, Fig. 11.2.

# Advice to readers

This book has been edited to present data at a rather high density. Most people will find it necessary to read slowly and to be sure that they understand at each stage.

We have included three 'aids' for the reader: Appendices, Glossary and Preambles. Appendix A gives the classification of allergic tissue damage according to Coombs and Gell (1963), a classification which is used throughout this book and which is recommended by the Editors. Appendix B is a guide to the genetic terms used in the book. Most of our readers will have heard of these, but many will retain only a hazy memory of them. The terms have precise meanings which represent real distinctions. Any reader finding himself 'out of his depth' on genetic matters should read Appendix B in an attempt to restore his understanding.

The Glossary attempts to provide accurate, exemplary or pungent definitions for the special terms used in immunology. Consult it if you are not fully happy about the meaning of a term.

The book is divided into four sections covering Immunochemistry, Immunobiology, Immunogenetics and Immunopathology. Each section is preceeded by a Preamble providing a directory of what is to be covered and in the cases of Sections II and III some background information. Chapter 1 is a species of signed preamble on immunoglobulin structure! Readers with some knowledge of immunology may find these preambles unnecessary.

# SECTION I
# IMMUNOCHEMISTRY

As all our readers must be aware, much of the discipline of immunology is concerned with the production of antibodies. Over the past 15 years there has been a very intensive effort to understand the structure of the antibodies, which belong to a class of proteins known as immunoglobulins. This effort has been recognized by the scientific community by the award of the Nobel Prize for Medicine to Porter and Edelman in 1972. As so often happens, this award came at a time when the emphasis of the subject was changing. The basic sequences were known for most of the immunoglobulins, and enough was known of the sequence of the variable regions (which contribute to the binding site) for it to be clear that the problem of the origin of antibody diversity was not going to be easily solved by the accumulation and analysis of the sequences of immunoglobulins. Thus the focus of attention has shifted slightly, predominantly in the direction of the cellular basis of the allergic response.

The state of play as far as immunoglobulin is concerned is crudely summarized in Chapter 1, which is not intended for those who already know some immunology. Were this ruthless approach not taken, the subject could easily fill the whole book. Chapter 2 is concerned with some of the still unresolved arguments concerning the genetic origin of the diversity of the variable region sequences. The recent advances in the field of the three-dimensional structure of antibodies, and a superbly elegant example of the stochastic approach to molecular biology in the building of a model for IgM, occupies Chapter 3. It should be emphasized that much of this work is published in full for the first time here. The thermodynamics, chemistry and three-dimensional structure of the antibody combining site are discussed in Chapter 4. Chapter 5 should give the lie to the widespread view that complement is all witchcraft, or, at best, unintelligible. The section closes with a largely speculative account of how the genes which code for immunoglobulins and complement might have evolved, together with a simplified view of their current genetics.

# Chapter I
# Immunoglobulins as Proteins

## M. J. Hobart

## 1.1 Introduction

There is such a large and excellent review literature on this topic
that to attempt to repeat it would be redundant. Rather, this
chapter intends to provide some reference facts at hand for the
understanding of subsequent chapters, and to point out some of the
more interesting aspects of our knowledge of the structure of
immunoglobulin.

### 1.1.1 Basic anatomy

Immunoglobulins are made up of equal numbers of heavy and light
polypeptide chains (general formula $(H_2L_2)_n$), held together by

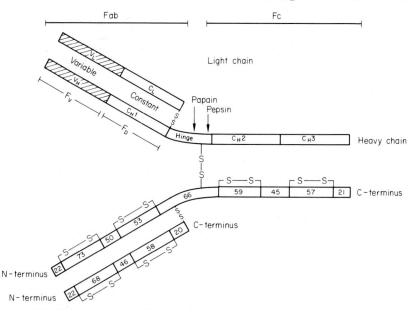

**Fig. 1.1.** A typical IgG molecule.

In the upper part of the figure, the names of the various parts of the
molecule are given, while in the lower part, the number of amino acids in
typical domains, and the arrangements of the intrachain disulphide bridges
are shown. (Adapted from Milstein and Svasti, 1971.)

noncovalent forces and usually by interchain disulphide bridges. Each chain is made up of a number of loops (domains) of rather constant dimensions held together by disulphide bridges (Fig. 1.1) (Fleischmann *et al.*, 1963; Edelman *et al.*, 1969).

The N-terminal domain of each chain shows much more variation in amino acid sequence than the others and is known as the variable region to distinguish it from the less variable constant regions. The region where the variable and constant regions join is called the 'switch' region.

Immunoglobulins are in general rather resistant to proteolytic enzymes, but are most easily cleaved about half-way along the heavy chain. If papain is used, the molecule falls into three parts of similar size: (a) two Fab fragments which include the variable regions of both chains, the constant region of the light chains and the $C_H1$ domain of the heavy chain and (b) an Fc fragment composed of the C-terminal halves of the heavy chains. If pepsin is used, the digestion occurs a little closer to the C-terminus than with papain, the inter-heavy chain disulphide bridge is preserved and the large $F(ab')_2$ fragment is released. The Fc fragment is extensively degraded. The region joining the Fab and Fc parts of the molecule is known as the 'hinge' region. Using careful conditions, it is sometimes possible to split off the variable regions, this fragment being known as Fv. The portion of the heavy chain in the Fab fragment is known as Fd.

## 1.2 Heterogeneity of immunoglobulins

It is a necessary corollary of the specificity of antibodies that their structure be heterogeneous with respect to their combining sites (see Chapters 2, 8). Since they are molecules with two functions, in as much as they recognize antigen and also initiate a variety of secondary phenomena like complement fixation and histamine release by mast cells, we should expect heterogeneity in structures related to both functions.

This heterogeneity presents problems for the protein chemist, but plasmacytomas of both men and mice provide homogeneous immunoglobulins which have greatly facilitated the study of the amino acid sequence.

### 1.2.1 Light chain types

Light chains exist in two forms, kappa and lambda, whose multiple structural differences are reflected in antigenic differences. The sequence homologies between human and mouse kappa chains are much greater than those between the kappa chain and the lambda chain, indicating an early separation of the two types during evolution, antedating that of the divergence of mammalian species.

**Table 1.1.** Physicochemical and biological properties of immunoglobulin classes

| Class | Heavy chain | | Whole molecule | | | Placental transfer | Complement fixation | Serum conc. (mg/ml) |
|---|---|---|---|---|---|---|---|---|
| | Class | m.w. | Sedimentation coefficient | m.w. | Carbohydrate content | | | |
| IgM | $\mu$ | 70,000 | 19S | 900,000 | 12% | − | + | 0·6–2·0 |
| IgG | $\gamma$ | 50,000 | 7S | 150,000 | 3% | + | + | 8–16 |
| IgA | $\alpha$ | 55,000 | 7S etc. | $(160,000)_n$ | 7·5% | − | − | 1·5–4 |
| IgD | $\delta$ | 65,000? | 7 | 180,000? | 12% | − | ? | trace |
| IgE | $\varepsilon$ | 65,000 | 8 | 180,000 | 12% | − | − | trace |

*Section I: Immunochemistry*

**Table 1.2.** IgG Subclasses in man and animals

| Species | IgG subclasses | γ chains | Relative electrophoretic mobility pH 8·6 | Relative conc. as % serum IgG | Complement activation | | Placental transfer | Heterologous skin sensitizing | Other |
|---|---|---|---|---|---|---|---|---|---|
| | | | | | Classical | Alternative | | | |
| Human | IgG1 | γ1 | slow | 70 | ++ | | + | + | binds to macrophages |
| | IgG2 | γ2 | slow | 20 | ± | | ± | – | |
| | IgG3 | γ3 | slow | 7 | +++ | | + | + | binds to macrophages |
| | IgG4 | γ4 | fast | 3 | – | +? | + | + | |
| Mouse | IgG1 | γ | fast | | – | | | – | |
| | IgG2a | | slow | | + | | | | |
| | IgG2b | | slow | | | | | | |
| Guinea-pig | IgG1 | γ1 | fast | app. 25 | – | + | | + | |
| | IgG2 | γ2 | slow | app. 75 | +++ | | | – | |
| Cow/Sheep | IgG1 | γ1 | fast | app. 75 | +++ | (+) | – | + | in colostrum |
| | IgG2 | γ2 | slow | app. 25 | – | + | – | – | |

The proportion of kappa to lambda chain synthesis varies from species to species, being about 2 : 1 in men.

### 1.2.2 Heavy chain classes

Five classes of heavy chains have been found in humans, $\mu$, $\gamma$, $\alpha$, $\delta$ and $\varepsilon$. The class of the heavy chain of the immunoglobulin determines the class of the immunoglobulin. Thus, two $\mu$ chains with either two $\kappa$ or two $\lambda$ chains constitute an IgM subunit; two $\gamma$ and two light chains an IgG. Table 1.1 shows the physicochemical and biological properties of the immunoglobulin classes. The $\mu$ and $\alpha$ chains are notably rich in carbohydrates, and the $\mu$ and $\varepsilon$ chains are characterized by the possession of five domains, compared with the four of $\alpha$ and $\gamma$ chains (see Chapters 3 and 6).

### 1.2.3 Subclasses of chains

In many species there is more than one version of some of the heavy chain classes, although by antigenic, physical, sequence and carbohydrate content criteria they can be shown to be more closely related to each other than to the other classes. In some species (e.g. guinea-pig, cow and horse) the charge spectra of the IgG subclasses differ, permitting physicochemical isolation of the subclasses. In the human, the IgG subclasses are recognized principally by the existence of myelomas, as the charge spectra largely overlap. The biological and physical characteristics of some of the IgG subclasses are set out in Table 1.2.

A notable aspect of the differences between the immunoglobulin subclasses is the number and arrangement of the interchain disulphide bridges (Fig. 1.2). In IgA2, the light chains are not covalently linked to the heavy chains. In other immunoglobulins the light to heavy bridge may be formed close to the junction of the $V_H$ and $C_H1$ domains or alternatively at the junction between $C_H1$ and $C_H2$ (e.g. IgG1, IgM).

The $\lambda$ chain in man exists in at least three and possibly four forms (subtypes), apparently tandem gene duplicates (see Chapters 2 and 6). At position 191 in the $\lambda$ chain there may be lysine or arginine which constitute the Oz markers, originally thought from studies on myeloma proteins to be allotypes, but now shown to be present in all normal individuals. Further similar variation occurs at position 153 which may be either glycine or serine (Kern markers).

### 1.2.4 Allotypes

Allotypes are variants which are inherited as alternatives (i.e. as alleles). In the same position but in contradistinction to the Oz markers on the lambda chain, the human kappa chain exists in

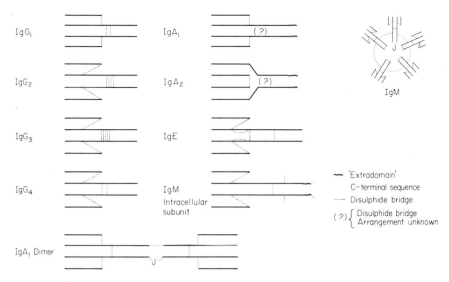

**Fig. 1.2.** Arrangement of chains and interchain disulphide bridges in human immunoglobulins.

Note that the IgA2 subclass does not have a heavy-light disulphide bridge and that IgA and IgM have a C-terminal additional sequence including a cysteine residue. Note also the additional intrachain disulphide bridge in the Fd region of IgE. (Adapted from Milstein and Pink, 1970.)

a number of allelic forms known as Inv allotypes (see Table 1.3). A large number of allotypic markers, recognized by specific antisera in haemagglutination inhibition assays, are found in the $\gamma$ and $\alpha$ chains of humans (see Chapter 6). They are known as Gm and Am markers.

**Table 1.3.** Sequences correlated with INV allotypes

| INV allotype | Amino acid at position No: | |
| | 153 | 191 |
| --- | --- | --- |
| 1, 2 | Ala | Leu |
| 3 | Ala | Val |
| 1 | Val | Leu |
| ?— | Val | Val |

(Data from Milstein *et al.*, 1974.)

Rabbits have complex allotypic systems (*a* and *b*) detected by precipitating antisera. For immune precipitation to take place with divalent antibody, the antigen needs to be at least trivalent. Lattice formation, and hence precipitation, does not take place with divalent antigens, which instead make small complexes (Fig. 1.3). Since the rabbit $a$ and $b$ locus allotypic systems are defined by precipitin analysis, the allotypes cannot be single point amino-acid substitutions, since this would give rise to only two determinants per molecule, immunoglobulins being bilaterally symmetrical. There must be at least two mutations, giving four determinants per molecule, for the allotypes to be detected by precipitation.

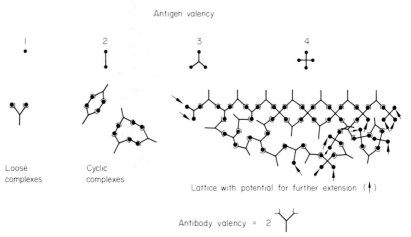

**Fig. 1.3.** The effect of antigen valency on complex size.

The capacity of a system to make an extended lattice depends on one of the reactants being at least divalent, and the other at least trivalent. Thermodynamic considerations limit the extent of cyclic oligomers.

Notwithstanding this strange situation, it is a remarkable finding that IgM, IgA and IgG all share a set of heavy chain allotypes, the $a$ locus markers. These appear to be located in the variable region and to be correlated with multiple differences in the amino-acid sequence.

### 1.2.5 Idiotypes

Idiotypic differences are those related to the individual variable region sequences produced by each clone of antibody forming cells, and were originally identified by specific antisera. If the antibody raised by a rabbit to a bacterium is used to coat organisms which are injected into another rabbit of identical allotype, the second rabbit may make antibodies against the coating antibodies. These antibodies will recognize the 'foreign' variable regions of some of the injected antibody, and the antiserum will react with only a restricted population of immunoglobulins in the serum of the first rabbit. In some cases, the anti-idiotypic antisera raised against an anti-hapten can be inhibited by the presence of the hapten, indicating that the idiotypic antigenic determinants are close to or in the antibody combining site. An antibody to the idiotypic determinants can be regarded as an immunological marker for the antibody combining site.

It seems legitimate to extend the term 'idiotype' to the 'unique' product of any clone of antibody-forming cells, that is any combination of a particular light chain variable sequence with a particular heavy chain variable sequence. Like the *a* locus allotypes, idiotypic determinants may be shared by different antibody classes, but they are very rarely found to be the same among different individuals, especially when the anti-idiotype is raised against an antiserum in which there was a normal polyclonal response (see Chapter 2).

### 1.2.6 Other polypeptide components of immunoglobulins

(a) *J chain*. The J chain is a 15,000 MW polypeptide rich in cysteine, which is structurally unrelated to the basic immunoglobulin domain but which is invariably found in association with the polymeric immunoglobulins IgM and IgA. In both the IgM pentamer and the IgA dimer, there is one J chain. J chain is synthesized by the antibody-forming cell, and is made even by those cells which are secreting non-polymeric immunoglobulins such as IgG. The secretion of unpolymerized IgM and IgA in mutant mouse plasmacytomas is associated with a failure of J chain synthesis.

(b) *Secretory component*. The IgA dimers of the external secretions (gut, saliva and milk), carry a 60,000 molecular weight polypeptide, secretory component, which is not secreted by the antibody-forming cell, but by epithelial cells, and is attached during the secretion process. The function of this molecule is not known, but may be related to protection against the hostility of the external environment.

## 1.3 The variable region

The N-terminal 110 amino acids of the light and heavy chains are not uniformly variable. While no two human myeloma chains have been found to have identical sequences in the V region, the extent of the variability is restricted in two respects: its location and the presence of discernible subgroups.

### 1.3.1 V-region subgroups

When the sequences of the variable regions of kappa chains are compared, four subgroupings can be made which have substantial homologies. The subgroups differ principally in the length and position of the insertions and deletions (Fig. 1.4). Similar subgroup similarities are seen in the heavy chain variable regions and the lambda chain variable regions. In mice, however, the sequences

Amino terminal position

| | 10 | 20 | 30 | 40 |

**Vκ₁ Subgroup**

| | 1 | 5 | 10 | 15 | 20 | 25 | 30 | 35 | 40 | 43 |
|------|---|---|----|----|----|----|----|----|----|----|

```
                 1         10          20          30            35         40
Vκ I Subgroup
ROY    D I Q M T Q S P S S L S A S V G D R V T I T C Q A S Q D I S – – – – I F L N W Y Q Q K P
AG     D I Q M T Q S P S S L S A S V G D R V T I T C Q A S Q D I N – – – – H Y L N W Y Q Q G P
EU     B I Z M T Z S P S T L S A S V G B R V T I T C R A S Z Z S I B – – – T W L A W Y Z Z K P
BJ     D V Q V Q S P S S T L S V S V G D R V T I T C Q A S Z S I – – – – – K Y   W Y Z Z K P
OU     D I Q M T Q S P S S L S A S V G D R V T I T C Q A S Q N I N – – – – S   W L B W Y Z (Z K P)
HBJ4   D I Q M T Q S P S S L S A S V G D R V T I T C R A S Q B I – – – – – B W L A W Y Q E L P
DAV    D I Q M T Q S P S S L S A S T V G D R V T I T C R A S Q B I S – – – S W L I W Y Q Q Y P
FIN    D I Q M T Q S P S S L S A S V G D R V T I T C D A S Q B I B – – – S W L I W Y Q Q Y P
KER    D I Q M T Q S P S S L S A S V G D R V T I T C Q A S Q B I K – – – D F
TRA    D I Q M T Q S P S S L S A S V G D R V T I T C
CON    D I Q L T Q S P S F L S A S V G D R V T I T C
LUX    D I Q L L T Z S P S S L S A S V G D R V T I T C
BEL    B I Z M T Q S P S S L S A S V G D R V T I T C Z A S B I S – – – K S S L A W Y Z Z K P
PAUL   D I Q M T Q S P S S L S A S V G D R V T I T C R A S Q S I – – – – S S L A W Y Z Z K P

Vκ II Subgroup
Ti     E I V L T Q S P G T L S L S P G E R A T L S C R A S Q S V S – – – N S F L A W Y Q Q K P
FR4    E(L) V V L D Q S P G T L S L S P G E R A T L S C R A S Q S V R – – – N N Y L A W Y Q Q R P
B6     Z I V L T Q S P G T L S L S P G Z R A A T L S C R A S Q S L S S – – G N Y L A W Y Q Q K P
RAD    E I V L T Q S P G T L S L A T L S C R A S Q S V – V S – S N Y L A W Y Q Q K P
CAS    E I V L T Q S P G A L S L S P G D R A T L S C R A S Q – V S Q S – – S N S
SMI    E I V L T Q S P G T L S L S P G D R A T L S C R A S Q – V S
DIL    E I V L T Q S P A T L S L S P G E R A T L S C R A S Q S L S – – – S K S L S W Y Q Q K P
NIG    K I V L T Q S P A T L S V S P G E R A T L S C
GRA    E M V L T Q S P A T L S M S L L S P G E R A T L S

Vκ III Subgroup
CUM    E D I V M T Q T P L S L P V T P G E P A S I S C R S S Q S L L A S G D G N T Y L N W Y L Q K A
TEW    D I V M T Q S P L S L P V T P G E P A S I S C R S S Q – H(G B)S – – F L N W Y L Q K P
MIL    D I V L T Q S P L S L P V T P G E P A S I S C R S S Q N L L Z S – B G B – Y L D W Y L Z K P
MAN    D I V M T Q S P L S L P V T P G E P A S I S C R S S Q S L L H(S)B G B B – Y L B ? Y L Z K P
BATES  D I V M T Q S P L S L P V T P G E P A S I S G R S S G R S S Q(S)L L H(S)B G B B – Y L B ? Y L Z K P
```

of the kappa chain are so variable as to demand at least nineteen sub-groups.

### 1.3.2 Hypervariable regions

Some parts of the variable regions display much more variation than others. A plot of the known variations versus position in the sequence shows three or four peaks, depending on the class of chain (Fig. 1.5). These regions are known as hypervariable regions and can be shown to be intimately involved in the formation of the combining site (see Chapter 4). Two of the hypervariable regions are close to the cysteine residues forming the intrachain disulphide bridge of the variable domains.

## 1.4 Biological activities

As noted above (1.2), immunoglobulins are bifunctional molecules which not only bind to antigens but also initiate a number of other biological phenomena, activities in which the antibody acts as the directing agency for an otherwise 'blind' process. These two kinds of activity can each be localized to a particular part of the molecule: antigen binding to the variable region of the Fab (see Chapter 4) and most of the other activities to the Fc.

### 1.4.1 Complement fixation

The role of the different parts of immunoglobulin in complement activation is complicated by the existence of (at least) two pathways of complement activation (see Chapter 5). The 'classical' pathway, involving the numbered complement components, is initiated by the binding of C1q to antibody. IgM can bind C1q and one IgM molecule alone bound to an antigen is sufficient to initiate the complement reaction (see Chapter 3). Most IgG is also complement fixing by the classical pathway, especially IgG3 and IgG1 in

---

Fig. 1.4. N-Terminal sequences of Human Kappa chains.

Sequence data on the N-terminal residue of human $\kappa$-chains showing how they can be classified into three subgroups on the basis of sequence homology. Subgroup specific residues are underlined and deletions are shown by dashes.

*Key to one letter amino acid code:*

| | | | | | | | |
|---|---|---|---|---|---|---|---|
| A | Ala | G | Gly | N | Asn | V | Val |
| B | Asx | H | His | P | Pro | W | Trp |
| C | Cys | I | Ile | Q | Gln | Y | Tyr |
| D | Asp | K | Lys | R | Arg | Z | Glx |
| E | Glu | L | Leu | S | Ser | | |
| F | Phe | M | Met | T | Thr | | |

(From Hood and Prahl, 1971, for reference see Chapter 6.)

*Chapter 1: Immunoglobulins as Proteins*

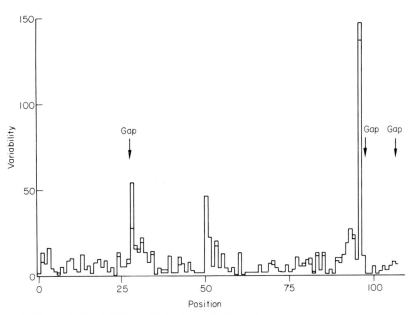

**Fig. 1.5.** Variability within the variable region.

Variability at different amino acid positions for the variable region of the light chains. GAP indicates positions at which insertions have been found. (From Wu and Kabat, 1970.)

humans. Human IgG2 binds C1q weakly and IgG4 apparently not at all. In the case of IgG, it seems that the binding of two molecules of antibody in close proximity is a necessary condition for complement activation. The specific location of the C1q binding site on the IgG molecule seems to be in the $C_H2$ domain. IgA, IgD and IgE seem not to bind to C1q.

The initiation mechanisms for the 'alternative' pathway of complement are not well understood, largely because of the existence of a positive feedback loop whose action is liable to mask the micro-events which are involved in the triggering of the system (see Chapter 5). Nevertheless, it seems clear that the F(ab')$_2$ of some IgGs and at least some 'non-complement fixing' IgG subclasses can trigger complement activation by the alternative pathway in certain favourable circumstances and that the complement activation sites, in a broad sense, are not restricted to the Fc. It remains unclear how many of the other immunoglobulin classes can initiate complement action, at least under physiological conditions.

### 1.4.2 Transfer across membranes

The transfer of immunoglobulins across epithelial membranes is of particular importance in providing antibody for the external

12                                          *Section I: Immunochemistry*

surfaces of the body, and for the provision of an adequate repertoire of antibody to the newborn, providing it with antibodies specific for the dangerous organisms in its own environment.

(a) *The external secretions* of the alimentary, respiratory and reproductive tracts are relatively richly supplied with IgA, in the form of dimers with secretory component. Much of this IgA is locally secreted, and it seems probable that the Fc of the molecule is important in the transfer process. An intriguing feature of the external secretions is that there are differences in the specificities of the antibodies secreted in different sites, even in the apparent absence of any local antigenic stimulation.

(b) *The colostrum of ruminants* is very rich in the IgG1 subclass, almost all of which is derived from the plasma. The placentae of ruminants are impermeable to macromolecules, and the colostrum is the principal source of maternal antibody for the young. The intestine of the newborn ruminant is specially adapted to transfer wholesale the undigested macromolecules which it receives, although this facility disappears after a suitable quantity of protein has been transferred. The subclass specificity of the secretion of IgG in these animals confirms that the structure of the heavy chain is important for transfer across membranes.

(c) *The transplacental transfer* of immunoglobulins in man is subclass specific, and in the rabbit is a feature of the Fc fragment and not of the Fab fragment. The adaptive value, if any, of subclass-specific transfer to fetal or neonatal animals is obscure.

### 1.4.3 Cell-binding immunoglobulins

There seems to be a wide variety of mechanisms by which immunoglobulins bind to cell surfaces. A number of cell types have Fc receptors, thus permitting them to take up antibodies synthesized by other cells for 'use' as specific receptors. IgG administered intradermally may persist at the site of injection for days, but the pre-eminent cell-binding immunoglobulin is IgE, which has a very high affinity for mast cells. The ability to bind antigen is passively conferred on the mast cell for very long periods (weeks). The Fc receptor of macrophages exhibits specificity for the IgG1 and IgG3 subclasses of human IgG.

## 1.5 Integration and biosynthesis

'Well, immunoglobulins break *all* the rules'—famous geneticist.

The dual role of immunoglobulins, as antigen binding and secondary phenomenon directing molecules, seems to have produced evolutionary advantages for two remarkable phenomena: allelic exclusion and the coding of a single polypeptide chain by two genes.

*Chapter 1: Immunoglobulins as Proteins*

### 1.5.1 Allelic exclusion, isotypic and idiotypic selection

Individual antibody secreting cells from animals heterozygous for immunoglobulin allotypes synthesize only a single allotype (allelic exclusion). Furthermore, they make only one pair of variable region sequences in the light and heavy chain respectively, one light chain type, and (usually) only one class and subclass of heavy chain to yield a homogeneous product. Thus, each cell uses only a fraction of the information carried in the *haploid* chromosome set. While it is usual for cells to translate only a fraction of their genetic potential, the only parallel to allelic exclusion is the suppression of one of the X chromosomes in the cells of females (Lyon phenomenon), but this effect is applied to all the genes on one chromosome, and not a specific set of genes on a number of chromosomes.

### 1.5.2 Integration

The random association of V-region subgroups, allotypes and idiotypes with different constant regions is evidence for a situation hitherto unique in molecular biology: that two genes code for a single polypeptide chain. This is a very economical solution to the need to marry a large heterogeneous set of combining sites with a smaller heterogeneous set of Fcs.

The question can be raised as to what stage does integration of the V- and C-regions occur: DNA, DNA to RNA transcription, RNA to protein translation, or by the formation of a peptide bond between two preformed polypeptides. The last two possibilities are eliminated by the discovery that both the light and heavy chains are synthesized without interruption on polyribosomes of about the expected size. It has now been possible to isolate the messenger RNAs for both chains, and to show that they are translated by either cell-free systems or by frog oocytes. Both messengers are rather longer than is required to code for the protein chain, even allowing for the characteristic poly-A sequence which seems to be a common feature of messenger RNA. This discrepancy is even more marked in the case of heavy chain messenger isolated from the nucleus, and the function of much of the additional sequence is not known. There is some evidence, however, that in the case of light chains some of the additional sequence is translated but subsequently removed by proteolysis from the N-terminal end of the chain.

### 1.5.3 Synthesis, assembly and secretion

The chains are synthesized separately and the nascent chains are released into the cysternae of the rough endoplasmic reticulum of the plasma cell. Here the chains assemble themselves by non-covalent interactions between the constant region of the light

*Section I: Immunochemistry*

chain and $C_H1$ domain of the heavy chain, and between the domains of the Fc. The interchain disulphide bridges form as the chains assemble, and a variety of partially assembled molecules have been isolated from within cells—$H_2$, $H_2L$ and HL. The formation of large $H_n$ aggregates is inhibited by the presence of an excess light chain pool within the cell.

Carbohydrate is attached after the heavy and light chains have been assembled, and, although the process is not genetically coded, there is some degree of specificity as to which of the potential sites have carbohydrate attached to them, and which variety of carbohydrate complex is attached (see Chapter 3).

The polymeric immunoglobulins IgM and IgA assemble themselves shortly before secretion, the J chain being attached at this time. It seems that the J chain has some function in stabilizing the initial phase of the polymerization process, though sub-units derived from polymers can be reassociated without J chains.

## References

EDELMAN G.M., CUNNINGHAM B.A., GALL W.E., GOTTLIEB P.D., RUTISHAUSER U. & WAXDAL M.J. (1969) The covalent structure of an entire $\gamma$G immunoglobulin molecule. *Proc. Nat. Acad. Sci. U.S.A.* **63**, 78–85.

FLEISCHMANN J.B., PORTER R.R. & PRESS E.M.M. (1963) The arrangement of the peptide chains in $\gamma$-globulin. *Biochem. J.* **88**, 220–228.

MILSTEIN C.P., STEINBERG A.G., MCLAUGHLIN C. & SOLOMON A. (1974) Amino acid sequence change associated with genetic marker Inv 2 of human immunoglobulins. *Nature (Lond.)* **248**, 160.

WU TAI TE & KABAT E.A. (1970) An analysis of the sequence of the variable regions of Bence Jones proteins and myeloma light chains and their implications for antibody complementarity. *J. exp. Med* **132**, 211.

## Further reading

BEVAN M.J., PARKHOUSE R.M.E., WILLIAMSON A.R. & ASKONAS B.A. (1972) Biosynthesis of immunoglobulins. *Prog. Biophys. Molec. Biol.* **25**, 131–162.

EDELMAN G.M. (1973) Antibody structure and molecular biology (Nobel lecture). *Science* **180**, 830–840.

MILSTEIN C. & PINK J.R.L. (1970) Structure and evolution of immunoglobulins. *Prog. Biophys. Molec. Biol.* **21**, 209–263.

MILSTEIN C. & SVASTI J. (1971) Expansion and Contraction in the Evolution of Immunoglobulin Gene Pools. In AMOS B. *Progress in Immunology* **1**, 33. Academic Press, New York.

PORTER R.R. (1973) Structural studies of immunoglobulins (Nobel lecture). *Science* **180**, 713–716.

PORTER R.R. (1973) Immunoglobulin structure. In PORTER R.R. *Defence and Recognition*, pp. 159–197. MTP and Butterworth, London.

WILLIAMSON A.R. (1973) Biosynthesis of immunoglobulins. In PORTER R.R. *Defence and Recognition*, pp. 229–255. MTP and Butterworth, London.

# Chapter 2
# Genetics of Immunoglobulin Diversity

# A. J. Munro

## 2.1 Introduction

This chapter outlines the problem of the number and arrangement of the genes coding for the immunoglobulins, and of the time-span of their generation.

It is assumed that a specific amino acid sequence in a polypeptide implies the existence of a gene coding for the polypeptide within the genome of the antibody forming cell.

## 2.2 Alleles, tandem genes and linkage

### 2.2.1 The distinction between alleles and tandem genes

If a protein occurs in two forms, it may be assumed that an individual who synthesized the two forms carried two DNA sequences corresponding to the two forms of the protein. In such a case there is either a single copy of each DNA sequence, one on each of a pair of chromosomes, or each chromosome may carry both the DNA sequences as tandem genes (Fig. 2.1). The two situations are resolved by examining the proteins made by a number of individuals, most usefully the offspring of individuals who synthesize both forms. Examinations of the offspring permit inferences to be made as to the gametes formed by the parents (Fig. 2.1). If all the offspring carry both markers, then all gametes similarly carry both markers, and hence the genes are tandem. If half the offspring carry both markers, but the other half carry only one or the other, the genes are alleles. Allotypes are markers of this sort (e.g. Inv on human kappa chains). IgG subclasses on the other hand are examples of tandem genes (e.g. IgG1–4) as are the Oz markers on human lambda chains (Fig. 2.2).

### 2.2.2 Linkage

Where there are two genetic markers in close proximity on a chromosome, crossing over during meiosis occurs between them rather rarely and they usually segregate to the gametes as a pair.

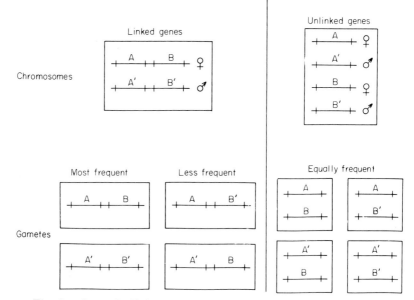

Fig. 2.1. A test for linked genes.

The diagram shows two genes, A and B of maternal origin, each with allelic forms A' and B' of paternal origin. It is possible to determine if A and B are linked or unlinked by the distribution of the allelic forms in the gametes. With linked genes, occasional recombinants give a pattern of markers not found in either parental chromosomes. The frequency of occurrence of these recombinants is a measure of the distance between the genes. Adjacent genes have a very low recombination frequency. (From Milstein and Munro, 1973.)

When they are far apart, the frequency of crossing over is much increased, and if they are in different chromosomes they segregate quite independently. Linkage studies are directed at determining the frequency of segregation events, to see if they are random, or if there is linkage. If there is linkage they also seek to determine the frequency of the crossing over events (recombinations) leading to genes on the paternal chromosome being transmitted with genes from the maternal chromosome. The results are usually expressed as recombination percentage. Unlinked genes recombine at a rate of 50 per cent. The smaller the crossover rate, the closer together in the genome are the genes under investigation (Fig. 2.1).

## 2.3 Arrangement of immunoglobulin genes

Using the tests set out above, the arrangement of the immuno-globulin constant region genes can be shown to be as in Fig. 2.2. The constant region genes for the heavy chains are linked to each other so closely that no recombinants have been found in 5,000 mice tested. They are not linked to either type of light chain gene.

*Chapter 2: Genetics of Immunoglobulin Diversity*

| Man | V-genes | | C-genes |
|---|---|---|---|
| Light chains — κ | Ia Ib II III | | — |
| Light chains — λ | I II III IV | | Arg Lys Gly |
| Heavy chains | I II III | | γ4 γ2 γ3 γ1 α1 α2 μ2 μ1 δ ε |

| Mouse | V-genes | C-genes |
|---|---|---|
| Light chains — κ | I II III IV V VI VII etc. | — |
| Light chains — λ | I (II) | I II |

**Fig. 2.2.** Possible arrangement of the minimum number of genes for human Ig and mouse light chains.

The genes on each horizontal line are thought to lie on the same chromosome. In mice the minimum of kappa V-genes is probably well above 8 and the existence of a second lambda V-gene is uncertain. (From Milstein and Munro, 1973).

Further, the genes for the lambda chain are not linked to the gene for the kappa chain.

The variable regions of immunoglobulins exist as a variety of subgroups, differing from each other in length and position of deletion or insertion (see Chapter 1). There are 4 V-region subgroups of human kappa chains expressed in all normal individuals, indicating that they are tandem genes (1a, 1b, II, III). Similar subgroups exist for the lambda and heavy chain variable region genes. In rabbits the $a$ allotype markers reside in the heavy chain variable region, and behave in all respects as an allelic system. They appear to be related to multiple structural differences in the variable region (Mole *et al.*, 1971). Using the $a$ heavy chain variable region and $d$ and $f$ heavy chain constant region markers, two recombinants have been observed in about 400 crosses. The preliminary recombination frequency of 0·5 per cent suggests that the variable and constant region genes of heavy chains are fairly closely linked but not immediately juxtaposed.

Since the immunoglobulin chains are synthesized as a single unit, there is considerable interest in the mechanism of integration of the variable and constant region genes. It is especially interesting to see if the variable region genes on one chromosome can be integrated with the constant region gene on the other chromosome. In rabbits, where genetic markers for both the variable and constant regions are available, the proportion of molecules in which this *trans*-integration of genetic information seems to have occurred is less than 1 per cent.

A second type of marker for particular variable region sequences is the idiotypic marker, recognized by an antiserum against a product of a single clone of antibody producing cells (see Chapter

1). If an idiotype can be shown to be genetically transmitted, it should be renamed a variable region allotype. Krause (1970) raised monoclonal antisera to bacterial polysaccharides in rabbits, and showed that the idiotype of the monoclonal antibody was to some extent inheritable. Eichman (1972) extended this work to mice, and found that when an antiserum was raised to the antibody from one mouse, 6 out of 6 mice of the same strain shared the idiotypic determinant, whereas monoclonal antibodies to the same antigen produced in a different strain of mice, failed to react with the anti-idiotype antiserum. This marker can be shown to be closely linked to the heavy chain constant region allotype by backcross analysis with animals which do not carry the gene for making the idiotype.

## 2.4 The number of variable region genes: arguments from proteins

### 2.4.1 How many 'genes' do we 'need'?

Since we believe that for each polypeptide chain sequence there must be a corresponding DNA sequence, if we can estimate the number of V-region sequences which are needed to give a large enough antibody repertoire to cover all eventualities, we shall have an estimate for the number of different DNA sequences needed to encode for this. This question is rather more complicated than might be thought. Since both the heavy and the light chain variable regions are involved in the combining site, the largest number of possible antibodies would arise if there were fully random association of light and heavy chain V-regions, i.e. if there are p heavy chain V-regions and q light chain V-regions, there might be pq different combining sites. However, there is no evidence as to how many of these combinations 'work' as antibodies. Therefore $2.\sqrt{pq}$ gives an untested, but certainly minimal, figure for the number of 'genes' (for further discussion of this topic see Chapter 8).

Cross reactions certainly occur in the antibody population and this might lessen the number of antibodies needed to 'cover' the antigenic universe. In mice, a surprisingly large number of myelomas occur which have respectable affinity, e.g. for haptens, but many of them also have affinity for other test antigens, notably DNA (Eisen, 1971). It is not clear, however, if this population of induced tumour immunoglobulins is a fairsample of the normal antibody population.

### 2.4.2 How many proteins do we make?

Attempts have been made to estimate the heterogeneity of the antibody population by estimating the frequency of occurrence of a myeloma idiotype in normal sera. An anti-idiotypic antiserum raised against a mouse myeloma protein is used in a radioimmuno-assay to estimate the quantity of myeloma idiotype in the sera of normal mice (Iverson, personal communication). These experiments suggest that on average one of every $2 \times 10^5$ normal immunoglobulin molecules carries the myeloma idiotype. The experiment may be criticized on the ground that it may measure not only these molecules which are truly identical with the myeloma, but also those which have similar antigenic determinants and react with lower affinity. Indeed Kunkel (1970) has found a figure of about $1 \times 10^7$ with human myelomas and in normal human serum.

In another method to estimate the heterogeneity of antibodies, antibody forming cells from hapten primed mice (e.g. NIP–BSA) are transferred in limiting numbers to irradiated syngeneic recipients and a secondary anti-NIP response is evoked in these recipients (Kreth & Williamson 1973) (see Chapter 9 for methods). The recipients make a response of restricted heterogeneity, since they have been transplanted with only one or a few viable clones of cells. The heterogeneity of the anti-NIP in their sera is estimated by isoelectric focusing in a thin polyacrylamide gel slab, in which the hapten-binding antibodies are detected by autoradiography. In this way a catalogue of the clonal products of a single mouse can be compiled from analysis of the antibody clones in the recipients. From 4 donor mice, 337 clones were found, of which 5 were common to two mice. This is a frequency about 20 times greater than the calculated resolving power of the system, and this number of clones requires a minimum of 140 different V-regions to make the mouse anti-NIP repertoire.

In addition to the technical problems involved in these methods, the intrinsic problems of using arguments from whole immunoglobulins as a method for estimating the V-gene pool size are set out in 2.4.1 above.

By an immunofluorescent method the number of plasma cells synthesizing a particular lambda chain V-region idiotype in human spleens has been estimated (Pernis, 1967). From this it appears that there are at least 25,000 different lambda V-regions.

## 2.5 Germ line versus somatic mutation

Since the variable region is not uniformly variable but has hypervariable regions, one can propose that there are special mechanisms which increase the rate of mutation in the hypervariable regions. Alternatively, normal random mutational events are responsible but there are selective pressures which make these the most common sites for observed variation. What is still open to question is the time scale over which these processes occur and what the selective pressures are. The somatic mutation hypothesis proposes that the variants arise from a small gene pool during the development of the individual. The selective pressures are unknown but it has been proposed that they are associated with the internal antigenic experience of the individual (see Chapter 8). The germ line hypothesis proposes that coding for the variants is predominantly carried out in the genome of the individual and that mutation and selection occurred during the evolution of the species. There remain widely diverse views among immunologists as to the relative importance of genes carried in the germ-line for the formation of specific variable region sequences.

If an extreme germ-line position is taken, then it would be necessary to postulate the existence of, say, $10^3$ germ line genes for each of the types of light and heavy chains. To explain the existence of V-region sub-groups, each subgroup would have to be the result of a massive tandem duplication of a primordial gene with its own particular deletion or insertion, to give perhaps 300 copies. Where such multiple copies occur, such as the genes for making ribosomal RNA, there is a high frequency of large-scale deletion of the genes presumably by unequal crossing over (see Chapter 6), and a special case must be made for the stability of the V region genes in the germ line (Milstein & Munro 1973).

To the somatic mutationist, the finding of inheritable idiotypes would become a severe embarrassment if the number of such inheritable idiotypes became too large, since there would have to be a large number of genes in the germ-line to account for the observation. The present number may be explained as being the few genes which are carried in the germ-line, and on which the process of somatic mutation acts to produce the full antibody repertoire.

A balanced view at the present time is that there will probably be a number of germ-line genes depending on the class of chain and the species of animal. It is already clear in the case of the mouse kappa chains that there may be at least 50 copies of the variable region gene in the genome, since the known sequence cannot be fitted into a smaller number of subclasses, as is the case in the human kappa chain. It seems possible that factors such as the gestation time available for a fetus to generate a sufficient antibody repertoire might demand a heavier dependence on multiple germ-line specificity in the mouse than in man.

## 2.6 The number of germ-line genes: annealing studies with nucleic acids

Annealing studies measure the rate of association of labelled copies of the nucleic acid sequence which codes for a particular polypeptide chain with single-stranded DNA from the parent genome. The rate of annealing depends on the chances of a labelled copy finding a section of the DNA with which it has homology: the more duplicates of a particular gene there are, the more rapidly will the labelled copies anneal.

Messenger RNA is prepared which codes for one of the immunoglobulin chains, in most cases the light chain. This messenger has approximately 660 nucleotides which code for the secreted protein, and in addition 350 nucleotides whose function is unknown, and which may make the interpretation of annealing data difficult. The messenger RNA may be procured in a labelled form for the annealing study, or alternatively, a labelled single stranded DNA copy (cDNA) may be made from the RNA by means of the reverse transcriptase. Two techniques give different results: the cDNA anneals slowly indicating that there are only a few copies, and that they are homogenous in sequence. However, it is not known what section(s) of the messenger have been transcribed, though certainly it is not all, since different transcription systems work with different efficiencies.

Probably the best available data comes from the use of labelled messenger RNA. This, it is generally agreed, anneals at two different rates, one of which indicates the presence of 50 to 500 copies per genome (fast), the other about 2 to 5 copies (slow). An interesting approach is that of Tonegawa (1974), who has made light chain messenger RNA from three mouse myelomas, two belonging to one V-region subgroup of kappa chain (1 and 1*) and a third (2) to a different subgroup. He investigated the inhibition of the annealing of labelled mRNA from (1) by the other unlabelled mRNAs. Both 1* and 2 compete with 1 in the high annealing rate experiments, though fibroblast mRNA does not. It seems therefore, that the fast annealing phenomenon is related to a large number of copies of a nucleotide sequence which, though probably specific for immunoglobulins, are not V-region specific. It seems reasonable to speculate that the portion of the messenger whose function is unknown may be responsible. However, when competition for slow annealing sites was investigated, 1* competed with 1, but 2 did not. This clearly suggests that slow annealing phenomenon is related to the sequence coding for the variable region, and that there are only a few copies of the V-region in the genome. If mRNAs for a further 10 light chains in the same V-region subgroup are all shown to compete with 1, then the repertoire of V-region sequences which will compete will substantially exceed the estimate for the number of gene copies in the genome, and this will argue firmly in favour of a somatic mutation model.

Recent evidence using labelled cDNA also suggests a small number of V-genes (Rabbitts and Milstein, 1975).

### References

EICHMAN K. (1972) Idiotypic identity of antibodies to streptococcal carbohydrate in inbred mice. *Europ. J. Immunol.* **12,** 1.

EISEN H.N. (1971) Combining sites of Anti-2,4-Dinitrophenyl Antibodies. In AMOS, B. *Progress in Immunology* **1,** 243. Academic Press, New York.

KRAUSE R.M. (1970) The search for antibodies with molecular uniformity. *Adv. Immunol.* **12,** 1.

KRETH H.W. & WILLIAMSON A.R. (1973) The extent of diversity of anti-hapten antibodies in inbred mice: Anti-NIP antibodies in CBA mice. *Europ. J. Immunol.* **3,** 141.

MILSTEIN C. & MUNRO A.J. (1973) Genetics of Immunoglobulins and of the Immune Response. In PORTER R.R. *Defence and Recognition.* MTP & Butterworths, London.

MOLE L.E., JACKSON S.A., PORTER R.R. & WILKINSON J.M. (1971) Allo-typically related sequences in the Fd fragment of rabbit immunoglobulin heavy chains. *Biochem. J.* **124,** 301.

PERNIS B. (1967) Relationship between the heterogeneity of immunoglobu-lins and the differentiation of plasma cells. *Cold Spring Harbor Symp. Quant. Biol.* **32,** 333.

RABBITTS T.H. & MILSTEIN C. (1975) Mouse immunoglobulin genes: studies on the reiteration frequency of light-chain genes by hybridisa-tion procedures. *Eur. J. Biochem.* **52,** 125.

TONEGAWA (1974) In BRENT L. & HOLBORROW J. *Progress in Immunology II.* **1,** 236. North-Holland, Amsterdam.

# Chapter 3
# The Three-dimensional Structure of Immunoglobulins

## A. Feinstein

### 3.1 Introduction

Two direct methods have been used in the investigation of the three-dimensional structure of immunoglobulins: electron microscopy and X-ray diffraction crystallography. The former has been used since the early 1960s, while the latter has produced high resolution results only in the 1970s. For the interpretation of the data obtained, much use is made of knowledge of the chemical structure of immunoglobulins, and of a number of hydrodynamic and other physical methods.

### 3.2 Electron microscopy

Studies of the structure of immunoglobulins started with electron microscopic examination of antigen–antibody complexes using the negative staining technique (see reviews by Green, 1969, and Feinstein et al., 1971). The molecules and particles under investigation are embedded in an electron dense stain, for instance sodium phosphotungstate, and are visualized because they exclude stain to present a less opaque path for the electron beam. In very thick layers of stain, the contrast between the electron translucent molecules and the stain is diminished, usually resulting in a diminution of the apparent dimensions of the molecules. Hence, there are advantages in the use of small complexes leading to smaller depths of stain. In addition, there are frequently problems of failure of the molecules to completely exclude stain, often as a result of partial denaturation.

The earliest electron micrographs were of virus particles linked by antibody. They were followed by the use of ferritin: IgG anti-ferritin complexes which were made under controlled conditions (Feinstein & Rowe, 1965). Precipitates were first made at optimal proportion, washed, and then redissolved in antigen excess (Fig. 3.1). The molecule was seen to be Y-shaped, with a variable angle between the arms. It is probable that the 'clicked-open' T-shaped form seen in large lattices is responsible for the initiation of complement fixation. When pepsin digested antibody was used, the free

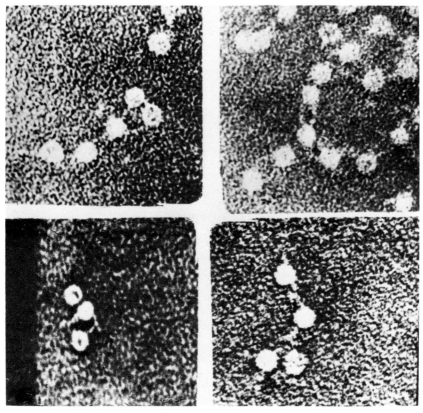

**Fig. 3.1.** Complexes of IgG and F(ab′)₂ antibody and ferritin.
The angle between the Fab arms is variable. The Fc can be distinguished in the IgG complexes (lower pictures). Note cyclic oligomers.

arm of the Y-shaped molecule was lost, and the precipitates re-dissolved on reduction. The ferritin molecules were then left with the individual Fab′ arms attached.

Valentine and Green (1967) introduced the elegant technique of using a bifunctional hapten as antigen. The haptenic determinants are separated by a short aliphatic chain, about 20 Å in length. This system leads to the formation of cyclic oligomeric structures made up of two, three, four and sometimes more IgG molecules linked together by the hapten via their combining sites (Fig. 3.2). The principal advantage of this system is the absence of bulky antigen molecules around which the stain accumulates. It gives results of good resolution and contrast.

IgM has a characteristic starfish-like appearance when examined in free purified form (Fig. 3.3a). In some molecules, the five arms are seen to be bifid (Fig. 3.3b), and these appear to be the Fab parts, which are attached to a central disc-like structure about 100 Å in diameter. When complexed with antigen, for instance the flagella of Salmonella (Fig. 3.4), the IgM molecules assume a variety of shapes. Where they are cross-linking widely separated flagella, the

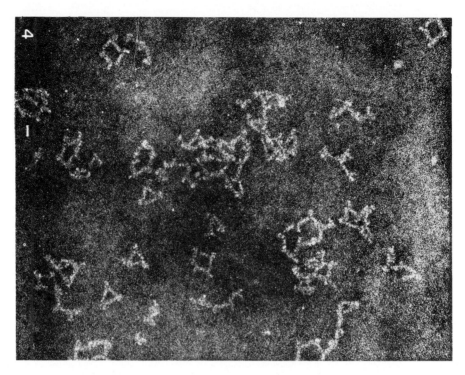

**Fig. 3.2.** Complexes with a bivalent hapten.

In this technique, introduced by Valentine and Green, the antigen is very small, and 'invisibly' binds the antibodies together into cyclic oligomeric complexes. Again, the angles between the Fab arms vary, and the Fc protrudes from the corners of the complexes.

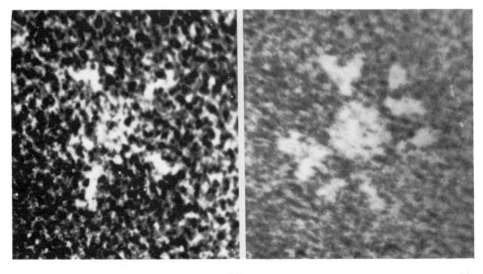

(a)                                                                         (b)

**Fig. 3.3.** Free IgM.

The IgM molecule shows a central disc with five protruding arms. In some cases, these are seen to be bifid. (From Feinstein *et al.*, 1971).

*Section I: Immunochemistry*

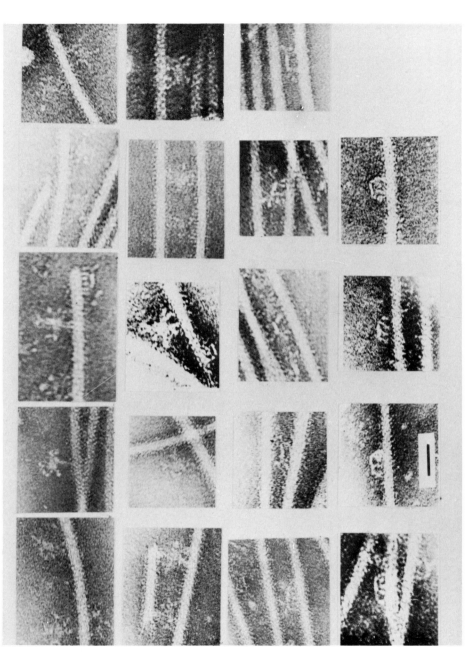

**Fig. 3.4.** The reaction of IgM antibody with Salmonella flagella. For description, see Fig. 3.5 and text. (From Feinstein *et al.*, 1971.)

characteristic star shape is seen, but when many combining sites are attached to a single flagellum, the molecule has a 'staple' appearance. Transitional forms are also seen (Figs. 3.4 and 3.5). The staple form shows a highly contrasted bar, which represents the central disc in profile, held up to 100 Å from the surface of the flagellum by the Fab arms which are bent down from the plane of the central disc. It should be noted that the Fab arms have the facility to bend either up or down, and that they have a distinct tendency to move together as a rigid F(ab)$_2$ pair, with fixed angles being maintained between them.

Unlike IgG, a single molecule of IgM complexed with antigen is capable of binding C1q to initiate complement activation, the binding site probably residing in the C$\mu$3 domain. In order for the triggering of complement activation to be specific for bound IgM, one must imagine that antigen-binding causes a change in the properties of the molecule, probably by the exposure of a new site.

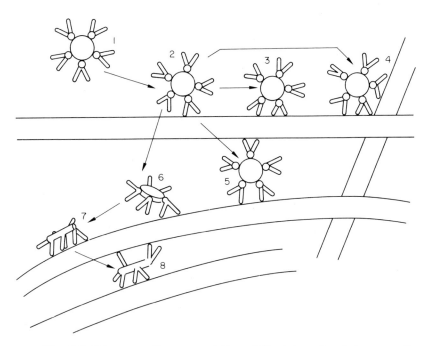

**Fig. 3.5.** Diagrammatic representation of the interaction between anti-flagella $\gamma$M antibody and the antigen.

The diagram is based on electron micrographs of the type shown in Fig. 3.4. A possible sequence by which one form is converted to another is indicated: The free molecule (1) first binds to a flagellum at one point (2); subsequently, further attachments are formed to the one flagellum (3) or, if another flagellum is within range, cross-linking occurs (4) and (5). It is envisaged that the staplelike form (7) is derived via a transient intermediate (6). The conversion of a staple to a cross-linking staple (8) is also shown. Clearly, other sequences are possible and the process is reversible. (Feinstein *et al.*, 1971.)

*Section I: Immunochemistry*

This could be achieved either by a structural rearrangement of the central disc which contains the Cμ3 domain, or the exposure of previously sterically hindered sites by the folding away of the F(ab)₂ arms. We have some evidence that there is no *gross* rearrangement of the central disc on antigen binding. Beale (1974) has prepared a very hydrodynamically homogeneous Fcμ fragment. On examination of this molecule by electron microscopy, two extreme forms are seen: weakly contrasted pentagons and highly contrasted bars. A variety of intermediate orientations are also seen (Fig. 3.6a). The pentagons and bars are comparable in appearance with the central disc of the free IgM molecule (Fig. 3.6b) and the bar in the 'staple' (Fig. 3.6c). Thus, both appearances of the central disc in whole molecules are seen in a preparation in which there is no hydrodynamic evidence for shape heterogeneity, and suggests that there is no gross shape change in the central disc when the molecule is combined with antigen.

If the complement binding site is exposed by the flexion of the

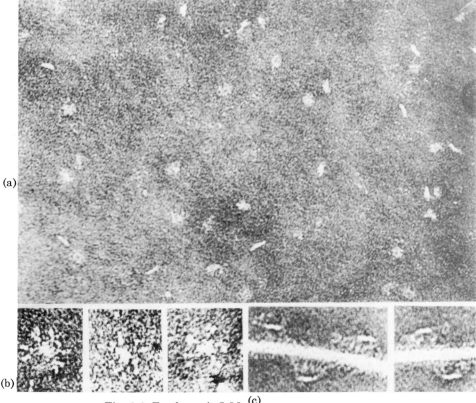

(a)

(b)

(c)

**Fig. 3.6.** Fcμ from pig IgM.

Fig. 3.6a shows isolated Fcμ 'central discs' prepared from pig IgM by pepsin digestion. The disc forms, seen face on, compare with the central discs of free IgM (3.6b), while the bar forms, seen edge on, compare with the bar of the IgM 'staples' (3.6c).

29 *Chapter 3: The Three-dimensional Structure of Immunoglobulins*

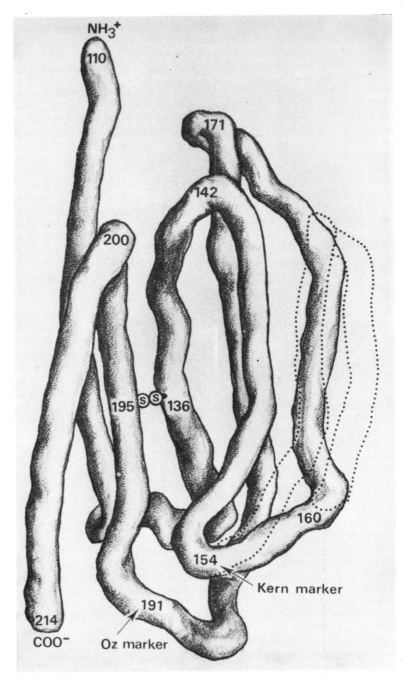

**Fig. 3.7.** The folding of the polypeptide chain of a single immunoglobulin domain (from Poljak *et al.*, 1973).

Diagram of the basic 'immunoglobulin fold'. Solid trace shows the folding of the polypeptide chain in the constant subunits of Fab ($C_L$ and $C_H1$). Numbers designate light ($\lambda$)-chain residues, beginning at 'NH$_3^+$', which corresponds to residue 110 for the light chain. Broken lines indicate the additional loop of polypeptide chain characteristic of the $V_L$ and $V_H$ subunits.

*Section I: Immunochemistry*

F(ab)$_2$ arms, the site of flexibility should be close to the C$\mu$3 domain in which it resides. If the Fab arms were flexible at a junction between the V and C domains or between the C$\mu$1 and C$\mu$2, the degree of flexion transferred to the critical C$\mu$2:C$\mu$3 junction might be insufficient. In fact, as noted above, the F(ab)$_2$ arms of IgM do seem to move as a rigid unit with respect to the central disc (Figs. 3.4 and 3.5).


## 3.3 X-ray crystallographic studies of immunoglobulins

Poljak *et al.* (1973), Davies (Padlam *et al.* 1974) and Edmondson (Schiffler *et al.*, 1973) have recently had success in the examination of the crystallized parts of the IgG molecule. Poljak and Davies have worked with Fab′ derived from human and mouse myelomas respectively, and Edmondson with a light chain dimer (Bence–Jones protein). All these workers have developed models for the backbone structure of the polypeptide chains, although the side chains of the individual amino-acids are not yet fully resolved.

The most obvious feature of this work is that the polypeptide chains of any domain have a characteristic pattern of folding which is essentially similar, irrespective of their origin (Fig. 3.7). The V-domains usually have an additional small loop, shown dotted in Fig. 3.7. For much of its length, the chain is thrown into a series of antiparallel (see glossary) folds which form two surfaces which are held together by a disulphide bridge. One surface is made up of three 'runs' of the chain, the other of four. Adjacent 'runs' on each surface are antiparallel (see Fig. 3.8).

This basic shape permits non-covalent interaction between pairs of domains in two different ways:

(a) '*Apart pairing*'. The V-region domains are apposed such that their three-chain surfaces face each other and that both the N- and C-terminal ends of the domains are well apart in space (Fig. 3.9a).

(b) '*C-together pairing*'. The constant domains of the Fab′ and light chain dimer interact through the four-chain surfaces, with the N-termini of the domains apart. The C-termini are closely approximated, permitting the formation of interchain disulphide bridges, such as the light to heavy chain bridge in human IgG1 (Fig. 3.9b). It should be noted, however, that the carboxyl end of the N-terminal 'run' of the domain is also close by, permitting the alternative light to heavy bridge found between the C-terminus of the light chain and a position not far in the sequence from the N-terminus of the C$_H$1 domain (131 in rabbit IgG). This arrangement is seen in human IgG2, IgG3, IgG4 and in IgM.

The V and C domains of the light chain, or the V and C$_H$ domains of the heavy chain interact at approximately right angles (Fig. 3.8). The variable and constant domains of the light chain meet at a different angle from the variable and constant domains of

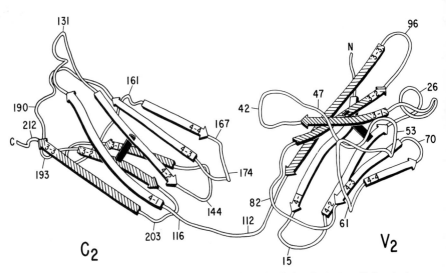

Fig. 3.8. The relationships of the domains of a light chain in a light-chain dimer. (From Edmonson *et al.*, 1975.)

The white arrows correspond to segments of the four-chain surfaces and the striated arrows represent segments of the three-chain surfaces.

the heavy chain in the Fab', and in the light chain dimer, one of the light chains acts as a 'surrogate' Fd, showing that there is some flexibility in the configuration of an individual molecule. It seems likely that in all immunoglobulins, irrespective of their class or subclass, the known homologous domains will be somewhat similarly folded, and the relationships of the domains will be similar to those seen in the Fab'.

### 3.4 A stochastic approach

The construction of a model for IgM can be used as an example of the way in which we can arrive at a structure for polymeric immunoglobulins in the absence of high resolution X-ray crystallographic data. There are three sorts of data used in the construction of this model: Electron microscopic, X-ray crystallographic (see above) and chemical (described below).

---

**Fig. 3.9.**

The pairing of immunoglobulin domains is shown by using a pair of model $C_H1$ domains (Fig. 3.9a). They are arranged (Fig. 3.9b) so that when either is lifted and placed on the other, without rotational movement, they pair 'apart' (3.9c) and 'C-together' (3.9d). The approximate main contact areas on the upper surfaces of the lower domains are 'shaded' in the accompanying drawing. Interacting domains in the real Fab' show detailed adaptation to give better fit and greater and more diverse contact areas.

*Section I: Immunochemistry*

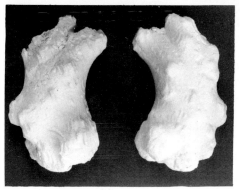

(a)

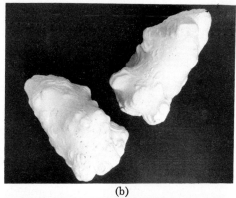

(b)

(c)

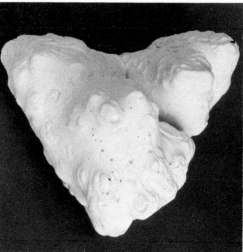

(d)

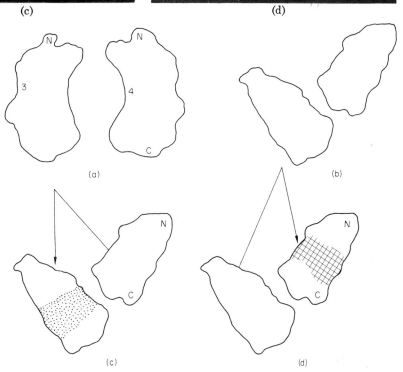

(a)

(b)

(c)

(d)

**33** *Chapter 3: The Three-dimensional Structure of Immunoglobulins*

### 3.4.1 Sequence data

The sequence of the $\mu$ chain from two different laboratories (Putnam *et al.*, 1973, Watanabe *et al.*, 1973) agree in showing five homologous regions or domains, which have arisen by the tandem duplication of a gene coding for an original precursor immunoglobulin domain (Fig. 3.10). The variable domain forms part of the antigen binding site (see Chapter 4), and the four constant domains are numbered from the N-terminus to C-terminus as $C\mu 1$ to $C\mu 4$. IgM differs from IgG in having four constant domains rather than three, but like IgG the $V_H$ and $C\mu 1$ domains interact with the V and C domains of the light chain. Further differences between the $\mu$ and $\gamma$ chains are that although the domains are almost equal sequence length, the $\gamma$ chain has an additional 'hinge' region sequence between the $C\gamma 1$ and $C\gamma 2$ domains and the $\mu$ chain an additional nineteen residues at the C-terminus.

### 3.4.2 Carbohydrate

While carbohydrate is commonly disregarded as structural feature of proteins, it is highly quantitatively significant in IgM and IgA. There are 5 carbohydrate moities on the $\mu$ chain, three complex and two simple. (Putnam *et al.*, 1973). Two are on the $C\mu 3$ domain, one of which is analogous to that on the $C\gamma 2$ domain of IgG. The locations of the other moities are indicated in Fig. 3.10. The carbohydrate groups are quite large, each having a molecular weight of the order of 2000, and they are probably quite bulky since they are branch-chained structures.

### 3.4.3 Dissociation of IgM

IgM may be dissociated into 7S subunits either by the reduction of the disulphide bridges which hold the subunits together or by

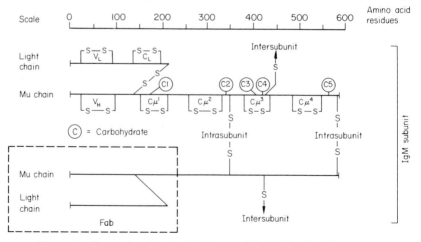

**Fig. 3.10.** The major chemical features of the IgM subunit.

*Section I: Immunochemistry*

limited papain digestion. If carefully controlled conditions of reduction are used, and the thiol groups released are labelled with radioactive iodoacetamide, the labelled peptides may be recovered and identified from the sequences. Two methods are used to determine the effects of the reduction of the disulphide bridges on the integrity of the molecules: ultracentrifugation is used to determine what proportion of the molecules have spontaneously dissociated and SDS gel electrophoresis is used to determine the proportion of molecules which dissociate when non-covalent interactions are abolished.

In human IgM, the intersubunit bridge between the $C\mu3$ domains is the most labile, but the molecules can remain intact (19S) until dissociated in SDS, indicating that there are strong non-covalent forces holding them together. If higher concentrations of reducing agent are used, the IgM dissociates into subunits in aqueous media, possibly due to reduction of the disulphide bridge linking a single J chain to $\mu$ chains, and subsequent rearrangement of domain interactions.

IgM breaks down to subunits when mildly treated with papain (Inman & Hazen, 1968), conditions which appear to digest the additional C-terminal sequence of the heavy chains (Feinstein *et al.*, 1971). The concentration of cystein used to activate the enzyme is not sufficient to break the intersubunit bridges, but following digestion, disulphide interchange may be encouraged and the molecule dissociates into subunits.

IgM subunits may be reassociated in the absence of J chain. Intracellular IgM subunits seem to need both J chain and a disulphide promoting enzyme to assemble into polymers (Della Corte & Parkhouse, 1973).

It should be noted that the disulphide bridge of IgM nearest the Fab is on the C-terminal side of the $C_H2$ domain, unlike IgG in which it is on the N-terminal side.


## 3.5 Rules for immunoglobulin model building

As mentioned above (3.3), the similarity in both the folding of all the domains hitherto examined by X-ray crystallography and their interactions seems to justify the assumption that these features have been conserved in the evolution of the different immunoglobulin chains and the domains which make them up. If this is true, then rules can be deduced which will permit the building of immunoglobulin models.


### 3.5.1

Where the existence of the disulphide bridge demands that the C-terminal ends of pairs of domains be close together, they will pair in the same manner as the constant region domains in the Fab′ (C-together).

### 3.5.2

Since the domains paired C-together have their N-termini separated, in the absence of additional inter-domain sequences, sequential 'C-together' pairing of neighbouring domains along the chain is not possible where the C-termini are disulphide bridged together. In the absence of an interchain disulphide bridge, it is conceivable that the sections of chain which would have approached each other to form the disulphide bridge could diverge sharply to meet the N-termini of a subsequent 'C-together' pair.

### 3.5.3

Neighbouring domains along the chain will interact approximately at right angles, in a zig-zag fashion, unless contact between them is prevented, for instance by bulky oligosaccharides. Where the interaction is prevented, there may be more flexibility in the molecule.

### 3.5.4

The positions of salient features on the basic immunoglobulin fold is shown in Fig. 3.11. Note that there is an additional polypeptide sequence at the C-terminus of IgM, whose three-dimensional structure is unknown, and which is probably unlike any other part of the immunoglobulin.

## 3.6 A model for IgM

Figs. 3.12 and 3.13 show preliminary models for IgM, built up by the application of the rules, which incorporate all the features discussed above. It is the numerous constraints in the arrangement of the disulphide bridges which allow the model to be built with some confidence. The central disc of the IgM molecule is seen to be made up of a densely packed complex of the $C\mu3$ and $C\mu4$ domains. The $C\mu3$ domains lie circumferentially around the disc, arranged almost to enclose their maximum circle. Both the inter-heavy chain bridges between the C-terminus of the $C\mu2$ domains and the inter-subunit bridges between the C-termini of the $C\mu3$ domains are close to the periphery of the disc (Fig. 3.12). The spatial position of the single J chain is not known, since it is attached to the penultimate cysteine in the additional sequence beyond the $C\mu4$ domain.

A striking feature of the model is the arrangement of carbohy-

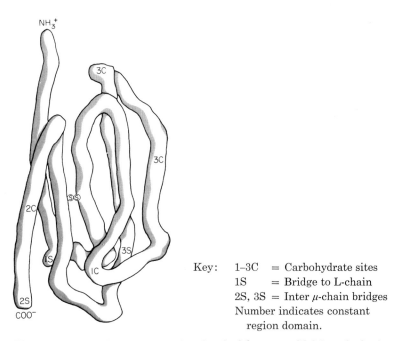

Key:  1–3C = Carbohydrate sites
      1S    = Bridge to L-chain
      2S, 3S = Inter μ-chain bridges
      Number indicates constant
             region domain.

**Fig. 3.11.** The position of the major chemical features of IgM on the basic domain.

The positions of the major chemical features of the μ chain are mapped onto the basic domain: nC indicates the position of a carbohydrate moiety, and the domain on which it is found. Similarly, nS represents an interchain disulphide bridge.

drate moities close to the periphery of the central disc. Their role may well be in the prevention of interactions between adjacent domains which would either lead to the incorrect assembly of the IgM, or prevent the free movement of the F(ab)$_2$ arms with respect to the central disc. Concordant with the electron microscopic evidence is the lack of flexibility of the F(ab)$_2$ arms themselves, whose binding sites appear to be held firmly in an antiparallel relationship.

## 3.7 Discussion

The observation that IgM frequently seems to have only five *effective* antibody binding sites when it interacts with large antigens is probably to be explained by the lack of flexibility of the F(ab)$_2$ arms. Even when two antigenic determinants are sufficiently close to each other to permit binding by both the combining sites, this must often be prevented by their antiparallel arrangement.

Consideration of the model makes possible some speculation as to the mechanism of action of J chain in promoting the formation of

Diagram of the arrangement of the domains
in the IgM molecule

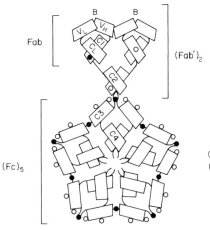

Fab

(Fab')₂

(Fc)₅

Only one of the five
(Fab')₂ arms is shown

●    Interchain disulphide bridge

○    Carbohydrate

B    Antigen – binding site

Regions of polypeptide chains
folded into domains

**Fig. 3.12.** From Feinstein, A., 1974.

IgM polymers. The J chain promotes the polymerization of IgM
through a residue remote from its site of attachment, since the
intersubunit bridge is at the C-terminus of the Cμ3 domain. It seems
that the portion of the μ-chain which is C-terminal to the Cμ4
domain can fold back to form an intrachain disulphide bridge with
the residue which would otherwise have formed the intersubunit
bridge (Fig. 3.14), and that J chain prevents this. This intrachain-
bridged form probably occurs naturally in the 7S IgM of elasmobranchs, and possibly as the IgMs receptor on lymphocytes.

The model for IgM gives some insights into the structure and
function of other classes of immunoglobulins. It seems probable
that IgG and IgA have each evolved from ancestral IgM by deletions
of one of the heavy chain domains, the Cμ2 in the case of IgG and
the Cμ3 in IgA. IgA has retained the C-terminal tail of IgM with
its cystein residue. IgG has developed its flexibility by the retention
of the carbohydrate on the domains adjacent to the hinge region.
The additional length of polypeptide characterizing the hinge
region of IgG may not be required for flexibility at the hinge, but

*Section I: Immunochemistry*

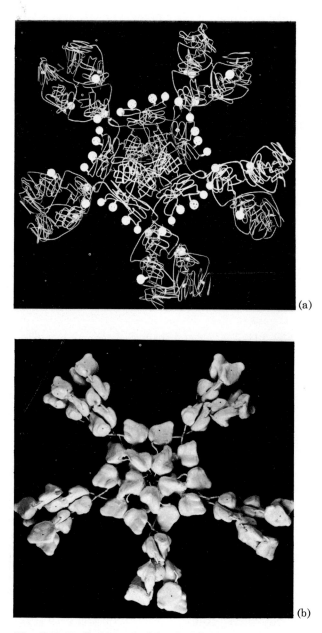

(a)

(b)

**Fig. 3.13.** Preliminary models of IgM.

Figure 3.13a shows the polypeptide-chain backbone and
carbohydrate of IgM assembled as a complete model, according to the 'rules' set out in 3.5. Note that the carbohydrate
(balls) is concentrated at the margin of the central disc.
Figure 3.13b shows a preliminary space-filling model.

39 *Chapter 3: The Three-dimensional Structure of Immunoglobulins*

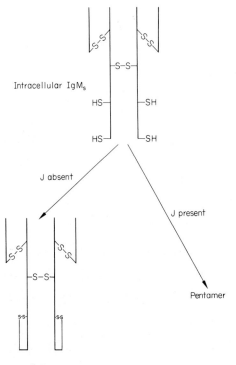

Intracellular IgM$_s$

J absent

J present

Pentamer

IgM$_s$

**Fig. 3.14.** The role of J chain in determining the assembly of IgM pentamers.

rather to bring the $\gamma$ chains together to form the interheavy chain disulphide bridges.

## References

ANDERSON T.F. & STANLEY W.M. (1941) Study by means of electron microscope of reaction between tobacco mosaic virus and its antiserum. *J. Biol. Chem.* **139**, 339.

BEALE D. (1974) A porcine immunoglobulin Fc$\mu$ polymer that has no J chain. *Biochim. Biophys. Acta,* **351**, 13.

DELLA CORTE E. & PARKHOUSE R.M.E. (1973) Biosynthesis of Immunoglobulin A (IgA) and Immunoglobulin M (IgM). Requirement for J chain a disulphide-exchanging enzyme for polymerisation. *Biochem. J.* **136**, 597.

EDMUNDSON A.B., ELY K.R., ABOLA E.E., SCHIFFER M. & PANAGIOTOPOULOS N. (1975) Rotational allomerism and divergent evolution of domains in immunoglobulin light chains. *Biochemistry* **14**, 3953.

FEINSTEIN A. (1974) Conclusions: and IgM model. In BRENT L. & HOLBOROW J. *Progress in Immunology* II, **1**, 115. North-Holland, Amsterdam.

FEINSTEIN A., MUNN E.A. & RICHARDSON N.E. (1971) The three dimensional conformation of γM and γA globulin molecules. *Ann. N.Y. Acad. Sci.* **190**, 104.

FEINSTEIN A. & ROWE A.J. (1965) Molecular mechanism of formation of an antigen–antibody complex. *Nature (Lond.)* **205**, 147.

INMAN F.P. & HAZEN R. (1968) Characterisation of a Large Fragment Produced by Proteolysis of Human Macroglobulin M with Papain. *J. Biol. Chem.* **243**, 5598.

PADLAM E.A., SEGAL D.M., COHEN G.H. & DAVIES E.R. (1974) The Three-Dimensional Structure of the Antigen Binding Site of McPC 603. In SERCARZ E., WILLIAMSON A.R. & FOX F. *The Immune System, Genes, Receptors, Signals.* Academic Press, New York.

POLJAK R.J., AMZEL L.M., AVEY H.P., CHEN B.L., PHIZACKERLY R.P. & SAUL F. (1973) Three-dimensional structure of the Fab′ fragment of a human immunoglobulin at 2·8 Å Resolution. *Proc. Nat. Acad. Sci. U.S.A.* **70**, 3305.

PUTNAM F.W., FLORENT G., PAUL C., SHINODA T. & SHIMIZU A. (1973) Complete amino acid sequence of the Mu heavy chain of a human IgM Immunoglobulin. *Science* **182**, 287.

SCHIFFLER M., GIRLING R.L., ELY K.R. & EDMONDSON A.B. (1973) Structure of a λ-Type Bence-Jones Protein at 3·5 Å Resolution. *Biochemistry* **12**, 4620.

STOTT D.I. & FEINSTEIN A. (1973) Biosynthesis and assembly of IgM. Free thiol groups present on the intracellular subunits. *Eur. J. Immunol.* **3**, 229.

VALENTINE R.C. & GREEN N.M. (1967) Electron microscopy of an antibody–hapten complex. *J. Molec. Biol.* **27**, 615.

WATANABE S., BARNIKOLO H.U., HORN J., BERTRAM J. & HILSCHMANN N. (1973) Die primärstructur eines monoclonalen IgM-immunoglobulin (Macroglobulin Gal) II Die aminosäursequenze der H-Katte (μ-Typ, subgruppe H$_{III}$), Structur des gesamten IgM-Molecüls. *Hoppe Seyler's Z. Physiol. Chem.* **243**, 1505.

## Further reading

FEINSTEIN A., MUNN E.A. & RICHARDSON N.E. (1971) See above.

GREEN N.M. (1969) Electron Microscopy of the Immunoglobulins. In DIXON F.J. & KUNKEL H.G. *Advances in Immunology* **11**, 1. Academic Press, New York.

# Chapter 4
# The Antibody Combining Site

# M. J. Taussig

## 4.1 Introduction

In this chapter, three aspects of the antibody combining site are discussed: its affinity for antigen, and how this is measured; the specificity of the reaction with antigen; and finally studies on the structure of the binding site.

## 4.2 Antibody affinity

Affinity is a measure of the binding of an antigen at a single binding site. An exact definition derives from the fact that the reaction between antigen and antibody is a reversible one and may be expressed as:

$$H + B \rightleftharpoons HB$$

where $H$ represents antigen (hapten), $B$ the antibody binding site, and $HB$ the complex. The association constant of this reaction at equilibrium is given by:

$$K = \frac{\text{concentration of complex}}{\text{concentration of free antigen} \times \text{concentration of free antibody}}$$

or

$$K = \frac{[HB]}{[H] \times [B]}$$

where $K$ is the affinity of the antibody combining site.

An important corollary of this relationship is that the extent of an immunological reaction ($\alpha$) can be calculated from the equation:

$$\alpha = \frac{K \cdot c}{(1 + K \cdot c)}$$

where $\alpha$ is the fraction of antigen or antibody reacted (at equilibrium) and $c$ is the equilibrium concentration of the *corresponding* free antibody or antigen respectively. This expression shows that the extent of an immunological reaction, $\alpha$, depends on the product of a concentration, $c$, and a constant, $K$. For example, the degree to which an infectious virus will be neutralized by antibody is governed by the affinity of the antibody and the antibody concentration. Immunity to the infection might be improved by increasing either the amount of antibody or its affinity. In this case, $\alpha$ is the fraction of virus (antigen) combined with antibody and $c$ is the equilibrium concentration of free antibody. Another illustrative example is the triggering of antigen sensitive cells by antigen. The fraction of cells in a population that are triggered will depend on the affinity of the cell receptors for the antigen and on the antigen concentration. The more antigen is administered, the lower the affinity of the cell receptor needs to be to ensure sufficient antigen binding to trigger the cell; and consequently the lower the average affinity of the antibody produced by the population.

**Table 4.1.** Variation in affinity of antibodies isolated from serum. (From Karush F., 1970)

| Amount DNP-BGG injected (mg) | Rabbit No. | Time after injection of DNP-BGG | |
|---|---|---|---|
| | | 2 weeks | 8 weeks |
| | | $K_0$ (liters/mole $\times 10^{-6}$) | $K_0$ (liters/mole $\times 10^{-6}$) |
| 5 | 3 | 0·32 | 20·0 |
| 5 | 4 | 1·0 | 250·0 |
| 5 | 5 | 0·78 | 80·0 |
| 50 | 7 | 0·21 | 0·97 |
| 50 | 8 | 0·26 | 1·4 |
| 50 | 9 | 0·78 | 32·0 |
| 100 | 13 | 0·17 | 0·23 |
| 100 | 14 | 0·87 | 0·55 |
| 100 | 15 | 0·26 | 0·37 |

These conditions underlie the well-known increase in affinity of antisera with time after immunization. A classical experiment by Eisen & Siskind (1964) showed that the later one bled an animal following administration of an antigen, the higher was the affinity of the serum antibody. Table 4.1 shows the anti-DNP affinity of the sera at two and eight weeks following the administration of different quantities of DNP–BGG. There was a large increase (about 100-fold) when a small dose (5 mg) was administered, but this effect was much less evident when the dose was larger. This is explained by the persistence of a large amount of the antigen in the high dose animals, which remained above the triggering threshold of a large

*Chapter 4: The Antibody Combining Site*

number of cells with low affinity receptors. In the low dose animals, the antigen concentration decays more quickly to levels which will trigger only a small population of cells with high affinity receptors. Presumably, if the animals given large doses were bled very much later, their antigen levels, too, would have fallen to levels low enough to stimulate only high affinity antibody production.

### 4.2.1 Measurement of affinity

It is useful here to rewrite the expression for affinity as

$$K = \frac{\text{molar concentration bound hapten}}{\dfrac{\text{molar concentration}}{\text{free hapten}} \times \dfrac{\text{molar concentration}}{\text{freebinding sites}}}$$

at equilibrium. In essence, methods for determination of $K$ measure the amount of hapten bound and free at equilibrium; since a known amount of antibody is used, $K$ can readily be calculated.

A classical method for the measurement of affinity is *equilibrium dialysis*. Two chambers of equal size are set up, separated by a dialysis membrane which is freely permeable to the hapten, but not permeable to the antibody. The apparatus used and the principle of the method are shown in Fig. 4.1. A known quantity of antibody in solution is placed in one chamber, and a solution of hapten is placed in the other chamber. The system is allowed to come to equilibrium and the concentration of hapten in the hapten chamber is measured. This is most conveniently done if the hapten is coloured or radioactive. Since the compartments contain an equal quantity of free hapten, the total free hapten can be calculated, and the bound hapten determined by subtraction of the total free hapten from the hapten offered. In practice, a series of experiments is performed over a range of hapten concentration. For each concentration of free hapten, $c$, the ratio, $r$, of hapten bound per mole of antibody is calculated. $r$ and $c$ are related to $K$, the affinity, and $n$, the valency of the antibody, by the relationship

$$r/c = nK - rK$$

A plot of $r/c$ versus $r$ therefore gives a graph of slope $K$ and intercept $n$. This is known as a Scatchard plot, and yields both the affinity of the antibody and its valency, which in the case of IgG is usually 2 (Fig. 4.2). The slope is usually not a straight line, since antisera generally contain a heterogeneous mixture of antibodies of different affinities, thus necessitating the use of a range of hapten concentrations for the determination of the (average) affinity of the antibody population. In the case of divalent antibody.

$$r/c = 2K - rK$$

Therefore, when half the antibody combining sites are filled, the ratio $r$ becomes equal to 1, and $r/c$ becomes $K$. $K$ may thus be found

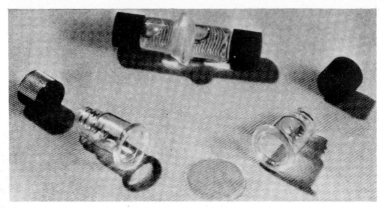

**Fig. 4.1a.** Equilibrium dialysis cell of the type designed by Carsten and Eisen. (*J. Am. Chem. Soc.* **77** (1955), 1273.)

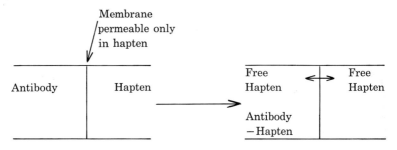

Free Hapten−measured

Bound Hapten=Total Hapten−2×Free Hapten

**Fig. 4.1b.** The principle of equilibrium dialysis.

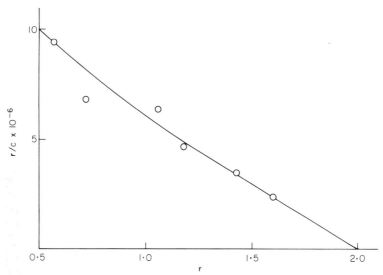

**Fig. 4.2.** Binding of DNP-lysine by rabbit anti-DNP antibody at 37°. Scatchard plot. (From Karush, F., 1970.)

*Chapter 4: The Antibody Combining Site*

by reading the value of $r/c$ from the graph when $r = 1$ (Fig. 4.2). Hence, a secondary definition of affinity is 1/the free hapten concentration required to fill half the antibody combining sites.

An index of heterogeneity, $a$, of the antibody population may be found from the relationship:

$$\log (r/n - r) = a \log c - a \log K$$

and by plotting $\log (r/n - r)$ against $\log c$, the Sips plot (Fig. 4.3). A heterogeneity index of 1 indicates a homogeneous population.

While equilibrium dialysis can be applied to a wide variety of haptens, and the affinity of antibody in whole serum can be measured, where pure antibody can be obtained, the method of *fluorescence quenching* provides a quicker method for the measurement of

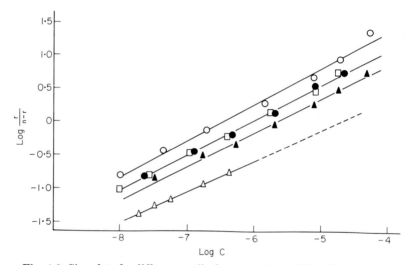

**Fig. 4.3.** Sips plots for different antibody preparations. (From Schechter, I. 1971.)

affinity. This method depends on the intrinsic fluorescence of tryptophan residues in the immunoglobulin. When antibodies are irradiated with ultraviolet light at 280 nm the tryptophane residues are excited to emit light at 340–350 nm. If the antibody binds a hapten which has an absorption at 350 nm, the energy which would have been emitted as light by the tryptophan residues in the region of the combining sites will be absorbed by the hapten. This will produce a reduction in the emission of fluorescent light, hence the term fluorescence quenching. DNP (the dinitrophenyl group) is a convenient hapten for such purposes since it has an absorption at 350 nm. The method is rather restricted in respect of choice of hapten, but has the advantages of speed and requirement for only a minute amount of antibody.

In practice an antibody solution is placed in the cuvette of a spectrofluorophotometer, and the fluorescence is measured at a

*Section I: Immunochemistry*

range of added hapten concentrations (Fig. 4.4). Maximum quenching ($Q_{max}$), usually about 70%, occurs when all the combining sites are occupied by hapten, and the amount of quenching at lower hapten concentrations ($Q_i$) indicates the proportion of combining sites occupied by hapten. Hence the bound hapten concentration for a divalent antibody must be $Q_i/Q_{max} \times 2$ [Antibody,] and the values for construction of a Scatchard or Sips plot may be readily calculated from knowledge of the amount of hapten added to the mixture.

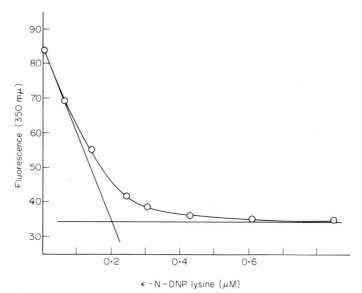

**Fig. 4.4.** Fluorescence quenching.

The titration of 0·02 mg of anti-DNP antibody with ε-DNP-lysine as measured by fluorescence quenching. (From Velick S.F., Parker C. W. and Eisen H.N., 1960.)

### 4.2.2 Avidity

Antibody molecules are usually multivalent, having one combining site for each heavy and light chain pair. Thus IgG has two combining sites, and IgM 10. If the antigen has multiple antigenic determinants which are presented so as to be sterically available to more than one of the binding sites of antibody, the strength of the binding of antibody will be much higher than would be predicted from the affinity of a single binding site. Once a single binding site of the antibody has attached to the antigen, the other is much more likely to come into contact with a suitable antigenic determinant on the surface of a repeating structure such as a virus or a bacterial surface. Furthermore, the probability of both the binding sites dissociating from their antigenic determinants at the same time is much less than the probability of a single combining site dissociat-

*Chapter 4: The Antibody Combining Site*

ing. This total combining power of the intact antibody with a particular multideterminant antigen is called avidity. The avidity (*Km*) of an antigen antibody system is given by the expression:

$$Km = \frac{F(K^n)}{2}$$

where *Km* is the association constant of the molecular interaction between a divalent antibody molecule and an antigen possessing a number of combining sites. A typical difference between the affinity of a divalent antibody and its avidity is of the order of ten thousandfold (Karush, 1970).

## 4.3 Size and specificity of the combining site

### 4.3.1 Size

The size of the combining site has been estimated by the technique of inhibition of antigen binding by using small fragments of antigen as inhibitors. A convenient system for this investigation is the

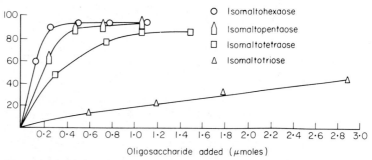

**Fig. 4.5.** Inhibition by isomaltose oligosaccharides of precipitation by dextran of the antidextran in a human antiserum. (From Kabat and Mayer's *Experimental immunochemistry*, 2nd ed.,1961).

inhibition of the precipitation reaction between anti-dextran antibodies and dextran which may be inhibited by glucose oligomers (Kabat, 1968). The degree of inhibition of a series of oligomers of different sizes at equal molar concentrations is estimated, and plotted against oligomer size (Fig. 4.5). Oligomers consisting of 6 glucose units gave optimal inhibition, and any increase in their size above this value failed to improve the inhibition. Hence the antibody combining site appears to be able to accommodate six glucose units. Similar experiments may be carried out with peptides, and it has been shown that the optimal inhibitor of anti-poly-l-alanine is a pentapeptide (Sela 1970).

48

*4.3.2 Specificity*

It is clear, however, that not all the members of such oligomers are of equal importance in the combination with antibody. Table 4.2 shows the protocol for testing which member of a tetra-alanyl peptide is most important in its reaction with anti-polyalanine antibody (raised to poly-alanyl-BSA). The side chains of alanine to which the antiserum was raised are replaced in the assay system with peptides of alanine and glycine in which a single glycine residue has been substituted for alanine at defined positions in the tetramer. When the glycine is substituted at the carboxyterminal end, by which the synthetic polyalanyl side chain was linked to the carrier protein in the original immunogen, the inhibitory power of the complex is little affected. As the position of substitution approaches the N-terminus of the side chain, the inhibitory power decreases, until, when glycine is the N-terminal residue, the inhibitory power is reduced to 40%. The term 'immunodominant group' is used to signify that portion of the determinant which is most important in determining binding with antibody, and, in the case cited, it is the *N*-terminal alanine.

**Table 4.2.** Inhibition of anti-polyalanyl antibodies by related peptides

| Inhibiting peptide | Inhibitory power (approx.) (%) |
|---|---|
| $NH_2$-Ala-Ala-Ala-Ala-$CONH_2$ | 100 |
| $NH_2$-Ala-Ala-Ala-Gly-$CONH_2$ | 95 |
| $NH_2$-Ala-Ala-Gly-Ala-$CONH_2$ | 90 |
| $NH_2$-Ala-Gly-Ala-Ala-$CONH_2$ | 70 |
| $NH_2$-Gly-Ala-Ala-Ala-$CONH_2$ | 40 |

An early hypothesis was that the N-terminal amino acid was always immunodominant, but it is evident that in the above experiment, it is merely the most exposed of the amino-acids in the side chain. Accessibility is very important in determining which groups will react with antibody, as has been demonstrated with synthetic polypeptides, antigens which can be 'custom made'. Side chains of poly-L-alanine (A) are attached to a backbone of poly-L-lysine (L), to form a molecule which is itself non-immunogenic. Short co-polymers of tyrosine (T) and glutamic acid (G) can be attached to the alanine side-chains to yield an immunogenic molecule (T,G)-A--L (Fig. 4.6a) which stimulates the production of anti-(T,G) antibodies. A similar molecule can be synthesized in which the (T,G) residues are attached to the polylysine backbone directly, and then covered with a 'fur' of polyalanine side-chains (Fig. 4.6b).

This molecule is not immunogenic, suggesting that only the outermost components of the polymer are important for antibody production. However, a similar molecule to Fig. 4.6b in which the TG residues are still on the inside of the molecule, but in which the poly-alanine side chains are more widely spaced can evoke the production of anti-TG antibodies, clearly demonstrating that the important factor is the accessibility of the groups and not their chemical position.

Landsteiner (1945) examined the reactivity of antibodies against native and denatured proteins, and showed that antibodies against native proteins reacted only with native proteins and that this reaction was abolished when the protein was denatured. Similarly, antibody to denatured protein fails to react with the same protein

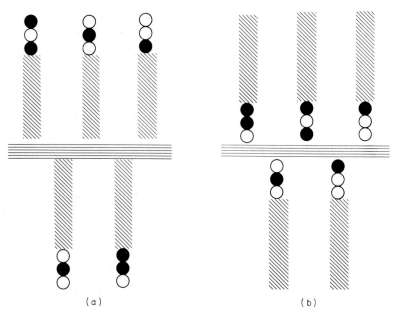

(a)                                    (b)

**Fig. 4.6.** Peptides of L-tyrosine (●) and L-glutamic acid (○) were attached in (a) to poly-DL-alanine (diagonal hatching) coupled to poly-L-lysine (horizontal hatching) and in (b) directly to poly-L-lysine and then covered up with poly-DL-alanine. (From Sela, 1969.)

in the native form. The amino acid sequence of the protein is not altered by the denaturation, and it follows that the antibody reacts with particular conformations of the polypeptide and fails to recognize the sequence itself. Another elegant example of the specificity of antibodies for the shape of proteins was shown by Crumpton (1972) who raised antisera against metmyoglobin and apomyoglobin, molecules which differ in their haem content:

Metmyoglobin⇌Apomyoglobin+haem

Anti-metmyoglobin reacts with metmyoglobin to give a red precipitate containing haem, but anti-apomyoglobin reacts with the apomyoglobin in a metmyoglobin solution to give a colourless precipitate and free haem in solution. It appears that the anti-apomyoglobin shifts the equilibrium to the right either by stabilizing conformational changes in the protein part of the metmyoglobin, such that the haem escapes and the molecule is converted to the apo- form. Alternatively, the apomyoglobin is removed from the free phase by precipitation, and the equilibrium drifts to the right.

Sela and Mozes (1966) have shown that an inverse relationship exists between the net charge of an immunogen and the net charge of the antibodies produced. Acidic antigens, such as diphtheria toxoid, stimulated production of basic antibodies, and, vice versa, basic antigens such as lysozyme and RNAse, caused formation of acidic antibodies. However, this charge difference between antibodies does not apparently relate directly to the combining site. Thus, a hapten such as DNP can be attached to acidic or basic carriers and will stimulate populations of anti-DNP antibodies of opposite charges, but of apparently identical combining sites. The opposite net charges of the antigen and antibody are probably best understood in terms of the close approach of the molecules to one another before specific interaction at the binding site takes place, rather than reflecting any electrostatic interaction at the specific combining site itself.

## 4.4 The structure of the combining site

### 4.4.1 Sequence information

Within the variable region of both heavy and light chains (see Chapter 1), are regions which exhibit very great variability, the 'hypervariable' regions. The light chain has three hypervariable regions involving residues 24–34, 50–56 and 89–97. The first and third of these regions are close to the cysteine residues making up the interchain disulphide bridge and so must be close to each other in space. It seems reasonable to assume that these hypervariable regions will be involved in the antibody combining site, as has recently been confirmed by X-ray diffraction studies (see Chapter 3 and 4.4.3 below).

### 4.4.2 Affinity labelling

Information regarding the specific portions of the light and heavy chains involved in the combining site can be derived from experiments in which a chemically reactive analogue of an antigen (hapten) is allowed to bind to antibody and to form a covalent bond with it. Such a molecule is termed an affinity labelling reagent. The principle of affinity labelling is shown in Fig. 4.7. The choice of affinity labelling reagents is important: they should not be so reactive as to give high labelling of parts of the immunoglobulin distant from the combining site, and they should resemble the hapten to which the antibody was raised as closely as possible, so that a very high saturation of the binding sites will occur at fairly low affinity label concentrations. The nature of the reactive group should be such that the covalent binding will occur under mild conditions, not likely to alter the conformation of the antibody to expose groups not in the binding site, and not likely to weaken the affinity of the antibody for the affinity labelling reagents. The ideal affinity labelling reagent will also have the ability to bind to any residue in the polypeptide chain, thus giving a more accurate indication of the position in which it was most closely opposed.

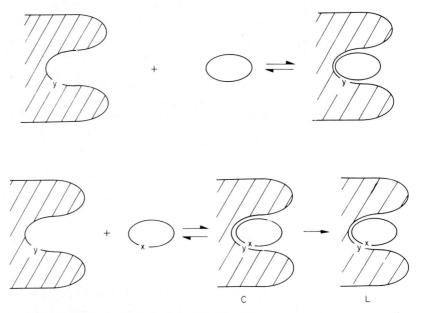

**Fig. 4.7.** The method of affinity labelling illustrated. At the top, the typical reversible combination of a hapten with its specific antibody site is represented. At the bottom, the hapten, modified by the attachment of the group $x$, first combines reversibly with the specific site to give a complex $C$; while in the site, the group $x$ reacts to form a covalent bond with a suitable amino acid residue $y$ in the site, yielding the labelled product $L$. (From Singer & Doolittle, 1966.)

Provided that the affinity labelling reagent is radioactive, the amount bound to different parts of the immunoglobulin molecule may be readily determined. Thus, the amount bound to the heavy and light chains can be determined by separating them, and the position of binding within them may be found by isolating the labelled peptides following, for instance, cyanogen bromide cleavage of the polypeptide chains at methyonyl residues.

*Section I: Immunochemistry*

Among the first affinity labels used were the diazonium derivatives of various haptens. Anti-DNP and anti-ABA (azobenzenearsonate) antibodies will react with the diazonium derivatives of DNP and ABA respectively (Table 4.3). These affinity labels always bind to both the heavy and light chains, though not in equal amounts—the heavy chain is generally more heavily labelled (Table 4.3). They are almost always found to be attached to tyrosine residues, typically for example, that in the third hypervariable region of the heavy or light chain showing that this is in the region

**Table 4.3.** Affinity-Labelling Systems. (From Singer *et al.*, 1971)

| Species of antibody | Antibody to | Labelling reagent | Mole ratio of label (H:L chain) |
|---|---|---|---|
| Rabbit | $AsO_3H - \langle\bigcirc\rangle - N=N -$ { tyr / his / lys } | $AsO_3H - \langle\bigcirc\rangle N_2{}^+$ | 2·1 |
| Rabbit | $(CH_3)_3N^+ - \langle\bigcirc\rangle - N=N -$ { tyr / his / lys } | $(CH_3)_3N^+ \langle\bigcirc\rangle N_2{}^+$ | 1·5 |
| Rabbit | $NO_2\langle\bigcirc\rangle - NH(CH_2)_4 -\overset{}{C}H$, $NO_2$ | $NO_2\langle\bigcirc\rangle N_2{}^+$ | 1·3 |
| Rabbit | $\langle\bigcirc\rangle N_2{}^+$, $NO_2$ | $\langle\bigcirc\rangle N_2{}^+$, $NO_2$ | 2·4 |
| Sheep | Same | Same | 4·5 |
| Guinea-Pig γ1 | Same | Same | 2·5 |
| Guinea-Pig γ2 | Same | Same | 3 |
| Mouse | Same | Same | 2 |
| Pig | Same | Same | 2 |

of the binding site. However, these reagents do not fulfil the last criterion of a good affinity labelling reagent since they can only be expected to react with tyrosines, histidines or lysines.

A more ingenious affinity labelling reagent, the NAP (nitroazidophenyl) group, was developed by Fleet, Knowles and Porter (1969) which does fulfil the third criterion very well. In this case, the hapten and the affinity labelling reagent are the same molecule, the reactive group being generated by exposure of the hapten to light, converting an aryl azide group to a highly reactive nitrene

*Chapter 4: The Antibody Combining Site*

group (Fig. 4.8). Further, this activated compound will insert itself into any carbon bond and is therefore entirely non-residue specific. Experiments with this reagent confirm that the binding site involves both the heavy and light chains and that the areas of the hypervariable regions are involved in the reaction with the antigen.

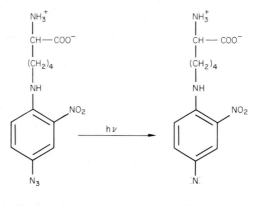

E - 4 - azido - 2 - nitrophenyl lysine
( NAP – lysine )                                    Nitrene

**Fig. 4.8.** The activation by light of NAP-lysine to give the nitrene derivative. (From Press *et al.*, 1971).

### 4.4.3 X-ray diffraction data

The recently published X-ray diffraction data on the three-dimensional structure on immunoglobulins (see Chapter 3) show that there are a number of possible shapes for the antibody combining site. In the human Fab' molecule examined by Poljac and his colleagues, the combining site forms a shallow depression with the side chains of some of the 'variable' amino acids extending into it to give a specific mosaic of hydrophilic and charged groups. The mouse Fab' examined by Davies and his colleagues has a cleft in addition to a broad depression similar to that of the Poljac Fab'.

It is not yet possible to draw firm conclusions as to the shapes that can be assumed by various combining sites. It is, however, clear that variations and deletions in the hypervariable region can give rise to major differences in shape.

### References

CRUMPTON M.J. (1972) In JAENICKE R. & HELMREICH E. *Protein–protein interactions.* Springer-Verlag, Heidelberg, 395.
EISEN H.N. & SISKIND G.W. (1964) Variations in affinities of antibodies during the immune response. *Biochemistry* **3,** 996.

FLEET G.W.J., KNOWLES J.R. & PORTER R.R. (1969) Affinity labelling of antibodies with Aryl Nitrene as reactive group. *Nature* **224,** 511.

KABAT E.A. (1968) *Structural concepts in Immunology and Immunochemistry.* Holt, Rinehart and Winston Inc., New York.

KARUSH F. (1970) Affinity and the immune response. *Annals N.Y. Acad. Sci.* **169,** 56.

LANDSTEINER K. (1945) *The Specificity of Serological Reactions,* 2nd edn. Harvard Univ. Press, Cambridge, Mass.

PRELS E.M., FLEET G.W.J. & FISHER C.E. (1971) Affinity labelling of rabbit antibodies with ε-4-azido-2-nitrophenyl-lysine. In AMOS B. *Progress in Immunology* **1,** 233. Academic Press, New York.

SCHECHTER I. (1971) Mapping of the combining sites of antibodies specific to polyalanine chains. *Ann. N.Y. Acad. Sci.* **190,** 394.

SELA M. (1969) Antigenicity: some Molecular Aspects. *Science* **166,** 1365.

SELA M. (1970) Structure and specificity of synthetic polypeptide antigens. *Annals N.Y. Acad. Sci.* **169,** 23.

SELA M. & MOZES E. (1966) Dependence of the chemical nature of antibodies on the net electrical charge of antigens. *Proc. Nat. Acad. Sci. U.S.A.* **55,** 455.

SINGER S.J. & DOOLITTLE R.F. (1966) Antibody active sites and immunoglobulin molecules. *Science* **153,** 13.

SINGER S.J., MARTIN N. & THORPE N.O. (1971) Affinity labelling of the active sites of antibodies and myeloma proteins. *Annals N.Y. Acad. Sci.* **190,** 342.

VELICK S.F., PARKER C.W. & EISEN H.N. (1960) Excitation Energy Transfer and the Quantitative Study of the Antibody Hapten Reaction. *Proc. Nat. Acad. Sci. (Wash.)* **46,** 1470.

**Further reading**

CRUMPTON M.J. (1973) In PORTER R.R., *Defence and Recognition,* p. 133. MPT & Butterworths, London.

GOODMAN J.W. (1969) Immunochemical specificity: recent conceptual advances. *Immunochemistry* **6,** 139.

PORTER R.R. (1973) In PORTER R.R., *Defence and Recognition,* p. 159. Butterworths, London.

WEIR D.M. (1973) *Handbook of Experimental Immunology,* 2nd edn., Chapter 16. Blackwell Scientific Publications, Oxford.

Articles in: Specificity of Serological Reactions: Landsteiner Centennial. *Annals N.Y. Acad. Sci.* **169** (1970), 1–293.

Articles in: Immunoglobulins. *Annals N.Y. Acad. Sci.* **190** (1971).

# Chapter 5
# The Immunochemistry of Complement

## P. J. Lachmann

### 5.1 Introduction

'A system of factors occurring in normal serum activated characteristically by antibody–antigen interactions and which subsequently mediate a number of biologically significant consequences',
WHO Definition.

#### 5.1.1 History

It was noticed at the end of the nineteenth century that immune
haemolysis and immune bacteriolysis needed, in addition to antibody, a heat labile cofactor that was present in unimmunized serum.
Buchner in 1889 was probably the first to make this observation
but Bordet in 1895 gave the first clear description of 'alexin'. The
current name 'complement' was given because the factor 'comple-
mented' the action of antibody. It was soon found that complement
was multifactorial, Ferrata in 1907 showing that both the euglobulin and the pseudoglobulin components of serum were needed for
the action of complement. By the middle of the twentieth century,
at least four factors were recognized, but it was with the application of the newly available biochemical separation methods
(notably by Müller-Eberhard and his colleagues) in the early 1960s
that the details of the composition and action of the system
became clear.

Complement belongs to the group of plasma systems termed triggered enzyme cascades by McFarlane (1969), which also include the
coagulation and fibrinolytic systems and the kinin generating
systems. They are all effector mechanisms which can produce a
rapid and amplified response to a trigger stimulus. Such mechanisms have adaptive value if invoked in appropriate circumstances,
but may be harmful if triggered in inappropriate circumstances.
They are complex systems both in their reaction pathways and in
the homeostatic mechanisms which have evolved to control them.

#### 5.1.2 Glossary of complement terminology

E   represents Erythrocyte

A       represents Antibody (capable of activating complement, e.g. IgM)

C1–C9   represents the 'classical' complement components, i.e. those needed in the lysis of Sheep E coated with rabbit A by dilute guinea-pig or human serum.

The factors involved in the alternative pathway are denoted by capital letters—B, D, and P (properdin).

Cñ         The bar over a component represents an activated state, usually enzymatic, generated during the complement sequence.

Cn*       The asterisk represents the presence of an evanescent binding site.

Cni        The postscript i represents the inactive state of a previously active component.

Cna & Cnb   represent the fragments of a component derived by proteolytic cleavage, the 'a' fragment being the smaller.

For historical reasons, the subcomponents of C1 are also represented by the use of the postscript letters, q, r and s.


### 5.1.3 The complement components

The published approximate molecular weights, electrophoretic mobilities, labilities, serum concentrations, sites of synthesis and synonyms of the major components of the complement system are shown in Table 5.1. It should be noted that all are fairly large proteins, and that C3 has a serum concentration in excess of 1 mg/ml, being, after the immunoglobulins, albumin and transferrin among the most abundant of serum proteins. It appears that the complement components are not all synthesized by a single cell type.


### 5.1.4 The activation of the complement system

The components of the complement system, at least as far as the C3 step, resemble triggered enzyme systems in that they circulate in an inactive form as proenzymes, awaiting the action of their predecessor in the sequence to convert them to their active form, frequently by a proteolytic step.

The complement sequence may conveniently be thought of as occurring in three main stages:

(i) *The generation of C3 splitting enzymes.* There are at least two of these produced as a consequence of immunological reactions and their interactions and homeostasis occupy much of this chapter.

(ii) *The activation of C3.* This is the central event of the complement sequence and its bulk reaction, analogous to the conversion of fibrinogen to fibrin in blood coagulation. It appears also to be

**Table 5.1.** Properties of complement components

| Component | Approx. serum concentration (μgms/ml) | Electrophoretic mobility (pH 8·6) | Sedimentation coefficient (Svedbergs) | m.w. | Lability to Heat | Lability to NH₃ | Synthesized by | Other |
|---|---|---|---|---|---|---|---|---|
| C1q | 150 | γ | 11 | 400,000 | + | − | Intestinal epith. | 6 subunits, 3 chains each |
| C1r | | β | 7 | 170,000 | ++ | − | Intestinal epith. | |
| C1s | 20 | α | 4 | 79,000 | − | − | Intestinal epith. | |
| C4 | 450 | β | 10 | 240,000 | − | ++ | Macrophage | |
| C2 | 30 | β | 5·5 | 120,000 | ++ | − | Macrophage | |
| C3 | 1200 | β | 9·5 | 180,000 | − | + | Liver | Genetic markers |
| C5 | 75 | β | 8·7 | 200,000 | − | (+) | Spleen cells | |
| C6 | 60 | β | 5·8 | 150,000 | + | − | Liver | Genetic markers |
| C7 | 50–100 | β | 5·7 | 140,000 | − | − | | |
| C8 | 50–100 | γ | 8·0 | 150,000 | + | − | Cells in spleen | |
| C9 | 150 | α | 4·5 | 79,000 | − | − | Liver | |
| C1 inhibitor | | α2 | 3·7 | 90,000 | − | − | | |
| C3b inactivator | 10–20 | β | 6·0 | 90,000 | − | − | | |

*Section I: Immunochemistry*

biologically the most significant part of the sequence (see Chapter 19).

(iii) *The activation of the terminal components.* This step is initiated by the activation of C5 which seems to be the last enzymatic reaction in the complement sequence. Thereafter the remaining components—C6–C9—combine to form a multi-molecular complex which mediates the most characteristic *in vitro* event of the complement system: the generation of membrane lesions leading to cell lysis.

## 5.2 The generation of C3 converting enyzmes

Table 5.2 lists the enzymes known to be capable of splitting C3. The 'non-immunological' enzymes are serine/histidine esterases, sensitive to DFP. They all seem to split the C3 molecule at a particular

**Table 5.2.** C3 Converting Enzymes

| Non-Immunological | | Immunological |
|---|---|---|
| Trypsin | $\overline{C42}$ | 'Classical pathway' C3 convertase |
| Thrombin | $\overline{C3b, B_b}$ | 'Alternative pathway' C3 convertase |
| Plasmin | $\overline{CVF, B_b}$ | 'Cobra venom factor' C3 convertase |
| Leucocyte cathepsins | | |

point to yield C3a and C3b fragments, which are largely similar irrespective of the enzyme used. The splitting of C3 *in vivo* by thrombin and plasmin, and especially by the leucocyte proteases, is probably of importance in antibody-independent inflammatory reactions (see Chapter 19).

There are two 'immunological' C3 converting enzymes which are the end products of the so-called 'classical' and 'alternative' pathways of complement activation.

### 5.2.1 The 'classical C3 convertase'

In the presence of antigen/antibody complexes, C1 is converted to $\overline{C1}$. C1 has three subcomponents, C1q, C1r and C1s. It is C1q which binds to some antibodies, for instance IgM and some IgG subclasses (see Chapter 1) but not to IgA, IgD and IgE. C1q has a characteristic appearance in the electron-microscope (Fig. 5.1) which can be likened to a bunch of 6 flowers. It is known that the molecule has multiple binding sites for IgG, probably 5 or 6, and

*Chapter 5: The Immunochemistry of Complement*

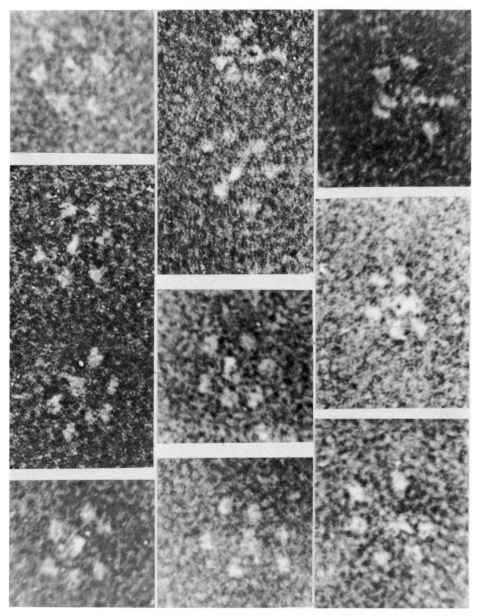

**Fig. 5.1.** Electron micrographs of C1q. By courtesy of Dr E. A. Munn.

it seems likely that the binding sites will be found to be in the 'flower heads'. An extraordinary feature of C1q is the presence of a collagen-like portion of the polypeptide chains making up the sub-units (Reid, Lowe and Porter, 1972), and this is probably seen as the 'stalk' in the electron microscope. The mechanism of the con-version of C1 to C$\bar{1}$ following the interaction of C1q with antibody is not fully understood but involves the other two sub-components

*Section I: Immunochemistry*

of C1, C1r and C1s, together with calcium ions. The proenzyme is C1s which becomes activated to give $\overline{C1s}$ or 'C1 esterase' which splits acetyl tyroinse ethyl ester and *in vivo* acts on C4 and C2.

$\overline{C1}$ acts on C4 to split off a small C4a fragment, and to expose an evanescent hydrophobic binding site on the larger C4b, some 10–15 per cent of which is bound in the region of the complement activation site (Fig. 5.2). C2 binds reversibly to C4b in the presence of magnesium ions, even in the absence of $\overline{C1}$: however in its presence a fairly large fragment is split from the C2 yielding $\overline{C42}$ which has a half life of about 5 mins at 37°C, and C2b. After this stage, C1 and antibody are no longer required for the completion of the complement sequence. C1 may be removed by EDTA, inactivated by DFP, or 'cold' antibody may be removed by washing in warm buffer, all without affecting subsequent lysis (Fig. 5.2).

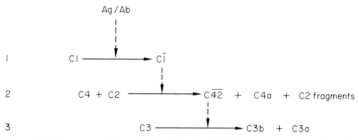

**Fig. 5.2.** The generation of the 'classical' C3 convertase has the characteristics of an enzyme cascade, whose bulk product is C3b.

There is an inhibitor of $\overline{C1}$, the α2-neuraminoglycoprotein, which acts stoichiometrically on $\overline{C1}$ and which also inhibits plasmin, kininogenase (kallikrein), activated Hageman factor (XIIa) and activated plasma thromboplastin antecedent (XIa). The inhibitor is important in preventing the unrestrained action of $\overline{C1}$ on C4 and C2 in free solution but has little inhibitory effect on the on-going complement sequence. Heterozygous genetic deficiency of the inhibitor in man produces the disease of hereditary angio-oedema which is due to extensive local activation of C1, and the production of pharmacologically active fragments from (C4), C2, C3 and C5 (Chapter 19).

### 5.2.2 The 'alternative pathway'

It has long been recognized that there are certain substances which fix large amounts of complement, especially the late components C3–9, but very little or no C1, C4 or C2. The best known of these substances are yeast cell wall polysaccharide (zymosan), gram negative endotoxin and a factor from cobra venom (Table 5.3). In addition, there are various immunoglobulin aggregates and antigen–antibody complexes which behave similarly. These include

*Chapter 5: The Immunochemistry of Complement*

aggregates of human IgA, guinea-pig IgG1 and ruminant IgG2.

The known components of the alternative pathway are listed in Table 5.4 with their synonyms and physical characteristics. Properdin was first described by Pillemer *et al.* (1954) as a factor which was capable of activating C3 in the absence of antibody on addition of zymosan to serum. The work on properdin was criticized in relation to its supposed non-specificity but more recently the molecule has been isolated. It is found in serum at low concentration, is characterized by a highly asymmetric shape and is involved, with other factors listed here, in the conversion of C3.

Pillemer and his colleagues also described two further factors (A

**Table 5.3.** A comparison of the classical and alternative complement activation sites

|  | Classical | | Alternative (or C3b-feedback pathway) |
|---|---|---|---|
| Activating agents | | | |
| Aggregates of human | IgG1 & 3 (&2); IgM | | IgA |
| rabbit | IgG | IgM | F(ab')$_2$ |
| guinea-pig | IgG2 | | IgG1 |
| ruminant | IgG1 | | IgG2 |
|  | | | Inulin |
|  | (Lipid A) | | Zymosan |
|  | | | Endotoxin LPS |
|  | | | CVF |
| Factors required to generate | C1 | | Properdin, factor D |
| C3 convertase | C4 | | C3 |
|  | C2 | | factor B |
| Total serum requirement | Dilute | | Concentrated |
| Ion requirements | Ca and Mg | | Mg |
| Capacity to generate C$\overline{56}$ in acute phase serum (reactive lysis) | Low | | High |

and B) needed in the properdin system. Factor A was thought to be C4-like in view of its sensitivity to hydrazine and has now, surprisingly, been shown to be C3. Factor B, hydrazine stable but heat sensitive, was also known as C3 proactivator (C3PA) or glycine rich beta glycoprotein (GBG).

On activation this molecule is split into fragments of alpha and gamma mobility termed Ba and Bb respectively. At least one further factor is now known to be involved. This is known as Factor D and in man is a 3S $\alpha$2 euglobulin.

**Table 5.4.** Factors involved in the alternative pathway

| Factor | Same as | Approx. serum concentration (μgms/ml) | Electrophoretic mobility (pH 8·6) | Sedimentation coefficient (Svedburgs) | m.w. | Lability to heat | NH₃ | Other |
|---|---|---|---|---|---|---|---|---|
| Properdin | | 10– 20 | γ | 5·2 | 220,000 | | | |
| Factor A | C3 | | | | | | | |
| Factor B | C3Pa GBG | 100–200 | β | 6·2 | 80,000 | + | − | Genetic markers |
| Factor D | pro-GBGase | | α2 | 4 | 25,000 | − | − | |

Besides using different components to generate a C3 splitting enzyme, the classical and alternative pathways also have different reaction requirements. The classical pathway functions in dilute serum and has been widely exploited *in vitro* for its economy, lack of interference by low titre antibodies in the complement source and its suitability for the complement fixation tests. The alternative pathway, by contrast, works satisfactorily only at high serum concentration. The classical pathway requires both calcium and magnesium ions whereas the alternative pathway requires only magnesium ions. The alternative pathway has a more rigorous requirement for high temperatures at least in the case of normal sera.

The action of the alternative pathway may be conveniently distinguished from the classical pathway in normal serum by the specific chelation of calcium by the magnesium salt of ethyleneglycoltetracetic acid (EGTA) or in sera genetically deficient in C4 or C2.

### 5.2.3 The C3b feedback cycle

While the details of the initiation mechanism of the alternative

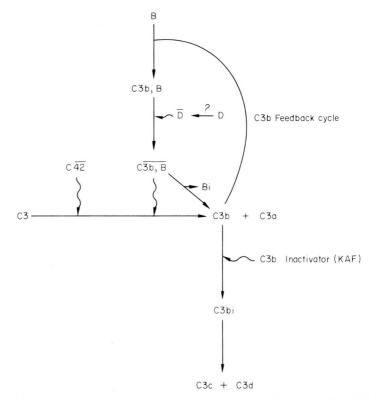

**Fig. 5.3.** The generation of C3b leads to the activation of a self-amplifying positive feedback cycle. This is damped by the action of the C3b inactivator (KAF) which inactivates C3b with very high turnover.

*Section I: Immunochemistry*

pathway are still incompletely understood, it has recently become clear that the main events observed in alternative pathway activation of C3 are due to a positive feedback cycle. C3b, no matter how produced, will form a loose complex with Factor B in the presence of $Mg^{++}$. This is cleaved by Factor $\overline{D}$ to form $\overline{C3b,Bb}$ which is the alternative pathway C3 convertase and splits C3 to C3a and C3b, 'pushing the cycle on another turn'! (Müller-Eberhard & Götze, 1972) (Fig. 5.3). Clearly such a mechanism demands a homeostatic mechanism, or the splitting of a single C3 molecule would lead to massive complement activation.

The homeostasis is achieved by the action of the C3b inactivator (KAF), an enzyme which destroys much of the biological activity of C3, notably its ability to fire the feedback cycle, to take part in the activation of C5, and some of its adherence properties.

### 5.2.4 The cobra venom factor

The action of cobra venom on complement was first noticed by Flexner and Noguchi in 1903 and it was soon recognized that it

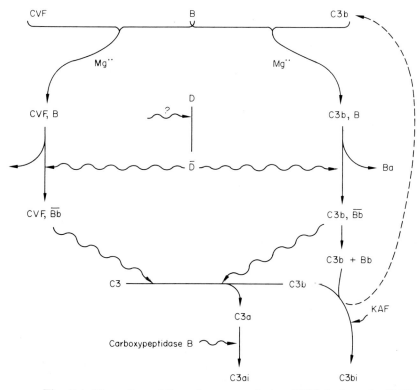

**Fig. 5.4.** The action of the cobra venom factor (CVF) is that of a KAF-resistant analogue of C3b. The complex CVF,$\overline{Bb}$ is stable and does not itself lead to turnover of Factor B.

*Chapter 5: The Immunochemistry of Complement*

acted on C3, but spared C1, C4 and C2. Müller-Eberhard & Fjell-ström (1971) showed that the factor in cobra venom would not split pure C3, but required a cofactor present in normal serum, which they named C3 proactivator (C3PA) which is Factor B. It is now clear that cobra venom factor is cobra C3b and acts on B in the same way as mammal C3b, except that it does not 'turn it over' but instead forms a stable product of $\overline{CVF,B}$ which is also insusceptible to KAF (Lachmann & Nicol, 1973, Alper & Balavitch, 1976) (Fig. 5.4).

In summary, the major event of the 'alternative pathway' is the feedback cycle, which can potentially be entered at a number of steps but which is inevitably triggered by any mechanism which converts C3 to C3b, be it $\overline{C42}$, $\overline{C3b,B}$, $\overline{CVF,B}$ or extrinsic enzymes.

The mechanism by which the initiators and properdin trigger the feedback cycle is not clearly known. It has been claimed (Schreiber

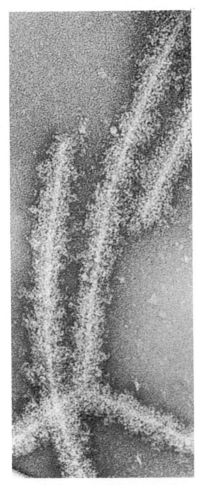

**Fig. 5.5.** C3 coating Salmonella flagella. (From Feinstein A. & Munn E.A., 1966.)

*Section I: Immunochemistry*

*et al.*, 1975) that an initiating enzyme is formed by the interaction of native C3, native Factor B, Factor D and activated Properdin (or C3 nephritic factor). Activated Properdin combines with C3b and seems to enhance the activity of the feedback C3 convertase.

## 5.3 The C3 step

### 5.3.1 Activation

The activation of C3 is quantitatively the major event of the complement sequence, as might be expected from its serum concentration and from the manifold and self-amplifying mechanisms for its activation. There is visible evidence for this also from electron-micrographic studies (Feinstein & Munn, 1966) in which particles coated with antibody and exposed to complement are seen to be ensheathed in a thick amorphous layer consisting principally of C3 (Fig. 5.5).

The action of the C3 converting enzyme is to cleave peptide bonds at a restricted site in the molecule, rendering it unstable, such that a C3a fragment may be eluted in weak acid, or spontaneously released in serum. C3a has biological activity as an anaphylatoxin and as a chemotactic factor, and a molecular weight of about 7,000. C3b, like C4b has an evanescent hydrophobic binding site, permitting its firm attachment to local structures: be they proteins, phospholipid membranes or polysaccharides. This form of C3 binding is to be distinguished from the much weaker and more specific adherence sites on the C3 molecule involved in immune and opsonic adherence which are much longer lived features of the fixed C3 molecule.

### 5.3.2 Inactivation

C3b is inactivated by the C3b-inactivator also known as the conglutinogen activating factor or KAF for short. KAF acts enzymatically on C3b splitting off a peptide about 25,000 m.w. As a consequence the carbohydrate determinant in C3 which reacts with conglutinin becomes exposed (hence the name conglutinogen activating factor); and the C5 splitting, feedback activating, and adherence activities are lost. A further 14,000 m:w. fragment is split off from KAF-reacted C3b by traces of tryptic enzymes and the remaining large fragment is C3c (see Fig 5.6) (Gitlin *et al.*, 1975). KAF, unlike the other complement components, seems to be an enzyme present in active form in normal serum with a high specificity for its substrate and a high turn-over. It is therefore an ideal homeostatic system.

There exists a unique, genetically KAF deficient, patient who was observed to have a gravely disordered complement system (see Alper & Rosen, 1971), whose deficiency has helped to characterize the biologlcal function of KAF (Alper *et al.*, 1972). He has a low serum antigenic C3 level and no C3 function. His C3 is present in the circulation largely as C3b, an otherwise unknown event, since it is usually rapidly broken down by the action of KAF. Further, the patient's erythrocytes carry bound C3 antigens and there is $\overline{D}$ but no Factor B in his serum. His serum is not capable of producing a cobra venom dependent C3 convertase, presumably for lack of Factor B. C1, C4 and C2 levels in this patient are normal. An accurate *in vitro* model for the situation in this patient is provided by the immunochemical depletion of KAF from normal serum using a pure $F(ab')_2$ anti-KAF (Nicol & Lachmann, 1973).

In the absence of KAF, the homeostatic control of the feedback control of the feedback cycle is removed and it fires spontaneously until one or more of the components are exhausted.

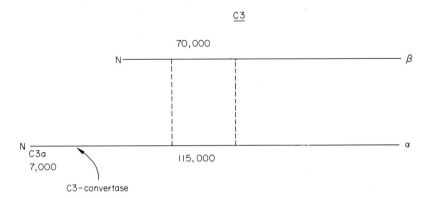

Fig. 5.6. The outline structure of C3 is shown, although the position of the disulphide bridges is not known. All the enzymes which attack C3 seem to act on the heavy ($\alpha$) chain: the C3 convertases removing a 7,000 m.w. fragment, probably from the N-terminus. Short (3 min) incubation with purified KAF removes a further 25,000 m.w. from the $\alpha$ chain, leaving the molecule exquisitely susceptible to the action of trypsin, which removes a further 14,000 m.w. from the $\alpha$ chain. This reaction also occurs on prolonged incubation with KAF, possibly due to trace contamination with other proteases. The final product is composed of the 70,000 m.w. remainder of the heavy chain and the 70,000 m.w. light ($\beta$) chain, held together by disulphide bridges. (Gitlin *et al.*, 1975.)

### 5.3.3 Control of C3 biosynthesis

It appears from both *in vivo* measurements of the turnover of C3 in normal subjects and in patients with chronic complement activation (Alper & Rosen, 1971; Charlesworth *et al.*, 1974) as well as from studies on the *in vitro* synthesis of C3 by liver slices (Colten *et al.*, 1973), that the terminal breakdown products of C3 are able to inhibit its biosynthesis. In the turnover studies, when the fractional catabolic rate of C3 is plotted against plasma C3 concentration, a theoretical line can be drawn showing the expected C3 level for varying degrees of hypercatabolism. It can be seen (Fig. 5.7) that virtually all patients with C3 hypercatabolism have C3 levels which fall well below this line, the exception being the KAF-deficient patient, who is completely unable to degrade his serum C3b.

This negative feedback inhibition of C3 synthesis by the products of its breakdown may serve to limit the extent of C3 activation in chronic complement activating diseases.

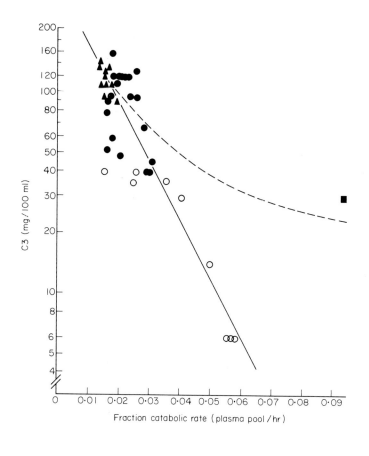

△     Normal

●     Disease

○     Disease with C3d

■     Patient T.J. of Alper *et al* 1970

**Fig. 5.7.** Serum C3 concentrations vs. fractional catabolic rate of C3. The interrupted line indicates the calculated fall in plasma C3 if no change in intravascular pool size, distribution or synthesis occurred. The value for the KAF-deficient patient T.J. falls close to this line. $r - 0.96$; $P < 0.001$. (From Charlesworth *et al.*, 1974.)

       *Chapter 5: The Immunochemistry of Complement*

## 5.4 The terminal complement sequence

The only step in this sequence which is part of the enzyme cascade is the splitting of C5 into C5a (15,000 m.w.) and C5b with a weak binding site for membranes. C5b has for a short time the capacity to react with C6 to give the complex C$\overline{56}$. The complex C$\overline{56}$ may be released from the complement binding site. It binds C7 stoichiometrically to give the trimolecular complex C567* which will bind firmly to membranes with a measurably long half-life at 37°. As a result there is significant 'contagion' of complement activity from the initial activation site at this stage, and innocent bystander cells may become involved in the terminal lytic events.

### 5.4.1 Reactive lysis

It is possible to generate free C$\overline{56}$ in solution by the action of zymosan on sera with a relative excess of C5 and C6. Such sera include the sera of patients in the 'acute phase' of inflammation including those who have recently had major surgery or given birth— and the extremely rare persons genetically deficient in C7 (Pondman et al., 1974). When activated, there is an excess production of C$\overline{56}$ over the available C7, and this excess remains in the fluid phase, while the C567* is bound or decays. The C$\overline{56}$ may be isolated and used with C7 to generate the C$\overline{567}$ on red cells or on liposomes having neither antibody nor C1–C3 on them. This is the phenomenon underlying reactive lysis (Thompson & Lachmann, 1970).

### 5.4.2 Generation of the lytic lesion

The site of the terminal complement lesion leading to the lysis of erythrocytes seems to be the site of attachment of the C567 complex. The C567 complex binds one molecule of C8 and six molecules of C9 to produce a complex of about $10^6$ Daltons (Kolb & Müller-Eberhard, 1973). There is, for human complement, no absolute necessity for the presence of C9, since iron chelating agents such as phenanthrolene and bipiridine can substitute for it.

The complement of some species show marked specificity for the substrate cells which they are to lyse. For example, horse complement fails to lyse sheep cells, but will lyse guinea-pig cells quite well. This specificity can be shown by the use of the reactive lysis system, in which human C567 is bound to the cells and the efficiency of lysis is measured for the sera, or in some cases, the isolated C8, of different species. These results further confirm the importance of C8 as the principal agent of lysis, and might be thought to suggest that it has a specific enzymic activity. However, strenuous efforts to detect the enzymic action of C8 have been uniformly unsuccessful, and it appears that the mechanism of formation of the complement lesion is by some kind of insertional event of the

*Section I: Immunochemistry*

C5–9 complex into the lipid bilayer of the membrane. Certainly, the efficiency of the complement system is much greater than any other known mechanism for inducing cell lysis, needing as little as one C8 molecule per cell for its action, compared with $10^7$ of molecules of, for instance, the naturally occurring detergent antibiotic filipin.

## 5.5 The complement lesion on membranes

The lesion has a characteristic appearance in the electron microscope (Fig. 5.8) with a dark, stain-penetrated centre, and a sur-

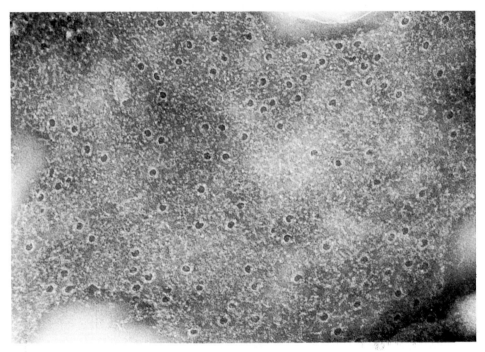

**Fig. 5.8.** Complement lesions in erythrocyte membrane. Electron micrograph by courtesy of Dr E. A. Munn.

rounding ring, often apparently incomplete, of material which excludes stain and is about 30Å thick (see Humphrey & Dourmashkin, 1969). Complement does not demand a complex membrane for its action, since typical lesions may be formed in liposomes made wholly of lecithin (Fig. 5.9), or of sphingomyelin/cholesterol. Such liposomes show not only the characteristic lesions, but are also rendered leaky for low molecular weight markers.

Lesions can sometimes be dissociated from the membrane in which they were formed: 'the grin without the cat' phenomenon (Fig. 5.9) indicating that they are stable structures, not simply

*Chapter 5: The Immunochemistry of Complement*

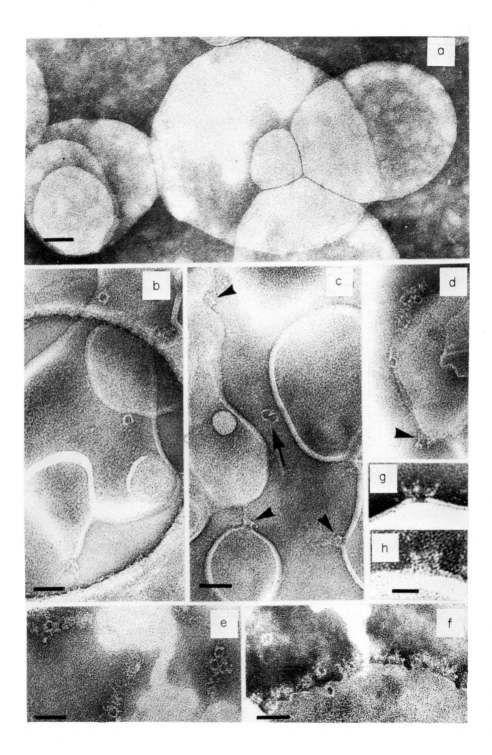

micellar rearrangements of the lipid bilayer. In profile, a few lesions have been well resolved (Fig. 5.9) showing a funnel-shaped structure through which there may be a hole leading through the lipid bilayer.

### 5.5.1 The lytic event

The release of haemoglobin from red cells by immune haemolysis requires osmotic swelling of the cells, showing that the initial lesion is too small to allow protein to pass. If the colloid osmotic pressure of the medium is raised to equal that inside the cell (e.g. by using a solution of 30 per cent albumin), complement lysed cells lose their intracellular potassium, but do not rupture or release haemoglobin (Green et al., 1954).

## 5.6 Kinetics

The analysis of the kinetics of complement lysis was undertaken by Mayer et al. in the 1940s (see Mayer, 1961) and provided a useful tool in the understanding of the action of complement. It was observed that a plot of the fraction of cells lysed versus the complement concentration has a sigmoid shape. The most obvious interpretation of this was that the phenomenon depended on multiple hits on the cells. However, when lower concentrations of complement were used, it was found that the number of cells lysed was independent of the number of cells offered, a phenomenon which is only compatible with a single hit phenomenon. In other words, the multiple event in the complement system is the large number of reaction steps between the components, and not the cumulative effect of a single kind of event. When the single hit nature of complement lysis was first appreciated it was thought that this reflected an analysis of the reaction of the molecular level, i.e. that one

---

Fig. 5.9 a–h are electron micrographs of preparations negatively stained with 2 per cent sodium phospho-tungstate pH 7·3. Similar pictures were obtained when the preparations were stained with 4 per cent ammonium molybdate, pH 6·9. In a–f the bar represents 500 A; in g–h it represents 250 A.

(a) Sphingomyelin + cholesterol liposomes + $C\overline{567}$.

(b)(c)(d) Sphingomyelin + cholesterol liposomes + $C\overline{567}$ + C8 and C9. The characteristic structures (lesions) associated with complement lysis are seen in top view, (b, d) and in profile (arrowheads, (b, c, d)). Two lesions (arrow c) appear to be detached.

(e) Sphingomyelin-cholesterol liposomes + $C\overline{567}$ + C8 + C9 to show groups of lesions in top view detached from the liposomes.

(f) Lecithin liposome + $C\overline{567}$ + C8 + C9 showing lesions in top view, profile and detached.

(g)(h) Higher magnification views of lesions seen in profile (g) from a lecithin liposome, (h) from a sphingomyelin-cholesterol liposome. It is noteworthy that in (g) the negative stain appears to be continuous through the lesion to the hydropohilic space underlying the first bilayer. (From Lachmann et al., 1973)

molecule of complement or of a particular component contributed to the single hit. However, with the newer methods of studying complement by physicochemical techniques it soon became apparent that for many components this was not true. The term 'functional molecule' was then introduced for the amount of a component that by kinetic analysis is responsible for single hit lysis. In the case of some components, for example C3, this represents a very large number of real molecules although it seems quite possible that a single C56789 multimolecular complex is in fact responsible for producing a lesion.

The one-hit concept predicts from the Poisson distribution that the number of cells which have no hits when there is an average one hit per cell is 37 per cent, i.e. 63 per cent lysis is given by one functional molecule per cell.

## 5.7 Summary

The complement system is seen to be a remarkably complex interacting system even by comparison with other triggered enzyme systems. The early part of the cascade up to and including the fixation of C3 is in many ways a typical enzyme cascade although the multiplicity of C3 splitting enzymes and the complicated feedback enhancing cycles are unusual features. In the later part of the complement sequence, the process leading to lysis is the formation of a self-associating multimolecular complex. The evolutionary significance of the fusing of these two quite different mechanisms is unknown and it is not so far even clear which came earlier in evolution. However, if the complexity of an effector mechanism can be regarded as a measure of its biological importance then the complement system must certainly have some value.

## References

ALPER C.A. & BALAVITCH D. (1976) Cobra venom factor: Evidence for its being altered cobra C3 (the third component of complement). *Science* **191,** 1275.

ALPER C.A. & ROSEN F.S. (1971) Genetic aspects of the complement system. *Adv. Immunol.* **14,** 252.

ALPER C.A., ROSEN F.S. & LACHMANN P.J. (1972) Inactivator of the third component of complement as an inhibitor of the properdin pathway. *Proc. Nat. Acad. Sci.* **69,** 2910.

BORDET J. (1895) Les leukocytes et les proprietes actives du serum chez les vaccine. *Ann. Inst. Pasteur.* **9,** 462.

BUCHNER H. (1889) Uber die bakterientodtende Wirkunk des zellenfrien Blutserums. *Zbl. Bakt. Parasit. Kde.* **6,** 1.

CHARLESWORTH J.A., WILLIAMS D.G., SHERINGTON E. & PETERS D.K. (1974) Metabolism of the third component of complement (C3) in normal human subjects. *Clin. Sci. molec. Med.* **46,** 223.

COLTEN H., LEVEY R., ROSEN F.S. & ALPER C.A. (1973) Decreased Synthesis of C3 in Membranoproliferative Glomerulonephritis. *J. Clin. Invest.* **52,** 20a.

FEINSTEIN A. & MUNN E.A. (1966) An electron-microscopic study of the interaction of immunoglobulin (IgM) antibodies with bacterial flagella and the binding of complement. *J. Physiol.* **186**, 64.

FERRATA A. (1907) Die Unwirksamkeit der komplexen Hämolysine in salzfreien Losungen und ihre Ursache. *Berl. Klin. Wschr.* **44**, 366.

FLEXNER S. & NOGUCHI H. (1903) Snake venom in relation to haemolysis, bacteriolysis and toxicity. *J. exp. Med.* **6**, 277.

GITLIN J., ROSEN F.S. & LACHMANN P.J. (1975) The mechanism of action of the C3b inactivator (conglutination activating factor) on its natural substrate the major fragment of the third component of complement (C3b). *J. exp. Med.* **141**, 221.

GREEN H., BARROW P. & GOLDBERG B. (1959) Effect of antibody and complement on permeability control in ascites tumour cells and erythrocytes. *J. exp. Med.* **110**, 699.

HUMPHREY J.H. & DOURMASHKIN R.R. (1969) The lesion in cell membrane caused by complement. *Adv. Immunol.* **11**, 75.

KOLB W.P. & MÜLLER-EBERHARD H.J. (1973) The membrane attack mechanism of complement. Verification of a stable C5–9 complex in free solution. *J. exp. Med.* **138**, 438.

LACHMANN P.J., BOWYER D.E., NICOL P., DAWSON R.M.C. & MUNN E.A. (1973) Studies on the terminal stages of complement lysis. *Immunology* **23**, 135.

LACHMANN P.J. & NICOL P.A.E. (1973) Reaction mechanisms of the alternative pathway of complement fixation. *Lancet* **1**, 465.

MAYER M.M. (1961) Complement and Complement Fixation. In Kabat E.A. *Kabat and Mayer's Experimental Immunochemistry*, 2nd. ed. p. 133. Thomas, Springfield.

McFARLANE R.G. (1969) A discussion on triggered enzyme systems in blood plasma. (Chairman's Introduction). *Proc. Roy. Soc. B* **173**, 259.

MÜLLER-EBERHARD H.G. & FJELLSTRÖM K.E. (1971) Isolation of the anticomplementary protein from cobra venom and its mode of action on C3. *J. Immunol.* **107**, 1666.

MÜLLER-EBERHARD H.G. & GÖTZE O. (1972) C3 proactivator convertase and its mode of action. *J. exp. Med.* **135**, 1003.

NICOL P.A.E. & LACHMANN P.J. (1973) The alternate pathway of complement activation: the role of C3 and its inactivator (KAF). *Immunology* **24**, 259.

PILLEMER L., BLUM L., LEPOW I.H., ROSS O.A., TODD E.W. & WARDLAW A.C. (1954) The properdin system and immunity. I. Demonstration and isolation of a new serum protein, and its role in immune phenomena. *Science* **120**, 279.

PONDMAN K.W., HANNEMA A.J., DOHMANN U., GODNER H. & DOOREN L.J. (1975) A deficiency of the 7th component of complement in man. *New Engl. J. Med.* (in press).

REID K.B.M., LOWE D.M. & PORTER R.R. (1972) Isolation and characterisation of C1q, a sub-component of the first component of complement from human and rabbit sera. *Biochem. J.* **130**, 749.

SCHREIBER R.D., MEDICUS R.G., GÖTZE O. & MÜLLER-EBERHARD H.J. (1975) Properdin and nephritic factor dependant C3 convertases: requirement of native C3 for enzyme formation and the function of bound C3b as properdin receptor. *J. exp. Med.* **142**, 760.

THOMPSON R.A. & LACHMANN P.J. (1970) Reactive lysis: the complement-mediated lysis of unsensitised cells. I. The characterisation of indicator factor and its identification as C7. *J. exp. Med.* **131**, 629.

*Chapter 5: The Immunochemistry of Complement*

# Chapter 6
# The Evolution and Genetics of Antibody and Complement

# M. J. Hobart

## 6.1 Introduction

The evolution of a system of adaptive immunity is a vertebrate characteristic, and represents a very much more sophisticated system of defence than that of lower animals, which are equipped with phagocytes alone. The unique characteristics of the adaptive immune response are specificity, dissemination, amplification and memory. It is rather like ideas which (can) show specificity, be spread and accepted, and stored for future use. These features have enormous advantages in repelling invading organisms, which elicit an accelerated response on second exposure, even at a site remote from the first exposure. In the phagocyte-alone system every experience of an antigen is a 'first' experience (see Chapter 23).

The existence of a common set of signals (antibodies) which can be applied to any foreign particle offers the opportunity for the development of powerful effector mechanisms. The complement system is one of these, which without direction might be dangerous. The selective pressures acting in favour of the present interaction between antibody and complement is clear. It is less obvious by what mechanism the genetic potential for their synthesis arose, at least in the case of the complement system.

### 6.1.1 Evolutionary origins

The evolutionary origin of a protein is most surely determined from a comparison of its amino acid sequence with that of structurally related proteins derived from living representatives of ancestral life forms. The immunoglobulins of mammals are among the most extensively studied of all proteins, but there is relatively little data on most complement components or primitive immunoglobulins.

Both antibody and complement are found in elasmobranch fishes. Efforts to find them in lower animals have given conflicting results, and the elasmobranchs will be taken as the most primitive possessors of both. IgM seems to be the first class of immunoglobulin which evolved, and as will be shown below (6.3.1) it forms a plausible basis for the evolution of other classes. Part of this chapter explains mechanisms by which this could be achieved.

## 6.2 Gene duplication

The immunoglobulins are a classical example of the evolution of proteins by gene duplication. Much of this section attempts to summarize the arguments on the role of gene duplication in evolution, which have so elegantly been put forward by Ohno (1970).

### 6.2.1 Polyploid duplication

When there is a partial or complete failure of the process of meiosis, there is the possibility of the development of a strain of individuals with duplicate sets of chromosomes (Fig. 6.1). At any duplicated

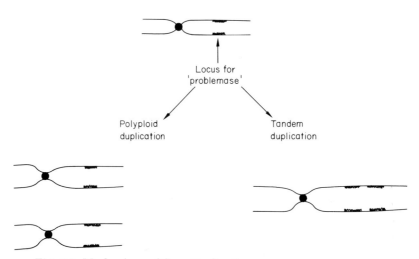

**Fig. 6.1.** Mechanisms of Gene Duplication.
A typical pair of chromosomes are shown, with the locus for an enzyme ('problemase'). Polyploid duplication, due to partial failure of meiosis results in the complete duplication of the chromosome, and perhaps all the other chromosomes. The four copies of 'problemase' are *all* alleles. Tandem duplication, probably due to unequal crossing over during meiosis (see Fig. 6.2), results in the elongation of the DNA strand, with a tandem duplicate of the gene close to the original.

locus, the individual has not two but four gene copies, and, if they are different, four alleles. Polyploidy is relatively common in fishes, but is incompatible with reproduction in species which use chromosomal sex determination, since XXXX, XXXY and XXYY individuals are sterile.

In polyploid duplication, the genes of the duplicate set of chromosomes are free to mutate to serve new functions and to evolve new control mechanisms different from those which operate on the parental genes. Subsequent polyploid duplication could give rise quite rapidly to a large number of related gene copies carrying out different functions.

### 6.2.2 Tandem duplication

Tandem duplication of genes involves the partial or complete doubling of a stretch of DNA on a chromosome. It can give rise to a gene which codes for a polypeptide chain larger than its parent, or to a complete identical duplicate gene. Unequal crossing over is probably the most common mechanism for tandem duplication. When the chromatids pair during meiosis, the DNA strands align themselves homologously. If the alignment is imperfect, crossing

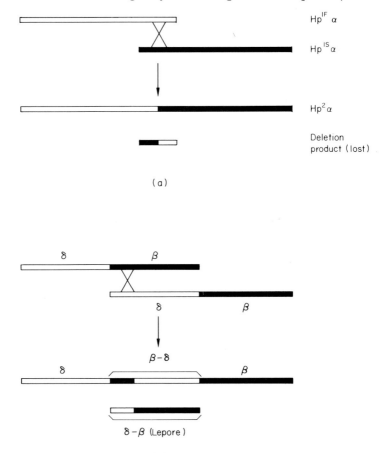

(a)

(b)

**Fig. 6.2.** Unequal Crossing Over.

Unequal crossing over is the probable mechanism for the generation of the genes for $Hp^2\alpha$ and Hb Lepore. The first is an almost complete duplication product, the latter a deletion product.

over will give rise to two daughter chromatids of unequal length, one with a gene, or part of it, deleted, and the other with a tandem duplicate. Surviving examples of both kinds of product are well known: haptoglobin 2 is a result of the *fusion* of a large part of the $Hp^{1F}$ allele with the $Hp^{1S}$ allele (Fig. 6.2a). Haemoglobin Lepore has an abnormal globin chain whose N-terminal sequence is that of the $\delta$ chain and C-terminal sequence of the $\beta$ chain. The genetic event which led to this involved the deletion of a part of the gene cluster coding for the globin chains (Fig. 6.2b).

The presence of tandem gene copies permits mutation to occur without compromising the essential function of the gene but tandem duplication is not without risks. There may be problems of gene dosage, for instance if the gene for one of the globin chains was duplicated, it might be difficult to make stable $\alpha_2\beta_2$ haemoglobin tetramers. The duplication may not include the controlling portion of the operon, leading to runaway synthesis, or the initiating sequence, leading to asynthesis. Further, since the net DNA content of the gametes is not altered by unequal crossing over, some will be deprived of the genetic potential which has gone into the duplicate.

Duplication of the genes, to give a large number of homologous sequences of DNA closely arranged on the chromosome, increases the likelihood of non-homologous pairing and unequal crossovers. In the case of the nucleolar organizer genes of the frog Xenopus laevus, the very large number of copies carried in the germ-line (200–300) give rise to a grave instability in the numbers carried by each oocyte. A significant proportion of these are deficient mutants, becoming sterile ova, a situation tolerable only where a species is prolific (Brown & David, 1968).

Gene duplication is essential to provide the 'raw material' on which mutation and selection can act, but tandem duplication is unstable. The two types of gene duplication can be likened to features of a capitalist economy, which evolves by overproduction, adaptation and new overproduction. Tandem duplication is the stock-exchange bubble, confidence breeding overconfidence, then collapse. Polyploid duplication is the opportunity for the tea-boy to make good, freed by emigration from old restraints and associations.

## 6.3 The evolution of immunoglobulins

Both polyploid and tandem duplication processes have been at work in the evolution of the immunoglobulins. We may imagine that a primordial immunoglobulin chain evolved by the tandem duplication of a gene which coded for a single domain. One of the copies specialized and may have reduplicated to provide a variable domain. The whole system seems to have undergone polyploid duplication to give rise to $\kappa$, $\lambda$ and heavy chain precursor gene clusters on different chromosomes (Fig. 6.3). The primordial heavy chain constant region gene evolved into classes by multiple tandem duplication (see 6.3.1).

It is of interest that there is a molecule associated with the histocompatibility antigens, $\beta_2$ microglobulin, which has substantial homologies with an immunoglobulin domain (Cunning-

*Chapter 6: Evolution of Antibody and Complement*

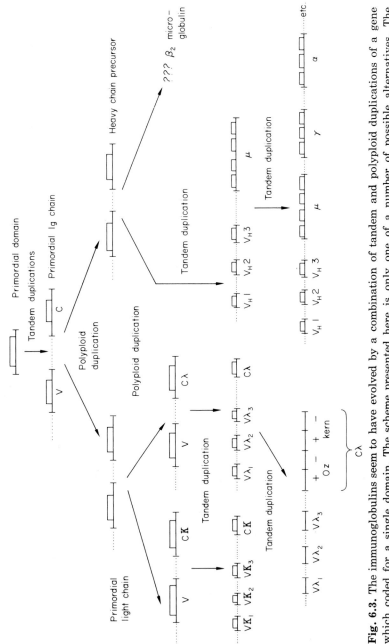

**Fig. 6.3.** The immunoglobulins seem to have evolved by a combination of tandem and polyploid duplications of a gene which coded for a single domain. The scheme presented here is only one of a number of possible alternatives. The evolution of the V-regions is not represented.

*Section I: Immunochemistry*

ham *et al.*, 1973). There must have been at least two polyploid duplication events to give rise to the three imumnoglobulin gene clusters, and if these both involved all the chromosomes, there should be four gene clusters. It is interesting to speculate that $\beta_2$ microglobulin is a product of the 'missing' gene cluster (Fig. 6.3).

### 6.3.1 Evolution of heavy-chain classes

It appears that IgG and IgA might have evolved from IgM by the loss of a single domain from the heavy chain (see Chapter 3). Loss of the C$\mu$2 domain seems to have given rise to the $\gamma$ chain, and of the C$\mu$3 domain to the $\alpha$ chain. These events are readily achieved by unequal crossing over (Fig. 6.4). It appears that the $\varepsilon$ chain may be a tandem duplicate of the $\mu$ chain.

### 6.3.2 Evolution of heavy chain subclasses

As noted above (6.2.2) tandem gene duplication is an unstable method for the generation of new genes. The existence of duplicates favours unequal crossing over, with consequent loss and duplication of genes. The number of subclasses of IgG varies widely from species to species, with four in humans, two in guinea-pigs and cows, and apparently only one in rabbits. This disparity in numbers itself suggests that the number of $\gamma$ chain genes fluctuates rapidly during evolution, and that speciation is often accompanied by either a collapse in the number of heavy-chain subclasses, or by the establishment of new subclasses. There is clear evidence for the recent evolution of subclasses in the case of the cow. The amino acid sequences of the two $\gamma$ chain subclasses are shown in Table 6.1. Since both chains have species-specific residues at positions 2 and 6 from the C-terminus, they must have a common cow-like ancestry. The $\gamma$2 subclass has a unique methionine residue at position 10, clearly indicating that this chain has evolved from a primordial cow-like $\gamma$1 chain. Subclasses seem to represent the 'current experiments' of immunoglobulin evolution and most are probably of neutral selective advantage. What is essential is that the capacity to synthesize classes of adaptive value is not lost.

Some rearrangements of the immunoglobulin genes which are of no (or negative) value are described in the next section, together with the human heavy-chain allotypes.

## 6.4 Allotypes and sporadic events

### 6.4.1 Human heavy-chain allotypes

I have always found this to be a disaster zone in my understanding of immunology, and I offer the following excuses.

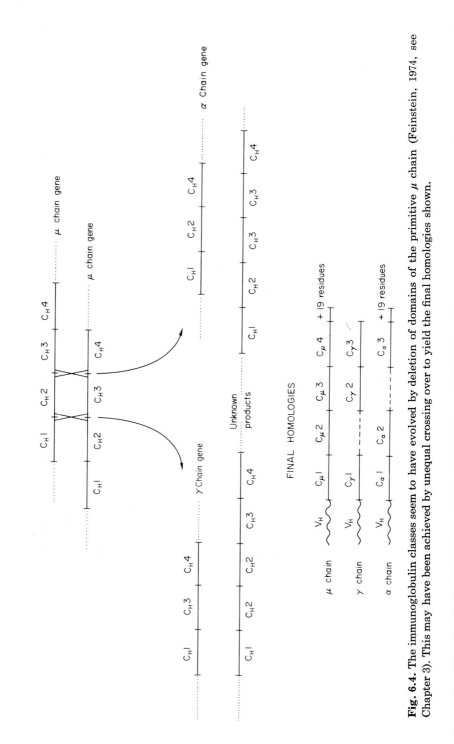

**Fig. 6.4.** The immunoglobulin classes seem to have evolved by deletion of domains of the primitive μ chain (Feinstein, 1974, see Chapter 3). This may have been achieved by unequal crossing over to yield the final homologies shown.

**Table 6.1.** C-terminal sequences of heavy chains

| Chain | Sequence | | | | | | | | | | | | | | | | | | |
|---|---|---|---|---|---|---|---|---|---|---|---|---|---|---|---|---|---|---|---|
| | 19 | 18 | 17 | 16 | 15 | 14 | 13 | 12 | 11 | 10 | 9 | 8 | 7 | 6 | 5 | 4 | 3 | 2 | 1 |
| Human γ1, γ2 | (Met) | His | Glu | Ala | Leu | His | Asn | His | Tyr | Thr | Gln | Lys | Ser | Leu | Ser | Leu | Ser | Pro | Gly-COOH |
| Human γ3 Gm (–5) | | | | | | | | Arg | | | | | | | | | | | |
| Human γ4 | | | | | | | | | | | | | | | | | | | Leu |
| Rabbit γ | | | | | | | | | | | | | Ile | | | Arg | | | |
| Horse IgG(T) γ | | | | | Val | Glu | | | | | | | Asn | Val | | His | | | |
| Horse IgG γ | | | | | | | | | | | | | | Val | | Lys | | | |
| Bovine γ1 | | | | | | | | | | Met | | | | Thr | | Lys | Ala | | |
| Bovine γ2 | | | | | | | | | | | | | | Thr | | Lys | | Ala | |

All sequences identical to human γ1 except where shown.
(From Milstein and Feinstein, 1968).

(a) The nomenclature has undergone recent revision (at least officially), and does not make clear what is an allele of what.

(b) The latter is a real problem as well as a semantic one, since it seems that the Gm types reflect single amino acid substitutions which are the reflection of point mutations in the DNA sequence which codes for the $\gamma$ chains ($\gamma$-chains cistrons). Intracistronic recombinations, resulting from crossing over within the cistron, are rare events, and in their absence mapping of markers by genetic methods is impossible. In classical genetic terms, any unit which does not exhibit internal recombinations is a locus, and the markers in the locus are alleles. In molecular terms, this is not a very satisfactory definition, since if one looks long enough, a recombination will be observed within the cistron, provided that suitable markers are available with a space between them. The term 'homo-allele' has been used to describe the two DNA sequences which at a particular point are mutually exclusive. As shown in Table 6.2, Gm 4 and Gm 17 (at $\gamma$ 1, 214) are homoalleles in this sense since they seem to reflect two alternative amino acids at a single position within the chain. Gm 1 and Gm 1- reflect two amino acid substitutions close together. In practice, though we seek till Judgement Day, we shall probably not observe the recombination of the sequences at this point because they are so close.

(c) Since accurate location of the Gm markers is essentially impossible by genetic methods, they must be correlated with amino acid sequences. These will almost certainly have to be those of myeloma proteins, since homogeneity will be essential (see (d) below), but a number of proteins of each Gm type will have to be sequenced before the correlations can be regarded as firm, since individual proteins may have unique and unrepresentative point mutations. Not many complete sequences are yet available.

(d) Both allotypic markers and $\gamma$ chain subclasses are relatively recent evolutionary events, and as a result, most of the individual Gm markers are confined to one subclass, but others, for instance Gm 1-, are expressed on *all* $\gamma$2 and $\gamma$3 molecules. This means that $\gamma$1, $\gamma$2 and $\gamma$3 are tandem duplicates, but in $\gamma$1, a mutant has arisen (Gm 1), which is an allele.

(e) Probably as a result of their recent evolution and close linkage, the Gm types tend to be inherited as groups of markers. Where a new mutant arises close to a pre-existing marker, it will be passed on in coupling linkage with that marker until a recombination occurs between them. There will be a tendency for the new marker to occur in the population in coupling rather than repulsion for many generations, a situation which makes the mapping problems severe throughout the system, but it does permit certain rare events to be very evident, for instance the discovery of the 'Lepore' immunoglobulins (6.4.2).

(f) The assay system for Gm markers (haemagglutination inhibition) is not quantitative, so that the heterozygote cannot be dis-

**Table 6.2.** Gm allotypes in man

| Chain | γ4 | γ2 | γ3 | γ1 |
|---|---|---|---|---|
| Arrangement of genes (not to scale) | | | 436 | 214  356, 358 |
| Sequences of Homoalleles | | | Phe / Tyr | Arg / Lys  AspGluLeu / GluGluMet |
| Old nomenclature | N O  M A R K E R S | n | c b $^a$b $^\beta$b $^\gamma$b $^3$b $^4$b s t ; b g | r$^5$xb$^2$ Rouen 2, 3, SF2 ; f z ; a non-a |
| New nomenclature | | 23 | 6 10, 11, 12, 13, 14, 15, 16 ; 5 21 | 7 2 3 18, 19, 20 ; 4 17 ; 1 1- |
| Non-allelic markers | | non-a or 1-  non-g | non-a or 1- | |

tinguished from the homozygote who carries the markers, except, of course, where there are antisera to both the homoalleles.

Table 6.2 shows the arrangements of the Gm markers as presently understood. Probably many of the unlocated markers will turn out to be either homoalleles of other markers, and will move to the lower lines in the way that 21 has recently paired with 5. Others will disappear when it is shown that they are the same marker, but that the antisera behave a little differently, and probably those that disappear will be replaced with new markers.

There are also genetic markers for the IgA2 subclass: the Am markers.

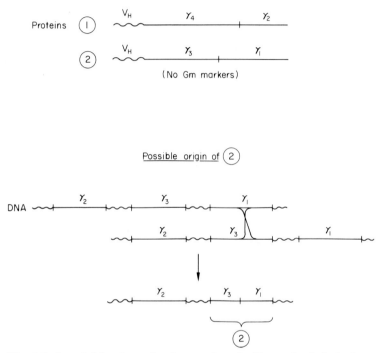

Fig. 6.5. A probable scheme for the creation of a 'Lepore' γ chain is shown in the lower part of the figure.

### 6.4.2 'Lepore' heavy chains

'Lepore' immunoglobulins are proteins which, like the classical haemoglobin Lepore, have the N-terminal sequence of one chain and the C-terminal sequence of another (Fig. 6.5). The 'Lepore' immunoglobulins are the best evidence that the human γ subclass genes are arranged in the order 4-2-3-1.

### 6.4.3 Heavy chain disease proteins

Heavy-chain diseases are unusual forms of myeloma in which the cells secrete immunoglobulins without light chains. These proteins

*Section I: Immunochemistry*

are noticeable for their lack of light-chain antigens and low molecular weight. The malignant cells are like lymphoma cells.

Most of the cases so far reported involve a deletion of part of the $C_H1$ domain, which is responsible for the attachment of the light chains. A peculiar feature of many of the proteins is that the deletion begins or ends at residue 216 (Eu numbering). Whatever the mechanism for the generation of the abnormal genes, this position seems to have a special instability, perhaps because of the high density of proline-coding triplets. The high incidence of deletions on the $C_H1$ domain may be due to the ease of finding this lesion with its profound size effects. Naturally-occurring mutants of plasmacytoma cell lines maintained *in vitro* include two with partial heavy-chain deletions. One of these involves the $C_H1$ domain, the other does not (Secher *et al.*, 1974). In these experiments, the ascertainment is essentially complete.

## 6.5 Complement

As indicated earlier (6.1.1) there is a dearth of structural information on complement components. However, there is growing knowledge of their genetics. This will be covered first as some of the speculation as to their evolution derives from it.

### 6.5.1 Complement deficiencies

The known deficiencies of the complement system are set out in Table 6.3. Most of the deficiencies are well tolerated, those which

Table 6.3. Genetic deficiencies of the complement system

| Species | Factor deficient | No. of pedigrees | Clinical |
|---------|------------------|------------------|----------|
| Man | C1r | 2 | Renal & skin dis. |
| | C2 | Several | Most healthy, SLE? |
| | C3 | 2 | Immunity deficiency |
| | C4 | 1 | Skin disease |
| | C5 | 1 | Skin disease |
| | C6 | 1 | Healthy |
| | C7 | 2 | Healthy |
| | C1̄-inh. | many | HAE |
| | C3b-inactivator(KAF) | 1 | Immunity deficiency |
| Guinea-pig | C4 | 1 | Healthy |
| | A component C3-9 | 1 | Healthy but extinct |
| Mouse | C5 | Many inbred | Healthy |
| Rabbit | C6 | Several | Healthy |
| Hamster | C6 | 1 | Healthy |

*Chapter 6: Evolution of Antibody and Complement*

are clearly associated with human disease are described elsewhere (KAF deficiency in Chapter 5; C3 deficiency and CĪ inhibitor deficiency in Chapter 19). There is a high incidence of SLE-like disease in C2 deficient individuals. The association will probably prove to be real, although it may be argued that the ascertainment of the incidence of C2 deficiency is disturbed by the fact that SLE patients are among those whose complement function is most commonly investigated.

CĪ inhibitor deficiency is expressed as a disease in heterozygotes and this is inherited as a dominant trait. There is no recorded case of homozygous CĪ deficiency although this may not be very good evidence for its being lethal, since the frequency of the event must be very small, perhaps $10^{-7}$ or fewer zygotes, and would usually demand the union of two affected individuals.

Functional deficiency of complement components is the result of either lack of synthesis, hypercatabolism (which is usually a secondary phenomenon) or synthesis of a dysfunctional molecule. CĪ inhibitor deficiency can be caused by genetic defects of the first or third kind, and can cause deficiency of C4 and C2 of the second kind. In the cases of C6 deficiency in rabbits and C4 deficiency in guinea-pigs, potent antisera can be raised against the missing component. These antisera cross-react with the homologous component of a large number of species, indicating that the asynthetic defect is complete.

### 6.5.2 Complement allotypes (polymorphisms)

Table 6.4 shows the complement components for which genetically determined charge polymorphism has been demonstrated. The C4

**Table 6.4.** Genetic markers on complement components

| Component | No. of variants | Gene frequencies (Caucasians) | | | Null allele | Linked to |
|---|---|---|---|---|---|---|
| | | Commonest | Second commonest | Remainder | | |
| C3 | 20 + | 0·75 | 0·25 | rare | + | ? |
| C6 | 6 | 0·63 | 0·36 | 0·01 | + | ? |
| Factor B | 4 | 0·71 | 0·28 | 0·01 | ? | HL-A |

of different individuals shows differences, but it has not been possible to demonstrate their mode of inheritance.

Investigation of C3 polymorphism produced evidence for the existence of a null (asynthetic) allele before any case of C3 deficiency had been discovered.

Factor B's less common alleles represent mutants in a different

*Section I: Immunochemistry*

part of the molecule from the common allelic differences, since on natural cleavage during the activation of the alternative pathway, the common alleles go with the a fragment, the rare ones with the b fragment.

### 6.5.3 Complement evolution: a wild speculation

The complement system divides into three function groups of components: the early numbered components (C1, 4 and 2), the alternative pathway (including factors B and D), and the terminal lytic sequence (C5–9), the whole linked around C3 (see Chapter 5). It is quite conceivable that the three groups evolved independently, but it is hard to conceive that the individual components did not evolve in a co-ordinated way within the groups. For example, there would be no evolutionary advantage to retaining the genetic potential for making C7 without the possibility of its use in a lytic event, nor in making KAF without C3b, its apparently unique substrate. However it would be hazardous to evolve the alternative pathway factors without the homeostatic mechanism of KAF.

Speculation about the origin of the complement system should try to explain at least the following facts.

(i) The physiochemical similarity of C4, C3 and C5; of C2 and factor B; and of C6 and C7.

(ii) The apparent convergency of the generation of two separate mechanisms for cleavage of C3, the 'classical' and 'alternative' pathways.

(iii) C2 deficiency and the structural genes for Factor B and C2 are linked to the major histocompatibility complex (Fu *et al.*, 1974; Allen, 1974; Alper, 1976; Hobart & Lachmann, 1976).

It would be attractive to think that the 'classical' and 'alternative' pathways were the result of polyploid duplication, for this would give a complete working and coordinated system which could specialize its function. Such a model now seems most unlikely as C2 and factor B are both linked to the HLA complex, and thus to each other. In fact, it seems most likely that they will prove to be tandem duplicates, and perhaps this will also prove to be true for the other similar proteins mentioned in (i). Deficiency of a number of other complement components (e.g. C4 and C8) seems to be linked to the major histocompatibility complex. This may be a significant finding since there is evidence that both C8 and Factor B are expressed on cell surfaces.

### References

ALLEN F.H. (1974) Linkage of HL-A and GBG. *Vox. Sang.* **27**, 382.
ALPER, C.A. (1976) Inherited structural polymorphism in human C2:

evidence for genetic linkage between *C2* and *Bf*. *J. exp. Med.* (in press).

BROWN D.D. & DAVID I.B. (1968) Specific gene amplifications in oocytes. *Science* **160,** 272.

CUNNINGHAM B.A., WANG J.L., BERGGARD I. & PETERSON P.A. (1973) The complete amino-acid sequence of *β2* microglobulins. *Biochemistry* **12,** 4811.

FU S.M., KUNKEL H.G., BRUSMAN H.P., ALLEN F.H. & FOTINO M. (1974) Evidence for linkage between HL-A histocompatibility genes and those involved in the synthesis of the second component of complement. *J. exp. Med.* **140,** 1108.

MILSTEIN C.P. & FEINSTEIN A. (1968) Comparative studies of two types of bovine immunoglobulin G heavy-chains. *Biochem J.* **107,** 559.

OHNO S. (1970) *Evolution by gene duplication*. Springer Verlag, Berlin.

SECHER D.S., COTTON R.G.H., COWAN N.J. & MILSTEIN C. (1974) Spontaneous mutation in immunoglobulin genes. In *The Immune System: Genes, Receptors, Signals*. SERCARZ E., WILLIAMSON A.R. & FOX C.F. Academic Press, New York.

## Further reading

OHNO S. (1970) *Evolution by Gene Duplication*. Springer Verlag, Berlin.

FUDENBERG H.H., PINK J.R.L., STITES D.P. & AN-CHUANG WANG (1972) *Basic Immunogenetics*. Oxford University Press, London.

NATVIG J.B. & KUNKEL H.G. (1973) Human immunoglobulins: classes, subclasses, genetic variants and idiotypes. *Adv. Immunol.* **16,** 1.

HOOD L. & PRAHL J. (1971) The immune system: a model for differentiation in higher organisms. *Adv. Immunol.* **14,** 291.

ALPER C.A. & ROSEN F.S. (1971) Genetic aspects of the complement system. *Adv. Immunol.* **14,** 252.

HOBART M.J. & LACHMANN P.J. (1976) Allotypes of complement components in Man. *Transplantation Rev.* (in press).

McCONNELL I. & LACHMANN P.J. (1976) Complement components and cell membranes. *Transplantation Rev.* (in press).

# SECTION II
# IMMUNOBIOLOGY

## II.1 Introduction

This section is concerned with the central areas of immunology: the cells of the lymphoid system, their interactions, responses to antigenic stimulation, development and physiological environment. This preamble attempts to cover some of the general groundwork of this field and describes in a didactic way the nature of antigens and the consequences of exposure of animals to them.

## II.2 Antigens

In so far as antigens were considered at all in Section I, they were considered as structures which could fit into the combining site of an antibody molecule. In this section, we are concerned with the properties of an antigen which permit it to evoke an allergic response* when an animal is exposed to it.

### II.2.1 Rigidity

An antigenic determinant (or epitope) requires to be of consistent shape and charge pattern if it is to be recognized by a specific combining structure (e.g. antibody). Since the antibody combining site is relatively small, most large organic molecules and almost all biological molecules fulfil this criterion, with the possible exception of lipids. Antigens range from protein molecules (even immunoglobulin itself), polysaccharides, synthetic polypeptides and chemically modified proteins to entirely unnatural substances.

### II.2.2 Valency

Most natural antigens are multivalent. They are either large protein molecules with a large number of different epitopic struc-

* The term allergic is used to denote a state of altered reactivity. It is to be preferred to the term immune, which has connotations of protection.

91

tures on their surfaces, or are polymers of one kind of subunit, presenting the same few epitopes in a large array. Examples of such multivalent but unideterminant antigens are *E. coli* endotoxin (LPS), capsular polysaccharides from streptococci and pneumococci, polymerized flagellin and the synthetic antigen PVP (polyvinyl pyrrolidone). Haptens are small molecules with only one valency, the most commonly used haptens being substituted benzene derivatives like 2,4-Dinitrophenol (DNP) and 4-hydroxy-3-iodo-5-nitrophenacetyl (NIP).

If, as seems to be the case, the immune system is potentially capable of reacting to most biological molecules, it is essential that it can distinguish 'self' from 'not-self', since promiscuous response to all possible antigens would lead to self destruction. Conversely, it is essential that the system be capable of recognizing and responding to *all* foreign structures. The *information* required for these distinctions to be made demands that the antigen be recognized by more than one kind of receptor molecule or cell (see Chapter 8). To be recognized as foreign, the antigen molecule must present at least two recognizably different structures from any that exist in the recipient (Chapters 8 and 9). The experimental model which shows this best is the hapten-carrier system.

*II.2.3 Hapten-carriers*

Haptens alone are non-immunogenic. To evoke a response they have to be coupled to a larger molecule (carrier) which is usually a heterologous protein. The secondary anti-hapten response is much more vigorous when the animal has been previously injected (primed) with both hapten and carrier. Hapten-primed animals which have not been primed to the carrier give poor responses (Table II.1). The importance of these observations to the theoretical basis of modern immunology is discussed in Chapter 8.

**Table II.1.** The carrier effect in secondary anti-hapten responses

| Antigen used for | | Secondary response (IgG) | | |
| Priming | Secondary challenge | Anti-NIP | Anti-BSA | Anti-CG |
|---|---|---|---|---|
| NIP–BSA | CG | – | | – |
| NIP–BSA | BSA | – | + | |
| NIP–BSA | NIP–CG | – | | – |
| NIP–BSA | *NIP–BSA* | + | + | |
| NIP–CG | CG | – | | + |
| NIP–CG | BSA | – | – | |
| NIP–CG | *NIP–CG* | + | | + |
| NIP–CG | NIP–BSA | – | – | |

*Section II: Immunobiology*

## II.3 Antigen recognition and the allergic response

When antigen is injected into a normal animal, there is a 'lag' phase, followed by the appearance of antibodies in the serum. If the animal has not been exposed to the antigen before, the 'lag' phase of this response may last for up to 12 days (Fig. II.1). If the same antigen is reinjected, the 'lag' phase is very much shorter and the predominant antibody produced is IgG, which persists in the serum for weeks or months.

The first antigenic experience has primed the animal so that it can make a secondary response which differs both quantitatively and qualitatively from the primary response. This is the phenomenon of immunological memory.

The allergic response is mediated by a number of cell types, although the initial specific recognition of antigen is done by lymphocytes which carry specific membrane receptors for antigen.

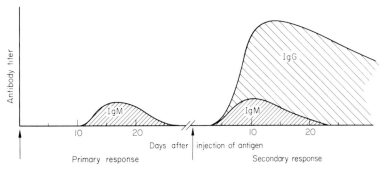

**Fig. II.1.** Primary and secondary antibody responses.

They are subdivided into T (for Thymus) lymphocytes and B (for Bursa or Bone marrow) derived lymphocytes. T cells* mediate a number of functions, notably the 'cell-mediated' immune responses, such as graft rejection and delayed (tuberculin type) hypersensitivity, whereas B cells are the direct precursors of mature antibody secreting cells. Both cell types are described in detail in Chapter 7.

Both T and B lymphocytes are required in the humoral (antibody) response to most antigens. Although both are specifically involved in antigen recognition, only the B cells differentiate into antibody secreting cells and this process is controlled by the T lymphocytes. Much of this section will be devoted to this phenomenon wherein T cells 'help' B cells to respond to antigen, a phenomenon also known as cell cooperation (Chapter 9).

The allergic response can be thought of as occurring in three phases termed initial, central and effector (Fig. II.2).

* The terms T lymphocyte and T cell (or B) are used interchangeably in this book. The reader is advised that the former is more correct.

*Preamble to Section II: Immunobiology*

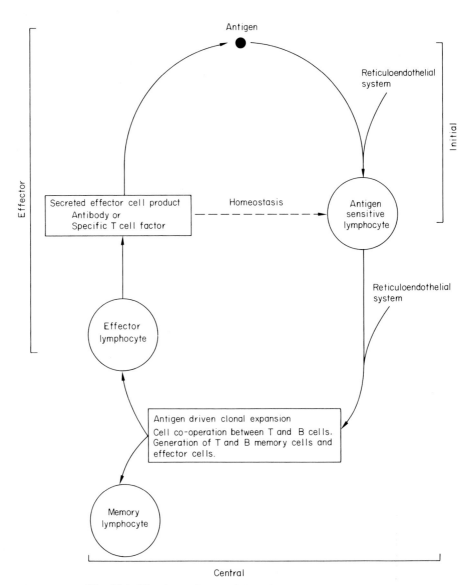

**Fig. II.2.** The three phases of the allergic response.

## II.3.1 Initial phase

The initial phase of the allergic response comprises the events between the entry of the antigen and its contact with the specific receptors of the lymphocyte membrane. The reticuloendothelial system and particularly the macrophages are essential to this phase. Macrophages used to be considered as the 'antigenic garbage disposal unit', concerned only with the phagocytosis and degradation of antigen. In the last few years, however, they have undergone considerable 'job evaluation', and are now recognized as playing an important role in the presentation of antigen to lymphocytes. They are also essential in cell cooperation.


## II.3.2 Central phase

The central phase of the response is to a large extent concerned with cell cooperation and is the most complex. It involves interactions of antigen, T and B lymphocytes, macrophages, specific soluble factors, antibody and probably more, all played out in a rather loosely organized four dimensions. While a substantial part of this book is concerned with these phenomena, it is difficult to make a clearcut statement of the events at present in this area which is even challenging complement in the complexity of its interactions.

The overall impression which should be taken away is that lymphocytes proliferate in response to antigen, giving rise to both primed (memory) and activated (or effector) cells (e.g. antibody secreting cells or specifically allergized T cells which carry out cell-mediated reactions). The distinction between these two maturation stages of a given clone presumably reflect the degree of antigen-induced proliferation. Lymphocytes in the memory stage only become activated cells on re-exposure to antigen, whereas effector cells express their reactivity irrespective of the presence or absence of antigen. The latter can be regarded as end cells with short half-lives (days) compared to the long-lived memory populations. Although memory cells may have no individual antigenic experience, it is possible that they have a 'folk memory' of antigenic experience, though what this means in real terms is unclear. Memory can be invested in both the T and B lymphocyte populations.

This positive type of response in the central phase is not the only possible consequence of antigenic stimulation. Sometimes the antigenic experience results in the specific elimination of the potential to make responses (see Chapter 10). This specific failure to respond to re-exposure to the same antigen is known as immunological tolerance.


## II.3.3 Effector phase

Antigen has no role in this phase of the response except as a target for destruction. The events of the central phase cause B lymphocytes with receptors for antigen to undergo clonal expansion. Some of the daughter cells differentiate into antibody secreting cells and plasma cells, short-lived end cells which execute their function of making antibody irrespective of the presence of antigen. T lymphocytes undergo similar proliferation, giving rise to their character-

*Preamble to Section II: Immunobiology*

istic effector cells. The secreted products of T cells might be thought of as homologues of the immunoglobulin secreted by B cells. They are defined, however, in terms like those in use for antibodies 20 years ago, when the antibodies were defined functionally as opsonins, antitoxins, neutralisins and reagins. The T cell products include a multitude of lymphokines and specific soluble cooperating factors (Chapters 9 and 12). These factors are of considerable importance for the full expression of T cell allergic reactivity and they amplify the cell-mediated reactions by promoting the action of other cell types, notably macrophages.

The T cell products have not been physicochemically characterized to any extent, but it is already clear that on the whole they are not structurally related to the immunoglobulins. It is quite likely that they will prove to be a structurally interrelated series of proteins serving the different functions by relatively minor differences in structure, just as the immunoglobulin classes serve their functions by means of quite subtle differences in structure.

## II.4 Homeostatic control of the allergic response

Like an ideally functioning capitalist economy, the allergic response is under homeostatic control. This leads to stabilization of the quantity of the response by, for instance, antigen elimination. The homeostatic process also causes the diversification of the response to provide antibody to antigenic determinants not adequately recognized in the initial stages of the response. This process may involve the competition between the secreted antibody and the antigen receptor on the B lymphocyte for the epitopes on the antigen.

Specific control of the antibody response is also exerted by T lymphocytes. These cells can specifically suppress the proliferation of B cells by mechanisms poorly understood, but described in Chapter 10. The presence of a multitude of antigenic determinants has an effect on the specificity of the antibody made by an animal. This is the phenomenon of antigenic competition which is described in Chapter 11.

## II.5 Lymphoid tissues

T and B lymphocytes are not isolated particles. They have their function within the lymphoid organs or 'lymphon'. This is a collective term to describe the lymphoid tissues and their constituent cells. Much of the physiology of this organ will be described in Chapters 13 and 14, and only the barest bones will be described here (Fig. II.3).

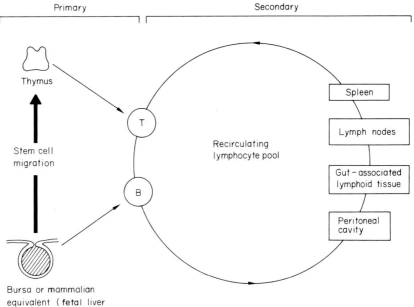

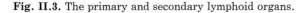

**Fig. II.3.** The primary and secondary lymphoid organs.

### II.5.1 Primary lymphoid organs

These are the thymus and the Bursa of Fabricius in birds and the thymus and fetal liver, followed later by the bone marrow, in mammals. The thymus and Bursa are both lymphoepithelial organs which support the extensive proliferation and differentiation of lymphoid stem cells into T and B lymphocytes respectively. The stem cells of the lymphoid system are derived from the same primordial precursors as those which give rise to erythroid and myeloid cells.

### II.5.2 Secondary lymphoid organs

In mammals these comprise the lymph nodes, spleen and gut associated lymphoid tissue (e.g. tonsil, Peyer's patches, appendix and peritoneal cavity). Birds have no lymph nodes. These organs are connected both by blood vessels and by lymphatics, and it is through these that the lymphocytes circulate and recirculate, responding to antigen and disseminating the specific 'experience' of it to all parts of the lymphoid system.

*Preamble to Section II: Immunobiology*

# Chapter 7
# T and B Lymphocytes

## I. McConnell

### 7.1 Introduction

Categorical statements often have the reverse effect from that expected: far from ending or discouraging research activity, they promote it. A good example of this about 1960 was the statement 'Lymphocytes are end cells'. Since then, these 'end cells' have been closely scrutinized and now, after some fifteen years and several thousand publications, one can say that to have called lymphocytes end cells was an understatement.

By morphological criteria, T and B cells are identical but by functional and other criteria they can be shown to have a large number of distinctive features. They arise in different primary lymphoid organs, colonize separate areas of the secondary lymphoid tissues, mediate distinct types of immunological function and express an array of characteristic surface markers. Much of this section will be concerned with the function of T and B lymphocytes and this chapter with their defining characteristics.

### 7.2 Lymphocyte markers

The analysis of lymphocyte populations has been facilitated by the detection of a large number of distinctive markers. Many of the markers are shown in Table 7.1 and some of the more interesting and useful are described below.

#### 7.2.1 Alloantigens and heteroantigens

Some lymphocyte alloantigens are expressed only on one of the subpopulations. To date these are best described in mice because of the availability of large numbers of inbred strains. The $\theta$ antigen (now called Thy 1.) is mainly present on thymus cells, peripheral T cells and brain, with small amounts being found on skin and fibroblasts. It is absent from B lymphocytes. $\theta$ is the product of a single locus with two alleles, $\theta$C3H (Thy 1.2), present in C3H, CBA and many other mouse strains, and $\theta$AKR (Thy 1.1), present in AKR and A/J mice. Anti-$\theta$ sera are raised by cross immunizing congenic mouse strains which differ at the $\theta$ locus. The routine check for specificity is the removal of anti-$\theta$ activity by absorbtion with brain of the appropriate strain (Reif & Allen, 1964; Raff, 1971).

The Ly series of alloantigens, Ly 1, 2, 3 and 5 are also restricted to the T lymphocyte subpopulation—although the fourth member of the series, Ly 4, is also found on B lymphocytes. Unlike $\theta$, Ly antigens (except Ly 4) are confined to thymus and thymus-derived cells (Boyse et al., 1968).

The TL alloantigen is present on normal cells only within the thymus of $TL^+$ strains and is lost as they differentiate to mature T cells. TL appears on leukaemic T cells in $TL^-$ strains, indicating that in these strains the gene is present but normally repressed (Boyse & Old, 1969).

Alloantibodies for human T cells are found in the sera of patients with diseases such as infectious mononucleosis and systemic lupus erythematosus (SLE) (Wernet & Kunkel, 1973). Many tissue-typing sera may prove to be T or B cell specific once tested on pure populations of T or B cells.

T lymphocytes can also be distinguished by heteroantisera to brain or thymus cells, which can be made T cell specific by extensive absorption with B cells (Golub, 1971). Lymphocytes from patients with chronic lymphocytic leukaemia (CLL cells) provide a source of B cells in humans. These cells can also be used to raise B cell-specific antisera.


### 7.2.2 Lymphocyte surface receptors (other than antigen receptors)

Receptors for a variety of structures are present on the lymphocyte surface. These range from receptors for erythrocytes of different species and certain viruses, mainly found on T lymphocytes, to receptors for the Fc of IgG and for C3b, predominantly found on B lymphocytes and other cell types.

The technique of rosette formation has provided a useful means of detecting many of the receptors on lymphocytes. For example, receptors for a variety of different structures (see 7.4) can be easily detected by gently centrifuging a mixture of lymphocytes and suitably sensitized erythrocytes (Fig. 7.1). The indicator red cells bind to the receptors on the lymphocyte surface, forming a rosette or mulberry of adherent erythrocytes around a central lymphoid cell (Fig. 7.1). Receptors for erythrocytes, Fc of IgG or C3b can all be detected using erythrocytes alone or sensitized with IgG (EA, for Fc rosettes) or IgM and complement (EAC for C3 receptors) respectively. In the latter case, mouse serum deficient in complement components beyond C3 is used, since this is non-lytic for EA.

The following receptors have been detected on lymphocytes by these and similar techniques.

*Chapter 7: T and B Lymphocytes*

**Table 7.1.** T and B lymphocyte markers

| Marker | Species | Distribution of marker on cells | | | Other features |
|---|---|---|---|---|---|
| | | T | B | Other | |
| **ALLOANTIGENS** | | | | | |
| θAKR (Thy 1.1) | Mouse | + | – | + | ⎰ Present on brain, small amounts on epidermal cells and |
| θC3H (Thy 1.2) | Mouse | + | – | + | ⎱ fibroblasts |
| Ly, 1, 2, 3, 5 | Mouse | + | – | – | Ly4 also on B cells |
| TL | Mouse | + | – | – | Present on thymus cells only |
| PC.1 | Mouse | – | – | + | Plasma cells only |
| Serum antibody in infectious mono-nucleosis | Human | + | – | | Some sera block T cell functions *in vitro*. This activity not absorbed out by red cells and platelets |
| s.L.E. | Human | + | – | | |
| **HETEROANTIGENS** | | | | | |
| Rabbit anti-brain or thymus sera | Human and mouse | + | – | + | Many sera also have antibodies to haemopoietic stem cells. Require extensive absorption with B cells before T cell specific |
| Rabbit anti-CLL cells | Human | – | + | | Require extensive absorption with T cells before B cell specific |

*Section II: Immunobiology*

## SURFACE RECEPTORS FOR

| | Species | | | | Notes |
|---|---|:---:|:---:|:---:|---|
| Sheep red cells | Human/pig | + | − | − | In humans neuraminadase treated B lymphocytes also form rosettes with SRBC |
| Rabbit red cells | Guinea-pig | + | − | − | |
| Guinea-pig red cells | Cat | + | + | − | |
| Fc of IgG | Most | − | + | + | Present on activated T cells, monocytes, macrophages and polymorphs. In humans IgG2 binds to lymphocytes but not macrophages |
| C3b | Most | − | + | + | Also present on monocytes, macrophages, rabbit platelets and primate red cells. These cells fail to bind KAF reacted C3b whereas some lymphocytes do |
| **Viruses** | | | | | |
| Measles [1] | Human | + | − | − | |
| Epstein Barr Virus [2] | Human | − | + | + | |
| **SURFACE IMMUNOGLOBULIN** | Most | − | + | − | |
| **MITOGEN RESPONSIVENESS** | | | | | |
| (a) Phytohaemagglutinin (PHA) | Most | + | − | − | Mitogens generally bind to both populations of lymphocytes but are selective in their mitogenicity. Many mitogens show a marked species variation |
| (b) Pokeweed mitogen (PWM) | Human/mouse | + | + | + | |
| (c) E. coli LPS | Mouse | − | + | + | |
| (d) Polymerized flagellin | Mouse | − | + | + | |
| **ELECTROPHORETIC MOBILITY** [3] | | High | Low | | |

References
(1) Valdimarsson et al. (1974)
(2) Jondal M. and Klein G. (1973)
(3) Zeiller and Pascher (1973)

*Chapter 7: T and B Lymphocytes*

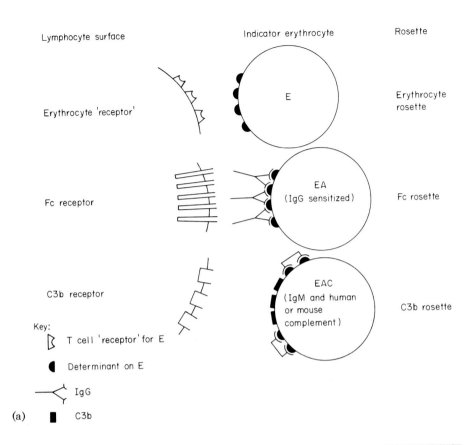

Lymphocyte surface       Indicator erythrocyte       Rosette

Erythrocyte 'receptor'      E       Erythrocyte rosette

Fc receptor       EA (IgG sensitized)       Fc rosette

C3b receptor       EAC (IgM and human or mouse complement)       C3b rosette

Key:

▷   T cell 'receptor' for E

◖   Determinant on E

⅄   IgG

(a)   ▮   C3b

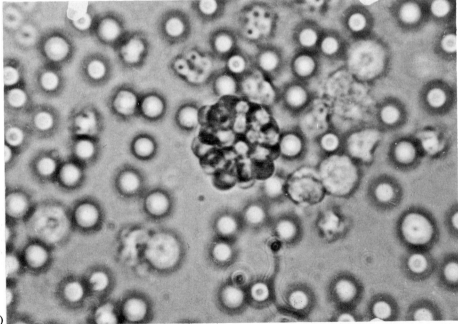

(b)

(a) *Receptors for heterologous erythrocytes*. Most T lymphocytes of several species will form erythrocyte (E) rosettes with the red cells of other species. These are *not* antigen rosettes (see 7.4.1) and do not involve immunoglobulin receptors. Activated T cells and thymus cells give stronger reactions than peripheral T cells. The expression of the receptor seems to be an energy-dependant process since it is sensitive to metabolic inhibitors and depends on cell viability.

E rosettes have proved to be useful markers for T cells in humans, pigs and guinea-pigs (Coombs *et al.*, 1970; Bach, 1973).

(b) *The Fc receptor*. This binds the Fc part of IgG (Basten *et al.*, 1972) but not 19S IgM although 7S IgM can bind to the receptor and block its reactivity for IgG. Fc receptors are present on B cells and many myeloid derived cells, but these may not be identical receptors since human macrophages do not bind the Fc of human IgG2 whereas B cells do. Activated T cells have now been shown to have receptors for the Fc of IgG (Yoshida & Anderson, 1972).

(c) *The C3b receptor* on B lymphocytes recognizes bound C3b and, to a lesser extent, KAF-reacted C3b (C3d) (Bianco *et al.*, 1970; Ross *et al.*, 1973). It is not clear whether these are different receptors, though there are fewer cells which bind C3d. Although C3b receptors are also present on polymorphs, rabbit platelets, human red cells and macrophages (Chapter 19), these cells all fail to bind C3d, suggesting that there are differences between C3b receptors on lymphocytes and the other cell types.

Since none of these receptors are inhibited by anti-immunoglobulin antisera and are present on large numbers of cells, not merely the few cells of individual clones, they are not immunoglobulin in nature.

The list of receptors on T and B lymphocytes is ever growing but, despite the ingenuity of investigators in adding to the list, their functional significance remains largely unknown.

### 7.2.3 Surface immunoglobulin

The antigen receptor on B lymphocytes is immunoglobulin (7.4) and the detection of freshly synthesized immunoglobulin on the surface of lymphocytes is a reliable marker for B cells in most species. Resynthesis of membrane immunoglobulin following its enzymatic removal distinguishes endogenous immunoglobulin from that passively acquired from the plasma and adhering via the

**Fig. 7.1** (a) Detection of lymphocyte membrane receptors by rosette formation. Indicator erythrocytes can be erythrocytes alone (E); IgG sensitized erythrocytes (EA) for Fc receptors and IgM and complement sensitized erythrocytes for C3b receptors.

(b) Erythrocyte rosette. The adherent erythrocytes obscure the lymphocyte within the rosette which expresses membrane 'receptors' for antigenic determinants on the erythrocytes.

*Chapter 7: T and B Lymphocytes*

**Table 7.2.** T and B lymphocyte status in disease

| Disease | Lymphocyte status | | Predominant lymphocyte phenotype | | | | |
|---|---|---|---|---|---|---|---|
| | T | B | SE-RFC | Ig | C3b | Fc | |
| Chronic lymphocytic leukaemia | N | ↑ | − | + | + | + | (Most) |
| Acute lymphoblastic leukaemia | ↑→ | N | + | − | − | − | (Some, not all) |
| Severe combined immunodeficiency | → | → | all low | | | | |
| di George syndrome ⎱ Thymic plasma ⎰ | → | N | − | + | + | + | |
| Sex-linked agammaglobulinaemia | N | →N | + | − | − | − | |
| Hypogammaglobulinaemia | N | N | + | + or − | + | + | |

Marked increase (↑) or decrease (↓) compared to normal (N) level

Fc receptor. The nature of the antigen receptor on T cells is controversial (see 7.6) and, to date, there is no distinctive marker for it.

### 7.2.4 Mitogen responsiveness

Certain plant lectins such as phytohaemagglutinin (PHA) and pokeweed mitogen (PWM) as well as certain bacterial lipopolysaccharides (LPS) readily induce mitosis and differentiation of lymphocytes (Greaves & Janossy, 1972). In addition to selectively stimulating DNA synthesis in T and B cells, certain mitogens like PHA will induce lymphokine production in T cells, whilst PWM, although stimulating both T and B lymphocytes, initiates IgM synthesis and secretion in human and mouse B lymphocytes.

### 7.2.5 Analysis of lymphocyte populations

The various lymphocyte markers have proved useful in a number of respects. They have permitted the enumeration of T and B lymphocytes in different lymphoid tissues, both in normal and diseased states (Table 7.2 and Fig. 7.2). Membrane receptors have

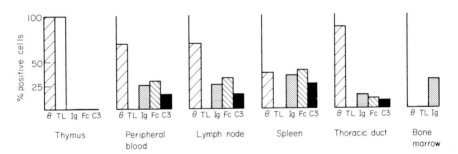

**Fig. 7.2.** Distribution of T and B lymphocytes in different lymphoid tissues of mice.

also been exploited in the preparation of pure populations of either cell type (7.4 and Chapter 9).

The evaluation of human T and B lymphocytes has important diagnostic significance. By using lymphocyte markers, it has been shown that chronic lymphocytic leukaemia is predominantly a B cell leukaemia and many of the lymphocytes simultaneously express IgM and IgD on their surface (Table 7.3) (Fu et al., 1974). Some cases of acute lymphoblastic leukaemia are T cell malignancies. A selective lack of either of the populations has been described in many immunodeficiency states (Chapters 13 and 23).

Although of promising diagnostic value, the evaluation of T and

*Chapter 7: T and B Lymphocytes*

B lymphocyte populations in disease states presents considerable problems for the following reasons.

1. Many of the markers only hold true for normal lymphocytes and their stability in abnormally differentiated or neoplastic lymphocytes is unknown. Even the surface phenotype of normally differentiating lymphocytes shows considerable variation (7.3).

2. Many of the markers for T or B lymphocytes overlap. Both Fc and C3 receptors are present on a variety of other cell types, notably non-phagocytic monocytes, macrophages and activated T cells. Human B lymphocytes also have a receptor for SRBC (a T cell marker) which is normally hidden but can be revealed by neuraminidase treatment of the lymphocytes.

3. Autoantibodies to T cells arise in certain diseases and in these circumstances T cells are detected as $Ig^+$. Discrimination from B lymphocytes is possible if the cells are first treated with pronase

**Table 7.3.** Lymphocyte surface immunoglobulin in chronic lymphocytic leukaemia

| Patient | Per cent immunofluorescent positive cells | | | | |
| | $\mu$ | $\delta$ | Fab | $\kappa$ | $\lambda$ |
|---|---|---|---|---|---|
| A | 88 | 89 | 94 | 6 | 86 |
| B | 73 | 67 | 74 | 70 | 2 |
| C | 12 | 87 | 93 | 6 | 93 |
| D | 80 | 3 | 86 | 83 | 2 |

Data from Fu *et al.* (1974)

to remove surface-bound immunoglobulin. Only B lymphocytes will resynthesize their surface immunoglobulin. Many T cell auto-antibodies are temperature sensitive and, like cold agglutinins, bind better to lymphocytes at 4°C. These antibodies can then be eluted from lymphocytes following their incubation for several hours at 37°C.

4. Many preparative lymphocyte separation methods lead to a differential loss of one or other of the lymphocyte populations.

5. The blood lymphocyte pool is not entirely representative of the total recirculating lymphocyte pool. Abnormalities of lympho-cyte traffic due to stress and other factors can convey a false impression of the total lymphocyte status (see Chapter 14).

Since evaluation of lymphocyte status is potentially an important clinical tool, especially in diseases with an immunological basis, it is of the utmost importance that the many problems associated with this approach are critically evaluated and properly under-stood before their routine application (Greaves, 1973).

## 7.3 Expression of surface markers during lymphocyte differentiation

There are both quantitative and qualitative differences in lymphocyte surface phenotype during lymphocyte maturation and activation (Fig. 7.3). As far as mouse T cells are concerned, the differentiation alloantigens ($\theta$ and TL) are not present on stem cells and only appear on the lymphocyte surface after a short residence in the thymus. The amount carried by individual cells varies;

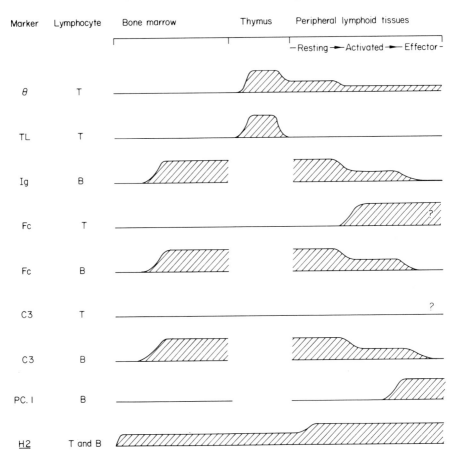

**Fig. 7.3.** Expression and relative amounts of surface markers on differentiating mouse lymphocytes. (For fuller discussion, see Aoki *et al.* (1969); Takahashi *et al.* (1971)).

cortical thymocytes having more of both antigens than medullary thymocytes. It is believed, although not conclusively demonstrated, that the cortical thymocytes are immature cells compared with the medullary thymocytes. Amongst peripheral T cells, TL is absent and the amount of $\theta$ antigen is also less. This is especially true of circulating T cells which may have been stimulated by antigen.

*Chapter 7: T and B Lymphocytes*

The Fc receptor, although a good marker for resting B cells, is also present on activated T cells.

Differentiating B cells, however, progressively lose most of their surface markers, including surface immunoglobulin, Fc and C3 receptors. Many mature plasma cells lack all three and in mice these cells also acquire a new alloantigen, PC.1, which is absent from their precursor lymphocytes. *H-2* alloantigens, however, are stable on cells at all stages but do show quantitative changes.

Thus, during differentiation, the surface phenotype of lymphocytes is extensively remodelled. There is evidence to show that at least one inductive factor within the microenvironment of lymphoid tissues can influence this. Bach *et al.* (1971) and Komura & Boyse (1973) have shown that soluble extracts from calf or mouse thymus can induce the appearance of $\theta$ and TL on some mouse bone marrow cells. These cells are presumably T cell precursors. It may be that the extensive remodelling of the cell surface which takes place during cell differentiation plays an important physiological role in lymphocyte differentiation, life-span, tissue localizing properties and functions in lymphocyte interactions (Chapter 9).

## 7.4 Recognition of antigen by lymphocytes

The induction of the allergic response requires that antigen be recognized by lymphocytes. The specificity of cell-mediated and humoral responses suggests that both T and B lymphocytes specifically recognize antigen. A variety of methods have been used for the detection of antigen-binding receptors on lymphocytes, all relying on the specific binding of antigen to the cell surface.

### 7.4.1 Techniques for identifying individual antigen-binding cells

The technique of rosette formation (see 7.2.2) has proved particularly useful for the identification of lymphocytes with receptors for particulate antigens or antigens which can be coupled to particles (e.g. red cells) (McConnell *et al.*, 1969). Cells with receptors for soluble antigens can also be identified by radioautography following exposure to radioactive antigen (Fig. 7.4) (Naor & Sulitzeanu, 1967; Ada, 1970). These techniques detect antigen binding B lymphocytes more readily than antigen binding T lymphocytes. Antigen-specific T cell rosettes readily dissociate either because there are fewer receptors on T cells than B cells, or because the receptors are of lower affinity or more readily dissociate from the cell surface (Haskill *et al.*, 1972; Ashman & Raff, 1973).

Only about 0·001–0·01 per cent of the lymphoid cells in unprimed animals have receptors for most antigens other than histocompatibility alloantigens. Antigenic stimulation raises the proportion to a maximum of 1–3 per cent.

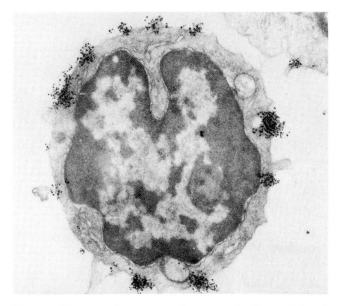

**Fig. 7.4.** Electron microscope radioautograph of a small lymphocyte from mouse spleen binding $^{125}$I-haemocyanin via antigen-specific membrane receptors. Magnification × 14,000. (By Dr T. Mandel, from Ada, 1970.)

### 7.4.2 Techniques for analyzing antigen-specific cell populations

The functional significance of antigen binding cells was first demonstrated by Wigzell & Andersson (1969). Passing a primed population of lymphoid cells through an antigen-coated glass bead column led to the specific depletion of antigen-reactive cells (Fig. 7.5). Both specific antibody forming cells and their precursors were removed by this method. Cells retarded by the column were shown, on elution, to be the specific precursors of antibody-secreting cells. Affinity chromatography of lymphocytes is essentially a preparative method. The separation of rosette-depleted or enriched cell populations by differential centrifugation (see Chapter 9) and the specific radiation killing of antigen-binding cells by *in vitro* exposure to antigen of very high specific activity (antigen suicide) can be used for similar purposes. These methods also show that antigen-binding B cells are the precursors of antibody-secreting cells. Antigen suicide techniques have also revealed that T cells possess specific receptors for antigen (Basten *et al.*, 1971).

## 7.5 Characterization of the B lymphocyte antigen receptor

### 7.5.1. Immunoglobulin nature

Antigen-binding reactions of B cells can be inhibited by anti-immunoglobulin antisera. Antisera to most of the antigenic

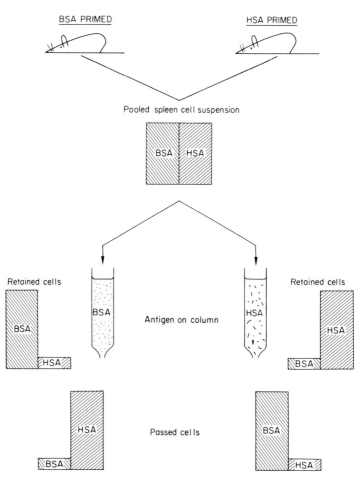

**Fig. 7.5.** Affinity chromatography of antigen-specific lymphocytes.

determinants on immunoglobulins are inhibitory, including class and subclass specific antisera (McConnell *et al.*, 1969; Greaves, 1971). Separate populations of cells expressing $\gamma$ and $\mu$ heavy chains together with $\kappa$ or $\lambda$ light chains have been detected by this method.

Immunoglobulin determinants can also be detected on the surface of B lymphocytes by the binding of fluoresceinated or radiolabelled antiglobulin sera to the lymphocyte surface. The percentage of Ig$^+$ cells in human peripheral blood shows a between laboratory variance and estimates ranging from 10 per cent to 30 per cent have been published. This wide discrepancy could reflect technical and serological differences. Controls to exclude passive uptake of serum immunoglobulin have not been done in all cases (Warner, 1974).

The proportion of lymphocytes expressing different classes and subclasses of surface immunoglobulin is quite different from the serum distribution of the classes and subclasses (Fig. 7.6). IgM$^+$

cells are more common than IgG$^+$ lymphocytes in humans and particularly in mice. Froland & Natvig (1972) have shown that IgG2$^+$ lymphocytes are the most common in humans. IgG2 is the second commonest immunoglobulin in serum. There is an even greater discrepancy with IgD, which is barely detectable in serum. Human cord blood, tonsil and, to a lesser extent, peripheral blood contain many IgD$^+$ lymphocytes (Rowe et al., 1973). The difference between cell surface and serum immunoglobulin concentrations is due to the fact that plasma cells and not lymphocytes make antibody. They may, however, ultimately derive from IgM and possibly IgD carrying precursors (see Chapter 13). The function of IgD on lymphocytes is unknown.

Isolation of surface IgM from normal mouse lymphocytes has shown that it is present as 7S monomer which lacks certain heavy

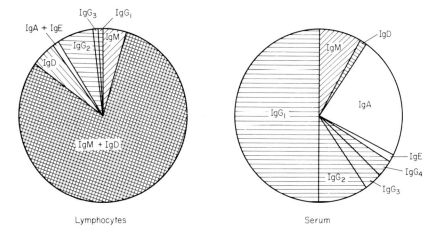

Lymphocytes                    Serum

**Fig. 7.6.** Class and subclass distribution of immunoglobulin amongst Ig$^+$ lymphocytes in human peripheral blood compared with serum immunoglobulin distribution.

chain carbohydrates. Either of these features may contribute to its retention in the membrane. Isolated light or heavy chains are rarely found on normal lymphocytes (Vitetta et al., 1971).

### 7.5.2 Class, subclass and allelic exclusion of surface immuno-
globulin

Plasma cells of a single clone synthesize a single homogeneous product of one class, subclass, allotype and idiotype. Since B lymphocytes are the direct precursors of plasma cells, it can be asked whether they also show similar restriction.

(a) *Class and subclass.* 30–40 per cent of cord blood and tonsil lymphocytes, though fewer peripheral blood lymphocytes, simultaneously express IgD and IgM on their surface, as do some chronic lymphocytic leukaemias (Table 7.3). Although large numbers of both $\kappa$ and $\lambda$ bearing cells are present, cells which express both heavy chain classes are *either $\kappa$ or $\lambda$*, strongly suggesting that neither class is passively acquired from plasma. IgD reappears on the membrane following its removal, suggesting its active synthesis (Rowe *et al.*, 1973). Simultaneous expression of IgM and IgG by one cell has also been described (see Chapter 13).

The likeliest explanation for these findings is that B lymphocytes can sequentially transcribe different heavy chain cistrons during their differentiation.

(b) *Allotype*. Although all plasma cells show allelic exclusion there is considerable controversy whether the same is true for B lymphocytes. In rabbits heterozygous for the *b* (light chain) locus allotypes (*b4,b6*) some investigators claim that B lymphocytes are all either *b4* or *b6* (allelic exclusion) (Pernis *et al.*, 1970), whilst others have produced evidence to show that a large proportion of blood lymphocytes simultaneously express both *b4* and *b6* (Wolf *et al.*, 1971). Peripheral blood lymphocytes also show allelic exclusion in humans heterozygous for Gm markers (Gm f and Gm z) (Froland & Natvig, 1972). The points of difference in these studies remains to be defined, in particular whether any lymphocyte-associated immunoglobulin is acquired from serum as immune complexes adhering via Fc or C3 receptors. In experiments which have shown that lymphocytes are not allelically excluded, rigorous attempts have been made to show that passive uptake of serum immunoglobulin is not the cause.

### 7.5.3 Distribution of cell surface immunoglobulin

The distribution of surface immunoglobulin on lymphocytes can be investigated by the use of fluoresceinated or radio-labelled anti-immunoglobulin sera (Fig. 7.7). If the reaction is carried out at low temperatures ($<4°C$), the antiglobulin is uniformly distributed indicating that the surface immunoglobulin is also uniformly distributed. At temperatures above $15°C$, the antiglobulin shows a patchy distribution due to the formation of small immune complexes (lattices) on the cell surface. This process depends on the antibody being divalent, Fab' antibody giving only a uniform distribution. It seems that above $15°C$, the cell membrane becomes much less viscous, permitting the movement of the cell surface determinants. Patch formation gives way in about 10–15 minutes to the formation of a cap of label over one pole of the cell. This is an energy-dependent process, and seems to be due to the normal active movement of the cell membrane bringing the patches together. The cap is internalized, the cell surface remaining denuded of immunoglobulin for 12–24 hours before freshly synthesized immunoglobulin can be detected (Taylor *et al.*, 1971; Unanue *et al.*, 1972). Exactly the same phenomenon can be demonstrated using antigen only and in this case the capping is observed *only* on the cells which express specific receptors for the antigen.

The ability of antisera to induce the redistribution of cell surface determinants including immunoglobulin (antigenic modulation) indicates that *individual* surface molecules are free to move within the plane of the membrane.

In this sense, the cell membrane is fluid rather than plastic with proteins floating either individually or in small aggregates in the membrane. This is the fluid mosaic model of Singer (Singer, 1974).

Capping of surface immunoglobulin has no effect on the distribution on histocompatibility antigens and other structures on the surface. Thus, immunoglobulin is not apparently associated with

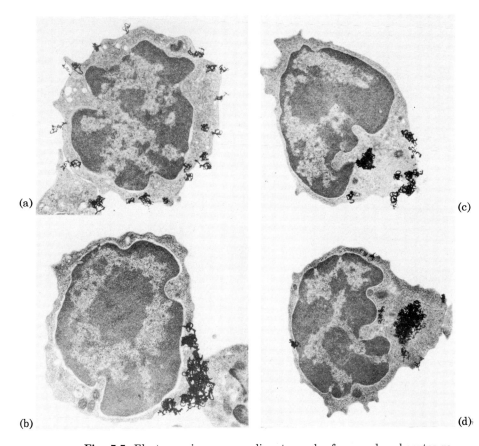

**Fig. 7.7.** Electron microscope radioautograph of mouse lymphocytes reacted with $^{125}$I-labelled anti-immunoglobulin at 4°C and then incubated:

(a) at 4°C. Magnification ×9,450.

(b) at 37°C for 1 minute. Note polar distribution of anti-immunoglobulin. Magnification ×12,250.

(c) at 37°C for 10 minutes. Magnification ×7,350.

(d) at 37°C for 10 minutes. Label now becoming internalized. Magnification ×12,250. (Unanue *et al.*, 1972.)

*Chapter 7: T and B Lymphocytes*

other known molecules in the cell membrane. Tests for co-capping of two determinants are useful for investigating their association in the membrane (see Chapter 15). Other surface structures like antigens and Fc receptors can also be capped on the cell surface, although less readily than immunoglobulin.

Since patch formation is solely dependent on the cross-linking of antigen, it should obey the same rules as apply to precipitate formation (Chapter 1). That is, for divalent antibodies, the antigen must have a valency of at least three, and failure to produce ring and patch formation may indicate that the structure being detected is only mono- or di-valent.

## 7.6 Characterization of the T lymphocyte antigen receptor

It is rational to assume that since nothing else recognizes antigen except antibody, then the T cell receptor must be an immunoglobulin. However, characterization of the T cell receptor has proved difficult and controversial, and opinion is sharply divided on whether it is immunoglobulin or a completely different type of recognition structure.

The arguments for and against the immunoglobulin nature of the T cell receptor are summarized below and in Table 7.4. Those interested in taking sides are referred to excellent reviews by Warner (1974), and Paul (1973).

### 7.6.1 Surface immunoglobulin

No immunoglobulin can be detected on the surface of thymus cells, but trace amounts, about $10^3$ molecules per cell; have been detected on the surface of activated T cells (Marchalonis et al., 1972). The possibility that this T cell 'immunoglobulin' is passively acquired from B cells (i.e. exogenous) is difficult to exclude (Hunt & Williams, 1974). It could adhere either via the Fc receptor on activated T lymphocytes, or in the case of specific antibody, by combining with antigen bound to the T cell by the true T cell receptor. However, in one experiment, it was shown that T cells will regenerate immunoglobulin after it has been capped off, suggesting active resynthesis (Roelants et al., 1974).

In the serological detection of surface immunoglobulin, it is apparent that only some and not all antisera give positive results. Nagging doubts arise as to the specificity of the sera and the possibility has not been fully excluded that they detect other cell surface determinants such as $\beta_2$ microglobulin or carbohydrate on the cell surface glycoproteins. Anti-light chain sera are often raised to urinary Bence-Jones proteins from mice and humans with myelomas. If, as a result of renal pathology, $\beta_2$ microglobulin (11,000 m.w.) was also excreted, care would have to be taken to

**Table 7.4.** Evidence for and against the immunoglobulin nature of the T cell receptor

| Assay | Immunoglobulin | Not immunoglobulin |
|---|---|---|
| A. Detection of surface Ig | | |
| 1. Immunofluorescence | Trace amount of Ig, $10^3$ molecules per cell | Trace Ig passively acquired from plasma |
| 2. Isolation of surface Ig | Pure T cells yield 7S IgM | 'Pure' T cells contaminated 1:400 with B cells |
| B. Inhibition of T cell function by anti-Ig sera | Anti-Fab inhibits antigen-binding T cells, MLC and GVH reactions. Some anti-$\mu$ sera also inhibit | Antigen-binding T cells have passively acquired specific antibody. Failure in many cases to inhibit T cell function with anti-Fab sera; inhibiting sera of doubtful specificity |
| C. Specificity characteristics of receptor | For serum protein antigens T and B cell receptor specificities are indistinguishable; i.e. lymphocytes have identical dictionaries | Many antigens not recognized by T cells, e.g. haptens, thymus independent antigens—therefore dictionaries not identical |
| D. Soluble specific factors | Specific factors from pure T cells which cooperate with B cells *in vitro* are 7S IgM (or IgT) | Specific T cell factors from educated T cells which cooperate *in vivo* with B cells are not Ig and are associated with histocompatibility antigens |
| E. *Ir* gene expression | Specific T cell associated *Ir* genes code for 'associative' recognition structures | Unlike V region genes, the *Ir* genes are linked to genes coding for the major histocompatibility systems and therefore unlikely to be immunoglobulin. These *Ir* genes code for the 'true' T cell receptor |

separate it from free light chains (25,000 m.w.) before any monospecific antiserum could be raised.

### 7.6.2 Characterization of soluble specific factors from T cells

By analogy with B cells, we may suppose that the antigen-specific soluble products of T cells are an accurate sample of the receptors on the T cell surface. Two firm attempts to characterize these products have given different results. *In vitro* studies by Feldmann and Basten (1972) have provided strong evidence for an antigen-specific soluble factor derived from T cells. This factor shows

*Chapter 7: T and B Lymphocytes*

specific T cell function *in vitro* (see Chapter 9) and its activity is removed by anti-$\mu$ sera. Rigorous attempts have been made to exclude B cells from the T-cell cultures which produce the factor. Using a semi-*in vitro* system, however, Munro *et al.* (1974) have evidence for another type of antigen-specific T cell factor. In contrast to the Feldmann and Basten system, the activity of this factor is not removed by anti-immunoglobulin columns but is removed by anti-*H-2* region antiserum columns. Its small molecular weight of about 50,000 also suggests that it is distinct from immunoglobulin. This raises the possibility that the T cell receptor is a non-immunoglobulin molecule associated with transplantation antigens—a suggestion first put forward by Crone *et al.* (1972).

### 7.6.3 *Specificity of antigen recognition by T cells*

If the T cell receptor is an immunoglobulin, then it is likely that its diversity is encoded by the immunoglobulin V-region genes. Since these also code for the combining sites of the B cell receptors, then both subpopulations should recognize and respond to the same antigens. However, T cells fail to respond to some antigens, for instance thymus independent antigens. Unless there are other reasons for this unresponsiveness (e.g. tolerance), it indicates major specificity differences in the T and B cell dictionaries (Chapter 8). This makes it unlikely that the same V-region genes are used by the two populations. The implication from this is that the T cell receptor uses non-immunoglobulin V-regions and is therefore a different type of recognition structure. Like all arguments in the T cell receptor debate, there is evidence that both T and B cell dictionaries are the same (see Chapter 8).

### 7.6.4 *Immune response* (Ir) *genes and T cells*

The discovery of the genetic control of specific immune responsiveness has been regarded as evidence that T cells have a different recognition system from B cells (McDevitt & Benacerraf, 1972). Many *specific* immune responses are controlled by genes linked to the major histocompatibility system (*H-2* in mice and HLA in man, see Chapter 16). Since immunoglobulin V-region genes are not linked to the *H-2* genes, this formally suggests that the H-linked *Ir* genes code for a different type of antigen recognition system, which is not immunoglobulin.

It is still unclear what the specific *Ir* genes code for. Proponents have argued strongly that since they code for specific receptors they are the 'true' T cell recognition system, while detractors have argued that the *Ir* genes code for 'associative, receptors involved in cell interactions between specific T and B lymphocytes (Chapter 9).

In summary, one fact is clear about the characterization of the T cell receptor—it is controversial. A different approach must now be adopted since repeated use of current methods, particularly serological ones in which the reagents are not fully characterized, seems likely to be increasingly unproductive of fact, if not argument. It seems likely that the truth must await the isolation and physicochemical characterization of the T cell receptor.

## References

ADA G.L. (1970) Antigen binding cells in tolerance and immunity. *Transplant Rev.* **5**, 105.

AOKI T., HAMMERLING V., DE HARVEN E., BOYSE E.A. & OLD L.J. (1969) Antigenic structure of cell surfaces. An immunoferritin study of the occurrence and topography of H-2, $\theta$ and Tl alloantigens on mouse cells. *J. exp. Med.* **130**, 979.

ASHMAN R.F. & RAFF M.C. (1973) Direct demonstration of theta positive antigen binding cells, with antigen-induced movement of thymus dependent cell receptors. *J. exp. Med.* **137**, 69.

BACH J.F., DARDENNE, M., GOLDSTEIN A., GUKA A. & WHITE A. (1971) Appearance of T cell markers in bone marrow rosette forming cells after incubation with thymosin, a thymic hormone. *Proc. Nat. Acad. Sci.* (Wash.) **68**, 2734.

BACH J.F. (1973) Evaluation of T cells and thymic serum factors in man using the rosette technique. *Transplant Rev.* **16**, 196.

BASTEN A., MILLER J.F.A.P., WARNER M.L. & PYE J. (1971) Specific inactivation of thymus-derived (T) and non thymus-derived (B) lymphocytes by [125]I-labelled antigen. *Nature New Biol.* **231**, 104.

BASTEN A., MILLER J.F.A.P., SPRENT J. & PYE J. (1972) A receptor for antibody on B lymphocytes. I. Method of detection and functional significance. *J. exp. Med.* **135**, 610.

BIANCO C.R.P. & NUSSENSWEIG V. (1970) A population of lymphocytes bearing a membrane receptor for antigen-antibody-complement complexes. I. Characterization and separation. *J. exp. Med.* **132**, 702.

BOYSE E.A., MIYAZAWA M., AOKI T. & OLD L.J. (1968) Ly-A and Ly-B: Two systems of lymphocyte isoantigens in the mouse. *Proc. roy. Soc. B.* **178**, 175.

BOYSE E.A. & OLD L.J. (1969) Some aspects of normal and abnormal cell surface genetics. *Ann. Rev. Genet.* **3**, 269.

COOMBS R.R.A., GURNER B.W., WILSON A.B., HOLM G. & LINDGREN B. (1970) Rosette formation between human lymphocytes and sheep red blood cells not involving immunoglobulin receptors. *Int. Arch. Allergy* **39**, 658.

CRONE M., KOCH C. & SIMONSEN M. (1972) The elusive T cell receptor. *Transplant. Rev.* **10**, 36.

FELDMANN M. & BASTEN A. (1972) Cell interactions in the immune response *in vitro*. III. Specific collaboration across a cell impermeable membrane. *J. exp. Med.* **136**, 49.

FROLAND S.S. & NATVIG J. (1972) Class, subclass, and allelic exclusion of membrane bound Ig of human B lymphocytes. *J. exp. Med.* **136**, 409.

*Chapter 7: T and B Lymphocytes*

Fu S.M., Winchester R.J. & Kunkel H.G. (1974) Occurrence of surface IgM, IgD and free light chains on human lymphocytes. *J. exp. Med.* **139,** 451.

Golub E.S. (1971) Brain-associated θ antigen: reactivity of rabbit anti-mouse brain with mouse lymphoid cells. *Cell. Immunol.* **2,** 353.

Greaves M.F. (1971) The expression of immunoglobulin determinants on the surface of antigen-binding lymphoid cells in mice. I. An analysis of light and heavy chain restrictions on individual cells. *Eur. J. Immunol.* **1,** 186.

Greaves M. & Janossy G. (1973) Elicitation of selective T and B lymphocyte responses by cell surface binding ligands. *Transplant Rev.* **11,** 87.

Greaves M. (1973) Surface markers for human T and B lymphocytes. *Current Titles in Imm. Transpl. and Allergy.* **1,** 193.

Haskill J.S., Elliott B.E., Kerbel R., Axelrad M.A. & Eidinger D. (1972) Classification of thymus derived and marrow derived lymphocytes by demonstration of their antigen binding characteristics. *J. exp. Med.* **135,** 1410.

Hunt S.V. & Williams A.F. (1974) The origin of cell surface immunoglobulin of marrow derived and thymus derived lymphocytes of the rat. *J. exp. Med.* **139,** 479.

Jondal M. & Klein G. (1973) Surface markers on human B and T lymphocytes. II. Presence of Epstein-Barr virus receptors on B lymphocytes. *J. exp. Med.* **138,** 1365.

Komura K. & Boyse E.A. (1973) Induction of T lymphocytes from precursor cells *in vitro* by a product of the thymus. *J. exp. Med.* **138,** 479.

Marchalonis J.J., Cone R.E. & Atwell J.L. (1972) Isolation and partial characterisation of lymphocyte surface immunoglobulins. *J. exp. Med.* **135,** 956.

McConnell I., Munro A., Gurner B.W. & Coombs R.R.A. (1969) Studies on actively allergized cells. I. The cytodynamics and morphology of rosette forming lymph node cells in mice and inhibition of rosette formation with antibody to mouse immunoglobulins. *Int. Arch. Allergy* **35,** 209.

McDevitt H.O. & Benacerraf B. (1969) Genetic control of specific immune responses. *Adv. Immunol.* **11,** 31.

Munro A.J., Taussig M.J., Campbell R. & Williams H. (1974) Antigen specific T cell factor in cell cooperation: physical properties and mapping in the left hand (K) half of *H-2. J. exp. Med.* **146,** 1579.

Naor D. & Sulitzeanu D. (1967) Binding of radioiodinated bovine serum albumin to mouse spleen cells. *Nature (Lond.)* **214,** 687.

Paul W.E. (1973) Antigen recognition and cell receptor sites. In Porter R.R. *Defence and Recognition* p. 329. Butterworth–MTP, London.

Pernis B., Forni L. & Amante L. (1970) Immunoglobulin spots on the surface of rabbit lymphocytes. *J. exp. Med.* **132,** 1001.

Raff M.C. (1971) Surface antigenic markers for distinguishing T and B lymphocytes in mice. *Transplant Rev.* **6,** 52.

Reif A.E. & Allen J.M.V. (1964) The AKR thymic antigen and its distribution in leukaemias and nervous tissues. *J. exp. Med.* **120,** 413.

Roelants G.E., Ryden A., Hagg L. & Loor F. (1974) Active synthesis of immunoglobulin receptors for antigen by T lymphocytes. *Nature (Lond.)* **247,** 106.

Ross G.D., Polley M.J., Rabellino E.M. & Grey H.M. (1973) Two different complement receptors on human lymphocytes. One specific for C3b and one for C3b inactivator-cleaved C3b. *J. exp. Med.* **138**, 798.

ROWE D.S., HUG K., FORNI L. & PERNIS B. (1973) Immunoglobulin D as a lymphocyte receptor. *J. exp. Med.* **138**, 965.

SINGER S.J. (1974) Molecular biology of cellular membranes with applications to immunology. *Advanc. Immunol.* **19**, 1.

TAKAHASHI T., OLD L., MCINTIRE R. & BOYSE E. (1971) Immunoglobulin and other surface antigens of cells of the immune system. *J. exp. Med.* **134**, 815.

TAYLOR R.B., DUFFUS P.H., RAFF M.C. & DE PETRIS S. (1971) Redistribution and pinocytosis of lymphocyte surface immunoglobulin molecules induced by anti-immunoglobulin antibody. *Nature New Biol.* **233**, 225.

UNANUE E.R., PERKINS W.D. & KARNOVSKY M.J. (1972) Ligand induced movement of lymphocyte membrane macromolecules. I. Analysis by immunofluorescence and ultrastructural radioautography. *J. exp. Med.* **136**, 885.

VALDIMARSSON H., AGNARSDOTTIR G. & LACHMANN P.J. (1974) Cellular immunity in subacute sclerosing panencephalitis. *Proc. roy. Soc. Med.* **67**, 1125.

VITETTA E.S., BAUR S. & UHR J.W. (1971) Cell surface immunoglobulin. II. Isolation and characterisation of immunoglobulin from mouse splenic lymphocytes. *J. exp. Med.* **134**, 242.

WARNER N.L. (1974) Membrane Immunoglobulins and antigen receptors on B and T lymphocytes. *Advanc. Immunol.* **19**, 67.

WERNET P. & KUNKEL H.G. (1973) Antibodies to a specific surface antigen of T cells in human sera inhibiting mixed leucocyte culture reactions. *J. exp. Med.* **138**, 1021.

WIGZELL H. & ANDERSSON B. (1969) Cell separation on antigen-coated columns. Elimination of high rate antibody-forming cells and immunological memory cells. *J. exp. Med.* **129**, 23.

WOLF B., JANEWAY J.C.A., COOMBS R.R.A., CATTY D., GELL P.G.H. & KELUS A.S. (1971) Immunoglobulin determinants on the lymphocytes of normal rabbits. III. AS4 and AS6 determinants on individual lymphocytes and the concept of allelic exclusion. *Immunology* **20**, 931.

YOSHIDA T.O. & ANDERSSON B. (1972) Evidence for a receptor recognizing antigen complexed immunoglobulin on the surface of activated mouse thymus lymphocytes. *Scand. J. Immunol.* **1**, 401.

ZEILLER K. & PASCHER G. (1973) Detection of T and B cell specific heteroantigens on electrophoretically separated lymphocytes of the mouse. *Europ. J. Immunol.* **3**, 614.

# Chapter 8
# Theories of Antibody Formation

## P. J. Lachmann

### 8.1 Introduction

The ability of an animal to synthesize specific antibody molecules is such a remarkable phenomenon that theories about its mechanism have been expressed since the turn of the century. This chapter will review these theories and discuss current views of antibody formation.

### 8.2 Selective versus instructive theories

#### 8.2.1 Ehrlich's selective hypothesis

In the first selective theory of antibody formation, Ehrlich (1900) proposed that toxin molecules (antigen) combined with pre-existing specific side chains on the surface of cells, thus stimulating them to generate more of these specific side chains which then appeared in the serum as antibody (Fig. 8.1). Apart from terminology, this is a very modern hypothesis. Later studies by Landsteiner, on antibody formation to non-biological antigens, created problems for Ehrlich's selective hypothesis since it seemed difficult to envisage that side chains could pre-exist to diverse non-biological entities such as DNP, NIP and Nickel ions. The Ehrlich theory thus fell into disrepute.

#### 8.2.2 Instructive or template hypothesis

There followed a prolonged flirtation from about 1935–55 with instructive theories of antibody formation (see Haurowitz, 1973) which proposed that antigen 'instructed' the antibody forming apparatus as to what specific patterns it should make. It was suggested that there was 'non-specific gamma globulin' present in serum which folded itself around antigen, thus giving rise to specific antibody. Difficulties for this hypothesis arose when it was shown that antibody specificity lay within the primary structure of the antibody molecule. Haber (1964) showed that if antibody molecules were unfolded to their primary structures in 6 M urea and subsequently allowed to refold to their tertiary structures on dialysis, an appreciable amount of antibody activity was recovered. Studies on protein biosynthesis also demonstrated that antibody molecules were newly formed in response to antigen and not derived from pre-existing macromolecules.

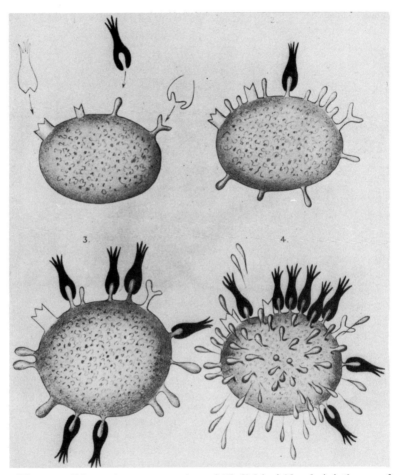

**Fig. 8.1.** Schematic representation of Ehrlich's 'side chain' theory of antibody formation. The antigen (black) combined with its corresponding 'side chain' or receptor, finally resulting in the excess regeneration of this receptor.

To overcome these objections indirect template hypotheses were then put forward. Antigen specificity was believed to be 'copied' into DNA which then coded for the specific antibody. However the sequence of events in protein synthesis is DNA→RNA→protein (or RNA→DNA→RNA→protein as in the case of reverse transcription), and has never been described as occurring in the reverse

*Chapter 8: Theories of Antibody Formation*

direction. Antibodies are formed to three dimensional determinants and the only way known to recognize such a shape would be to make use of a structure which is spatially complementary to it. Thus to make antibody one requires a pre-existing structure which has the essential properties (specificity and shape) of the molecule that is to be made. This is like the arguments of George Bernard Shaw on the existence of God, in which to make a God one needs a creature which has all His essential attributes, the argument thereby becoming circular.

Although instructive hypotheses are now virtually untenable there are occasional experiments which provide evidence for them. RNA extracted from the lymphoid cells of a rabbit of one immunoglobulin allotype can confer the ability to synthesize immunoglobulin of that allotype on lymphoid cells from rabbits of a different allotype (Bell & Dray, 1971). These results, however, are difficult to interpret unless there were found to exist some form of 'immunoglobulin transducing virus'.

### 8.2.3 Clonal selection hypothesis

In 1955 Jerne proposed the first of the modern selective theories of antibody formation. The kernel of all these theories is that the diversity of antibody receptors involved in the initial recognition of antigen arises spontaneously in the absence of antigen. The role of antigen is to select these receptors, thereby initiating antibody formation. Burnet (1957, 1959) and Lederberg (1959) proposed that these pre-existing receptors were associated with cells which underwent specific clonal proliferation on meeting antigen. This became known as the clonal selection hypothesis (CSH) for which there is now overwhelming evidence.

### 8.2.4 Accurate sample hypothesis

Mitchison (1967) stated parts of the CSH in more formal terms which can more easily be tested by experiment. This is known as the 'Accurate Sample Hypothesis'.

## 8.3 The accurate sample hypothesis

### 8.3.1

An animal has a population of cells, the virgin antigen sensitive cells, which express membrane receptors capable of reacting specifically with antigen. Both B and T cells have specific membrane receptors for antigen (Chapter 7).

*8.3.2*

One cell expresses only one receptor specificity. Numerous experiments have shown that cells cannot simultaneously bind two antigens to their surface. This clearly indicates that lymphocytes do not express all receptor specificities but does not totally exclude the possibility that B cells can express at least two specificities. This is unlikely because when antigen binding receptors are 'capped' on the lymphocyte surface by multivalent antigen (polymerized flagellin) all surface Ig is also capped (Raff *et al.*, 1973). Thus, if there are more than two receptor specificities for antigen on the lymphocyte surface, the second one is not immunoglobulin.

*8.3.3*

One cell expresses only one allotype and one isotype. Mature plasma cells synthesize immunoglobulin of only one allotype (allelic exclusion) and one heavy chain isotype. Opinion is divided as to whether lymphocytes also always show allelic exclusion (Chapter 7).

The simultaneous expression of both IgM and IgD by one lymphocyte is however firmly established. The combination of membrane IgM with cytoplasmic IgG in the same cell is also well recognized (Chapters 7 and 13). A possible explanation for this is that during B cell differentiation cells may switch from transcribing DNA necessary for synthesizing one immunoglobulin class to another, there being residual RNA which still codes for the first heavy chain isotype.

On balance this third tenet of the accurate sample hypothesis is basically correct, but may have to be slightly modified.

*8.3.4*

Antigen plays no part in the generation of diversity which gives rise to cells with different antigen receptors. There is currently much speculation about the generator of diversity and how clonal development takes place in the absence of antigen. This is discussed in detail later (8.4 and 8.5).

*8.3.5*

The product eventually produced by the cell is of identical specificity and affinity to the antigen-receptor originally present on the lymphocyte membrane (i.e. the receptor is an accurate sample of what the cell eventually secretes). It has been shown that if mice are treated with anti-idiotype antibody the *in vivo* synthesis of this idiotype is inhibited. Since the idiotype is the immunological marker of the antibody combining site, this is good evidence in support of this tenet.

*8.3.6*

The interaction between the receptor and the antigen is the event which triggers the cells to either differentiate and proliferate into effector lymphocytes or to become eliminated or inactivated, thus producing a state of tolerance.

At first sight the carrier effect in antibody formation (Chapter 9) is at variance with this tenet of the accurate sample hypothesis. To elicit an anti-hapten response to a hapten-carrier conjugate requires specific cellular recognition of both the hapten and the carrier. Hapten alone is non-immunogenic. Once produced, anti-hapten has equal affinity for the hapten irrespective of the carrier (either as free hapten or conjugated to another carrier). From this it was argued that the specificity of the cell receptor was different from that of secreted antibody (the one receptor theory, see Fig. 8.2). To overcome this objection to the accurate sample hypothesis,

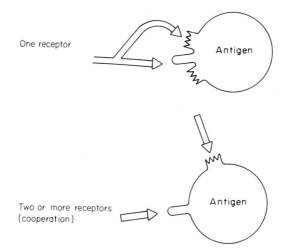

**Fig. 8.2.** Alternative hypotheses to account for the carrier effect. (From Mitchison A., 1967.)

Mitchison postulated that there must be two receptors involved in anti-hapten responses, one specific for the hapten (identical to secreted antibody) and one specific for the carrier (the two receptor theory, Fig. 8.2). The latter specificity we now know to be dictated by specific T cells which help B cells with the hapten specific receptors to make anti-hapten antibody. This is the phenomenon of cell cooperation (Chapter 9).

## 8.4 The problem of antibody diversity—'immunotheology'

*8.4.1 The generator of diversity (GOD)*

To deal with the vast range of antigens present in the environment (the epitopic universe) requires a repertoire of specific antibody molecules. Just how this antibody repertoire is generated is a considerable problem. It has been proposed that to do this requires a generator of diversity (GOD) (Lennox & Cohn, 1967) whose ways are inscrutable.

### 8.4.2 The epitopic universe

There appears to be little restriction on the size of the epitopic universe to which B cells can respond. Antibodies can be made to proteins, carbohydrates, nucleic acids, complex lipids, non-biological haptens such as the Nickel atom and phenol derivatives like NIP and DNP. Physically, an epitope can be as large as 6 hexose units, must have a certain minimum half-life *in vivo*, and be sufficiently rigid in structure.

With regard to T cells, the epitope universe may be more restricted since there are antigens to which T cells fail to respond such as certain carbohydrates and most haptens (see below).

### 8.4.3 The antibody repertoire

There are some restrictions on the total number of antibody combining sites. The antibody combining site seems to be made up of the hypervariable regions of the heavy and light chains. If the hypervariable regions comprise about 10 amino acid locations which can be occupied by 10 to 15 of the 20 possible amino acids then there can be at least $10^{10}$ to $10^{15}$ different hypervariable regions possible per chain. If heavy and light chains contribute equally to the combining site this gives a figure of $10^{20}$ to $10^{30}$ different antibody molecules. A figure as large as $10^{20}$ different antibody molecules has never been postulated, nor has it ever been suggested that the lymphon requires this number of antibody combining sites to deal with the epitopic universe. A more frequent guess at the number required is $10^6$ to $10^7$. The total number generated could be much in excess of this. There may be a great degree of redundancy and only a fraction of the total number is probably ever used in the lifetime of an individual.

Jerne (1973) has likened the immune system to glove manufacturers who, rather than making gloves on demand which fit a given type of hand make a vast number of gloves to fit all conceivable forms of hand. Of this pool of different gloves only a small fraction are ever required.

### 8.4.4 One or two generators of diversity (GOD)

Since both T and B lymphocytes recognize antigen, this raises the question of whether there is one GOD for both cell types (a 'monotheistic argument') or whether there is one for T cells and one for B cells (a 'ditheistic argument').

There is good experimental evidence on both sides. Studies by Rajewsky & Mohr (1974) have shown that in mice the cross-reactivity shown by the helper T cells for a whole range of heterologous serum albumins exactly parallels the cross reactivity of serum antibody for these same antigens. This would tend to indicate that the antibody repertoire or dictionary of both T and B lymphocytes is the same, i.e. they both use the same GOD. The evidence that the T cell receptor may be an immunoglobulin (see Chapter 7) also carries with it the implication that there is only one GOD for both T and B cells.

The ditheistic view is supported by evidence which shows that there are considerable differences in T and B cell repertoires. T cells, unlike B cells, seem to be unable to recognize conventional haptens like NIP and DNP. L-Tyrosine-azobenze arsonate (RAT) however (400 m.w.) is an exception to this. It not only evokes good T-cell responses, but can act as a 'carrier' for a much larger molecule: poly-$\gamma$-D glutamic acid (PGA 35,000 m.w.) which is not recognized by T cells. Antibody formation to PGA is only possible if it is coupled to an immunogenic carrier which can be the hapten, RAT. RAT-PGA evokes a good anti-PGA response (Alkan et al., 1971).

If one assumes that the failure of either B or T cells to respond to certain antigens is not due to secondary phenomena such as antigen handling or concentration, then such observations imply that there are major deletions in the T dictionary.

It has proved extremely difficult to detect immunoglobulin on the surface of T cells, even when antibody against V-region determinants is used. However, a definite answer as to the nature of the T cell receptor must await its isolation.

While the question of the T and B cell dictionary remains unresolved, at the present time I would tend towards an 'agnostic ditheism'.

## 8.5 The origin of GOD

### 8.5.1 Somatic or germ line

In general, the difference between somatic and germ-line theories is less one of mechanism than one of time scale. Does diversification of the V-region gene pool occur during the ontogeny of an individual's lymphon or does it occur phylogenetically during the development of the species? As far as the mechanism is concerned one can ask the question of whether GOD is random and acts by chance or whether it is driven by some stimulus. Arguments on this topic have been explored by Jerne (1971; 1973).

## 8.5.2 Histocompatibility antigens as the driving stimulus to antibody diversity

The first speculation is based on the observation that a high percentage of cells in unstimulated animals recognize the transplantation antigens of other members of the same species. For alloantigens which differ at a single locus, the number of reactive lymphocytes is around 10 per cent. For other antigens there are 0·0001–0·01 per cent antigen-binding cells present in unstimulated animals (see Ford, 1973).

Since the potential number of alloantigens is very large, the estimate of 10 per cent reactive cells per locus must obviously lead to over-occupancy of the total lymphocyte pool. Alternatively, perhaps one single Mendelian transplantation difference is really a difference at a large number of antigenic loci which are extremely cross-reactive (Howard & Wilson, 1974).

Jerne's first theory on the origin of antibody diversity proposes that the germ line V-region genes code for antibodies specific for the transplantation antigens of the species. These cells react with the individual's own transplantation antigens and are driven into proliferation by auto-antigenic stimulation, during the course of which mutations arise. At some stage during the process, the non-mutated, self-reactive clones become suppressed and the mutated (non-self-reactive clones) remain as the lymphocyte pool reactive to antigens other than transplantation antigens. The cells reacting with allogenic transplantation antigens remain in substantial numbers.

## 8.5.3 The idiotype paradox and the network theory

Since every antibody combining site seems to carry its own idiotopes, (idioepitope) it follows that the entire antibody repertoire is of approximately the same order of magnitude as the idiotope repertoire. In fact, the magnitude of the idiotope repertoire is so great that it is difficult to find a given idiotype in normal gamma globulin (Kunkel, 1970). The ability of animals, within a species and even within a strain, to make antibody to the idiotopes of antibody molecules with which they are immunized is a widespread phenomenon and perhaps indicates that a given animal has the ability to recognize any other idiotope on the immunoglobulin molecules of another member of the same species.

From this Jerne has made the assumption that within one individual, the idiotopes expressed by a given clone of antibody molecules is recognized by another set of combining sites. These in turn have their own unique idiotopes which can be recognized by yet another set of combining sites and so on. That is, the entire specific immune system is viewed as being a network of interacting molecules and cell receptors. This recognition system is entirely

Chapter 8: Theories of Antibody Formation

self-driven by the idiotopes of the developing V regions, with 'external' antigen playing no part.

From the point of view of the generation of antibody diversity, this is a very ingenious model. By somatic mutation of a few germ-line specificities, an entirely self-perpetuating recognition system can be derived, without the need for any external antigenic stimulus. These events could occur during the ontogeny of the lymphon. Thus all immunoglobulins may really be anti-idiotope and all other antibody reactivity is simply cross-reaction.


## References

ALKAN S.S., NITECKI D.E. & GOODMAN J.W. (1971) Antigen recognition and the immune response: the capacity of L-tyrosine-azobenzonearsonate to serve as a carrier for a macromolecular hapten. *J. Immunol.* **107,** 353.

BELL C. & DRAY S. (1971) Conversion of non-immune rabbit spleen cells by ribonucleic acid of lymphoid cells from an immunised rabbit to produce IgM and IgG antibody of foreign heavy chain allotype. *J. Immunol.* **107,** 83.

BURNET F.M. (1957) A modification of Jerne's theory of antibody production using the concept of clonal selection. *Aust. J. Sci.* **20,** 67.

BURNET F.M. (1959) *The clonal selection theory of acquired immunity.* Cambridge University Press.

EHRLICH P. (1900) On immunity with special reference to cell life. *Proc. Roy. Soc. Lond.* **66,** 424.

FORD W.L. (1973) The Cellular Basis of the Immune Response. In PORTER R.R., *Defence and Recognition*, p. 65. Butterworth–MTP, London.

HABER E. (1964) Recovery of antigenic specificity after denaturation and complete reduction of disulfides in a papain fragment of antibody. *Proc. Nat. Acad. Sci. (Wash)* **52,** 1099.

HAUROWITZ F. (1973) The problem of antibody diversity. Immunodifferentiation versus somatic mutation. *Immunochemistry* **10,** 775.

HOWARD J.C. & WILSON D.B. (1974) Specific positive selection of lymphocytes reactive to strong histocompatibility antigens. *J. exp. Med.* **140,** 660.

JERNE N.J. (1955) The natural selection theory of antibody formation. *Proc. Nat. Acad. Sci. (Wash.)* **41,** 849.

JERNE N.K. (1971) The Somatic Generation of Immune Recognition. *Europ. J. Immunol.* **1,** 1.

JERNE N.K. (1973) The immune system. *Sci. Amer.* **229,** 52.

KUNKEL H.G. (1970) Experimental approaches to homogeneous antibody populations. Individual antigenic specificity, cross specificity and diversity of human antibodies. *Fed. Proc.* **29,** 55.

LEDERBURG J. (1959) Genes and antibodies. *Science* **129,** 1649.

LENNOX E.S. & COHN M. (1967) Immunoglobulins. *Ann. Rev. Biochem.* **36,** 365.

MITCHISON N.A. (1967) Antigen recognition responsible for the induction *in vitro* of the secondary response. *Cold Spr. Harb. Symp. Quant. Biol.* **32,** 431.

PERNIS B., FORNI L. & AMANTE L. (1970) Immunoglobulin spots on the surface of rabbit lymphocytes. *J. exp. Med.* **132,** 1001.

RAFF M.C., FELDMANN M. & DE PETRIS S. (1973) Monospecificity of bone marrow derived lymphocytes. *J. exp. Med.* **137,** 1024.

RAJEWSKY K. & MOHR R. (1974) Specificity and heterogeneity of helper T cells in the response to serum albumin in mice. *Europ. J. Immunol.* **4,** 11.1

WOLF B., JANEWAY C.A. JR., COOMBS R.R.A., CATTY D., GELL P.G.H. & KELUS A.S. (1971) Immunoglobulin determinants on the lymphocytes of normal rabbits. *Immunology* **20,** 931.

# Chapter 9
# Cell Interactions in the Allergic Response

# I. McConnell

## 9.1 Introduction

The ability of T lymphocytes to modulate B lymphocyte function has consumed immunologists (not to mention mice) for the last seven years. T cells are now known to play a major role in the triggering and differentiation of B lymphocytes, and are particularly involved in promoting the IgG response to thymus-dependent antigens.

T–B cell cooperation involves an interaction between both populations of lymphocytes as well as macrophages. It is likely that this three-cell interaction in the allergic response is our first glimpse of a whole network of cellular interactions within the lymphoid system. This chapter describes the current state of the art, but the reader is forewarned that this is a rapidly-moving field where today's hypothesis might be tomorrow's fairy story! To understand the mechanisms involved in cell interactions requires a knowledge of the model systems used and these are described first.

## 9.2 Experimental models

### 9.2.1 The adoptive transfer system

Many of the *in vivo* assays for lymphoid cells are based on testing their reactivity after transfer to syngeneic recipients, usually mice. The recipients are made immunologically unresponsive by whole body irradiation which destroys lymphoid tissue but does not cause immediate death. Unless reconstituted with haemopoetic stem cells from bone marrow or spleen, the mice die within ten days from haemopoetic failure. They nonetheless provide living 'test tubes' for measuring the reactivity of cell innocula (Fig. 9.1). Transfer of cells to such animals is termed 'adoptive transfer' (Mitchison, 1957).

### 9.2.2 Graft versus host reactions (GVH)

A GVH reaction occurs when the adoptively transferred cells (the graft) are histoincompatible with the irradiated recipients. The lymphoid cells attempt to reject the host (graft versus host). The injected lymphoid cells proliferate in the spleen, giving rise to splenomegaly. GVH reactions can also be elicited in non-irradiated animals which are genetically incapable of rejecting the transfused cells (Fig. 9.1). This is achieved by transfer of parental cells to $F_1$ recipients which are naturally tolerant of the parental alloantigens. The other set of parental alloantigens in the $F_1$ are recognized as foreign by the inoculated cells and a GVH reaction occurs.

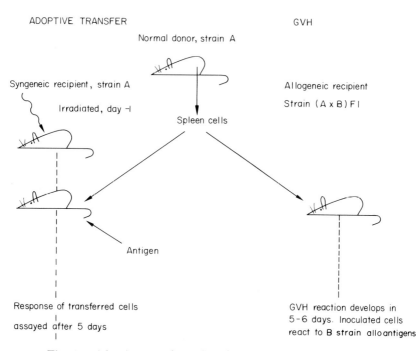

**Fig. 9.1.** Adoptive transfer and graft versus host (GVH) reaction.

## 9.3 Cell populations

The cell populations generally tested in the above assays are thymus, bone marrow, spleen and thoracic duct lymphocytes. Although these populations contain T and B cells in different ratios, relatively pure populations of either cell type can be prepared from them using *in vitro* and *in vivo* procedures. Some of the current *in vitro* methods are shown in Fig. 9.2.

It must be remembered that some tissues contain significant numbers of other lymphoid cells apart from T and B lymphocytes, for instance spleen which contains macrophages and K cells (see Chapter 12). These often remain in the 'purified' populations, depending on the technique used.

*Chapter 9: Cell Interactions in the Allergic Response*

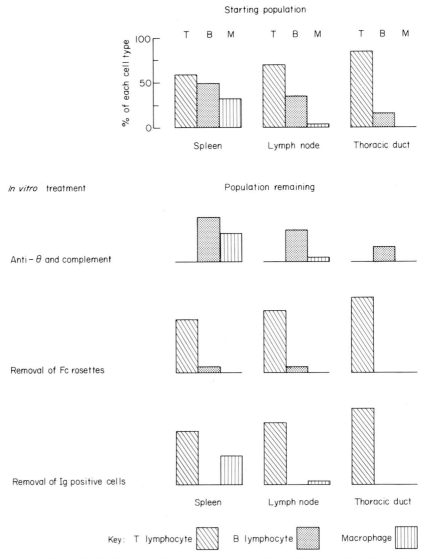

Fig. 9.2. *In vitro* methods of preparing 'pure' populations of T or B lympho-cytes.

### 9.3.1 *T lymphocyte populations*

The *thymus* contains a large proportion of thymocytes in different stages of differentiation. Mature immunocompetent thymocytes can be selected by pre-treating mice with hydrocortisone, which selectively destroys the immature T cells.

Thymus cells cannot be used in *in vitro* assays for antibody formation and spleen cells have to be used. *Spleens* can be en-riched for T cells by transferring cortisone resistant thymus cells to lethally irradiated recipients. Since no haemopoetic cells are given, these mice are dying 'test tubes', but provide a suitable

132                                    *Section II: Immunobiology*

source of splenic T cells about six days after transfer. *In vivo* challenge with antigen leads to priming of these T cells ('T educated') cells generally denoted $T_{SRBC}$ when sheep erythrocytes (SRBC) are used as antigen.

### 9.3.2 T lymphocyte enriched populations

These can be prepared from normal spleens, lymph nodes and thoracic duct cells by *in vitro* procedures which selectively deplete B lymphocytes.

For example, cells bearing Fc receptors can be selectively removed from a mixed population by passing it through an immuno-adsorbent column carrying immune complexes. Cells with Fc receptors are retained whilst T cells lacking these surface features pass through. B cells bearing immunoglobulin determinants can be similarly removed using columns carrying anti-immunoglobulin serum. Alternatively, rosettes formed either by T cells (E rosettes with SRBC in humans) or B cells (Fc or C3 rosettes) can be separated from the non-rosetting population by differential centrifugation on a discontinuous gradient.

### 9.3.3 B lymphocyte populations

The bone marrow of adult mice is a source of both B and T stem cells. In short-term reconstitution experiments, however, adult bone marrow can be regarded as a source of B cells. If the irradiated recipients are also thymectomized, then the T stem cells fail to differentiate. Populations of mature B cells can be derived by treating spleen or lymph node cell suspensions with anti-$\theta$ serum and complement to lyse the T cells. Finally, the thoracic duct lymph of B rats or mice (see below) is largely devoid of T cells and hence a useful source of mature recirculating B lymphocytes.

### 9.3.4 B mice

'B' mice is a term used to describe mice which are largely devoid of mature T cells. This can be achieved by:

(a) *Neonatal thymectomy* which prevents dissemination of mature T cells in mice.

Neonatally thymectomized mice are largely devoid of T cells by 6–8 weeks of age (Miller, 1962).

(b) *Adult thymectomy* followed by lethal irradiation is a convenient method of eliminating most lymphoid cells. Such animals may be reconstituted with bone marrow cells, the absence of the thymus preventing maturation of T stem cells in the innoculum. Perfectionists treat the bone marrow cells with anti-$\theta$ serum and complement before injection to remove the few residual T cells or reconstitute with fetal liver cells (super B mice!).

133  *Chapter 9: Cell Interactions in the Allergic Response*

(c) 'Nude' mice are homozygous for a recessive allele (Nu/Nu) which controls this condition. Since they are sterile, they have to be bred from heterozygotes which carry the allele. They are congenitally athymic, have no hair growth and endocrine abnormalities. Their spleens often contain T stem cells which fail to differentiate in the absence of the thymus (Pantelouris, 1968).

The absence of T cell function in B mice can be shown by their failure to reject skin grafts, or produce antibody to thymus dependent antigens.

### 9.4 *In vitro* systems for antibody formation

There are several systems which support the *in vitro* induction of antibody formation (Fig. 9.3).

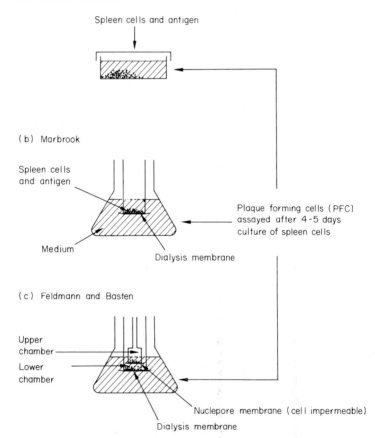

Fig. 9.3. *In vitro* systems for antibody formation. In (c) the double chamber cultures are formed by concentric glass tubes suspended in a reservoir of medium. T cells are placed in the upper chamber and B cell containing populations in the lower chamber.

### 9.4.1 Mishell & Dutton culture

If a suspension of spleen cells is cultured together with antigen in a small Petri dish under defined conditions, specific antibody forming cells (plaque forming cells, see 9.4.3 below) arise within five days (Mishell & Dutton, 1967). This tissue culture system has shown that macrophages are essential to the *in vitro* antibody response. It has also permitted an analysis of the mechanism of T–B cell cooperation, which can be studied by co-culturing T and B spleens.

### 9.4.2 Marbrook culture (Marbrook, 1967)

In this system the spleen cell culture is separated from the main bulk of the tissue culture medium by a dialysis membrane, thus permitting the diffusion of nutrients to and metabolites away from the culture. Good culture conditions are thus maintained without dilution of the macromolecular environment of the cells (Fig. 9.3b). Feldman and Basten (1972) have modified this by using a double-chamber culture formed by concentric glass chambers suspended in the reservoir of medium (Fig. 9.3c). The two chambers are separated by a nuclepore membrane which permits the free diffusion of macromolecular products between the chambers but keeps the cells separate. The activities of specific soluble products of T cells involved in cell cooperation have been analyzed by placing educated T cells in one chamber and B cells and macrophages in the other. The response of the B cells is measured by the Jerne plaque assay.

### 9.4.3 Jerne plaque assay

This is an ingenious and widely used assay for antibody formation by single cells (Fig. 9.4) (Jerne *et al.*, 1963). Spleen cells making antibodies to sheep erythrocytes (SRBC) are mixed with the antigen and plated out in agarose. During incubation the spleen cells release antibody and those red cells in the immediate vicinity become sensitized with antibody. These are lysed in the presence of complement, leaving a hole (or plaque) in the red cell layer around the single antibody forming cell (or plaque forming cell, PFC). As described, this assay detects IgM antibody forming cells (direct PFC), but IgG and any other class of antibody-secreting cell can be detected if the plate is overlayed with anti-immunoglobulin antibody before the addition of complement. This amplifies the lytic reaction on sensitized cells which would not otherwise be lysed (indirect plaques).

Most of the techniques are fully described in Weir (1973).

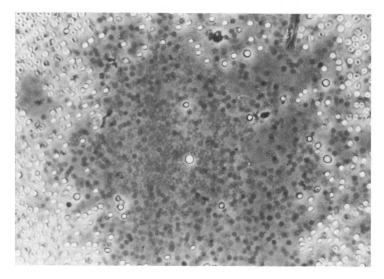

**Fig. 9.4.** Typical IgM plaque-forming cell.

The spleen cell secreting antibody to SRBC is readily visible in the centre of a zone of lysed erythrocytes. (Agarose-free modification of the Jerne plaque technique. For description, see 9.4.3.)


## 9.5 Lymphocyte cooperation

Cell cooperation between lymphocytes during the immune response was originally defined by *in vivo* experimental approaches. More recently, *in vitro* studies have been of considerable importance in understanding the mechanisms involved.


### 9.5.1 Restoration of response to SRBC in immunologically unresponsive mice

The immunological responsiveness of mice to SRBC can be severely impaired by neonatal thymectomy, adult thymectomy and irradiation alone. This failure to respond can be corrected by reconstituting the mice with thymus cells alone or together with bone marrow cells, depending on the experimental design. Using this type of approach, Claman *et al.* (1966) first showed that thymus cells and bone marrow cells act synergistically in the restoration of immune responsiveness in irradiated mice and that if either population was omitted, no response took place.

In an elegant series of papers, Miller and Mitchell (1968) first analysed the role of various cell populations in restoring immune responsiveness to mice which had been made unresponsive by neonatal thymectomy (i.e. 'B' mice). The increase in direct (IgM) plaque forming cells in the spleen in response to SRBC was measured. As shown in Fig. 9.5, the poor response of neonatally thy-

*Section II: Immunobiology*

mectomized mice to SRBC could be corrected by injecting them with $5 \times 10^7$ syngeneic normal thymus cells prior to antigenic challenge. Similarly, Mitchell & Miller (1968) showed that adult thymectomized, lethally irradiated mice, had to be repopulated with both thymus and bone marrow cells before they could produce a response to SRBC. Table 9.1 lists the essential points which emerged from their studies.

(a) The full restoration of an antibody response to SRBC in immunologically unresponsive mice requires viable, intact T cells. Additional bone marrow cells are without effect, as are thymus extracts and even irradiated thymus cells.

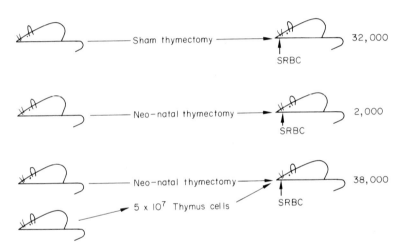

TREATMENT

RESPONSE

(IgM PFC/spleen day 4)

Sham thymectomy — SRBC → 32,000

Neo-natal thymectomy — SRBC → 2,000

Neo-natal thymectomy — SRBC → 38,000

$5 \times 10^7$ Thymus cells

**Fig. 9.5.** Effect of thymus cells on restoring immunological responsiveness to neo-natally thymectomized mice.

(b) B cells are the specific precursors of the antibody forming cells. If neonatally thymectomized CBA mice are reconstituted with $F_1$ (CBA × C57Bl) or allogeneic (C57Bl) T cells, all the PFC arising in the spleen can be lysed by treatment with anti-CBA serum and complement. Similar treatment with anti-C57Bl serum is without effect, showing that no PFC carry the donor alloantigens and are thus not derived from the T cell innoculum. Similarly, in a syngeneic system in which recipient mice carrying a chromosomal marker (the T6 chromosome in CBA/T6T6 mice) are reconstituted with T cells from mice which lack the T6 chromosome (CBA/--), all the PFC carry the T6 marker, indicating that they are host and not donor (Nossal et al., 1968).

(c) Even though T cells do not differentiate into PFC, they are *specifically* involved in enhancing the PFC response. T cells divide

*Chapter 9: Cell Interactions in the Allergic Response*

in response to antigen (Davies *et al.*, 1966), can be specifically educated to antigen in T mice and fail to cooperate in the antibody response to SRBC if they are derived from mice tolerant to this antigen (see Chapter 10). In the latter case their ability to specifically cooperate in the response to a non-cross-reacting antigen such as horse erythrocytes (HRBC) is normal.

The general conclusion from these and many similar studies (see review by Katz & Benacerraf, 1972) is that the IgM response to

**Table 9.1.** Reconstitution of immune responsiveness to SRBC in immunologically unresponsive mice

| Pretreatment (CBA strain) | Reconstitution with | PFC response[1] *in vivo* after challenge with SRBC |
|---|---|---|
| Sham thymectomy | No cells | + |
| Neo-natal thymectomy | No cells | − |
| | CBA thymus cells | + |
| | CBA TDL[2] | + |
| | CBA TDL from SRBC tolerant mice | − |
| | Thymus extract | − |
| | Bone marrow cells | − |
| | (CBA × C57Bl) $F_1$ thymus cells | + |
| | | (all PFC have CBA allo-antigens *only*) |
| Adult thymectomy and lethal irradiation | No cells | − |
| | CBA thymus cells | − |
| | Bone marrow cells | − |
| | Thymus cells and bone marrow cells | + |

(1) In neonatally thymectomized mice + = 20,000 PFC/spleen, − = 2,000 PFC/spleen.

(2) Thoracic duct lymphocytes.

Summary of data from Miller & Mitchell (1968) and Mitchell & Miller (1968).

SRBC in mice requires the specific cooperation between T and B cells. Both cell types recognize antigen but only the B lymphocytes give rise to antibody-forming cells.

This phenomenon of cell cooperation was then also demonstrated *in vitro*. Munro and Hunter (1970) showed that the poor response of spleen cell cultures derived from CBA 'B' mice could be restored by the addition to the culture of a small number of BALB/c spleen cells. All the PFC, however, were identified as CBA and not BALB/c. In this experiment the T cells were provided by the BALB/c spleen. Hartmann (1971) found that T cells were specifically in-

*Section II: Immunobiology*

volved since the addition of T cells educated to SRBC ($T_{SRBC}$) specifically enhanced the response of B spleen cell cultures to SRBC. Uneducated T cells failed to enhance the response. Similar *in vitro* studies also revealed that primed T cells could cooperate with B cells without undergoing division. If T cells have recently proliferated in response to antigen, their ability to cooperate is not abolished by high doses of irradiation given *in vitro* (1000 Rads). Since B cells have to proliferate to give rise to antibody forming cells, they are radiation sensitive.

### 9.5.2 Analysis of the response to hapten-carrier conjugates

Contemporary with the experiments on cell cooperation in the response to SRBC, attempts were being made to solve the hapten-carrier problem (Mitchison, 1969 and 1971; Katz *et al.*, 1970; Paul

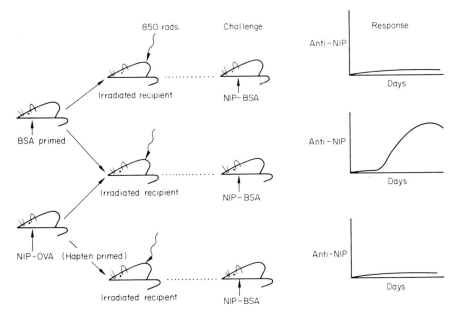

**Fig. 9.6.** Reconstitution of a secondary anti-hapten response in irradiated recipients with separate populations of hapten and carrier-primed spleen cells (Mitchison, 1969).

*et al.*, 1970). Rather than abandon the one-cell–one-receptor theory (Chapter 8), Mitchison (1967) postulated that in a secondary anti-hapten response two receptors are involved, one specific for hapten, the other for the carrier.

It was shown by adoptive transfer that two populations of cells are necessary for the effective reconstitution of a secondary (IgG) anti-hapten response to a hapten-carrier conjugate (Fig. 9.6). In Mitchison's experiments, the donor populations used in reconstitution were *separately* primed to *either* the carrier (BSA) *or* the hapten on a non-cross reacting carrier (NIP-OVA). Challenge of the recipient mice with NIP-BSA produced a brisk anti-NIP response, even although neither population had been previously exposed to the test conjugate (NIP-BSA). No anti-hapten response took place if the reconstituted mice were challenged with hapten or carrier alone, or if only one of the primed populations were used.

A similar phenomenon was demonstrated in normal guinea-pigs in the response to hapten-carrier conjugates (Katz *et al.*, 1970; Paul *et al.*, 1970). DNP-OVA primed guinea-pigs fail to make a secondary anti-DNP response on challenge with hapten on a different carrier, DNP-BGG (the carrier effect). If the DNP-OVA-primed guinea-pigs are separately injected with BGG or reconstituted with syngeneic BGG primed cells prior to challenge with DNP-BGG, then a good anti-DNP response takes place.

**Table 9.2.** Reconstitution of secondary anti-hapten response.

| Mice reconstituted with cells separately primed to | Anti-NIP response to NIP-BSA |
|---|---|
| NIP-CG | − |
| BSA | − |
| NIP-CG and BSA | + |
| NIP-CG (anti-$\theta$ and complement treated) and BSA | + |
| BSA (anti-$\theta$ and complement treated) and NIP-CG | − |

Reconstitution of secondary anti-hapten response in irradiated recipients using hapten and carrier-primed spleen cells. Evidence that carrier specificity is at the T cell level.

The significance of these experiments using the hapten-carrier systems lies in the demonstration that in a secondary anti-hapten response two receptors are involved; one hapten-specific, the other carrier-specific and these receptors are clearly on different cells.

The essential difference between these experiments and those described in 9.5.1 is that the different cell populations were defined as carrier-specific and hapten-specific rather than T or B cells. By the use of anti-$\theta$ serum and complement to eliminate T cells from either population, it was later shown that carrier specificity was expressed in T cells and hapten-specificity in B cells, the latter being the precursors of the anti-hapten producing cells (Raff, 1970). Most of the points made in 9.5.1 are also true for this model (Table 9.2).

The possibility that cell cooperation was due to information transfer from T to B cells was convincingly eliminated using this system. In experiments where carrier-specific (T) cells and hapten-specific (B) cells came from mice which carried different immuno-

*Section II: Immunobiology*

globulin allotype genes, all the anti-hapten antibody produced in the recipient was of the allotype of the B cell donor (Mitchison, 1971).

## 9.6 Possible mechanisms of lymphocyte cooperation: I Specific cooperation

### 9.6.1 Hypothesis

A plausible role for T cells in promoting B cell triggering is that they provide an antigen concentration mechanism for B cells. The concentration of free antigen in body fluids is usually so *low* that one would expect B cells to have receptors of very *high* affinity if

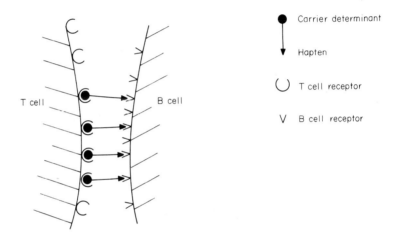

**Fig. 9.7.** Possible mechanism of cell cooperation: direct T–B cell bridging by antigen.

they were to be stimulated. This derives from the fact that the extent of an immunological reaction (in this case B cell activation) is proportional to the product of the affinity of the receptor and the free antigen concentration (see Chapter 4). Since we may assume that the secreted antibody is an accurate sample of the B cell receptor (see Chapter 8), the secreted antibody should have a similar, very high, affinity. That this is not the case suggests that the B cell experiences antigen at relatively high local concentrations.

T lymphocytes have been imagined as concentrating the antigen directly on the B cell surface by an antigen bridging mechanism (Fig. 9.7). The carrier-specific T cells combine with carrier determinants on the hapten-carrier molecules and thus present an array of haptenic determinants to the hapten-specific B cells (Mitchison, 1969 and 1971: Rajewsky *et al.*, 1969). An alternative model which

*Chapter 9: Cell Interactions in the Allergic Response*

eliminates the need for direct T–B cell bridging is that T cells secrete a specific soluble factor which attaches cytophilically to the surface of macrophages. The macrophages then present the hapten to the B cells (Fig. 9.8). In view of the well-documented association between antigen and macrophages and their role in the antibody response, this seems a reasonable hypothesis (Lachmann, 1971; Feldmann & Basten, 1972).

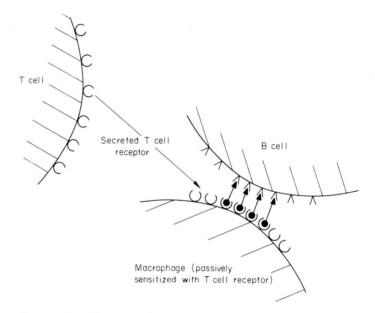

**Fig. 9.8.** Possible mechanism of cell cooperation involving presentation of antigen to B cells via macrophages.

### 9.6.2 Experimental evidence

Evidence was provided by Feldmann & Basten (1972) that cell cooperation is mediated by soluble specific factors derived from T cells. They showed that specific cell cooperation still took place when T cells and B cells were separated from one another by a cell-impermeable membrane in a double chamber version of the Marbrooke culture system (9.4.2, Table 9.3). B spleen cells which have been primed to DNP were shown to make a good anti-DNP response if challenged with DNP-KLH in the presence of T cells educated to KLH ($T_{KLH}$). The same cooperative response also took place when the hapten and carrier specific cells were separated by a cell impermeable membrane; $T_{KLH}$ being in the upper compartment of the tissue culture chamber and DNP primed B cells in the lower compartment. DNP-KLH was present in both compartments. No response occurred if T cells were omitted from the upper compartment or if T cells educated to another antigen were used. Since the two cell populations were separated, the only explanation is that the T cells release a specific soluble factor which diffuses from the upper (T) to the lower (B) cell compartment and there cooperates with the hapten-primed population.

Feldmann (1972) went on to show that the specific T cell factor is cytophilic for macrophages. Macrophages, rather than B cells, were placed in the lower chamber and recovered after several days culture with $T_{KLH}$ and KLH in the upper compartment. Addition of these macrophages and DNP-KLH to hapten-(DNP)-primed B cells stimulated an anti-hapten response to DNP-KLH. These experiments strongly support the view that cell cooperation can take

Table 9.3. Demonstration of cell cooperation via specific soluble T cell factors

| Upper chamber | Cell-impermeable Nuclepore membrane | Lower chamber | Response of spleen cells in lower chamber to DNP-KLH |
|---|---|---|---|
| None | | $T_{KLH}$ + DNP-primed spleen | + |
| $T_{KLH}$ | | DNP-primed spleen | + |
| $T_{KLH}$ | | DNP-primed spleen (anti-$\theta$ and complement treated) | + |
| T (not educated) | | DNP-primed spleen | − |
| None | | DNP-primed spleen | − |
| $T_{FGG}$ | | DNP-primed spleen | − |

For culture system, see Fig. 9.3c.

place *in vitro* via a specific T cell factor which, alone or complexed with antigen, binds to the surface of the macrophage. These sensitized macrophages then specifically present antigen to the antigen receptors on B cells, thus triggering antibody formation.

## 9.7 Mechanisms of cell cooperation: II Non-specific cooperation

### 9.7.1 Hypothesis

Mechanisms of specific cell cooperation based on antigen bridging between T cells (or macrophages) and B cells requires that the hapten is linked to the molecule which the T cells recognize. However, there are both *in vitro* and *in vivo* experiments to show that T cells can enhance the response of B cells, even when the antigen which the T cells recognize is on a *separate* molecule from that which stimulates the B cells. In this situation, it is impossible to envisage how antigen-bridging between B cells and helper cells can take place (Fig. 9.9).

The mechanism for this non-specific enhancement of the B cell response to antigen is unknown. It has been postulated that the T

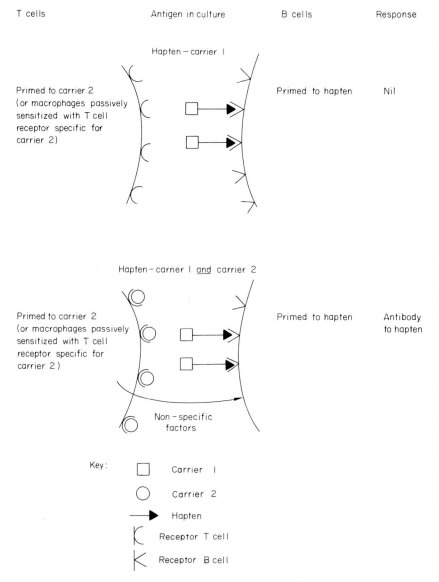

**Fig. 9.9.** Possible mechanism for non-specific cell cooperation.

cells (or macrophages carrying specific T cell factor) release mediators on reacting with antigen and that these mediators non-specifically enhance the response of B cells to thymus-dependent antigens (Dutton *et al.*, 1971).

### 9.7.2 In vitro *experimental evidence*

Evidence for a T dependent, non-specific enhancement of B cells comes from several studies. Hartmann (1971), Hunter *et al.* (1972) and Waldmann *et al.* (1973) have shown that the response of B spleens to SRBC can be enhanced by the addition to the culture of T spleen cells educated to a second non-cross-reacting antigen. The second antigen can be donkey erythrocyte antigen ($T_{DRBC}$) or protein antigens like KLH ($T_{KLH}$) which would be unlikely to cross-react with SRBC even at the T cell level. There is a strict requirement for the *educating* antigen to be present in the culture, since $T_{DRBC}$ or $T_{KLH}$ alone do not enhance the B cell response. Thus, the T cell factor is only produced by antigenic stimulation, but once produced this factor acts non-specifically in facilitating the response of B cells to a non-cross-reacting antigen.

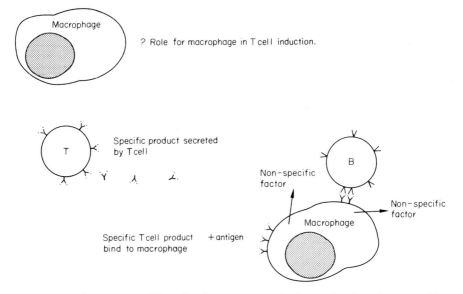

**Fig. 9.10.** Possible role of macrophages in the production of non-specific factor. (From Waldman and Munro, 1975.)

There is good evidence to show that this non-specific cooperation is mediated by soluble factors. Cell-free supernatants of T cells activated by protein and even alloantigens can facilitate the response of B cells to SRBC (Schimpl & Wecker, 1972; Waldmann *et al.*, 1972). Waldmann & Munro (1973) have shown that macrophages are involved in the production of the factor by T cells, although it is not clear which cell actually produces the factor(s). If macrophages synthesize the factor then its release may be triggered following interaction between antigen and passively acquired antigen-specific molecules derived from the T cells (Fig. 9.10).

## 9.7.2 In vivo *studies*

The allogeneic effect is another example of apparent non-specific activation of B lymphocyte function (Katz *et al.*, 1971; Katz & Benacerraf, 1972). The experimental protocol which reveals this phenomenon is shown in Fig. 9.11. In an *in vivo* anti-hapten response, the requirement for carrier recognition can be abrogated by a concomitant GVH reaction. The optimum time for hapten challenge is six days after transfer of allogeneic lymphocytes. Challenge before this time does not enhance the anti-hapten response but does lead to an enhanced memory cell population. Thus, when T cells are specifically activated *in vivo* within the immediate microenvironment of the B cell, they non-specifically promote a B cell response to a thymus-dependent antigen. The mechanism may be similar to that involved in the *in vitro* studies in being mediated by 'non-specific' factors released from activated T cells.

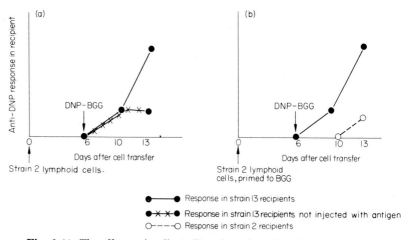

**Fig. 9.11.** The allogeneic effect. (Based on data from Katz *et al.* 1971.)
    Strain 13 guinea-pigs, primed to DNP-*OVA* were transfused with allogeneic strain 2 lymphoid cells and 6 days later the recipients were challenged with DNP-*BGG*. The resulting allogeneic cell interactions were found to abrogate the requirement for carrier recognition in the secondary anti-DNP response to DNP-*BGG*. Strain 13 animals produced a good anti-DNP response irrespective of whether the allogeneic cells were primed to BGG (b) or not (a). Some anti-DNP is also made without challenge with DNP-BGG (a). Both the magnitude and kinetics of the secondary anti-DNP response is different from that seen in a syngeneic system (b).

    The exact site of action of non-specific factors in cell cooperation is unknown. They either act during triggering of B cells or alternatively promote B cell differentiation and proliferation once this has been initiated (Askonas *et al.*, 1974) have shown that one of the non-specific factors derived from an allogeneic cell interaction can lead to increased proliferation of antibody forming cells triggered *in vitro* by antigen in the absence of the factor. T cell non-specific factors can thus promote B cell differentiation once it has been initiated.

### 9.8 *In vivo* significance of cell cooperation

We are ignorant of the detailed requirements for a B cell activation, and we know of some of the mechanisms which promote it. Any working model based on our present knowledge must seek to explain:

(a) Thymus independence.

(b) The relative lack of thymus dependence of the IgM response compared to the IgG response for certain antigens like haptens, proteins and heterologous erythrocytes. With the latter, the IgM and the IgG responses are thymus dependent.

The model can be based on the following facts:

(a) Antigen-specific T cell factors operating via macrophages.

(b) Non-specific factors produced by T cells/macrophages which facilitate the response of B cells.

(c) A slightly ill-defined requirement for a 'critical epitope density' in B cell triggering (Chapter 8)

A reasonable speculation is that the B cells require a minimum level of organized presentation of antigen, together with a certain total 'kick' of stimulation to lift them over an activation threshold. This threshold may vary considerably, depending on whether they are B memory cells, potential IgG or IgM secretors, etc. Thymus independent antigens seem to present both proper epitope density and 'kick', although neither is adequately defined, and they may, at least in some cases, be related.

The majority of antigens are thymus dependent, and will probably require both antigen-specific and non-specific factors for their activation. The former seem to act as antigen concentration devices on the macrophage surface, and it is possible that the latter serve to reduce the threshold of stimulation for the B lymphocyte population. Non-specific factors may be a separate family of molecules from the specific factors, or they may represent a secondary function of part of the specific T cell molecule; just as the Fc portion of an antibody molecule has a function separate from the antigen-binding function of the Fab. This function often amplifies the specific function of the antibody molecule and the same might apply to the T cell receptor. These concepts are embraced by the 'second signal' hypothesis, which states that the resting B cell requires both antigen and perhaps an amplifying signal for differentiation. If both are not sufficient then perhaps second, third, and more amplifying signals may be necessary. In this way, cell cooperation in its broadest sense can be viewed as a facilitating mechanism for promoting B cell triggering and differentiation to antigen.

### 9.9 Other levels of lymphoid cell interactions

#### 9.9.1 *T cell suppression*

The other levels of cell interaction which have also been described are as follows:

T–B cell cooperation is a positive interaction which leads to antibody formation. It has a negative counterpart in T cell suppression (Chapter 10) where B cells are tolerized after interaction with specific T cells or their products.

#### 9.9.2 *T–T-cell interaction*

Interactions between distinct sub-populations of T cells have been described in GVH and cytotoxic reactions to alloantigens. One of these subpopulations consists of a non-recirculating type of T cell, present in the thymus and the spleen ($T_1$). The second subpopulation ($T_2$) is recirculating and exists predominantly in peripheral blood and lymph nodes. Being recirculating, it is also found in spleen. $T_1$ and $T_2$ have been shown to act synergistically in the generation of cytotoxic effector cells (Cantor & Asofsky, 1970; Wagner, 1973).

#### 9.9.3 *Macrophage–lymphocyte interaction*

Most lymphocyte responses to antigen are macrophage dependent

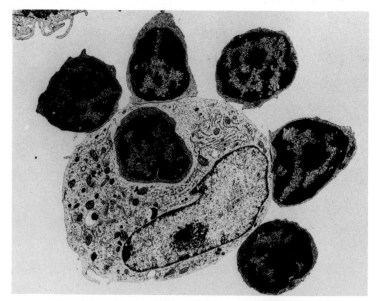

**Fig. 9.12.** The clustering of guinea-pig thymocytes about syngeneic glass-adherent macrophages. Broad areas of approximation between these cells were observed with little obvious specialization of the architecture adjacent to areas of contact. Magnification × 4550. (From Lipsky and Rosenthal, 1973.)

*Section II: Immunobiology*

(Unanue, 1972). Although macrophages are necessary for antigen-'handling' and presentation it has been shown that syngeneic combinations of antigen-bearing macrophages and T lymphocytes produces a greater proliferative response than allogeneic combinations (Rosenthal & Shevach, 1973). This suggests that macrophages may do more than physically present antigens and may interact with lymphocytes in some way. The clustering of lymphocytes around macrophages is often observed *in vitro* (Fig. 9.12). This phenomenon is antigen independent and requires metabolically active macrophages which may have surface 'recognition' structures for lymphocytes (Lipsky & Rosenthal, 1973).

### 9.10 Cell membrane requirements in cell interactions

Surface structures on lymphoid cells may be involved in cell interactions. In certain mouse models it can be shown that the cooperating cells have to be histocompatible within the *H-2* complex (Chapter 15). The exact *H-2* region involved is unknown, but recent experiments suggest that it is in the *I* region, wherein the *Ir* genes map (Benacerraf & Katz, 1975). Some non-specific factors also seem to act more effectively with syngeneic rather than allogeneic B lymphocytes, although this may not be a general truth. The array of surface receptors on lymphoid cells (Fc, C3, etc.) should not be forgotten in this context and it may be that some of these structures are membrane 'acceptor' sites for soluble factors involved in cell cooperation. For further discussion, see Chapter 16.

The apparent network of lymphoid cell interactions is daunting at first sight. However, it is known that other potent biological effector systems are under exquisite homeostatic control to prevent their untoward activation. It is equally likely that the immune system is under similar homeostatic control and lymphoid cell interactions are our first glimpse of cellular cascades analogous to the enzyme cascades of the complement and coagulation pathways.

### References

ASKONAS B., SCHIMPL A., WECKER E. (1974) The differentiation function of T cell replacing factor in nu/nu spleen cell cultures. *Eur. J. Immunol.* **4,** 164.

BENACERRAF B. & KATZ D. (1975) The histocompatability-linked immune response genes. *Advances in Cancer Research.* **21,** 121.

CANTOR H. & ASOFSKY R. (1970) Synergy among lymphoid cells mediating the graft-versus-host response. II Synergy in graft-versus-host reactions produced by Balb/c lymphoid cells of differing anatomic origin. *J. exp. Med.* **131,** 235.

CLAMAN H.N., CHAPERON E.A. & TRIPLETT R.F. (1966) Immunocompetence of transferred thymus-marrow cell combinations. *J. Immunol.* **97,** 928.

DAVIES A.J.S., LEUCHARS E., WALLIS V. & KOLLER P.C. (1966) The mitotic response of thymus derived cells to antigenic stimulus. *Transplantation* **4,** 438.

DUTTON R.W., FALKOFF R., HURST J.A., HOFFMAN M., KAPPLER J.W., KETTMAN J.R., LESLEY J.S. & VANN D. (1971) Is there evidence for a non-antigen specific diffusable chemical mediator in the initiation of the immune response? *Prog. Immunol.* **1**, 355.

FELDMANN M. (1972) Cell interactions in the immune response in vitro. V. Specific collaboration via complexes of antigen and thymus-derived cell immunoglobulin. *J. exp. Med.* **136**, 737.

FELDMANN M. & BASTEN A. (1972) Cell interactions in the immune response in vitro. III. Specific collaboration across a cell impermeable membrane. *J. exp. Med.* **136**, 49.

HARTMANN K.U. (1970) Induction of a hemolysin response *in vitro*. Interaction of cells of bone marrow origin and thymic origin. *J. exp. Med.* **132**, 1267.

HARTMANN K.U. (1971) Induction of a hemolysin response *in vitro*. *J. exp. Med.* **132**, 1267.

HARTMANN K.U. (1971) Induction of a hemolysin response *in vitro*. II. Influence of the thymus-derived cells during the development of antibody-producing cells. *J. exp. Med.* **133**, 1325.

HUNTER P., MUNRO A. & McCONNELL I. (1972) Properties of educated T cells for rosette formation and cooperation with B cells. *Nature New Biology.* **236**, 52.

JERNE N.K., NORDIN A.A. & HENRY C. (1963). In AMOS B. & KOPROWSKI H., *Cell Bound Antibodies*, p. 109. The Wistar Institute Press, Philadelphia, Pa.

KATZ D.H., PAUL W.E., GOIDL, E.A. & BENACERRAF B. (1970) Carrier function in anti-hapten immune responses. I. Enhancement of primary and secondary anti-hapten antibody responses by carrier preimmunization. *J. exp. Med.* **132**, 261.

KATZ D.H., PAUL W.E., GOIDL E.A. & BENACERRAF B. (1971) Carrier function in anti-hapten antibody responses. III. Stimulation of antibody synthesis and facilitation of hapten-specific secondary antibody responses by graft-versus-host reactions. *J. exp. Med.* **133**, 169.

KATZ D.H. & BENACERRAF B. (1972) The regulatory influence of activated T lymphocytes on B cell responses to antigen. *Adv. Immunol.* **15**, 1.

LACHMANN P.J. (1971) Lymphocyte co-operation. *Proc. R. Soc. Lond. B.* **176**, 425.

LIPSKY P.E. & ROSENTHAL A.S. (1973) Macrophage lymphocyte interaction: I. Characteristics of the antigen-independent binding of guinea pig thymocytes and lymphocytes to syngeneic macrophages. *J. exp. Med.* **138**, 900.

MARBROOK J. (1967) Primary immune response in cultures of spleen cells. *Lancet* **11**, 1279.

MILLER J.F.A. (1962) Effect of neonatal thymectomy on the immunological responsiveness of the mouse. *Proc. R. Soc. Lond. B.* **156**, 415.

MILLER J.F.A.P. & MITCHELL G.F. (1968) Cell to cell interaction in the immune response. I. Hemolysin-forming cells in neonatally thymectomized mice reconstituted with thymus or thoracic duct lymphocyte. *J. exp. Med.* **128**, 801.

MISHELL R.I. & DUTTON R.W. (1967) Immunisation of normal mouse spleen cell suspensions *in vitro*. *Science* **153**, 1004.

MITCHELL G.F. & MILLER J.F.A.P. (1968) Cell to cell interaction in the immune response. II. The source of hemolysin-forming cells in irradiated mice given bone marrow and thymus or thoracic duct lymphocytes. *J. exp. Med.* **128,** 821.

MITCHISON N.A. (1957) Adoptive transfer of immune reactions by cells. *J. Cell Comp. Physiol.* **50,** Suppl. I, 247.

MITCHISON N.A. (1967) Antigen recognition responsible for the induction *in vitro* of the secondary response. *Cold Spring Harbor Symp. Quant. Biol.* **32,** 431.

MITCHISON N.A. (1969) In LANDY M. & BRAUN, W. *Immunological Tolerance,* p. 149. Academic Press, New York.

MITCHISON N.A. (1971) Carrier effects in secondary responses to hapten protein conjugates. I. Measurement of the effect with transferred cells and objection to the local environment hypothesis. *Eur. J. Immunol.* **1,** 10.

MITCHISON N.A. (1971) Carrier effects on the secondary immune response. II. Cellular co-operation. *Eur. J. Immunol.* **1,** 18.

MUNRO A. & HUNTER P. (1970) *In vitro* reconstitution of the immune response of thymus-deprived mice to sheep red blood cells. *Nature (Lond.)* **225,** 277.

NOSSAL G.J.V., CUNNINGHAM A., MITCHELL G.F. & MILLER J.F.A.P. (1968) Cell to cell interaction in the immune response. III. Chromosomal marker analysis of single antibody forming cells in reconstituted, irradiated or thymectomised mice. *J. exp. Med.* **128,** 839.

PANTELOURIS E.M. (1968) Absence of thymus in a mouse mutant. *Nature (Lond.)* **217,** 370.

PAUL W.E., KATZ D.H., GOIDL E.A. & BENACERRAF B. (1970) Carrier function in anti-hapten immune responses. II. Specific properties of carrier cells capable of enhancing anti-hapten antibody responses. *J. exp. Med.* **132,** 283.

RAFF M.C. (1970) Role of thymus derived lymphocytes in the secondary humoral immune response in mice. *Nature (Lond.)* **226,** 1257.

RAJEWSKY K.V., SCHIRRMACHER V., NASE S. & JERNE N.K. (1969) The requirement of more than one antigenic determinant for immunogenicity. *J. exp. Med.* **129,** 1131.

ROSENTHAL A.S. & SHEVACH E.M. (1973) Function of macrophages in antigen recognition by guinea pig T lymphocytes. I. Requirement for histocompatible macrophages and lymphocytes. *J. exp. Med.* **138,** 1194.

SCHIMPL A. & WECKER E. (1972) Replacement of T cell function by a T cell product. *Nature New Biol.* **237,** 15.

UNANUE E.R. (1972) The regulatory role of macrophages in antigenic stimulation. *Advanc. Immunol.* **15,** 45.

WAGNER H. (1973) Synergy during *in vitro* cytotoxic allograft responses. I. Evidence for cell interaction between thymocytes and peripheral T cells. *J. exp. Med.* **138,** 1379.

WALDMANN H. & MUNRO A. (1973) T cell dependent mediator in the immune response. *Nature (Lond.)* **243,** 356.

WALDMANN H. & MUNRO A.J. (1975) The inter-relationships of antigenic structure, thymus independance and adjuvanticity. *Immunology* **28,** 509.

WALDMANN H., MUNRO A. & HUNTER P. (1973) Properties of educated T cells. The ability of educated T cells to facilitate the immune response to non cross reacting antigens *in vitro. Eur. J. Immunol.* **3,** 167.

WEIR D.M. (1974) *Handbook of Experimental Immunology,* 2nd ed. Blackwell Scientific Publications, Oxford.

# Chapter 10
# Immunological Tolerance and Unresponsiveness

## P. J. Lachmann

## 10.1 Introduction

The allergic response to an antigen includes not only the production of antibodies and specific effector T cells, but also the specific
failure to give rise to antibody or cell-mediated response. This state
of specific unresponsiveness to further challenge with antigen is
known as immunological tolerance. It is probably best to reserve
the term 'tolerance' for states in which lymphocytes capable of
responding to an antigen are absent (clonal elimination) or specifically inactivated. It should be remembered, however, that operational tolerance to an antigen may result from the absence of any one
population of specific cells (either T or B) which is needed for the
establishment of an immune response to the antigen : humoral
responses to T-dependent antigens will not occur if the requisite
specific T cell clones are absent.

The broader concept of unresponsiveness includes mechanisms
which interfere with the effector limb of the immune response.
These have recently been canvassed as the true mechanism by
which unresponsiveness occurs. Some of this chapter is devoted to
the arguments around this view.

From the clinical or operational, rather than the analytical,
viewpoint, these distinctions may not matter.

### 10.1.1 Historical

The first real description of tolerance arose from the observations
of Owen (1945) that dizygotic cattle twins which are naturally
parabiosed *in utero* as a result of placental fusion are permanent
chimeras with respect to their red cells. They also accept skin
grafts from each other but not from unrelated cattle. This phenomenon can be produced experimentally by injecting neonatal mice
of one inbred strain with tissues from other inbred strains (Billingham *et al.*, 1953).

These observations prompted a systematic investigation of
tolerance. It was shown to be highly specific and, under certain
regimes of antigenic stimulation, could be induced to most antigens,
including transplantation antigens and heterologous proteins. The

factors directing the allergic response towards tolerance rather than towards antibody production thus became an area of great interest.


## 10.2 Factors promoting tolerance induction

### 10.2.1 State of the lymphon

Early views on tolerance induction held that if the developing lymphon was confronted with antigen before a critical stage during embryogenesis, the antigen-reactive cells were inactivated or eliminated (clonal elimination, Burnet, 1959). Challenge at a later stage resulted in proliferation and antibody formation. This is not entirely correct, since fetal animals can produce antibody after antigenic challenge *in utero*, and tolerance can be induced in adults.

Despite this, it is true that tolerance is easier to induce in an immature or damaged lymphon. Simultaneous challenge of mice with antigen and cyclophosphamide, which depletes mainly the B cell population, or antigen and anti-lymphocyte serum, which depletes mainly the circulating T lymphocytes, results in tolerance to the antigen. In each case, only part of the lymphocyte pool is destroyed and it may be that it is failure to make antibody which leads to rapid tolerance induction, rather than there being an intrinsic change in the antigen-sensitive cells to a 'tolerance-prone' state.


### 10.2.2 Properties of antigen

The physical and chemical characteristics of an antigen can have a profound effect on whether it is a tolerogen or an immunogen.

(a) *Antigen size.* The removal of aggregates from IgG or albumin by ultracentrifugation confers tolerogenicity on these molecules at all dose levels. If uncentrifuged antigen is injected directly into the hepatic portal vein, aggregated material is removed by Kuppfer cells in the liver, where there is normally no antibody formation. That antigen which passes into the general circulation is aggregate-free and tends to be tolerogenic. Such antigen screening of material absorbed from the bowel may be an important physiological function of the liver.

Polymerized flagellin (POL, $10^7$ m.w.), the flagellar antigen from *S. adelaide*, is a thymus-independent antigen and potent immunogen. The monomer derived from it (MON, 40,000 m.w.), whilst antigenic at low doses, is tolerogenic at higher doses. Cleavage of MON by cyanogen bromide yields Fragment A (18,000 m.w.) which is tolerogenic at all doses. This phenomenon is not related to any change in antigenic specificity since flagellin is a molecule of repeating subunits.

(b) *Chemical characteristics of the antigen.* Different chemical forms of certain molecules are better tolerogens than immunogens. Thus, D-amino acid polymers are usually powerful tolerogens (Janeway & Sela, 1967). Chemical modification by acetoacetylation of monomeric flagellin converts it from an immunogen to a tolerogen without appreciably destroying its affinity for antibody (Parish, 1971). If this were also shown to be true for transplantation antigens, the clinical implications would be considerable.

(c) *Dose of antigen.* For protein antigens, there is a critical dose-dependency for either tolerance induction or antibody formation. As shown in Fig. 10.1, bovine serum albumin at $10^{-8}$ M will readily tolerize virgin antigen-sensitive cells (low-zone tolerance). At $10^{-7}$ M, this same antigen, especially if macrophage processed, will

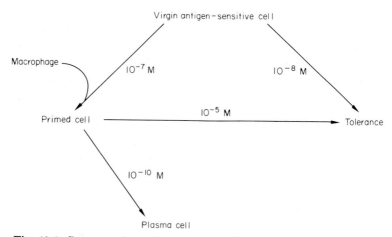

**Fig. 10.1.** Concentration of bovine serum albumin giving antibody formation and tolerance in mice.

generate primed cells which can subsequently be triggered into antibody formation by as little as $10^{-10}$ M antigen. In the presence of $10^{-5}$ M antigen the primed cells are tolerized (high-zone tolerance) (Mitchison, 1964; 1967). Thus, for some protein antigens there are two zones of antigen concentration wherein tolerance can be induced, but in intermediate ranges these antigens generally give rise to antibody formation.

An ultra-low zone tolerance for flagellin has been described by Shellam & Nossal (1968). Repeated neo-natal injections of POL, $10^{-8}$ g/g body weight (about $10^{-14}$ M), will produce low-zone tolerance in rats (Fig. 10.2). At these concentrations there is hardly enough antigen to reach all antigen-sensitive cells and the mechanism is unknown.

154

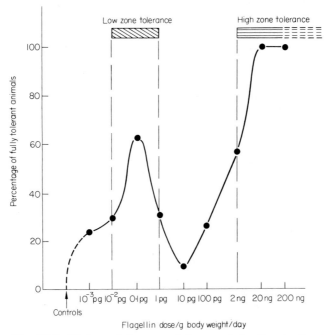

**Fig. 10.2.** High- and low-zone tolerance induction to flagellin in rats. Rats were repeatedly injected over an eight-week period with different concentrations of flagellin and then challenged with an immunogenic dose of flagellin. Tolerance was found to be induced in a high percentage of rats, low-zone tolerance being established with ultra-low doses of flagellin. (From Shellam and Nossal, 1968.)

### 10.3 Tolerance at the cellular level

#### 10.3.1 Tolerance induction in T and B cells

Since the response to most antigens requires the specific cooperation of both T and B cells, it could be predicted that tolerance in either one of these cell populations would result in tolerance at the whole animal level.

Experiments to test this hypothesis were done by Weigle *et al.* (1970) and Weigle (1973) who studied the kinetics of the induction and loss of tolerance in mouse T and B cells. Tolerance was assayed in T and B lymphocytes at various intervals after the induction of tolerance to Human Gamma Globulin (HGG). *Tolerant thymus* cells and normal bone marrow cells or *normal thymus* and tolerant bone marrow cells were adoptively transferred into irradiated mice. The response of these cell mixtures to HGG and non-cross reacting Turkey Gamma Globulin (TGG) was tested by challenging the recipients with immunogenic amounts of antigen (Table 10.1). As shown in Fig. 10.3, T cell tolerance was established within two days and persisted for about 150 days. B cell tolerance took about a

**Table 10.1.** Reconstitution of the response of irradiated mice to protein antigens using thymus and bone-marrow cells from normal and tolerant mice

| Cell population used for reconstitution | | Antibody response to | |
|---|---|---|---|
| Thymus | Bone marrow | HGG | TGG |
| Normal | Normal | + | + |
| HGG tolerant | Normal | − | + |
| Normal | HGG tolerant | − | + |
| HGG tolerant | HGG tolerant | − | + |

HGG = Human Gamma Globulin
TGG = Turkey Gamma Globulin

Data from Weigle *et al.* (1970)

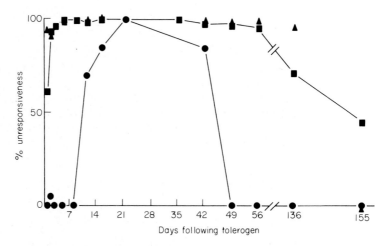

**Fig. 10.3.** Kinetics of the induction and loss of tolerance in mouse thymus and bone-marrow cells to HGG (Human Gamma Globulin).

Mice were injected with tolerogenic amounts of HGG and at various times thereafter, either the thymus or bone-marrow cells were assayed for responsiveness in an adoptive transfer system. Tolerant thymus (or bone-marrow) cells were transferred with normal bone-marrow (or thymus) cells respectively. Recipients were challenged with immunogenic HGG and their percentage unresponsiveness compared to animals receiving normal thymus and bone-marrow cells. (From Weigle, 1971.)

Key: ■ — Tolerant thymus
    ● — Tolerant bone marrow
    ▲ — Tolerant spleen

*Section II: Immunobiology*

week to become established and was lost again by 50 days. It is important to stress that, although the kinetics of induction and loss of tolerance are different for T and B cells, unresponsiveness in either of these populations leads to an operational tolerance at the whole animal level.

Tolerance to certain auto-antigens like thyroglobulin has been shown to be due to T cell tolerance alone. B cells specific for thyroglobulin antigen exist *in vivo* but cannot be triggered into antibody formation presumably because helper T cells specific for thyroglobulin are absent. Injection of heterologous thyroglobulin or thyroglobulin coupled to an immunogenic carrier provides 'immunogenic' T cell help for thyroglobulin specific B cells, which begin to make antibody (Fig. 10.4).

Injected with *rabbit* thyroglobulin having determinants: a,b,c,d,e

Result: No antibody to thyroglobolin because no T cell help

Injected with *heterologous* thyroglobulin having determinants: a,b,c   f,g

Result: Antibody to a,b,c because T cell help via foreign determinants: f,g

**Fig. 10.4.** Breaking of tolerance to thyroglobulins. Normal rabbit with self tolerance to rabbit thyroglobulin T cells but not B cells tolerant to thyroglobulin determinants a, b, c, d, e. (Schematic.)

This mechanism of by-passing tolerant T cells is believed to operate in inducing auto-antibody formation in certain auto-allergic diseases. As shown in Fig. 10.4, it may also explain circumvention of tolerance by cross-reacting antigens.

## 10.4 T cell mediated suppression and regulation

There are several examples of specific unresponsiveness being mediated by T cells.

### 10.4.1 Suppression via the B cell receptor

In rabbits or mice, the synthesis of a given immunoglobulin allotype can be suppressed if the animals are exposed prenatally to antisera against one of their allotypes. As shown in Fig. 10.5, if BALB/c mothers whose IgG allotype is 'a' (Ig-1a) are immunized with the 'b' allotype of SJL/J fathers (Ig-1b) before mating, the offspring (BALB/c × SJL/J) become exposed *in utero* to anti-'b' antibodies by the transplacental passage of maternal immunoglobulin. Although these offspring are *genetically* capable of making both 'a' and 'b' allotypes, the phenotypic expression is restricted to 'a'. (Jacobsen *et al.*, 1972; Jacobsen 1973).

Allotype suppression persists long after maternal anti-allotype antibody has disappeared from the offspring's circulation. By cell transfer experiments, it appears that suppression is an active process, since normal BALB/c × SJL spleen cells fail to secrete Ig-1b when transferred to the suppressed mice. It also appears to be T cell mediated since adoptive transfer of T cells from suppressed mice together with small numbers of normal $F_1$ spleen cells to irradiated $F_1$ mice also results in the suppression of Ig-1b secretion by the normal cells. It must be pointed out that this situation is best seen in mice of the SJL genotype. In the more established type of allotype suppression seen in rabbits, the mechanism is as yet unknown.

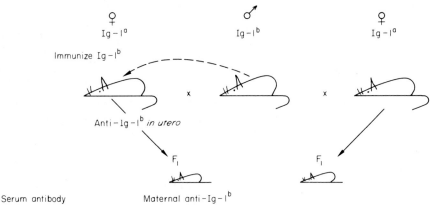

Fig. 10.5. Allotype suppression.

## 10.4.2 Suppression via antigen

Suppressor T cells which are antigen-specific have been demonstrated in several systems. Weber & Kolsch (1973) have shown that low-zone tolerance to bacteriophage can be transferred from tolerant to normal mice by T cells. A similar type of *in vivo* suppression of the response to SRBC has been described by Gershon (1974). The response of B cells *in vitro* is also suppressed in the presence of excess T cells or their specific T cell factor and antigen (Feldmann, 1974).

*Section II: Immunobiology*

### 10.4.3 Summary

The suppressor T cells recognize different structures in 10.4.1 and 10.4.2. In 10.4.1 the suppressor T cells are presumably specific for the allotype, and act directly on the B cell receptor. This system is interesting since it may be an experimental model for the Jerne network theory (Chapter 8). In 10.4.2 the T lymphocytes or their specific soluble factors recognize antigen just as they do in specific cooperation. It is unknown if specific suppressor factors are identical to specific cooperating factors or if they are functionally distinct molecules. If the former is the case tolerance induction rather than cooperation results perhaps because the T cell factors and their antigen are present in excess (prozone effect) at the B cell receptor. Such a mechanism would thus be analogous to antibody mediated tolerance (10.5.2).

## 10.5 Tolerogenic interactions between B cell receptor and antigen

Unresponsiveness in the B lymphocyte population can also be induced directly following the specific blocking of B cell receptors by antigen or antigen-antibody complexes.

### 10.5.1 Blocking of B cell receptors by antigen

Receptor blocking by antigen has recently been described by Mitchell *et al.* (1972). They showed that when hapten (DNP-) primed mice were challenged with the hapten linked to a thymus-independent antigen (DNP-SIII), the mice became unresponsive to further challenge with the same antigen on an immunogenic carrier (DNP-BSA). Since SIII is an antigen which is poorly degraded by the reticuloendothelial system, presumably DNP-SIII persists *in vivo*, blocking or inactivating DNP-specific B cells, thus preventing response to DNP-BSA.

The irreversible binding of antigen to the B cell receptor is another potent method of specifically inactivating B lymphocytes. Affinity labelled antigens bind irreversibly to the lymphocyte receptor. For unknown reasons, this specifically inactivates antigen-sensitive cells.

### 10.5.2 Influence of epitope density

*In vitro* studies by Diener & Feldman (1969) have shown that if the B cell is presented with a certain critical 'epitope' density, then it becomes tolerant. In the *in vitro* response to various conjugates of DNP-POL, it was shown that whilst $DNP_1$-POL is a good immunogen, $DNP_3$-POL is an obligate tolerogen. In the latter case, it was envisaged that tolerance is induced because a critical density of DNP-groups is presented to the B cell receptors. *In vivo* studies with DNP-BSA conjugates however have shown that there is no relationship between tolerance induction to the hapten and high epitope density of hapten on the carrier (Klaus & Cross, 1974).

*In vitro*, it has been shown that antigens normally immunogenic on their own become tolerogenic in the presence of small amounts of antibody. DNP conjugated to monmeric flagellin (DNP-MON) normally evokes an anti-DNP response in DNP-primed B cells. The addition to the culture of antibody to MON renders the DNP-specific B cells unresponsive to subsequent challenge with larger concentrations of DNP-MON. $F(ab')_2$ antibody to the carrier is equally effective, but univalent Fab' fragments do not induce tolerance in the antigen-binding B cells. Thus, the Fc part of the

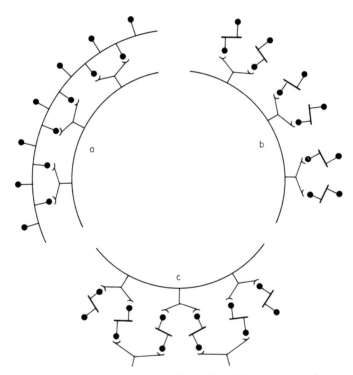

**Fig. 10.6.** Schematic drawing illustrating different ways of interaction on the cell surface between antigen or antigen and antibody with antigen recognition sites.

(a) Attachment to the recognition sites of a polymeric antigen. (b) Attachment to the recognition sites of a monomeric antigen. (c) Attachment to the recognition sites of a monomeric antigen in the presence of specific antibody.

*Note:* In situations (a) and (c) antigen-recognition sites become interlinked by the antigen alone or by antigen-antibody complexes, respectively. (From Diener & Feldmann 1969.)

*Section II: Immunobiology*

antibody has no apparent role in this type of tolerance induction. Possible mechanisms for the above types of tolerance induction are shown in Fig. 10.6.

## 10.6 Blocking factors

### 10.6.1 Immune complex blocking factors

The idea that serum antigen–antibody complexes may be a mechanism for producing tolerance was put forward by the Hellstroms (Hellstrom & Hellstrom, 1974, review). These 'blocking' factors were first described in *in vitro* models of tumour immunity. Lymphocytes from mice bearing certain virally induced sarcomas were shown, by an *in vitro* microcytotoxicity test, to be cytotoxic for the tumour line. This specific reactivity was blocked by serum from mice bearing the same but not different tumours. These 'factors' dissociated at low pH into two components, one of a much larger molecular size than the other. Separately, neither could block cytotoxicity but, when recombined, the original blocking activity was recovered. This has been taken as evidence that blocking factors are immune complexes. It must be pointed out that this is an operational tolerance or unresponsiveness, since the reactive cells clearly exist *in vivo* and the phenomenon is more one of effector cell block rather than clonal elimination.

## 10.7 Blocking factors *in vivo*

The conventional view of transplantation tolerance is that it is based on the clonal elimination of the reacting cells. The recent data on suppressor T cells and blocking factors is an obvious challenge to this view, and so Brent *et al.* (1972) have recently repeated an experiment first done twenty years ago. This time the role of blocking factors or suppressor T cells as the mediators of conventional transplantation tolerance was critically evaluated.

The model used involved the induction of tolerance in CBA mice to A strain alloantigens by the neonatal injection of $F_1$ spleen cells (A × CBA) into newborn CBA mice. $F_1$ cells were used to avoid a graft–versus host reaction. Several different experimental approaches were then adopted to test whether the tolerant state was based on suppressor cells or blocking factors.

### 10.7.1

Adoptive transfer of tolerant CBA spleen cells to $F_1$ mice produced no GVH reaction, whereas normal CBA spleen cells did. Since there are no blocking factors in the recipients, the absence of GVH reaction indicates that blocking factors are not involved in the maintenance of tolerance in the original CBA mice. However, it could be argued that suppressor cells or the cells which secrete antibody involved as a blocking factor are also transferred to the A strain mice along with the tolerant CBA spleen cells and these block the GVH reaction.

### 10.7.2

In a more critical experiment, it was shown that the GVH reaction in the $F_1$ mice given by a small number of normal CBA spleen cells was not abrogated when these cells were simultaneously transferred to $F_1$ recipients with excess syngeneic (CBA) tolerant cells. If transplantation tolerance was maintained by suppressor cells or blocking factors, one might expect the tolerant cells to reduce the GVH reactivity of a relatively small number of normally reactive cells. Similarly, Atkins & Ford (1972) have shown that thoracic duct lymphocytes from tolerant rats do not suppress the GVH reactivity of syngeneic non-tolerant lymphocytes. Both experiments argue against transplantation tolerance being due to suppressor cells or serum blocking factors.

### 10.7.3

Serum or cells from tolerant CBA mice did not prolong the survival of A-strain grafts on normal CBA mice, nor was serum from tolerant mice ever found to facilitate the induction of tolerance to small amounts of A-strain alloantigens.

### 10.7.4

When tolerant CBA mice were parabiosed to normal CBA mice, i.e. they now shared the same circulation, there was no evidence that tolerance to A-strain alloantigens was induced in the normal CBA partner of the parabiosed pair. On the contrary, tolerance was broken in the tolerant CBA partner because reactive cells migrated from the normal mouse.

In the face of this *in vivo* evidence, there seems little doubt that classical transplantation tolerance in mice is based on clonal inactivation or elimination. Suppressor T cells and blocking factors do not seem to be involved to any significant extent.

### 10.8 Conclusions and reservations

Soluble blocking factors may turn out to be more efficient at blocking effector-cell reactivity rather than inducing true 'central' tolerance in the antigen reactive cells. Antigen–antibody complexes

*Section II: Immunobiology*

which bind via the Fc or C3 receptor to B cells (or activated T cells) may interfere with their allergic reactivity. In tumour immunity, there is also substantial evidence for serum blocking factors which may simply be soluble tumour-specific antigens shed from growing malignancies which block effector cells *in vivo* and *in vitro* (see Chapter 21).

Finally, it can be asked to what extent any of the *in vitro* models of unresponsiveness are relevant to *in vivo* tolerance. It has been suggested that the microcytotoxic assay widely used in the *in vitro* investigations of blocking factors is so sensitive that it detects degrees of reactivity that are irrelevant *in vivo*.

Also, in the *in vitro* induction of tolerance by antibody, it is difficult to envisage that the concentration of antibody required for correct 'matrixing' of antigen is ever achieved at the lymphocyte surface *in vivo*. The view that this has any role *in vivo* is not widely held. Nevertheless, the possibility that cross-linking of receptors by antigen–antibody complexes can block specific cell is an intriguing one.

## References

ATKINS R.C. & FORD W.L. (1972) The effect of lymphocytes and serum from tolerant rats on the graft versus host activity of normal lymphocytes. *Transplantation* **13,** 442.

BURNET F.M. (1959) *The clonal selection theory of Immunity.* Cambridge University Press.

BILLINGHAM R.E., BRENT L. & MEDAWAR P.B. (1953) Actively allergised tolerance of foreign cells. *Nature (Lond.)* **172,** 603.

BRENT L., BROOKS C., LUBLING N. & THOMAS A.V. (1972) Attempts to demonstrate an *in vivo* role for serum blocking factors in tolerant mice. *Transplantation* **14,** 382.

DIENER E. & FELDMANN M. (1969) Relationship between antigen and antibody-induced suppression of immunity. *Transpl. Rev.* **8,** 76.

FELDMANN M. (1974) Antigen specific T cell factors and their role in the regulation of T–B interaction. In SERCARZ E., WILLIAMSON A.R. & FOX C.F. *The Immune System; Genes, Receptors, Signals.* p. 497. Academic Press, New York.

GERSHON R.K. (1974) T cell control of antibody production. In COOPER M.D. & WARNER N.L. *Contemporary Topics in Immunobiol.* **3,** 1. Plenum Press, New York.

HELLSTROM K.E. & HELLSTROM I. (1974) Lymphocyte-mediated cytotoxicity and blocking serum activity to tumour antigens. *Adv. Immunol.* **18,** 209.

JACOBSON E.M. (1973) *In vitro* studies of allotype suppression in mice. *Europ. J. Immunol.* **3,** 619.

JACOBSEN E.B., HERZENBERG L.A., RIBLET R. & HERZENBERG L.A. (1972) Active suppression of immunoglobulin allotype synthesis. II. Transfer of suppressing factor with spleen cells. *J. exp. Med.* **135,** 1163.

JANEWAY C.A. & SELA M. (1967) Synthetic antigens composed exclusively of L- or D-amino acids. I. Effect of optical configuration of the immunogenicity of synthetic polypeptides in mice. *Immunology* **13**, 29.

KLAUS G.G.B. & CROSS A.M. (1974) The influence of epitope density on the immunological properties of hapten-protein conjugates. III. Induction of hapten-specific tolerance by heavily and lightly hapten-substituted serum albumin. *Scand. J. Immunol.* **3**, 797.

MITCHELL G., HUMPHREY J.H. & WILLIAMSON A.R. (1972) Inhibition of secondary anti-hapten responses with the hapten conjugated to type 3 pneumococcal polysaccharide. *Europ. J. Immunol.* **2,** 460.

MITCHISON N.A. (1964) Induction of immunological paralysis in two zones of dosage. *Proc. Roy. Soc. B.* **161,** 275.

MITCHISON N.A. (1967) Immunological paralysis as a dosage phenomena. In CINADER B. *Regulation of the Antibody Response.* Thomas, Springfield, Illinois.

OWEN R.D. (1945) Immunogenetic consequences of vascular anastomoses between bovine twins. *Science* **102**, 400.

PARISH C.R. (1971) Immune surface to chemically modified flagellin. I. Induction of antibody tolerance to flagellin by acetoacetylated derivatives of protein. *J. exp. Med.* **134,** 1.

SHELLAM G.R. & NOSSAL G.J.V. (1968) Mechanisms of induction of immunological tolerance. IV. The effects of ultra-low doses of flagellin. *Immunology* **14,** 273.

WEBER G. & KOLSCH E. (1973) Transfer of low zone tolerance to normal syngeneic mice by theta-positive cells. *Europ. J. Immunol.* **3,** 767.

WEIGLE W.O. (1971) Recent observations and concepts in immunological unresponsiveness and autoimmunity. *Clin. exp. Immunol.* **9,** 537.

WEIGLE W.O. (1973) Immunological unresponsiveness. *Advanc. Immunol.* **16,** 61.

WEIGLE W.O., CHILLER J.B. & HABICHT G.J. (1970) Thymus and bone marrow cells in unresponsiveness. In MIESCHER P.A. *Immunopathology* **VI.** p. 109. Schwabe & Co., Basel.

## Further reading

Articles in 'Immunological Tolerance'. *Brit. Med. Bull.* **32** (1976).

# Chapter II
# Antigenic Competition

# M. J. Taussig

## 11.1 Introduction

Antigenic competition was discovered by Leonor Michaelis in 1902 when he injected rabbits with foreign serum and found that antibody was produced against globulins but not against albumin. In order to raise anti-albumin, he found it necessary to inject albumin alone. Michaelis suggested that the response to globulin inhibited that to albumin and called the effect 'antigenic competition'. It may be defined as the inhibition of the immune response to one antigen or determinant by the administration of another antigen or determinant.

Antigenic competition is of considerable interest for two main reasons:

(i) From a theoretical point of view, it is important to know how two non-cross-reacting antigens interfere with each other, especially if antigen sensitive cells are pre-committed to one specificity, as clonal selection demands. This has led to competition being used as an argument for the multipotentiality of antigen-sensitive cells.

(ii) Competition has important practical implications, especially in vaccination programmes where antigens are given as mixtures or in sequence. For example, diphtheria and tetanus toxoids interfere with each other and are given to babies as part of the 'triple vaccine'. Fortunately, by 'balancing' the mixture, competition can be circumvented. Competition is also an immunosuppressive phenomenon of some possible importance in disease processes—the immunosuppressive effect of certain viruses and the association between malaria and Burkitt's lymphoma may be among examples of the influence of antigenic competition on the course of infectious and malignant disease.

## 11.2 Mechanisms of antigenic competition

We now recognize that there are three possible ways in which antigens can interfere with one another (Table 11.1). Competition is said to be 'intermolecular' if the antigens involved are determinants on antigenic regions located on different immunogenic molecules

165

**Table 11.1.** Antigenic competition. The inhibition of the immune response to one antigen or determinant caused by the administration of another antigen or determinant.

1. *Intermolecular competition*
    (ii) Sequential e.g. Heterologous erythrocytes
                     Graft versus host reaction
    (ii) Mixtures  e.g. Globulin vs. albumin
                     Ferritin vs. albumin
                     Diphtheria toxoid vs. tetanus toxoid

2. *Intramolecular competition*
    e.g. Gamma globulin (Fc vs. Fab)
         Hapten (DNP vs. RAzo)
         Synthetic polypeptides ((Phe,G)-Pro--L)

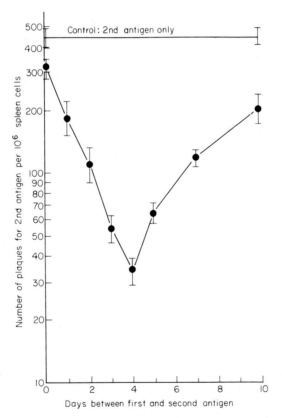

**Fig. 11.1.** Sequential competition. The response of mice to sheep red blood cell (S-RBC) at various time intervals after the injection of horse red blood cells (H-RBC). Vertical bars indicate standard error. (From Radovich & Talmage, 1967.)

*Section II: Immunobiology*

either (a) when one antigen is given a certain critical time before the other, an effect which will be referred to as 'sequential competition' or (b) when these are administered simultaneously as antigen mixtures as in the Michaelis example above. Intramolecular competition on the other hand occurs when the different antigens are located on the same immunogenic molecule.

### 11.2.1 Sequential competition

This is a very common event when antigens are given in sequence. It is frequently found that a response is made to the antigen administered first, but not to that given second. A typical experiment is to give non-cross-reacting red cells in series, for example sheep followed by horse, but in fact any antigens can be used, and the first response can also be a graft-versus-host reaction. Fig. 11.1 shows a typical example of sequential competition between sheep and horse erythrocytes. Note that there is a critical time interval between the administration of the two antigens and their relative doses—it can be as low as a few hours, or last up to two weeks. In Fig. 11.1, optimal competition occurred at the peak of the first response (4 days).

One suggested explanation for sequential competition was that antigen sensitive cells are multipotential, and that after contact with the first antigen they are all temporarily 'occupied'. Radovich & Talmage (1967) tested this in a transfer system. The hypothesis predicts that competition would be more marked when few cells are transferred than when many are transferred. They transferred increasing numbers of spleen cells into irradiated recipient mice together with horse red cells; 4 days later sheep red cells were given. It was found that the degree of suppression of the anti-sheep red cell response *increased* with the number of spleen cells transferred—the opposite of the expectation if cells were multipotential and able to recognize both sheep and horse antigens. The conclusion was drawn, therefore, that multipotent cells are not involved, and an alternative hypothesis was suggested, namely that as a result of the first response inhibitory substances are released which temporarily suppress the response to other antigens given shortly after (Radovich & Talmage, 1967). The idea that an immune response releases soluble inhibitors is now quite widely accepted. These inhibitors would function as regulators of the immune response by temporarily suppressing the division of T and B cells. Antigenic competition, of the sequential type, would be a side effect of this form of regulation.

Recently, Gershon and Kondo (1971) have shown that the cells responsible for sequential competition are T cells. A transfer system was again used. If irradiated mice were reconstituted with B cells only, they gave a thymus-independent IgM response to horse red cells, which could not be inhibited by prior injection of sheep

*Chapter 11: Antigenic Competition*

red cells (Fig. 11.2a). When T cells were present, in addition to B cells, the response to horse red cells was greatly improved, but could now be inhibited by the competitive influence of sheep red cells given first (Fig. 11.2b).

Thus the general view of sequential competition is that the first antigen stimulates the release from 'suppressor' T cells of inhibitors which regulate the immune response and consequently inhibit the response to a second antigen given shortly after. An inference from this is that thymus-independent antigens should not produce sequential competition, on the assumption that T cells for such

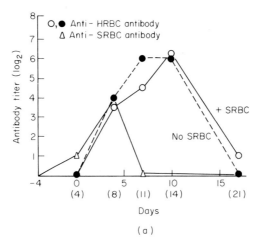

(a)

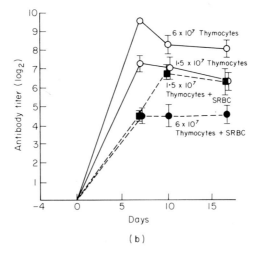

(b)

**Fig. 11.2.** Antigenic competition in thymus-deprived mice. SRBC inoculated day −4; HRBC day 0.

Antigenic competition in thymus-deprived mice reconstituted with different numbers of thymocytes. Total antibody response to HRBC. SRBC inoculated day −4; HRBC day 0. (From Gershon and Kondo, 1971.)

*Section II: Immunobiology*

antigens do not exist. The response to thymus-independent antigens, however, could be inhibited by competition from a thymus-dependent antigen, provided that the inhibitors produced by T cells affect the response of B cells. These predictions have been confirmed in the case of the thymus-independent SIII pneumococcal polysaccharide.

### 11.2.2 Intra- and intermolecular competition

(a) *Competition between Fc and Fab.* A good example of intra-molecular and intermolecular competition is provided by the IgG molecule when used as an antigen—in these studies, rabbit IgG was used as an immunogen in mice (Taussig, 1971; Taussig & Lachmann, 1972). From the point of view of IgG as an antigen, the important feature of the molecule is that it can be divided into two antigenic halves corresponding to the result of papain digestion, Fab and Fc. It is possible to follow antibody production to Fab and Fc independently. Thus when rabbit IgG is injected into mice, both anti-Fab and anti-Fc production may be expected. However, within the IgG molecule, competition seems to exist, such that a good primary response is made to Fc, but a much poorer response is produced to Fab. If the Fab fragment is injected alone on the other hand, mice make a good anti-Fab response. Therefore, it seems that intramolecular competition exists within the IgG molecule, with Fc being the more successful or 'dominant' antigen. This is illustrated in Fig. 11.3a, b. This type of competition seems to depend on the relative 'antigenic strength' of the antigens involved, since in mice made tolerant to rabbit Fc, the response to Fab is greatly improved, i.e. competition is abolished (Fig. 11.3d). Passive administration of anti-Fc antibodies has the same effect of enhancing the anti-Fab response by abolishing competition, presumably because anti-Fc prevents the immune recognition of Fc determinants (Fig. 11.3c). This effect—abolition of competition by antibody against the dominant antigen—may be of general physiological importance. It is very common for the body to be infected by multi-determinant antigens—bacteria, toxins, viruses, etc.—and the first antibodies which are made will often be directed principally against the dominant antigenic determinants. These antibodies may not always be best suited to removal or neutralization of a pathogen, for example, so a mechanism whereby the antibody response could be spread to other determinants on the same molecule or particle could be very important. This spreading of response can be accomplished by the first-formed antibody itself, which will act to abolish intramolecular competition and thus enhance the response to the less immunogenic determinants.

The intramolecular competition described above occurs when Fab and Fc are present on the same molecule. It is also possible to separate Fc from Fab by papain digestion of rabbit IgG followed by

*Chapter 11: Antigenic Competition*

chromatography, and then to administer them as a mixture rather than as one molecule. Here once again competition between Fc and Fab can be demonstrated, in this case termed intermolecular because the competing antigens are now on separate molecules. Table 11.2 shows that competition with antigen mixtures is critically dependent on the ratio of Fc:Fab in the mixture—an excess of Fc over Fab of 3:1 is required for competition. This relative dosage effect can be demonstrated with many other mixtures—an excess of one antigen in a mixture can inhibit the response to others in the mixture. The mixture can also be 'balanced'—the ratio of antigens in a mixture being adjusted so as to avoid competition between them. This is most important in vaccination with mixtures, of which the 'triple vaccine' of diphtheria and tetanus toxoids with pertussis vaccine is perhaps the best known. Diphtheria and

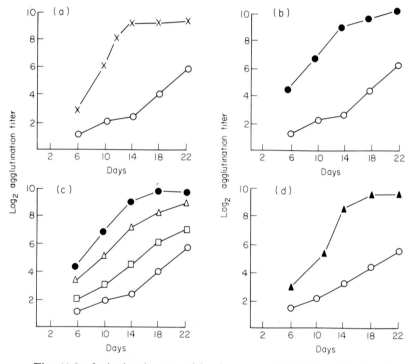

**Fig. 11.3a-d.** Antigenic competition between rabbit Fab and Fc in mice. (a) Primary anti-rabbit Fc ( × —— × ) and anti-rabbit Fab (o——o) responses in BALB/c mice after inoculation of 50 μg rabbit IgG in FCA. (b) Primary anti-rabbit Fab responses in BALB/c mice after inoculation of 50 μg rabbit IgG (o——o) in FCA or 35 μg rabbit Fab (●——●) in FCA. (c) Primary anti-rabbit Fab responses after inoculation of BALB/c mice with 50 μg rabbit IgG in FCA (o——o); 50 μg rabbit IgG in FCA with 25 μg anti-rabbit Fc administered passively (□——□); 50 μg rabbit IgG in FCA with 100 μg anti-rabbit Fc administered passively (△——△); or 35 μg rabbit Fab in FCA (●——●). (d) Primary anti-rabbit Fab responses after inoculation of 50 μg rabbit IgG in normal BALB/c mice (o——o) or in BALB/c mice tolerant to rabbit Fc (▲——▲). (From Taussig, 1973.)

*Section II: Immunobiology*

tetanus toxoids can be shown to compete with each other if the mixture does not contain a 'balanced' amount of each. It is also vitally important not to give a mixed vaccine to an individual who has received one component of the mixture alone on a previous occasion. The secondary response to that component would certainly compete successfully and suppress the primary responses to other antigens in the mixture, regardless of how the mixture was balanced.

(b) *Competition with synthetic polypeptides*. Recent work with synthetic polypeptide antigens has thrown light on the mechanism of competition (Taussig *et al.*, 1972; Taussig *et al.*, 1973). The structure of these materials, synthesized by Sela and coworkers, are

**Table 11.2.** The dose-dependence of intermolecular competition. (From Taussig, 1973)

| Day | Molar ratio Fc/Fab | | | |
| | 3/1 | | 1/1 | |
| | Anti-Fc titre | anti-Fab titre | anti-Fc titre | anti-Fab titre |
|---|---|---|---|---|
| 12 | 6·6(±0·7) | 2·6(±0·3) | 6·3(±0·5) | 6·0(±0·5) |
| 17 | 8·6(±0·7) | 4·1(±0·4) | 8·9(±0·8) | 7·8(±0·5) |
| 22 | 10·0(±0·6) | 6·9(±0·6) | 11·6(±0·6) | 10·3(±0·7) |

Anti-Fc and anti-Fab titres of groups of BALB/c mice immunized (on day 0) with mixtures of rabbit Fc and Fab in different molar ratios (in complete FREUND's adjuvant). Results as mean $\log_2$ agglutination titres; 10 mice per group.

shown in Fig. 11.4. The two polypeptides shown are designated (Phe,G)-A--L and (Phe,G)-Pro--L. Both are built on a backbone of poly-lysine (L) to which side chains are attached, in one case of poly-alanine (A) and in the other of poly-proline (Pro). This gives two types of macromolecule, abbreviated as A--L and Pro--L. At the tips of the side chains can be attached short sequences of 4–6 amino acids—in this case phenyl alanine and glutamic acid (Phe, G). Alternatively, another short hapten sequence of tyrosine and glutamic acid (T,G)- can also be used. From the immunological point of view, the molecules thus created—(Phe,G)-A--L and (Phe-G)-Pro--L- can be regarded as hapten-carrier complexes, with the hapten (Phe,G) attached to either A--L or Pro--L as carriers. A vital point is that A--L itself is a very poor immunogen, whereas Pro--L can be a good immunogen in some strains of mice. The hapten (Phe,G) can thus be attached to an antigen which is a good or a poor immunogen depending on strain and the effects of immunogenicity of the carrier thus studied in detail.

*Chapter 11: Antigenic Competition*

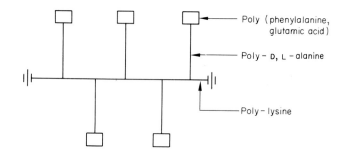

(a)  (Phe, G) – A – L

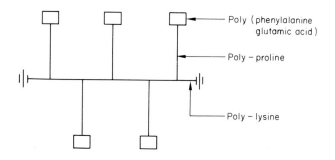

(b)  (Phe, G) – Pro – – L

**Fig. 11.4.** Diagrammatic structures of synthetic polypeptides used in studies of antigenic competition.

**Table 11.3.** Antigenic competition (intramolecular) between (PHE,G) and PRO--L regions of synthetic polypeptides in C3H/HeJ and DBA/1 mice. (From Taussig *et al.*, 1973.)

| Immunogen | C3H/HeJ | | DBA/A | |
|---|---|---|---|---|
| | Anti-(PHE,G) | Anti-PRO--L | Anti-(PHE,G) | Anti-PRO--L |
| (PHE,G)-A--L | 1/64–128 | — | 1/64–128 | — |
| (T, G)-PRO--L | — | 1/128–256 | — | 1/4–8 |
| (PHE,G)-PRO--L | 1/2–4 | 1/128–256 | 1/64–128 | 1/4–8 |

Results as $\log_2$ haemagglutination titres in secondary responses (10 mice per group).

*Section II: Immunobiology*

C3H/HeJ mice make a good response to the Pro-L component of both (T,G)-Pro--L and (Phe,G)-Pro- -L, showing that they respond to the carrier, whereas DBA2 mice do not. In the DBA2 strain both (Phe-G)-A--L and (Phe,G)-Pro--L give strong anti-(Phe,G) responses but C3H/HeJ mice respond well to the haptenic determinants only when they are attached to the poorly immunogenic carrier (Table 11.3). This is an important result for two reasons. First, it shows that for intramolecular competition to occur there must be a good response to the dominant antigen—hence there is no competition in the low responder strain. Secondly, if the cellular basis of the difference between C3H/HeJ and DBA/1 mice with respect to their response to Pro--L were known, it would provide the key to the mechanism of intramolecular competition. This cellular difference has now been established, and it has been shown by a technique known as 'limiting dilution analysis' that DBA/1 mice possess fewer cell precursors for Pro--L than C3H/HeJ. Moreover, this deficiency is found exclusively in the B cell line and not in the T cells. This seems, therefore, to establish a clear link between intramolecular competition and the B cells available for the competing antigens.

## 11.3 Models for intramolecular and intermolecular competition

### 11.3.1 Intramolecular competition

On the basis of this data, a model for intramolecular competition has been proposed in which B cells, carrying receptors for different determinants on a molecule, compete for antigen among themselves. The model is shown in Fig. 11.5 and is termed 'B cell competition' (Taussig et al., 1973). Consider, for example, an antigen with a carrier and two haptens (shown as → and ○). It will be presented to B cells, perhaps directly via T cells as shown,' though the bridging may be from a macrophage with carrier-specific 'cooperating antibody' on its surface. If the B cells recognizing the determinant → are present in larger numbers than those for ○, or have a higher affinity than cells recognizing ○, they will successfully compete for antigen as shown (Fig. 11.5a). Such a situation could occur if an animal had had prior contact with →, or if genetic control limited the number of precursors against ○ or for numerous other reasons (as in the response of DBA/1 mice to (Phe,G)-Pro-L). Thus there is no contradiction here with the clonal selection theory. It has been shown in the previous section that antibody against the dominant determinant abolishes intramolecular competition. Figure 11.5b shows how the B cell competition model explains this finding. Antibody against → will block the determinant specifically, preventing access by the B cells recognizing →, and thus allowing B

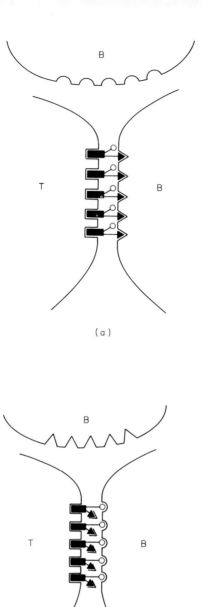

(a)

(b)

**Fig. 11.5.** (a) Competition between bone-marrow-derived (B) cells, of different specificities, for antigen. An antigen composed of a carrier ■ bearing two haptenic groups ↑ and ♀, is shown presented at the surface of a thymus-derived (T) cell (though this could also be a macrophage or dendritic cell). The antigen forms a multivalent bridge across to B cells. B cells for the ↑ specificity are present in larger numbers (or bear higher affinity receptors) than those for the ♀ specificity and are therefore more successful in competing for limited antigen. ↑ is thus the dominant determinant and antibody production to ♀ is suppressed. (b) Abolition of intramolecular

174

cells against ─○ to combine with antigen. Competition is therefore abolished by antibody.

### 11.3.2 Intermolecular competition

The B cell competition model thus accounts for intramolecular competition. However, it cannot explain intermolecular competition with antigen mixtures, because antigens which are not linked together should meet their respective T and B cells independently. It is therefore likely that competition between antigens in a mixture takes place by a quite different mechanism. Again, evidence has come from the use of synthetic polypeptides (Taussig *et al.*, 1972). The competing antigens were again Pro--L and (Phe,G) determinants, but they were administered as mixtures of (T,G)-Pro--L and (Phe,G)-A--L. The high and low responder for Pro--L strains, C3H/HcJ and DBA/1, were again compared. Results are shown in Table 11.4.

**Table 11.4.** Antigenic competition (intermolecular) between synthetic polypeptides in C3H/HeJ and DBA/1 mice. (From Taussig *et al.*, 1972.)

| Immunogens | | C3H/HeJ | | DBA/1 | |
|---|---|---|---|---|---|
| | | Anti-(PHE,G) | Anti-PRO--L | Anti-(PHE,G) | Anti-PRO--L |
| RATIO (T, G)-PRO--L / (PHE, G)-A--L | 5/1 | 1/2 –4 | 1/16–32 | 1/2 –4 | 1/2–4 |
| | 1/1 | 1/16–32 | 1/16–32 | 1/16–32 | 1/2–4 |
| | 1/5 | 1/16–32 | 1/16 | 1/32–64 | 1/2–4 |
| | 1/25 | 1/32–64 | 1/2 –4 | 1/32–64 | 1/2–4 |
| RATIO (T, G)-PRO--L A--L | 1/5 | — | 1/16–32 | — | — |
| | 1/25 | — | 1/2 –4 | — | — |

In the C3H/HeJ strain, an excess of Pro--L over (Phe,G)-A--L of 5:1 inhibited the response to (Phe,G), while there was a good response to Pro--L. An equimolar ratio did not give rise to competition —the anti-(Phe,G) response was much higher—showing once again the dependence of intermolecular competition on the relative amounts of the competing antigens in the mixture. In the low

---

competition by antibody against the dominant determinant. Antibody ∧ against the determinant ↑ specifically blocks the combination of that determinant with B cell receptors. B cells bearing receptors for the initially suppressed determinant ♀ are now able to combine with antigen. The result is suppression of antibody formation against ↑ and enhancement of that against ♀. (From Taussig *et al.*, 1973.)

*Chapter 11: Antigenic Competition*

responder DBA/1 strain, intermolecular competition was again achieved at a 5:1 excess of Pro--L over (Phe,G)-A--L. This is a key observation, when it is recalled that intramolecular competition within the (Phe,G)-Pro--L molecule, did not occur in the low responders (Table 11.4). Since the low responder DBA/1 mice are deficient specifically in the B cells, but not in the T cells, responding to Pro--L, the result suggests that intermolecular competition is not a B cell effect but rather a T cell phenomenon. Another finding in support of this is also shown in Table 11.4 namely competition between Pro--L and A--L. It was found that a large excess of A--L over Pro--L of 25:1 suppressed the response to Pro--L. A--L itself is an exceedingly poor antigen, even at the doses administered to achieve competition, but it does act as a carrier for haptens. It is therefore very likely recognized by T cells, but not by B cells, and it is probably this T cell recognition which leads to intermolecular competition.

In order to account for intermolecular competition, a model has been proposed involving the macrophage as an intermediary, and for which direct evidence has recently been obtained *in vitro* (Taussig & Lachmann, 1972; Schrader & Feldmann, 1973). It was suggested that the macrophage surface could be a common presentation mechanism for all thymus-dependent antigens, as shown in Fig. 11.6 (Taussig & Lachmann, 1972).

Presentation of antigen to B cells would take place via a special class of 'cooperating antibody' secreted for the purpose by T cells, the antibody having a binding site on its Fc for the macrophage surface as well as a specific antigen-combining site. Competition would occur if the sites on the macrophage surface for cooperating antibody were limited in number; competition for them could then ensue between cooperating antibodies of different antigen specificities. The antigen which stimulated the most cooperating antibody would become dominant in competition. This could account for the dependence of competition on the relative amounts of the antigens in the mixtures, and for the ability of antigens such as A--L and Pro--L to be dominant in competition without stimulating significant antibody production. Direct proof that such a mechanism is possible, at least *in vitro*, has been shown by the experiments of Feldmann and coworkers (see Chapter 9). An antibody-like factor obtained from T cells was shown to present antigen in a cooperative manner to B cells by adhering to the surface of macrophages and bridging across to B cells, much as in Fig. 11.6. However, when a macrophage population had been exposed to the cooperating antibody stimulated by one antigen, it could readily be functionally saturated and rendered unable to cooperate in the subsequent response to an unrelated antigen. Hence, competition for macrophage surface space between cooperating antibodies of different specificities may go a long way to resolving the problem of intermolecular competition between mixed antigens.

*Section II: Immunobiology*

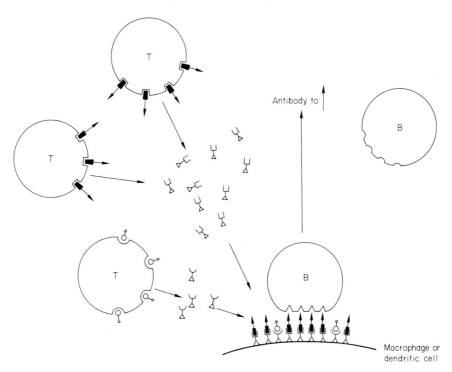

**Fig. 11.6.** A model for intermolecular competition.

Two antigens ■→ and ○○ , each composed of a carrier ■, ○, carrying a hapten →, —○. Specific T cells recognize carrier determinants and release specific 'cooperating antibodies' and . These in turn present antigen at the macrophage surface to B cells. Competition occurs between cooperating antibodies for macrophage presentation sites, as shown. (From Taussig, 1973.)

## 11.4 Conclusion

In conclusion, there seem to be three different manifestations of antigenic competition—intramolecular, intermolecular (antigen mixtures) and sequential—and very likely three independent mechanisms. Table 11.5 provides a summary of the proposed mechanisms of antigenic competition.

**Table 11.5.** Mechanisms of antigenic competition

| | |
|---|---|
| 1. *Intramolecular:* | 'B cell competition'—B cell populations of different specificities compete for antigen. |
| 2. *Intermolecular:* | 'T cell competition'. |
| (i) Mixtures | T cells produce cooperative antibodies of different specificities which compete for macrophage surface space. |
| (ii) Sequential | T cells produce non-specific inhibitors as regulators of the immune response. |

*Chapter 11: Antigenic Competition*

# References

GERSHON R.K. & KONDO K. (1971) Antigenic competition between heterologous erythrocytes. *J. Immunol.* **106**, 1524.

MICHAELIS L. (1902) *Dtsch. med. Wschr.* **28**, 733.

MICHAELIS L. (1904) *Dtsch. med. Wschr.* **30**, 1240.

RADOVICH J. & TALMAGE D.W. (1967) Antigenic competition: cellular or
humoral. *Science,* **158**, 512.

SCHRADER J.W. & FELDMANN M. (1973) The mechanism of antigenic competition. 1. The macrophage as a site of a reversible block to T–B
lymphocyte collaboration. *Euro. J. Immunol.* **3**, 711.

TAUSSIG M.J. (1971) Antigenic competition between the Fc and Fab fragments of rabbit IgG in mice. *Immunology* **21**, 51.

TAUSSIG M.J. & LACHMANN P.J. (1972) Abolition of antigenic competition
by antibody against or tolerance to the dominant antigen. A model for
antigenic competition. *Immunology* **22**, 185.

TAUSSIG M.J., MOZES E., SHEARER G.M. & SELA M. (1972) Studies on
the mechanism of antigenic competition: Analysis of competition
between synthetic polypeptide antigens. *Euro. J. Immunol.* **2**, 448.

TAUSSIG M.J., MOZES E., SHEARER G.M. & SELA M. (1973) Antigenic competition and genetic control of the immune response: A hypothesis of
intramolecular competition. *Cell. Immunol.* **8**, 299.

# Further reading

LIACOPOULOS P. & BEN EFRAIM S. (1974) Antigenic competition. *Progress in
Allergy.* **18**, 97.

NOSSAL G.J.V. & FELDMANN M. (1972) Tolerance, enhancement and the
regulation of interactions between T cells, B cells and macrophages.
*Transpl. Revs.* **13**, 3.

PROSS H.F. & EIDINGER D. (1974) Antigenic competition. A review of non-
specific antigen-induced suppression. *Adv. Immunol.* **18**, 133.

TAUSSIG M.J. (1973) Antigenic competition. *Current topics in microbiology
and immunology.* Springer-Verlag **60**, 125.

# Chapter 12
# Effector Mechanisms in Cellular Immunity

## H. Valdimarsson

### 12.1 Introduction

In recent years it has become increasingly evident that the expression of cell-mediated immunity (CMI) is primarily dependent on interaction between T lymphocytes and mononuclear phagocytes. The CMI effector response is initiated by antigen recognition and subsequent activation of a few specifically reactive T lymphocytes. This activation induces the production of various factors, 'lymphokines', which probably generate a multifactorial amplification phase involving non-specific recruitment of circulating lymphocytes and monocytes. Finally, the process reaches the level of allergic inflammation which is presumably largely mediated by phlogistic substances derived from macrophages, attracted and activated locally during the preceding steps of the reaction.

These mechanisms are thought to have evolved in vertebrates as a principal part of a homeostatic system which provides resistance to infections with facultative intracellular bacteria, fungi and many viruses. They have also been implicated as a surveillance device capable of eliminating abnormal and potentially malignant cells, a view which remains controversial. In this chapter the following three questions will be considered: first, how is specific activation of T lymphocytes translated into the delayed hypersensitivity reactions; second, how can this activation contribute to the killing and subsequent digestion of certain pathogens; and lastly, what operational evidence is there for mechanisms, not involving classical antibodies, which might be capable of eliminating abnormal cells?

These questions will be pursued by describing lymphocyte activation *in vitro* and the various biological activities released. An attempt will then be made to relate these activities to the *in vivo* manifestations of cellular immunity.

### THE EFFECTOR CELLS OF CMI

The principal effector cells of CMI reactions are T lymphocytes and mononuclear phagocytes. Another cell type, which brings about antibody-dependent cell-mediated cytotoxicity, has recently been defined. These mononuclear cells, which are called K cells, cannot be strictly regarded as a component of the CMI system, since the specificity of their cytotoxic activity is determined by antibodies (see later). The cytolytic mechanism of this reaction is cell-membrane-dependent, however, and closely related functionally to CMI cytotoxicity.

## 12.2 Mononuclear phagocytes

The mononuclear phagocyte system consists of several types of cells, widely distributed throughout the body (Table 12.1). These

**Table 12.1.** Mononuclear phagocytes

| | |
|---|---|
| Produced in | Bone marrow |
| Maturation | Bone marrow and other tissues |
| Mainly present in | Liver, spleen, lymph nodes, lungs, peritoneum |
| Main products | Lysosomal (hydrolytic) enzymes |
| | Lysozyme |
| | Complement components |
| | Interferon |
| Main function | Antigen 'presentation' |
| | Ingestion and digestion of pathogens and abnormal cells |
| | Accumulate in inflammatory reactions |
| Sub-Classes | Monocytes |
| | Kupffer cells |
| | Histiocytes |
| | Peritoneal macrophages |
| | Alveolar macrophages |
| | Sinusoid lining cells |
| | Osteoclasts |
| | ? Microglial cells |

cells, although somewhat heterogeneous both in function and morphology, have certain features in common, which distinguish them from other phagocytes.

### 12.2.1 Origin and maturation

Mononuclear phagocytes are produced by rapidly dividing precursor cells in the bone marrow (promonocytes). The daughter cells are released as monocytes into the bloodstream, where they circulate for approximately 22 hours (mice). Once they leave the blood they do not return but settle down in solid tissues and differentiate into the various types of fixed macrophages (Table 12.1) often surviving in the tissues for many months or even years. A characteristic feature of CMI reactions *in vivo* is the formation of granulomatous lesions, which are, to a large extent, made up of mononuclear phagocytes. It has been shown that only a small proportion of these cells are produced by a local proliferation of tissue macrophages, and the great majority are derived from circulating monocytes which are presumably attracted by factors released by the inflammatory process.

### 12.2.2 Lysosomal enzymes

Mononuclear phagocytes possess a wide spectrum of hydrolytic enzymes with acid pH optima. These hydrolases are organized within cytoplasmic vesicles, lysosomes, which are assembled in the region of the Golgi membranes and are capable of degrading a variety of protein, lipid, polysaccharide and nucleic acid structures. Following endocytosis of digestible material the stability of the lysosomal membranes is reduced, and this leads to a fusion between individual lysosomes and between lysosomes and the phagocytic vacuoles. At the same time, the hydrolytic enzymes are activated and production of more hydrolyses is induced.

### 12.2.3 Macrophage activation

Under suitable conditions macrophages can transform into activated ('angry') macrophages. These are characterized by enlargement, undulating (ruffled) plasma membranes, enhanced phagocytic capacity, activation of the hexose monophosphate pathway of glucose oxidation and increase in lysosomal enzyme activity. Macrophage activation can be induced by a variety of substances including bacterial endotoxins, double stranded RNA and many adjuvants. Factors derived from activated T lymphocytes can also activate macrophages and enhance their production of lysosomal hydrolases (see later).

### 12.2.4 Microbicidal mechanisms

The microbiocidal mechanisms of mononuclear phagocytes have not been subjected to much analysis. In contrast to PMN leucocytes the amount and composition of their lysosomal enzyme is variable and to some extent dependent on their tissue localization. Thus, considerable heterogeneity is found when different macrophage populations are compared (Cohn & Wiener, 1963). The killing and hydrolytic capacity of macrophages is also partially determined by their interactions with T lymphocytes. Therefore, it should be recognized that results obtained with purified macrophages *in vitro* may be misleading, since under these conditions their *in vivo* adaptability is not taken into account.

The microbicidal activities of PMN leucocytes are described in Chapter 23 and it is assumed that the intrinsic killing mechanisms of mononuclear phagocytes are basically similar. Several types of macrophages do not possess any peroxidase activity, however, and do not generate $H_2O_2$ during phagocytosis. The peroxidase—$H_2O_2$—halide system may therefore play a less important role in phagocytic killing by macrophages than it does in the PMN leucocytes where it is a major microbicidal pathway.

## 12.3 K cells

These cells have recently been defined as a distinct sub-population of lymphoid cells, capable of killing target cells sensitized with IgG antibodies. The killing does not require the presence of sensitized effector cells, but is mediated by lymphoid cells carrying membrane receptors for Fc of IgG. The cytotoxic activity is probably induced when these receptors react with the Fc part of the antibodies coating the target cells.

The nature of the K cells is still a subject of controversy, and may vary in different species (MacLennan & Harding, 1974). They are present in peritoneal exudates, blood, spleen and, to a lesser extent, in lymph nodes, whereas lymphoid cells derived from bone marrow, thymus and thoracic duct lymph show minimal K cell activity. Their absence from the thoracic duct lymph indicates that they do not re-circulate.

It has been convincingly demonstrated that these effector cells are not T lymphocytes, and the majority of B lymphocytes carrying surface immunoglobulins are not involved either. Moreover, K cell activity cannot be abolished by removing phagocytic and glass-adherent cells. We are therefore left with a distinct type of cyto-toxic lymphoid cells, equipped with Fc (and possibly also C3) receptors, which have some features in common with B lympho-cytes and mononuclear phagocytes, but which lack the cardinal characteristics of both, namely surface immunoglobulin and phagocytic capacity respectively. It should be pointed out, however, that macrophages themselves and possibly some B cells as well, are capable of mediating antibody-dependent killing.

It is now a matter of speculation whether the K cells represent a distinct type of fully differentiated effector cell or merely an immature form of either B lymphocyte or mononuclear phagocyte. Their paucity in bone marrow argues somewhat against the latter.

## LYMPHOCYTE ACTIVATION AND ITS CONSEQUENCES

Most circulating lymphocytes are inactive ($G_0$ phase) cells, which can be activated if they are suitably stimulated either by antigen or by non-specific mitogens. Fig. 12.1 illustrates schematically some of the features of lymphocyte activation. Most antigens require a pre-treatment by macrophages before being able to activate lymphocytes although phytomitogens like PHA can do so without the help of macrophages.

Lymphocytes which have been 'turned on' by a mitogenic stimulus are transformed into highly active cells which initiate production of the various mediators of immunity: i.e. antibodies if they are B lymphocytes and the mediators of cellular immunity if they are T lymphocytes.

## 12.4 Lymphokines

The generic term 'lymphokines' was coined by Dumonde *et al.* (1969) to cover all biologically active factors other than antibodies which can be detected in cell-free supernatants of stimulated lymphocytes.

The first lymphokine activity to be defined was the macrophage Migration Inhibitory Factor (MIF). The spontaneous migration *in vitro* of mononuclear cells from sensitized donors was shown to be specifically inhibited in the presence of antigens to which the donors had been sensitized. This inhibition correlated with delayed hypersensitivity and carrier specificity but not with humoral immunity. The phenomenon was therefore utilized for developing the MIF assay as the first *in vitro* test for CMI (Bloom & Bennett, 1966).

Many variants of this assay have been tried, but the original design, using peritoneal exudate from guinea-pigs as a source of indicator cells, is still the best standardized and most reliable method. Using such cell populations, containing approximately 60 per cent macrophages and 20 per cent lymphocytes, it has been shown that the macrophages are the principal target cells, whereas the lymphocytes are the effector cells which, on specific activation, release soluble factors that inhibit macrophage migration.

### 12.4.1 Classification and characterization of lymphokines

Over the last decade many lymphokine phenomena have been described in association with activated lymphocytes. Table 12.2 lists only some of the lymphokines that have been described together with their possible synonyms. Since none of these factors have been identified chemically, they can only be defined and classified in terms of biological activities. Their number and names

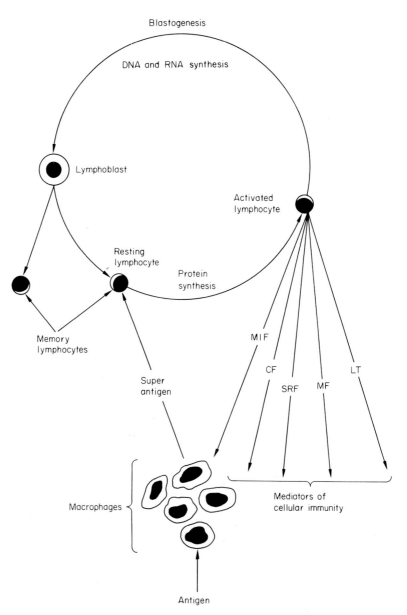

**Fig. 12.1.** The lymphocyte activation cycle. Lymphokines are mainly released during the $G_1$ phase of the cycle round. Their production stops when the cells begin to replicate (S phase). MIF: Migration Inhibitory Factor, CF: Chemotactic Factor, SRF: Skin Reactive Factor, MF: Mitogenic Factor, LT: Lymphotoxin.

*Section II: Immunobiology*

therefore merely reflect the assay systems available for their detection. Thus, migration inhibitory factors inhibit the movement of spontaneously migrating leucocytes, macrophage stimulating factors enhance various aspects of macrophage function, chemotactic factors attract migrating leucocytes and so forth.

It is evident from Table 12.3 that little is known about the physicochemical properties of most lymphokines and none have been isolated in a pure form. Therefore it should be recognized that the different activities as determined by the various assays may turn out to be due to one molecular entity. Conversely, more than one type of molecule may be required for producing some of the effects currently ascribed to a single factor.

### 12.4.2 Production of lymphokines

As indicated in Fig. 12.1. the production of lymphokines can be detected very early in the activation cycle ($G_1$ phase). Their production probably stops when the individual cells start to prepare themselves for division by replicating their nucleic acids and protein constituents. This is part of the cycle (S phase) when the lymphocytes undergo morphological transformation.

It is not clear whether the lymphocytes that release lymphokines are the same cells which proceed to division (M phase) and thereby give rise to clones of memory cells. It has not been established whether one lymphocyte is capable of releasing more than one mediator activity or whether each cell is committed to produce only one type of activity. There are some indications, however, that the repertoire of each cell may be limited to one or a few lymphokines, and it would not be surprising if T lymphocytes turned out to behave like B lymphocytes in this respect.

The cellular source of the great majority of lymphokine activities is still unknown. Although T lymphocytes have been shown to be the source of some lymphokines, it is by no means clear that this is their only source and lymphokine production by other cells has not been ruled out. Most workers have produced these factors by stimulating heterogeneous populations of lymphoid cells *in vitro* and *in vivo*. Recent techniques of lymphoid cell fractionation have only just begun to be used for establishing which sub-populations of lymphoid cells release the various types of lymphokine factors. Even when the production of a particular lymphokine activity can be abolished by eliminating T lymphocytes, other lymphoid cells could still be the main source, since T lymphocyte products might be required as a trigger mechanism. Macrophages passively sensitized with specific T cell factor could, for instance, release lymphokines on combining with antigen in much the same way as basophils release histamine in response to antigen.

It is well established both *in vitro* and *in vivo* that macrophages are needed for the induction, as well as expression, of immuno-

**Table 12.2.** A list of lymphokines

| Name | | Comment |
|---|---|---|
| 1. *Migration inhibitory factors* | | |
| (a) Antigen-independent macrophage Migration Inhibitory Factor | MIF | Has not been separated from MAF |
| (b) Antigen-Specific macrophage Migration Inhibitory Factor | SMIF | Possibly same as SMAF and PAF |
| (c) Buffy coat Leucocyte migration Inhibitory Factor | LIF | Has been separated from MIF |
| | | |
| 2. *Factors stimulating macrophage function* | | |
| (a) Macrophage Activating Factor | MAF | Has not been separated from MIF |
| (b) Specific Macrophage Arming Factor | SMAF | Possibly same as SMIF and PAF |
| (c) Pinocytosis Activating Factor | PAF | Possibly same as SMIF and SMAF |
| | | |
| 3. *Chemotactic factors* | | |
| (a) Chemotactic Factor for Macrophages | CFM | Has been separated electrophoretically from MIF and CFP |
| (b) Chemotactic Factor for Lymphocytes | CFL | Possibly distinct from CFM and CFP |
| (c) Chemotactic Factor for PMN leucocytes | CFP | Has been separated electrophoretically from CFM |
| | | |
| 4. *Mitogenic factors* | | |
| (a) Antigen independent Mitogenic Factor | MF | Possibly same as LTF |
| (b) Lymphocyte Transforming Factor | LTF | Possibly same as MF |
| (c) Antigen-dependent B Lymphocyte Mitogenic Factor | LMF | Possibly same as NSF |
| | | |
| 5. *Cytostatic factors* | | |
| (a) Lymphotoxin | LT | Acts only on certain target cells |
| (b) Proliferation Inhibitory Factor | PIF | ? chalone |
| (c) Colony Inhibitory Factor | CIF | Could be a PIF polymer |
| | | |
| 6. *Factors stimulating B lymphocyte maturation and antibody production (Thymus replacing factors)* | | |
| (a) Specific Factor | 'IgT' | Possibly same as SMIF and SMAF |
| (b) Non-specific Factor | NSF | Possibly same as LMF |
| (c) Allogenic T cell Replacing Factor | TRF | Possibly different from NSF |
| | | |
| 7. *Other factors* | | |
| (a) Skin Reactive Factor | SRF | The assay phenomenon is probably due to several factors |
| (b) Interferon | IF | |

*Section II: Immunobiology*

Table 12.3. Some available physico-chemical data on lymphokines

| | MIF* | SMIF* | LIF** | CFM* | MF/LTF** | LT* | MF** | NSF*** | IF** |
|---|---|---|---|---|---|---|---|---|---|
| Heat stability 56°C | + | + | | + | + | − | + | + | + |
| Susceptibility to neuraminidase | + | | | − | − | − | − | + | |
| Susceptibility to chymotrypsin | + | | | + | + | + | + | | + |
| Electrophoretic mobility | Pre-albumin | Albumin | | Albumin | | α-globulin | | | |
| Density | 1,44 | | | 1,34 | 1,34 | 1,34 | | | |
| Molecular weight | 25–50,000 | 60–70,000 | 60–70,000 | 50,000 | 20–45,000 | 45–90,000 | | 25–60,000 | 18–20,000 |
| Molecular species | Glycoprotein | Glycoprotein | | protein | protein | protein | protein | protein | protein |

\* As released by guinea-pig cells

\*\* As released by human cells

\*\*\*As released by mouse cells

logical reactions. In the mixed lymphocyte reaction, mononuclear phagocytes can enhance the proliferative response to antigen. Therefore, until proof has been provided to the contrary, macrophages should be considered as a probable contributory source of some lymphokine factors, notably the mitogenic and chemotactic activities.

## 12.5 Cytotoxicity

### 12.5.1 Direct cytotoxic activity of lymphoid cells

Allograft and tumour rejection is characterized by a specific destruction of large numbers of cells. Thus, it is clear that cytotoxic mechanisms operate *in vivo*, and it has been convincingly demonstrated by passive transfer experiments that these specific mechanisms are activated by small lymphocytes, whereas circulating antibodies are ineffective. Primary allograft rejection is, therefore, by definition, a cellular immune phenomenon.

There are undoubtedly many types of cytotoxic mechanisms which are involved in allograft rejection, and in recent years a wide variety of *in vitro* assays have been designed in order to elucidate these mechanisms. The complexity generated in this field may, however, partly reflect the idiosyncratic methodology developed by the individual investigators, and in Table 12.4 and Fig. 12.2 an attempt is made to simplify these phenomena by distinguishing four main types of reaction according to the activation mechanisms involved. It seems probable that to a varying degree, these four types of cytotoxic mechanism may be called upon in most cytolytic events of immunological homeostasis. The type 2 and 4 mechanisms may, however, be physiologically more important than the others.

### 12.5.2 Allograft cytotoxicity mediated by T lymphocytes (type 1)

It has been convincingly demonstrated in mice that *in vitro* cytotoxicity of lymphocytes sensitized against alloantigens is primarily mediated by T lymphocytes. Neither antibodies, B lymphocytes nor macrophages are required in this system, indicating that the T lymphocytes themselves possess the capacity to lyse other cells. The cytotoxic T lymphocytes appear in the donor within one week of immunization. The target cell destruction is strictly specific, since bystander cells carrying transplantation antigens different from those used for the immunization are never lysed (Bloom, 1971). The T lymphocyte-mediated cytotoxicity can only be consistently demonstrated if there is a histocompatibility difference between the effector and the target cells. Thus, in syngeneic systems, tumour antigens usually fail to induce direct cytotoxicity via T lymphocytes.

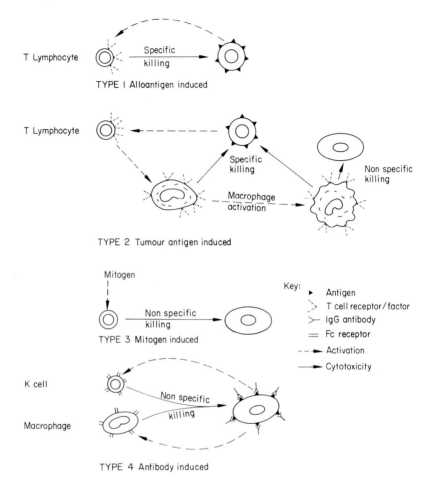

T Lymphocyte

Specific
killing

TYPE I Alloantigen induced

T Lymphocyte

Specific
killing

Macrophage
activation

Non specific
killing

TYPE 2 Tumour antigen induced

Mitogen

Non specific
killing

TYPE 3 Mitogen induced

Key:

▶   Antigen

〉   T cell receptor/factor

〉—   IgG antibody

=   Fc receptor

--▶   Activation

—▶   Cytotoxicity

K cell

Non specific
killing

Macrophage

TYPE 4 Antibody induced

**Fig. 12.2.** Four types of direct cytotoxic mechanism.

### 12.5.3 Tumour antigen-induced cytotoxicity mediated by T lymphocytes and macrophages (type 2)

While minor antigenic difference such as tumour-specific antigens do not alert syngeneic T lymphocytes to the extent that they alone become capable of eliminating the tumour cells, this effect can be achieved in a syngeneic system through an amplification involving cooperation between T lymphocytes and macrophages. This was

**Table 12.4.** Four main types of direct cytotoxicity reactions

| Type | Activating agents | Aggressor cells | Specificity | | |
|---|---|---|---|---|---|
| | | | Aggressor-cell activation | Target-cell destruction | |
| 1. Allograft induced | Alloantigens | T lymphocytes | Specific | Specific | |
| 2. Tumour antigen induced. (T lymphocyte directed macrophage-mediated (SMAF) cytotoxicity) | Cell membrane components including tumour specific antigens in syngeneic systems | T lymphocytes and 'armed' macrophages | Specific | Specific at first, becomes non-specific later | |
| 3. Mitogen-induced | Phytomitogens and soluble antigens | T lymphocytes (? B lymphocytes) | Non-specific (PHA) Specific (antigens) | Non-specific | |
| 4. Antibody-induced | 7S antibodies specifically bound to cell membrane antigens | K cells and macrophages | Non-specific | Specific, antibody-dependent | |

demonstrated by Evans & Alexander, who in 1970 reported that T lymphocytes from mice immunized with syngeneic tumour cells could be specifically activated to release a soluble factor which was taken up by macrophages from non-immune mice. (Evans & Alexander, 1970). These macrophages were now 'armed' to suppress the growth of the tumour cells *in vitro*. The tumour growth inhibition was initially specific, suggesting that the 'macrophage arming factor' (SMAF) might be T lymphocyte receptor molecules. Later, the 'armed' macrophages became cytotoxic to other tumour cells, indicating non-specific activation of the macrophages by T lymphocyte mediators.

### 12.5.4 Mitogen-induced cytotoxicity (type 3)

In these assays the target-cell killing is non-specific. The cytotoxicity induced by phytomitogens is non-physiological, but has been used as an *in vitro* test for T lymphocyte function. Mitogenic factor(s) might however amplify cytolytic reactions *in vivo*.

### 12.5.5 Antibody-induced K cell-mediated cytotoxicity (type 4)

It should be noted that this mechanism does not strictly belong to the CMI effector response, since neither T lymphocytes nor ordinary macrophages are involved, and the specificity is provided by classical (B lymphocyte-derived) antibodies. Antibodies bound to target cells can, however, also activate macrophages to become cytotoxic *in vitro*. It is therefore likely that this type of cytotoxicity, provided that it exists *in vivo*, is mediated by macrophages as well as the non-phagocytic K cells. The role of this system *in vivo* has recently been demonstrated in athymic (nude) mice which fail to reject allogeneic grafts. If grafted animals are passively transferred with alloantibodies specific for the graft, rejection rapidly occurs.

### 12.5.6 The requirement for effector-target cell contact

In most experimental systems designed to imitate graft rejection *in vitro*, cytotoxicity can only be achieved when direct membrane contact is established between the lymphoid effector cells and the target cells. While soluble factors capable of inhibiting target-cell function and multiplication can readily be detected in supernatants of stimulated lymphoid cells, cytolytic lymphokines are not consistently found in such supernatants. Cell killing is, therefore, dependent on an activity which is very closely associated with the aggressor cell membranes, and there is evidence that the cytolytic agent(s) may virtually be injected into the target cells through macrophage projections or lymphocyte uropods, thus confining the cytolytic activity to the immediate vicinity of the effector cells. In this way, cytolytic reactions can be selectively directed against the appropriate target, correlating with their exquisite specificity both *in vitro* (Cerottini, 1971) and *in vivo* (Billingham & Silvers, 1970).

One can think of a variety of reasons for the stringent requirement for effector target-cell contact in cytolytic reactions. The cytolytic component(s) may have a short half-life or not be released in an active state from the effector-cell membranes. It is also possible that killing requires a complex formation on the target-cell membrane of two or more molecules, and that such a complex formation can only take place or be sufficiently amplified at the effector-cell membrane. C8 has been implicated in cytotoxic reactions (Perlmann *et al.*, 1974), and more recently one of the factors of the alternative pathway (Factor B), has been found on lymphocyte membranes (Halbwachs & Lachmann, 1974; Bokisch, 1974). It is, perhaps, premature to present a unifying model which could account for all the phenomena observed in direct lymphoid cytotoxicity. One can speculate, however, that specific receptors ('IgT' or IgG) on binding to target-cell antigens might acquire the ability to react with and activate components in the effector-cell membranes (? complement) capable of inducing target-cell damage.

### 12.6 Attempts to relate *in vitro* phenomena to manifestation of cell-mediated immunity *in vivo*

Although some lymphokine activities are undoubtedly biological artefacts with little or no physiological pertinence, there is increasing experimental evidence that the mechanisms controlling CMI reactions *in vivo* involve factors which are identical or similar to those responsible for the *in vitro* phenomena. Only selective examples of this evidence can be given here.

#### 12.6.1 *Effects* in vitro *of factors produced* in vivo

Antigen-stimulated lymph nodes release into the efferent lymph factors which exert MIF and mitogenic activities *in vitro* (Chapter 14). MIF activity has also been found in serum shortly after intravenous injection of antigens to sensitized animals. Lastly, lymphokine activities have been extracted from DH reactions in the skin.

#### 12.6.2 *Effects* in vivo *of factors produced* in vitro

Intradermal injection of MIF-active lymphokine preparations produces a reaction which is similar both clinically and morphologically to the DH responses to antigens. The lymphokine reaction appears earlier, however, and this correlates with an observed acceleration of macrophage infiltration into the lymphokine reaction, as compared with antigen-induced DH response. Similarly, injection of lymphokines into afferent lymphatics produces lymph node enlargement, plugging of the medullary cords and proliferation of lymphocytes. It has also been demonstrated that intraperitoneal injection of MIF-active material reduces the yield of macrophages from the peritoneal cavity, and intravenous administration of MIF activity results in a prompt reduction of the number of circulating monocytes, associated with temporary anergy.

### 12.6.3 Clinical observations

A good correlation has been found in healthy individuals between DH reactivity *in vivo* and the ability of lymphoid cells to produce MIF activity *in vitro*. Furthermore, lymphoid cells from some patients with chronic candidiasis, who are not able to express any DH reactions, fail to release detectable MIF activity *in vitro*. Moreover, cells from patients with agammaglobulinaemia, but intact cellular immunity, are able to release MIF, whereas patients with selective T lymphocyte deficiency are unable both to produce DH reactions *in vivo* and MIF *in vitro*.

It has also been shown that *in vitro* MIF production is suppressed or absent in animals which have been immunized according to a schedule designed to induce high levels of antibody and minimal DH reactivity.

### 12.6.4 Histological studies of CMI reactions

The strongest evidence for the existence *in vivo* of non-specific recruitment of lymphocytes comes perhaps from experiments in which radio-labelled lymphocytes from sensitized donors are transferred to non-sensitive animals. The lymphoid cells which accumulate in the adoptive DH reactions elicited in the recipients are almost exclusively of recipient origin and it can be quite difficult to find the specific donor cells in the lesions. Controls where the recipient's cells are labelled confirm that the great majority of the infiltrating cells are derived from the recipient. Thus, the activation of specifically reactive donor cells must have initiated a recruitment reaction in the recipients.

## 12.7 Schematic translation of the *in vitro* activities into unified model for CMI mechanisms

The exact mechanisms whereby CMI reactions are generated and regulated *in vivo* are largely unknown, and the schematic model presented in Fig. 12.3 is therefore very hypothetical. The author has found this model useful, however, when confronted with the problem of analysing depressed cellular immunity in patients. It is, in fact, only an extension of the lymphocyte activation cycle presented in Fig. 12.1 and demonstrates some of the ingredients of

CMI effector mechanisms. While the model underlines the sequential nature of the many interdependent factors of these mechanisms, it gives a wrong dimensional impression, since every step of the process requires an intimate contact of the interacting cells.

It is convenient to divide the reaction sequence into three major components: specific recognition, an amplification phase and expression. Thus, antigenic material initially activates only a small number of specifically reactive lymphocytes. This activation leads to the production of chemotactic factor(s) which attracts other lymphocytes to the site. These 'unsensitized' lymphocytes are then 'turned on' by the mitogenic factor(s) and thereby start to

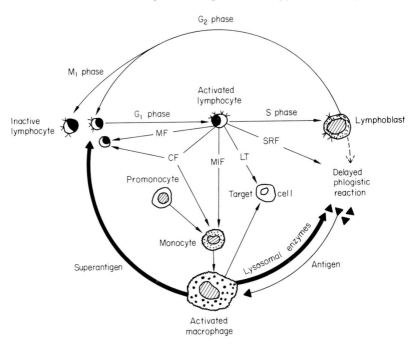

**Fig. 12.3.** Lymphokines released by antigen-activated lymphocytes and their effects on other cells.

amplify the reaction further by releasing activities which recruit and stimulate more lymphocytes. At the same time an increasing amount of factors are released which attract blood monocytes. The infiltrating monocytes are transformed into activated (or angry) macrophages by factors released by lymphocytes. These macrophages then show enhanced phagocytic and microbiocidal capacity, and increase in lysosomal enzyme activity.

The CMI reaction has now reached the level of expression. This may take the form of DH inflammatory reaction brought about, at least partly, by the release of lysosomal enzymes from the activated macrophages. Alternatively, the end point may be expressed as increased efficiency to kill and digest pathogens or as a co-opera-

194

tive cytotoxic effect of T lymphocytes and macrophages causing an allograft or tumour rejection.

## 12.8 Concluding remarks

The two features which distinguish the CMI effector response from manifestations of humoral immunity are the delayed and localized expression of the former. These features reveal a fundamental difference in the effector mechanisms involved. Whereas the expression of CMI requires *de novo* synthesis of mediators and subsequent amplifying interaction between T lymphocytes and macrophages, the humoral effector responses are brought about by an interaction of antigen with pre-formed molecules. Furthermore, in contrast to antibodies, the chemical signals which produce and regulate CMI effector responses are short-lived, and pre-dominantly confined to the immediate environment of the cells from which they originate. The reaction can, therefore, only proceed when a certain number of the reactive cells have been brought together and this local accumulation in turn depends on a gradual build up of lymphokine synthesis. This might explain the latency and the localized expression of the CMI responses.

It is tempting to speculate that lymphokine factors, especially the antigen-dependent activities, may have features in common with classical antibodies. If these factors are indeed antigen-specific T lymphocyte receptor molecules, made up, like classical anti-bodies, of variable and constant regions, the different lymphokine activities could be determined by the constant portion of the lymphokine molecules. This is the part of the antibody molecules which determines their class specificities as well as their ability to fix complement and react with certain cell types. In the case of lymphokines, an antigen could induce the release of T lymphocyte receptors, all possessing the same type of antigen specificity, while their constant regions would differ and thereby mediate several types of lymphokine activities. It was only after chemical analysis of monoclonal antibodies, that the physio-chemical basis of reaginic, cytophilic, agglutinating and complement-fixing activities could be established. Lymphokines will undoubtedly be similarly analysed.

Lymphoid tumours producing 'monoclonal' lymphokines in large quantities may be required for the long-awaited breakthrough in immunochemistry of cell-mediated immunity.

## References

BILLINGHAM R.E. & SILVERS W.K. (1970) Studies on the migrating behaviour of melanocytes in guinea pig skin. *J. exp. Med.* **131,** 101.

BLOOM B.R. (1971) *In vitro* approaches to the mechanism of cell-mediated immune reactions. *Adv. Immunol.* **13,** 102.

BLOOM B.R. & BENNETT B. (1966) Mechanisms of a reaction *in vitro* associated with delayed hypersensitivity. *Science* **153,** 80.

BOKISCH V. (1974) In BRENT L. & HOLBOROUGH J. *Progress in Immunology II*, **1,** 303. North-Holland, Amsterdam.

CEROTTINI J.C. (1971) (Discussion point.) In BLOOM B. & GLADE P. In vitro *methods in cell-mediated immunity*, p. 47. Academic Press, New York.

COHN Z.A. & WIENER E. (1963) The particulate hydrolases of macrophages. Comparative enzymology, isolation and properties. *J. exp. Med.* **118,** 991.

DUMONDE D.C., WOLSTENCROFT R.A., PANAYI G.S., MATTHEW M., MORLEY J. & HOWSON W.T. (1969) 'Lymphokines'. Non-antibody mediators of cellular immunity generated by lymphocyte activation. *Nature (Lond.)* **224,** 38.

EVANS R. & ALEXANDER P. (1970) Cooperation of immune lymphoid cells with macrophages in tumour immunity. *Nature (Lond.)* **228,** 620.

HALBWACHS L. & LACHMANN P.J. (1974) In BRENT L. & HOLBOROUGH J. *Progress in Immunology II* **1,** 303. North-Holland, Amsterdam.

MacLENNAN I.C.M. & HARDING B. (1974) Non-T cytotoxicity *in vitro*. In BRENT L. & HOLBOROUGH J. *Progress in Immunology II* **3,** 347. North-Holland, Amsterdam.

PERLMANN P., PERLMANN H. & LACHMANN P.J. (1974) Lymphocyte-associated complement: Role of C8 in certain cell-mediated lytic reactions. *Scand. J. Immunol.* **3,** 77.

VALDIMARSSON H. & GROSS N.J. (1973) Human skin responses to products of concanavalin A activated lymphocytes. *J. Immunol.* **111,** 485.

# Chapter 13
# B Lymphocyte Differentiation

## M. Cooper

### 13.1 Introduction

This chapter is concerned with a working model for B lymphocyte differentiation based on experimental studies and clinical observation of certain immuno-deficiency diseases as 'experiments of nature'.

The differentiation of B lymphocytes from multipotential stem cells to fully mature antibody-secreting cells can be divided into two distinct stages, each of which includes several steps (Fig. 13.1). In the first stage (*clonal development*) stem cells undergo a programmed sequence of differentiation within primary lymphoid organs to become immunocompetent lymphocytes that express immunoglobulins on their surface. The second stage (*clonal selection by antigen*) comprises the antigen-induced differentiation of B lymphocytes to mature plasma cells and memory-cell production.

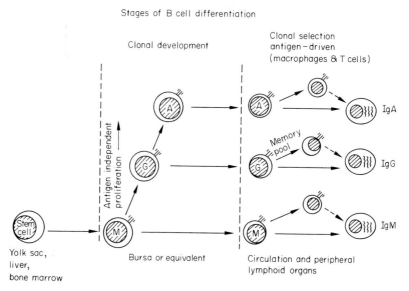

**Fig. 13.1.** Hypothetical model outlining the developmental states of a representative clone of B cells. (From Cooper *et al.*, 1973.)

197

## 13.2 Clonal development

This first stage appears to be entirely dependent on the inductive microenvironment of the primary lymphoid organs, the external antigenic environment playing no obvious role.

### 13.2.1 Primary site of B lymphopoiesis in chickens

The precursor cells of all immunocompetent lymphocytes arise in the blood islands of the yolk sac (Moore & Owen, 1967). These seed via the circulation to a primary lymphoid organ, the bursa of Fabricius, where they further differentiate into immunocompetent B lymphocytes.

Immunoglobulin synthesis by precursor cells begins early in ontogeny. B-stem cells first appear in the bursa about the 12th day of embryogenesis. Within 48 hours, these cells are induced to assume a lymphoid appearance and to express surface IgM. They undergo rapid proliferation with a doubling time of around 8 hours, and thus form small follicles of IgM-staining cells. Later IgG- and then IgA-containing cells arise within these developing follicles. Whether or not a single lymphoid follicle represents clonal expansion of a single B-stem cell is unknown.

One possible explanation for the sequential appearance of IgG- and IgA-containing cells within developing bursal follicles is that these cells arise from IgM precursors. Convincing evidence for this interpretation comes from the fact that if chick embryos are given specific heterologous antibodies to chicken IgM, the development of IgG and IgA as well as IgM is suppressed, and the chicks are agammaglobulinaemic for a while after hatching (Kincade *et al.*, 1970). Following a single injection of anti-$\mu$, the agammaglobulin-aemic state is transient, with recovery as the anti-$\mu$ is catabolized. Other B lymphocytes begin to differentiate from stem cells in the bursa and these seed to peripheral lymphoid organs. However, bursectomy at hatching prevents this recovery, rendering the anti-$\mu$ treated chicks permanently agammaglobulinaemic.

B lymphocytes seed to secondary lymphoid organs in the same sequence as they arise during bursal development (Kincade & Cooper, 1973). This seeding must begin about the 17th day of embryogenesis because bursectomy before this often results in complete and permanent agammaglobulinaemia. Bursectomy at 19 days regularly abrogates both IgG and IgA responses but not IgM. In some cases such chickens can make excessive amounts of IgM but they never repair their deficits in IgG and IgA. Similarly, bursectomy around hatching, when IgM and IgG cells have already appeared in the secondary lymphoid organs, results in a selective deficiency of IgA. The permanence of these dysgammaglobulin-aemic states also demonstrates that once B cells have reached the secondary lymphoid organs they are no longer capable of switching to synthesis of another class of immunoglobulin, this being entirely a bursal event in chickens.

A principal conclusion from these studies is that during clonal development in chickens, B lymphocytes can sequentially transcribe the $\mu$, $\gamma$ and $\alpha$ constant region genes. Thus IgM-producing cells are the precursors of lymphocytes which synthesize the other immunoglobulin classes.

### 13.2.2 Primary sites of B lymphopoiesis in mammals

Mammals have no bursa of Fabricius and it is pertinent to ask what structure serves this function in mammalian species. It has been argued that differentiation of stem cells into B lymphocytes occurs either in gut-associated lymphoid tissues (the GALT theory) (Cooper & Lawton, 1972), like appendix and Peyer's patches, or alternatively in the bone marrow. There is now evidence to indicate that neither of these tissues can be exclusive sites for induction of B cell differentiation. If the GALT theory were correct, removal of the entire gut sufficiently early in embryogenesis should arrest B cell differentiation. This was attempted in fetal lambs with the result that gutectomy at 8 weeks of gestation (i.e. before Ig-positive cells normally appear) makes no difference whatsoever to the subsequent differentiation of B cells (our unpublished observations). Kincade & Moore (personal communication) have shown that [89]Strontium-induced obliteration of haemopoietic activity of the bone marrow in adult or embryonic mice does not impair stem-cell differentiation along B cell lines either.

On the other hand, recent studies in mice have indicated that the fetal liver and spleen can generate B lymphocytes from immunoglobulin-negative precursors. If mouse fetal liver is removed as early as 5 days before B lymphocytes are scheduled to appear in the intact animal and is placed in an organ culture system, B lymphocytes of all immunoglobulin classes appear on a time scale virtually identical to their *in vivo* appearance. After 7 days in culture, immunoglobulin-bearing cells appear as they would have done *in vivo* (Owen *et al.*, 1974). These Ig-bearing cells have the usual morphology, surface antigens and surface receptors that are characteristic of B lymphocytes generated *in vivo*.

### 13.2.3 B lymphocyte differentiation in human fetal liver

In two infants who were born without circulating T or B lymphocytes, transfusion of a suspension of liver cells from a young unrelated fetus results in the appearance of mature B lymphocytes in the recipients' circulation together with increased serum levels of immunoglobulin (Cooper *et al.*, 1973; W. Hitzig, personal communication). Lymphocytes bearing donor histocompatibility antigens appeared in the circulation and erythrocyte chimerism occurred. Without stem-cell reconstitution these patients would soon have succumbed to overwhelming infection. These observations indicate that multipotent stem cells capable of giving rise to B lymphocytes are present in the liver of young human fetuses, as is known to be the case for mice.

B lymphocytes bearing IgM can first be found in the liver of human fetuses about the 9th week of gestation. Lymphocytes expressing surface IgG develop at nearly the same time, and by 11 weeks lymphocytes with IgA determinants arise. IgD expression is also an early event but its place in the developmental sequence has not yet been pinpointed. There is a rapid increase in numbers of B lymphocytes of all classes so that adult proportions are regularly attained by the 13th or 14th week (Fig. 13.2). The temporal consistency of this increase makes it seem likely that this is a

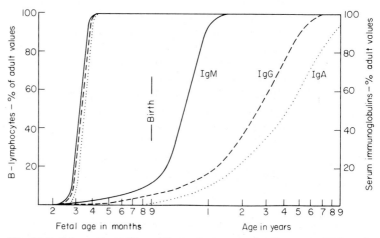

**Fig. 13.2.** Schematic outline of the early *in utero* development of B lymphocytes and the late development of serum immunoglobulins in humans. (From Cooper & Lawton 1972.)

genetically programmed event that is expressed independently of chance exposures to antigens from the external environment.

The facts mentioned above are consistent with the idea that B lymphocyte differentiation may also begin in the human fetal liver, but as yet there is no proof of this.

## 13.3 Mechanism for generation of Ig class heterogeneity among mammalian B lymphocytes

During mammalian B lymphocyte differentiation, $\mu$, $\gamma$ and $\alpha$ constant region genes appear to be transcribed sequentially during clonal expansion. The strongest evidence for this is the suppression of B cells of all classes and stages of maturity in mice given chronic injections of anti-$\mu$ beginning at birth (Lawton & Cooper, 1974). If the proposed switch sequence of IgM→IgG→IgA were correct, anti-$\gamma$ should suppress IgG and IgA but not IgM. This result has been achieved in only one experiment so far, and other experiments are needed to choose between this hypothesis and the most reasonable alternative (IgM $\nearrow$ IgG $\searrow$ IgA ).

To maintain *specificity* during a clonal development process which involves sequential transcription of constant region genes for each of the immunoglobulin classes, cells must continue to transcribe the same set of V-region genes. Evidence that this may occur comes from studies in selected individuals with multiple myeloma who produce two myeloma proteins, a situation which arises when there is abnormal clonal proliferation of both IgG- and IgM-secreting cells. In such patients, the light chains and V regions of both $\mu$ and $\gamma$ heavy chains have been shown to be identical in amino acid composition, although the two classes of myeloma proteins are being made by separate populations of malignant plasma cells (Wang *et al.*, 1970). Similarly, Oudin & Michel (1970) have shown that rabbit antibodies of different class can carry the same idiotype. This is strong evidence in support of the idea that at some point in clonal development cells can switch from synthesizing one class of immunoglobulin to another and yet at the same time transcribe the same V-region genes.

The genes coding for the constant regions of the heavy chains of IgD and IgE are thought to be activated in a similar way during clonal development, but as yet there is insufficient information to include them in the model. Recently IgD and IgM have been simultaneously detected on the surface of cord-blood lymphocytes (Rowe *et al.*, 1973), suggesting that activation of the gene for the $\delta$ constant region is a very early event (Chapter 7).


## 13.4 Antigen-induced B lymphocyte differentiation

The second stage of B lymphocyte differentiation from immuno-competent cells to mature antibody-secreting plasma cells is principally dictated by antigen, with T cells, macrophages and circulating antibodies playing regulatory roles (Chapter 9) (reviewed in Greaves *et al.*, 1973).


### 13.4.1 Role of antigen

When immunoglobulin-bearing B cells bind the appropriate antigen, the cells are stimulated to undergo clonal expansion giving rise to daughter memory cells, or they differentiate directly into mature antibody-secreting plasma cells. In contrast to memory cells, which may have a long life-span, plasma cells are relatively short-lived end cells whose half-life can be measured in days.

The class of immunoglobulin produced during an antibody response is critically related to the physical and chemical nature of the antigen. Thymus-independent antigens, like pneumococcal polysaccharide, lipopolysaccharide and polymerized flagellin usually trigger a profound IgM response without activating IgG producers in significant numbers. With T-dependent antigens on the other hand, both IgG and IgM antibody responses are produced. It is unknown why T-independent antigens fail to evoke an IgG response.

### 13.4.2 Role of T cells

T cells also play a crucial role in promoting B lymphocyte responses to antigens (Chapter 9) by providing in some way a mechanism for triggering terminal differentiation of IgG- and IgA-secreting cells. In congenitally athymic mice this hierarchy of requirement for T cell help is reflected by normal serum levels of IgM but low levels of IgG and IgA (Pritchard *et al.*, 1973). Paradoxically, the numbers of circulating B lymphocytes are normal or slightly increased in the athymic mice and there is no deficit in IgG- and IgA-bearing lymphocytes (Bankhurst & Warner, 1972). This paradoxical relationship may be related to the observation that little T cell help is needed for antigen-induced proliferation of memory B lymphocytes (Roelants and Askonas, 1972). Still unclear, however, is the role of T cells in the antigen-induced shift from a predominance of IgM antigen-binding cells in unprimed mice to an increase in IgG and IgA antigen-binding lymphocytes following immunization (Davie *et al.*, 1974). At present, there is insufficient evidence to choose between the two most attractive explanations for this: (i) T cells help antigens expand the relatively few pre-existing IgG- and IgA-committed members of the B cell clone, or (ii) in mammals, T cells and antigens generate IgG- and IgA- producing cells from IgM precursors.

T cells may play a much broader role in the overall homeostatic control of B cell function by exerting suppressor effects as well as helper effects (Chapters 8 and 9).

## 13.5 Defects of B lymphocyte differentiation in man

Certain immunodeficiency states in man provide a useful illustration of the two-stage concept of B cell differentiation. As shown in Figure 13.3 panhypogammaglobulinaemic patients fall into two general groups. In one group, there is a virtual absence of B cells at any stage in differentiation. This may result from a defect in the

*Section II: Immunobiology*

inductive microenvironment which promotes stem-cell differentiation along B lymphocyte lines (Stage 1A).

In contrast, other agammaglobulinaemic patients have normal levels of circulating B lymphocytes. B lymphocytes in such patients may recognize and proliferate in response to antigen but are incapable of terminal plasma-cell differentiation. The proliferative responsiveness to antigens in some of these patients can lead to B cell overgrowth which is probably because of absence of feedback control by circulating antibodies. In this group of agammaglobulinaemic patients, the findings clearly indicate that clonal development of B lymphocytes has occurred but that B lymphocytes for some reason fail to complete the second stage of differentiation. This 'block' in B lymphocyte differentiation (Stage 2a in Fig. 13.3) may result from a variety of specific defects. B lymphocytes from some of these patients undergo normal terminal differentiation *in*

Postulated sites for defects of plasma cell differentiation

First stage antigen independent · · · · · · · · · · Second stage antigen driven

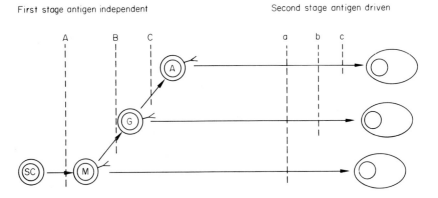

**Fig. 13.3.** The vertical lines represent possible sites for blocks in B cell differentiation leading to immunoglobulin deficiencies. With the possible exception of point C, phenotypic patterns consistent with each of these 'blocks' have been observed in patients. (From Cooper & Lawton 1973.)

*vitro* when stimulated by pokeweed mitogen (Wu *et al.*, 1973). The defect in these patients may therefore lie in the antigen-triggering mechanism. In other such patients, B lymphocytes fail to be stimulated by pokeweed mitogen to become immunoglobulin-secreting cells. Waldmann and co-workers (1974) have provided evidence that patients in this category may have an excess of suppressor T cells that can block differentiation of B lymphocytes from normal individuals as well. Still other agammaglobulinaemic patients may lack serum factors that are needed for B cell differentiation (Wernet *et al.*, 1974). With more information as to their precise nature some of these defects should be correctable.

*Chapter 13: B Lymphocyte Differentiation*

## 13.6 Summary

Both experimental studies and clinical observations support the hypothesis that B lymphocyte differentiation is a two-stage process beginning with clonal development, which is dependent on the inductive microenvironment of the primary lymphoid organs, and finishing with the antigen-driven proliferation and maturation of immunocompetent B lymphocytes. This model can be used as a map in charting and exploring the various defects in B cell differentiation.

## References

BANKHURST A.D. & WARNER N.L. (1972) Surface immunoglobulins on the thoracic duct lymphocytes of the congenitally athymic (nude) mouse. *Aust. J. Exp. Biol. Med. Sci.* **50**, 661.

COOPER M.D., KEIGHTLEY R.G., WU FRANK LIANG-YEH & LAWTON A.R. (1973) Developmental defects of T and B cell lines in humans. *Transplant. Rev.* **16**, 51.

COOPER M.D. & LAWTON A.R. (1972) The mammalian 'bursa-equivalent': Does lymphoid differentiation along plasma cell lines begin in the gut-associated lymphoepithelial tissues (GALT) of mammals? In HANNA M.G. *Contemporary Topics in Immunobiology*, pp. 49–68. Plenum Press, New York.

COOPER M.D. & LAWTON A.R. (1973) In JANKOVIC B.D. & ISAKOVIC K., *Microenvironmental Aspects of Immunity*. Plenum Press, New York.

DAVIE J.M. & PAUL W.E. (1974) Antigen binding receptors on lymphocytes. In Cooper Max D. & Warner Noel L. *Contemporary Topics in Immunobiology*, Vol. 3, pp. 171–192. Plenum Press, New York.

KINCADE P.W. & COOPER M.D. (1973) Immunoglobulin A: Site and sequence of expression in developing chicks. *Science* **179**, 398.

KINCADE P.W., LAWTON A.R., BOCKMAN D.E. & COOPER M.D. (1970) Suppression of immunoglobulin G synthesis as a result of antibody-mediated suppression of immunoglobulin M synthesis in chickens. *Proc. Nat. Acad. Sci.* **67**, 1918.

LAWTON A.R. & COOPER M.D. (1974) Modification of B lymphocyte differentiation by anti-immunoglobulins. In Cooper M.D. & Warner N.L. *Contemporary Topics in Immunobiology*, Vol. 3, pp. 193–225 Plenum Press, New York.

MOORE M.A.S. & OWEN J.J.T. (1967) Stem cell migration in developing myeloid and lymphoid systems. *Lancet* **ii**, 658.

OUDIN J. & MICHEL M. (1970) Idiotypy of rabbit antibodies. II. Comparison of idiotypy of various kinds of antibodies found in the same rabbits against Salmonella typhi. *J. Exp. Med.* **130**, 619.

OWEN J.J.T., COOPER M.D. & RAFF M.C. (1974) *In vitro* generation of B lymphocytes in mouse foetal liver—a mammalian 'bursa equivalent'. *Nature* **249**, 361.

PRITCHARD H., RIDDAWAY J. & MICKLEM H.S. (1973) Immune responses in congenitally thymus-less mice. II. Quantitative studies of serum immunoglobulins, the antibody response to sheep erythrocytes, and the effect of thymus allografting. *Clin. exp. Immunol.* **13**, 125.

ROELANTS G.E. & ASKONAS B.A. (1972) Immunological B memory in thymus deprived mice. *Nature New Biol.* **239**, 63.

ROWE D.S., HUG K., FORNI L. & PERNIS B. (1973) Immunoglobulin D as a lymphocyte receptor. *J. exp. Med.* **138**, 965.

WALDMANN T.A., BRODER S., BLAESE R.M., DURM M., BLACKMAN M. & STROBER W. (1974) Role of suppressor T cells in pathogenesis of common variable hypogammaglobulinaemia. *Lancet* **i**, 609.

WANG A.C., WILSON S.K., HOPPER J.E., FUDENBERG H.H. & NISONOFF A. (1970) Evidence for control of synthesis of the variable regions of the heavy chains of immunoglobulins G and M by the same gene. *Proc. Nat. Acad. Sci.* **66**, 337.

WERNET P., SIEGAL F.P., DICKLER H., FU S. & KUNKEL H.G. (1974) Immunoglobulin synthesis *in vitro* by lymphocytes from patients with immune deficiency: Requirement for a special serum factor (B-cell markers/B-cell differentiation/serum factor/T-cell influence/mitogen action). *Proc. Nat. Acad. Sci.* **71**, 531.

WU L.Y.F., LAWTON A.R. & COOPER M.D. (1973) Differentiation capacity of cultured B lymphocytes from immunodeficient patients. *J. Clin. Invest.* **52**, 3180.


## Further reading

COOPER M.D. & LAWTON A.R. (1974) The development of the immune system. *Scientific American* **231**, 559.

GREAVES M.F., OWEN J.J.T. & RAFF M.C. (1973) *T and B lymphocytes: Origins, Properties and Roles in Immune Responses.* Excerpta Medica, Amsterdam; American Elsevier, New York.

*Chapter 13: B Lymphocyte Differentiation*

# Chapter 14
# Structure and Function of Lymphoid Tissue

## I. McConnell

### 14.1 Introduction

The preceding chapters have adopted a 'gas law' approach to lymphocytes. They have been considered as interacting 'particles' whose behaviour might appear to be closer to 'gas law' rather than physiological principles. This chapter attempts to redress the balance and discusses the physiology of lymphocytes within their environment, the lymphon.

### 14.2 The lymphon

The lymphon is a collective term for primary and secondary lymphoid organs and their constituent cells. Its major function is to promote antigen recognition and disseminate both cellular and molecular memory of it. Lymphocytes do this by constantly moving through the tissues of the lymphon which, although anatomically discrete, are strategically placed accumulations of the circulating lymphoid mass. This traffic or recirculation of lymphocytes between and through the lymphoid tissue is probably essential for normal allergic responses and if it ceased or was in any way abnormal, the lymphon might function poorly, despite having a full complement of antigen-sensitive cells.

#### 14.2.1 Experimental models for analyzing lymphocyte traffic

Lymphocyte traffic has been investigated by cannulation experiments. In rats, mice and sheep the major posterior lymphatic trunk, the thoracic duct, can be cannulated and its cell population analyzed. In sheep, afferent and efferent lymphatics of single lymph nodes can be cannulated thus permitting analysis of cell traffic at a single lymph node, a technique pioneered by Morris.

To trace their migration and tissue distribution, lymphocytes are first labelled, either *in vitro* or *in vivo* with radioactive nucleotides, which are incorporated into DNA or RNA, or with $^{51}$Chromium *in vitro*. The cells can subsequently be identified by radioautography after their return to the original donor, or following adoptive transfer to syngeneic or irradiated recipients (Fig. 14.1).

By these techniques, Gowans & Knight (1964) first showed in rats that thoracic duct small lymphocytes (TDL) were constantly recirculating from blood to lymph. Removal of these cells through an indwelling thoracic duct cannula led to depletion of lymphocytes from the whole animal within 5–6 days. If the thoracic duct cells were radiolabelled and returned intravenously, within a short time they reappeared in the thoracic duct lymph. This established that the route of lymphocyte recirculation was predominantly from the blood to the lymph. Later studies by many other investigators showed that this is the major route of lymphocyte recirculation in most species (see reviews by Ford, 1975; Sprent, 1975).

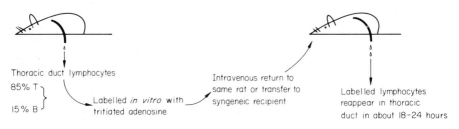

Thoracic duct lymphocytes
85% T
15% B
Labelled *in vitro* with tritiated adenosine

Intravenous return to same rat or transfer to syngeneic recipient

Labelled lymphocytes reappear in thoracic duct in about 18–24 hours

**Fig. 14.1.** Experimental models used for the analysis of lymphocyte recirculation in rats.

### 14.2.2 *Lymphocyte life-span*

The distinction between short- and long-lived lymphocytes can be determined *iv vivo* by labelling dividing cells with radioactive nucleic acid precursors. Clearly, cells which divide infrequently will require prolonged periods of exposure to the label before a significant proportion are labelled, whereas rapidly dividing cells label in a short period. Thus, the 'mix' of the labelled cells can be varied by altering the period over which the label is infused. The average interval between cell divisions for these populations can be estimated by measuring the rate of loss of labelled cells from the circulating population. Approaches like this have shown that resting T cells in the thoracic duct of mice are predominantly long-lived cells, with an average life of four to five months, with resting B lymphocytes being slightly less (Sprent & Basten, 1973). These are *minimum* estimates for the interval between mitoses and the average life span is probably greater, with T cells surviving for perhaps a year or more.

## 14.3 Cell content and cytoarchitecture of lymphoid tissues

### 14.3.1 *Cell content*

Different compartments of the lymphon contain different proportions of T and B lymphocytes as defined by their characteristic markers (Chapter 7, Table 7.1). In thoracic duct lymph, peripheral blood and lymph nodes, T cells greatly outnumber B lymphocytes, the difference being less marked in spleen.

TDL comprise about 95 per cent small non-dividing lymphocytes of which the majority (80–85 per cent) are T lymphocytes. In 'B' mice and rats (Chapter 9) although the overall number of circulating TDL is low, more than 90 per cent of them are B lymphocytes. In normal rats and mice, large lymphocytes in the thoracic duct are short-lived, non-recirculating cells thought to be mainly activated B lymphocytes (Fig. 14.2). Polymorphonuclear leucocytes monocytes and red cells are excluded from the lymph nodes and the thoracic duct.

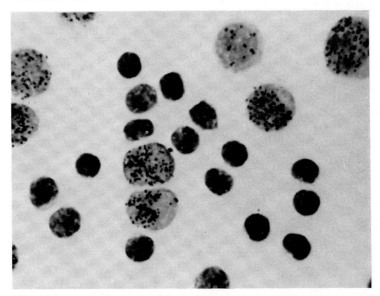

**Fig. 14.2.** Autoradiograph of thoracic duct lymphocytes from a rat which had received a continuous intravenous infusion of $^3$H-thymidine throughout the previous 24 hours. All the large lymphocytes were labelled but only 1 per cent of small lymphocytes (none in this field). (From Ford & Hunt, 1973, by permission of W. L. Ford.)

### 14.3.2 Thymus and Bursa of Fabricius

The thymus and Bursa of Fabricius are primary lymphoid organs which support extensive lymphopoiesis. During embryogenesis the site of stem-cell production originates in the yolk sac but later changes to fetal liver and finally bone marrow where it persists in adult life (Owen, 1973). The stem cells which seed to the thymus undergo extensive proliferation, giving rise in 5–6 days (in birds and mice) to large numbers of thymocytes which are organized into cortical and medullary areas. Cortical and medullary thymocytes differ in their expression of surface alloantigens and cortisone sensitivity *in vivo* (Chapter 7).

The number of stem cells which reach the thymus during the life

*Section II: Immunobiology*

of an individual may be small. Wallis *et al.* (1975) have shown that, following destruction of lymphoid tissue by whole body irradiation in mice, the thymus can be fully repopulated from only a few precursor cells.

The differentiation of B lymphocytes within primary lymphoid has been discussed (Chapter 13).

### 14.3.3 Lymph nodes

Lymph nodes have a framework of reticular cells and their fibres

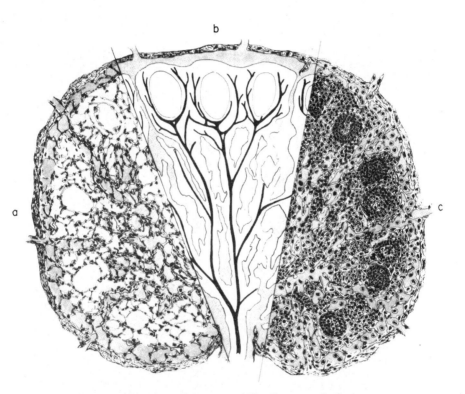

**Fig. 14.3.** Lymph node structure. The three panels depict:

(a) The 'skeleton' of the node. Nucleated reticular cells and their fibres are organized to form the follicular and perifollicular zones. These are separated by sinuses running radially from the supcapsular sinus which receives lymph and lymphocytes from the afferent lymphatics.

(b) Venous drainage. The first parts of the venous network are specialized parts of the vasculature known as the Post Capillary Venules (PCV). These predominate in the perifollicular areas and are the 'gates' through which lymphocytes enter nodes.

(c) Lymphocyte arrangement within the node. Follicles of B lymphocytes, some with germinal centres, are present in the cortex. Deep to this lies a narrow paracortical region which is a thymus dependent (T) area. (Osler & Weiss, 1972.)

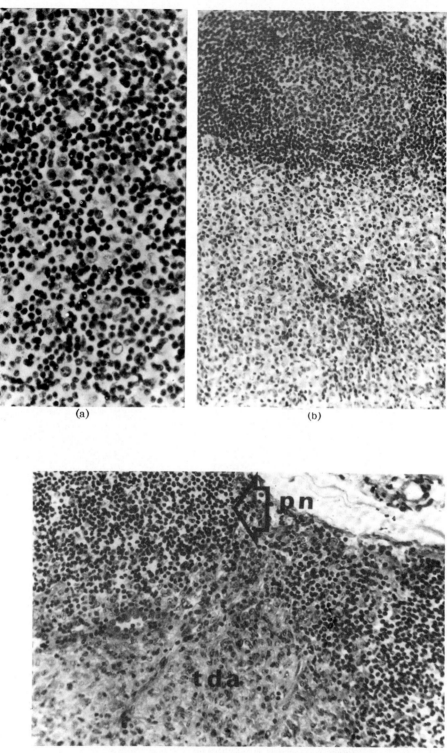

(a)

(b)

(c)

*Section II: Immunobiology*

which are organized into sinuses, the fibres also providing support for blood vessels and nerves (Fig. 14.3). The cortical region contains the germinal centres, which consist of a central pale staining area of large lymphoid cells and macrophage-like cells surrounded by concentric accumulations of the B lymphocytes. The entire structure is known as a secondary follicle or nodule. In unstimulated nodes, germinal centres are often not well defined the follicle consisting only of an accumulation of small lymphocytes (primary follicle). The medulla of the lymph node, especially after antigenic stimulation (see 14.9.2) often contains a large number of plasma cells. Both areas constitute the 'B'-dependent areas. By contrast T cells are confined to the paracortical regions or T-dependent areas. Antigens which evoke T cell responses cause blast transformation of lymphocytes within the paracortical region (Parrott et al., 1966; Davies et al., 1969). Procedures which deplete the circulating T cell population (neo-natal thymectomy, anti-lymphocyte sera, thoracic duct drainage) also result in the selective depletion of lymphocytes from the paracortical region of the lymph node (Fig. 14.4a, b & c.). In rats, thoracic duct drainage for about 4–5 days readily depletes the T-dependent areas of lymphocytes. B lymphocytes are less readily depleted by this procedure and no major depletion is seen until about 8–10 days after cannulation. Nude (athymic) mice and B mice have few lymphocytes in the T-dependent areas but normal numbers in the B-dependent areas (Fig. 14.4) (de Sousa et al., 1969).

### 14.3.3. Spleen

The major lymphoid mass of the spleen (the white pulp) is concentrated around arterioles as the periarterial lymphatic sheaths (PALS) (Fig. 14.5). Within the PALS lie the germinal centres and secondary follicles which, like those of lymph nodes, contain B cells. The white pulp is separated from the erythrocyte-filled red pulp by the marginal zones. In antigen-stimulated spleens, plasma cells are found mainly in the red pulp.

---

**Fig. 14.4.** T- and B-dependent areas of lymph nodes.

(a) Thymus-dependent area of a mouse lymph node three days after antigenic challenge. Blast cells are present in the paracortical region. (Davies et al., 1969.)

(b) Cortical and paracortical regions of a lymph node from a thymectomized, bone-marrow-reconstituted mouse. The cortical region has a normal appearance with a developing follicle compared to the relatively hypocellular paracortical region which has few T cells. (Davies et al., 1969.)

(c) Lymph node from Nude (athymic) mouse. There are few lymphocytes in the thymus dependent area (TDA). pn, primary nodule. (de Sousa et al., 1969.)

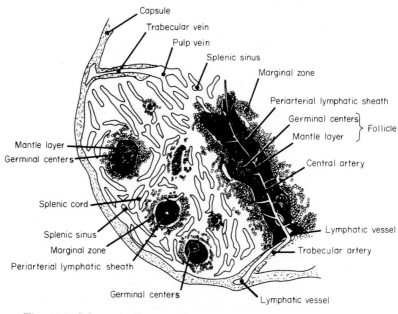

**Fig. 14.5.** Schematic diagram of the spleen. Description in text. (Weiss, 1972.)

### 14.3.4 *Gut associated lymphoid tissue (GALT)*

This includes the tonsils, small intestinal Peyer's patches and appendix, all of which show similar separation of lymphocytes into T- and B-dependent areas. In addition, there are many lymphocytes within the lamina propria of the small intestinal villi and between the epithelial cells of the intestinal mucosal surface (Ferguson & Parrott, 1972; Parrott & Ferguson, 1974).

## LYMPHOCYTE CIRCULATION

There are two major lymphocyte traffic patterns within the lymphon. The first involves migration to and from the primary lymphoid organs and includes the migration of stem cells from the yolk sac, fetal liver or adult bone marrow to the thymus or bursa (or its mammalian equivalent). Following their differentiation within the primary organs, the mature virgin immunocompetent cells then leave their breeder organs not re-entering these structures in substantial numbers.

The second bulk, traffic pattern is between and within the secondary lymphoid organs, via blood and lymphatic vessels. These major traffic routes are shown in Fig. 14.6.

212                                        *Section II: Immunobiology*

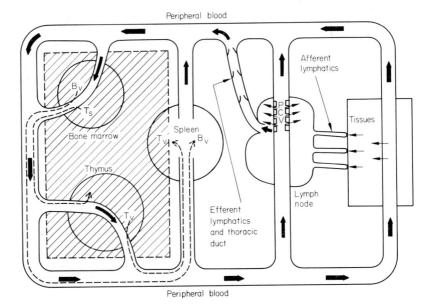

**Fig. 14.6.** Major lymphocyte traffic patterns within the mature lymphon. $T_s$ represents the migration of lymphoid stem cells (? precursor T cells) to the thymus. Virgin T and B lymphocytes ($T_v$ and $B_v$) are believed to preferentially migrate to the spleen where after antigenic stimulation (?) they give rise to recirculating lymphocytes. These then enter the recirculating lymphocyte pool. Lymphocytes entering the spleen return to the circulation via the splenic vein but lymphocytes entering lymph nodes or tissues return to the blood via the major lymphatic ducts.

*Key:* ↑↑↑ — recirculating lymphocyte pool
    ▨ — not part of recirculating lymphocyte pool
    $B_v$ — virgin B lymphocyte
    $T_v$ — virgin T lymphocyte
    $T_s$ — lymphoid stem cell (T)
    PCV — post-capillary venule.


## 14.4 Lymphocyte migration from primary lymphoid organs

### 14.4.1 Bone Marrow → Blood

About 80 per cent of bone marrow small lymphocytes are cells which have undergone recent division. Many are at different stages of differentiation and about 30 per cent acquire surface immunoglobulin about three days after undergoing division (Osmond & Nossal, 1974). These virgin B lymphocytes migrate preferentially to the spleen rather than lymph nodes. T precursor lymphocytes also arise in adult bone marrow and seed by haematogenous routes to the thymus.

A minority of lymphocytes in the bone marrow are part of the mature recirculating pool. In mice, a small proportion are T cells, since bone-marrow cells can elicit graft versus host reactions. In certain strains of rat, the bone marrow contains considerable numbers of T cells which are part of the recirculating population and can be depleted by chronic thoracic duct drainage. These are presumably present in the peripheral blood within the venous sinuses of the bone marrow and not intermingled with the stem-cell rich-haemopoetic tissue.

### 14.4.2 Thymus→Blood

It has been proposed that virgin T cells which leave the thymus preferentially migrate to the spleen to provide a population of non-recirculating T cells. These are short lived in the absence of antigenic stimulation which converts them to a long-lived re-circulating pool of memory T cells (Sprent, 1975). The functional subdivision of T cells into $T_1$ and $T_2$ cells (Chapter 9) lends weight to this possibility. It is unknown whether $T_1$ and $T_2$ are separately derived from different parts of the thymus (? cortical and medullary thymocytes respectively) or whether $T_2$ are derived from $T_1$ after antigenic stimulation in the spleen.

## 14.5 Lymphocyte recirculation between secondary lymphoid organs

The final common pathway of lymphocytes which enter efferent lymphatics is via the thoracic duct and right lymphatic duct and thence into the blood. This recirculating pool comprises about $2 \times 10^9$ cells in the adult rat and about $2 \times 10^8$ in mice. The rate at which these cells endlessly traffic from blood to lymph is consider-able, and in the adult rat and sheep about 1–2 per cent of the total pool emerges into the blood from the thoracic duct each hour.

The traffic patterns of the recirculating pool are:

### 14.5.1 Blood→Lymph Node→Lymph→Blood

Studies on the kinetics of lymphocyte output in the efferent lym-phatic from a single lymph node in sheep have shown that about 4 per cent of these cells are derived from recent division within the node, that about 10 per cent came to the node in the afferent lym-phatics and the remainder (about 90 per cent) from the blood (Hall & Morris, 1965). To achieve this efferent outflow requires an ab-straction rate of about 10 per cent of the blood lymphocytes passing through the node in the intravascular compartment (Figure 14.7). These efferent lymphocytes eventually flow into another lymph node and subsequently reach the thoracic duct, whence they enter the blood. The above quantitation is based on the first node of the

*Section II: Immunobiology*

chain (popliteal) and subsequent nodes may behave differently since they have a much higher afferent input.

An important physiological fact about lymph nodes is that irrespective of whether cells or macromolecules enter the lymph node from the blood or afferent lymphatic, their only apparent route back to the blood is via the efferent lymphatic from the node and eventually via the thoracic duct to the circulation. There is no direct transfer of either antigen or primed cells at the level of the lymph node back into the blood (Hall *et al.*, 1967). This is true for all mammalian species except the pig, where antigen and cells return to the blood at the level of the node (Binns, 1974).

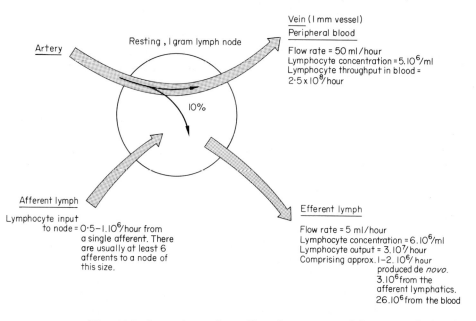

Fig. 14.7. Approximate flow of lymphocytes to and from a single lymph node in sheep.

The recirculation times for T and B lymphocytes to travel from blood to lymph have been separately analysed by Howard (1972) and Sprent (1973). The mean transit time for T lymphocytes to traverse the total lymph node mass and reappear in the thoracic duct is about 18–24 hours. B lymphocytes have a slightly longer transit time of about 30 hours. The reason for the longer time taken by B cells is not entirely clear. Either B cells enter the lymph nodes less readily than T lymphocytes or they migrate across them more slowly than T lymphocytes, which seems to be the case for the spleen. In splenectomized rats there is little change in the transit time for B lymphocytes, indicating that their longer transit time cannot be explained by splenic retention of B cells (Ford, 1975). The exact transit time for either cell type to cross a single lymph node has never been estimated.

*Chapter 14: Structure and Function of Lymphoid Tissue*

### 14.5.2 Blood→Tissues→Lymph Node→Blood

Lymphocytes which extravasate into the tissue spaces are returned to the lymph nodes via the afferent lymphatics. The cell population of the afferent lymphatics is unusual in that about 10 per cent of the cells are macrophages. In rabbits and sheep there are no B cells in the afferent lymphatics draining to the first node in a chain. It seems unlikely, therefore, that lymphocytes in the afferent lymphatics are a representative sample of the total circulating blood lymphocyte pool.

### 14.5.3 Blood→Spleen→Blood

Lymphocytes enter the PALS from the blood and eventually migrate to the red pulp, finally regaining the circulation via the splenic vein. Lymphocyte traffic from the spleen is thus markedly different from lymph nodes in that lymphocytes do not return to the blood via lymphatics.

## 14.6 Lymphocyte migration within spleen and lymph nodes

### 14.6.1 Lymph nodes

B and T lymphocytes enter lymph nodes via specialized parts of the postcapillary venules (PCV) many of which are situated in the paracortical region. The endothelial cells of the PCV are cuboidal rather than flat and lymphocytes gain access to the node by passing between these high endothelial cells. By using radioautographic techniques to distinguish the T and B lymphocytes in rats, Howard et al. (1972) have shown that, although both T and B lymphocytes enter the node together, they segregate shortly afterwards. The B lymphocytes preferentially migrate to the cortex where they accumulate around germinal centres, while the T cells remain confined to the paracortical region. The fact that plasma cells are not found in the cortex, but in the medulla indicates that activated B cells presumably have to migrate back across the thymus-dependent area. In normal mice, there is little evidence for B lymphocytes in this area, but in nude mice, B lymphocytes are seen within the thymus dependent area. The exit route for both T and B lymphocytes is via the medullary sinuses, and thence by the efferent lymphatics.

### 14.6.2 Spleen

Both T and B small lymphocytes enter the PALS from the marginal zone bounding the white pulp. Both T and B lymphocytes are intermingled in the peripheral areas of the PALS, but B lymphocytes seem to traffic differentially towards the germinal centre area. They accumulate around this, which, as in lymph nodes, excludes T lymphocytes. Lymphocytes exit from the PALS via the marginal zone bridging channels (Mitchell, 1972) thus reaching the splenic red pulp. The splenic transit time for T cells is about 5–6 hours with B cells taking slightly longer (Ford, 1969).

The factors which influence the selective entry of lymphocytes into lymphoid tissue and their distinct segregation within it are unknown. The high endothelial cells of the PCV, the various cell surface alloantigens and receptors on T and B lymphocytes as well as the micro environment within lymphoid tissue may all play a crucial role. Enzymatic treatment of lymphocytes with neuraminidase has a profound effect on lymphocyte traffic, suggesting that the surfaces of the lymphocytes directly dictate their *in vivo* behaviour (Woodruff & Gesner, 1969).

## 14.7 Uptake of antigen by lymphoid tissue

### 14.7.1 Access to lymphoid tissue

The reticuloendothelial system plays a major role in the uptake and presentation of antigen. Alveolar macrophages and liver macrophages screen and remove a large amount of antigen, thus preventing it from reaching lymphoid tissue. When the function of liver macrophages is impaired, as in chronic active hepatitis, the antibody titres to certain viral antigens like measles and rubella are extremely high. This could be due to failure to clear antigen or to the release of sequestered antigen from damaged cells.

Afferent lymphatics play a major role in conveying antigen to lymph nodes. Following skin sensitization with fluorodinitrobenzene (FDNB), much of the skin contactant, coupled to autologous protein, can be detected in the afferent lymph draining the sensitized site. In situations where afferent lymphatics are absent, either naturally, as in the hamster cheek pouch or anterior chamber of the eye, or experimentally, as in alymphatic skin pedicles, immune responses to antigens present at these sites takes a long time to develop, if at all (Barker & Billingham, 1973).

### 14.7.2 Localization in lymphoid tissue

On reaching nodes, antigen localizes in two sites. In the first case, antigen is taken up by macrophages which line the subcapsular and medullary sinuses. As early as thirty minutes after subcutaneous injection, antigen can be found within macrophage phagolysosomes and, in some cases, it persists there for up to six weeks. A second type of antigen localization takes place in the cortex of the lymph node. Antigen becomes localized to the surface of the dendritic processes of reticular cells within lymphoid follicles. This follicular localization is antibody-dependent, persists for several weeks and may be due to the adherence of antigen as an immune complex via Fc or C3 receptors on dendritic reticular cells (Ada et al., 1967).

## 14.8 Non-specific effects of antigen on lymphocyte traffic

### 14.8.1 Cell 'shutdown'

The arrival of antigen in lymph nodes has an almost immediate and profound effect on lymphocyte traffic through the node. This is

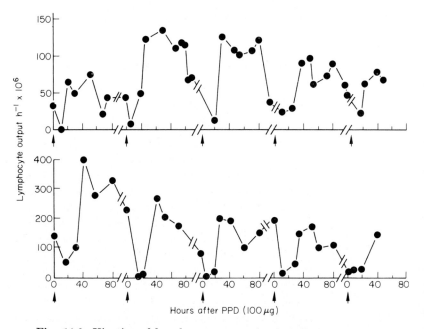

**Fig. 14.8.** Kinetics of lymphocyte output in the efferent lymph of two tuberculin sensitive sheep after repeated stimulation of the cannulated node with tuberculin (PPD). Heavy arrows indicate injection of 100 μg PPD in saline. Six hours after challenge of a node with antigen, the lymphocyte output in efferent lymph is markedly reduced, there being little change in lymph flow. Lymphokine release takes place mainly during this period of cell shutdown. There follows a biphasic increase in lymphocyte output with blast cells occurring during the second peak. (From McConnell et al., 1974.)

clearly defined in the sheep lymph node, where, six hours after the secondary challenge of the node with certain antigens, the lymphocyte output drops to 10–20 per cent of the resting level (Fig. 14.8). The phenomenon lasts from 5–20 hours depending on antigen and

Section II: Immunobiology

applies to the lymphocyte output, not to the lymph flow, which may be increased during 'cell shutdown'. Lymphokine release by lymphocytes, presumably T cells, takes place during cell shutdown (Hay *et al*, 1973).

The physiological significance of 'cell shutdown' is unknown. It is an obvious mechanism for promoting interaction between antigen and lymphocytes. Lymphokine release may also promote early cell interactions.

### 14.8.2 Lymphocyte recruitment

Immediately after the end of 'cell shutdown', the lymphocyte output from a stimulated node increases, frequently in a biphasic manner. The first wave of cells, mainly small lymphocytes, are almost entirely recruited from the blood, presumably a reflection of the large increase in blood flow to the node on antigenic stimulation. The second wave contains up to 20 per cent blast cells, produced *de novo* within the node. For antigens like tuberculin, the duration of this response is about 80 hours.

These physiological changes can also be demonstrated in intact animals. In mice, it can be shown that if syngeneic $^{51}$Cr-labelled lymphocytes are infused shortly after challenge of the lymph nodes with antigen, the labelled cells preferentially localize in large numbers in the stimulated nodes (Frost & Lance, 1974). This has been termed 'lymphocyte trapping' and is envisaged as being similar to the 'cell shutdown' seen in sheep lymph nodes. The paracortical and medullary sinuses of stimulated nodes become distended with lymphocytes at this time. However, the distinction between 'trapping' and increased lymphocyte flow through stimulated nodes would not be distinguished in the above experiment, and until excluded, this is an alternative explanation for the phenomenon. Many lymphokine preparations, when injected into lymph nodes via an afferent lymphatic, produce a similar increase in the flux of lymphocytes within the node.

## 14.9 Specific effects of antigen on lymphocyte traffic

### 14.9.1 Specific lymphocyte recruitment

The screening of the body for antigen by circulating lymphocytes is a rapid process. It has been demonstrated both in rats and mice that, 24 hours after antigen has first localized in spleen and lymph nodes, most lymphocytes specific for the antigen have been selectively depleted from the recirculating pool. This can be shown to occur for several antigens, including histocompatibility antigens and haptens (Ford & Atkins, 1972; Sprent & Miller, 1973). The depletion of specific antigen-reactive cells from the circulating pool is matched by a net increase in their numbers at the site of antigen localization. There is a peak of activated cells in the thoracic duct several days later, following their specific proliferation.

It is of interest to consider at what level antigen actually selects out specific cells from the circulating pool. One view, for which there is considerable evidence, is that lymphocytes enter the lymph nodes at random and that specific retention takes place within the parenchyma of the node as lymphocytes percolate past the antigen (Ford, 1975).

There is, however, preliminary evidence that this may not be the only mechanism. It has been shown in sheep that repeated challenge of a cannulated lymph node eventually leads to the depletion from the whole animal of lymphocytes specific for the challenge antigen. Lymphocytes specific for other antigens are not substantially depleted. This experiment cannot be explained *solely* on the basis of random entry of lymphocytes into the node which, if it were to lead to depletion, would be non-specific. The possibility arises that there is an antigen-specific mechanism acting at the level of stimulated nodes which specifically selects cells from the recirculating lymphocyte pool or conceivably returns cells which do not carry receptors for the antigen to the blood within the node. (McConnell *et al.*, 1974.)

## 14.9.2 Antigen-specific effects within lymphoid tissue

The specific cellular response to most antigens is first seen in the thymus-dependent areas. T lymphocytes differentiate into blast cells, giving rise to activated T lymphocytes which can later be detected in the circulating lymphocyte pool.

During the primary response similar proliferation is also seen in the B-dependent areas. Germinal centres expand, doubling their volume every 10–12 hours, mainly through rapid proliferation of cells. After about 3 weeks they begin to regress (Laissue *et al.*, 1971). The precise significance of germinal centre formation is unknown. These may be the sites where B lymphocytes are first activated and, although a few antibody forming cells can arise in the germinal centre, the majority of them are present within the medulla of the node as plasma cells.

## 14.9.3 T–B cell cooperation in vivo

The segregation of T and B lymphocytes within lymphoid tissue is difficult to reconcile with ideas of cell cooperation which envisage T–B cell bridging by antigen (see Chapter 9). It could be argued that in lymph nodes this takes place at their mutual point of entry near the postcapillary venules, where there is an obvious chance of T–B cell mixing. In spleen, T and B cells are mixed in the marginal zone and outer areas of the PALS.

The evidence that T–B cell cooperation is mediated by specific soluble factors which adhere to macrophages makes sense in view of the structure of lymphoid tissue. Specific T cell factor might attach cytophilically to the surface of reticular cells and localize antigen there in much the same way as antibody does. The passively sensitized reticular cells would then present antigen to the B lymphocytes as described for macrophages (Chapter 9).

### 14.10 Circulation of virgin, primed and activated lymphocytes

The overall traffic pattern of the circulating lymphocyte pool is well defined. It is, however, not surprising that lymphocytes in different stages of activation show different migratory behaviour, life span and tissue localizing properties.

Virgin lymphocytes, on leaving the thymus or bone marrow, seem to preferentially localize in the spleen rather than lymph nodes. In the responses to at least two antigens, diphtheria toxoid and ferritin, it has been shown that the B lymphocytes which propagate a primary immune response are rapidly dividing cells which are predominantly present in the spleen. Although they may be found in the thoracic duct, their capacity for recirculation is poor compared to primed cells (Strober, 1972).

Primed lymphocytes, by contrast, are mainly a recirculating, long-lived population. Both T and B memory lymphocytes recirculate from blood to lymph. The TDL of primed rats readily confers secondary immune responsiveness to irradiated recipients. It has been estimated in mice that the number of memory T and B lymphocytes in the thoracic duct are about 15 times greater than in unprimed animals (Sprent, 1975). By adoptive transfer it has been shown that plasma cells which arise in recipients following transfer of primed TDL carry the alloantigens of the donor (Ellis et al., 1969). Similarly it has been shown that anti-$\theta$ treated TDL can adoptively transfer secondary responsiveness. Both experiments clearly show that memory B lymphocytes are part of the recirculating lymphocyte pool.

The traffic of antigen-activated cells is the physiological mechanism whereby specific memory cells and their products are disseminated throughout the body following local antigenic experience. This is well defined in sheep where several days after challenge of a lymph node with antigen, the cells in the efferent lymph contain a very high proportion of primed and active blast cells, many of the latter containing specific antibody. If all of these cells are removed from the body, despite a vigorous response in the lymph node, priming of the whole animal for a secondary response fails to take place. On the other hand, if cells are washed free of antigen and returned intravenously, priming for a secondary response does take place, proving that lymphocytes in efferent lymphatics can be the carriers of immunological memory (Hall *et al.*, 1967).

Some activated or effector cells have apparently limited capacity for recirculation. In mice undergoing a GVH reaction following transfer of allogeneic T cells, activated donor T lymphocytes appear in the thoracic duct. Many of these cells fail to recirculate on subsequent transfer to second hosts and about 25 per cent of them migrate to the gut where they localize within the lamina propria and Peyer's patches (Sprent, 1975; Parrott & Ferguson, 1974). Activated B lymphocytes are also known to migrate to the gut. Why so many activated lymphocytes should preferentially migrate to the lymphoid areas of the gut is, like so many areas of immunology, a complete mystery.

## References

ADA G.L., PARRISH C.R., NOSSAL G.J.V. & ABBOT A. (1967) The tissue localisation, immunogenic and tolerance-inducing properties of antigens and antigen fragments. *Cold Spr. Harb. Symp. Quant. Biol.* **32,** 381.

BARKER C.F. & BILLINGHAM R.E. (1973) Immunologically privileged sites and tissues Corneal Graft Failure. *Ciba Foundation Symposium* **15,** p. 79. Elsevier, North-Holland.

BINNS R.M. (1973) Cellular immunology in the pig. *Proc. Roy. Soc. Med.* **66,** 1155.

DAVIES A.J.S., CARTER R.L., LEUCHARS E., WALLIS V. & KOLLER P.C. (1969) The morphology of immune reactions in normal, thymectomised and reconstituted mice. I. The response to sheep erythrocytes. *Immunology* **16,** 57.

DE SOUSA M.A.B., PARROTT D.M.V. & PANTELOURIS E.M. (1969) The lymphoid tissues in mice with congenital aplasia of the thymus. *Clin. exp. Immunol.* **4,** 637.

ELLIS S.T., GOWANS J.L. & HOWARD J.C. (1969) The origin of antibody forming cells from lymphocytes. *Antibiot et Chemotherapia* **15,** 40.

FERGUSON A. & PARROTT D.M.V. (1972) The effect of antigen deprivation on thymus dependent and thymus independent lymphocytes in the small intestine of the mouse. *Clin. exp. Immunol.* **12,** 477.

FORD W.L. (1969) The kinetics of lymphocyte recirculation within rat spleen. *Cell and Tissue Kinetics* **2,** 171.

FORD W.L. & ATKINS R.C. (1972) Specific unresponsiveness of recirculating lymphocytes after exposure to histocompatibility antigens in $F_1$ hybrid rats. *Nature, New Biol.* **234,** 178.

FORD W.L. & HUNT S.V. (1973) The preparation and labelling of lymphocytes. In WEIR D.M. *Handbook of Experimental Immunology* Chapter 23. Blackwell Scientific Publications, Oxford.

FORD W.L. (1975) Lymphocyte migration and immune responses. *Progr. Allergy.* **19,** 1.

FROST P. & LANCE E.M. (1974) The cellular origin of the lymphocyte trap. *Immunology* **26,** 175.

GOWANS J.L. & KNIGHT E.S. (1964) The route of recirculation of lymphocytes in the rat. *Proc. Roy. Soc. B* **159,** 257.

HALL J.G. & MORRIS B.J. (1965) The origin of the cells in the efferent lymph from a single lymph node. *J. exp. Med.* **121,** 901.

HALL J.G., MORRIS B., MORENO G. & BESSIS M. (1967) The ultrastructure and function of the cells in the lymph following antigenic stimulation. *J. exp. Med.* **125,** 91.

HAY J.B., LACHMANN P.J. & TRNKA Z. (1973) The appearance of migration inhibition factor and a mitogen in lymph draining tuberculin reactions. *Eur. J. Immunol.* **3,** 127.

HOWARD J.C. (1972) The life span and recirculation of marrow derived small lymphocytes from the rat thoracic duct. *J. exp. Med.* **135,** 185.

LAISSUE J., COTTIER M., HESS M.W. & STONER R.D. (1971) Early and enhanced germinal centre formation and antibody responses in mice after primary stimulation with antigen-isologous antibody complexes as compared with antigen alone. *J. Immunol.* **107,** 822.

MCCONNELL I., LACHMANN P.J. & HOBART M.J. (1974) The restoration of specific immunological virginity. *Nature (Lond.)* **250,** 113.

MITCHELL J. (1973) Lymphocyte circulation in the spleen. Marginal zone bridging channels and their possible role in cell traffic. *Immunology* **24,** 93.

OSMOND D.G. & NOSSAL G.J.V. (1974) Differentiation of lymphocytes in mouse bone marrow. I. Quantitative radioautographic studies of anti-globulin binding by lymphocytes in bone marrow and lymphoid tissues. *Cell Immunol.* **13,** 117.

OWEN J.J.T. (1972) The origins and development of lymphocyte populations. In Ontogeny of Acquired Immunity. *Ciba Foundation Symposium,* p. 35. Elsevier, North Holland.

PARROTT D.M.V., DE SOUSA M.A.B. & EAST J. (1966) Thymus dependent areas in the lymphoid organs of neonatally thymectomised mice. *J. exp. Med.* **123,** 191.

PARROTT D.M.V. & FERGUSON A. (1974) Selective migration of lymphocytes within the mouse small intestine. *Immunology* **26,** 571.

SMITH J.B. & MORRIS B. (1970) The response of the popliteal lymph node of the sheep to swine influenza virus. *Aust. J. Exp. Biol. Med. Sci.* **48,** 33.

SPRENT J. (1973) Migration of T and B lymphocytes in the mouse. I. Migratory properties. *Cell Immunol.* **7,** 10.

SPRENT J. & BASTEN A. (1973) Circulating T and B lymphocytes of the mouse II. Lifespan. *Cell Immunol.* **7,** 40.

SPRENT J. & MILLER J.F.A.P. (1973) Effect of recent antigen priming on adoptive immune responses. *J. exp. Med.* **138,** 143.

SPRENT J. (1975) Recirculating Lymphocytes. In MARCHALONIS J.J. *The Lymphocyte Structure and Function.* Marcel Dekker Inc., New York.

STROBER S. (1972) Initiation of antibody responses by different classes of lymphocytes. V. Fundamental changes in the physiological characteristics of virgin thymus-independant ('B') lymphocytes and 'B' memory cells. *J. exp. Med.* **136,** 851.

WALLIS V.J., LEUCHARS E., CHWALINSKI S. & DAVIES A.J.S. (1975) On the sparse seeding of bone marrow and thymus in radiation chimaeiras. *Transplantation* **19,** 1.

WEISS L. (1972) *The cells and tissues of the immune system: structure, functions, interactions.* (General editors, Osler & Weiss). Prentice-Hall, Inc., Englewood Cliffs, New Jersey.

WOODRUFF J.J. & GESNER B.M. (1969) The effect of neuraminadase on the fate of transfused lymphocytes. *J. exp. Med.* **129,** 551.

# SECTION III
# IMMUNOGENETICS

## III.1 Introduction

Most of this section is concerned with the genes in the major histo-compatibility region, their products and mode of action. Some of the products coded by the region are involved in the recognition and rejection of allografts. This preamble provides an introduction to the observed phenomena and the tools used for their investigation.

Most of our knowledge of the major histocompatibility systems (MHS) (Chapter 15) comes from genetic experiments and observations using the reactivity of the immune system as the tool of study. Some of the products coded by the genes in the region are present on the surfaces of tissue cells and are detected and analysed as antigens. They may evoke either antibody or cell-mediated responses. This approach to mapping is obviously limited, since failure to produce a response, due, for instance, to lack of helper function, does not mean that there are no differences. Nevertheless, these have proved valuable tools in mapping the genes of the MHS whose products are present on cell surfaces.

A more recent approach to the genetic analysis of the region has come from studies of the genetic control of immune responses to certain antigens (Chapter 16). This approach is also fraught with complications since many steps are involved before a response is produced, and suitable and sensitive assays must be used to measure the product.

It is important to remember that all of the genetic arguments in this section are on a much broader scale than is the case with molecular genetics of haemoglobin or even the immunoglobins. In the case of histocompatibility antigens detected by alloantisera, there is virtually no structural data to clarify the genetics, in the other cases there is absolutely none.

## III.2 Alloantisera to cell-surface determinants

Alloantisera reacting specifically with cell-surface alloantigens are prepared by cross-immunization of inbred strains of experimental

225

animals and, for greater specificity, the immunization of congenic strains differing at the relevant loci. In Man, naturally-occurring alloantisera are found in polytransfused individuals and multi-gravid women, both groups having been exposed to foreign tissue antigens. The alloantisera are tested in cytotoxicity assays, and are used to detect the serologically-defined (SD) antigens on the surface of lymphocytes which are commonly used as target cells.

### III.3 Graft rejection and its *in vitro* 'correlates'

Cells or tissues transferred between unrelated outbred individuals are rejected by virtue of an allergic response by the host to anti-genic structures on the cell surfaces. Analysis of these genetic differences by grafting or graft-versus-host reaction is tedious in experimental animals and unethical in humans, so a number of *in vitro* methods have been developed as models (Chapter 17).

Mixed lymphocyte cultures form the basis for defining histo-compatibility antigens: the mixed lymphocyte (proliferative) reaction (MLR), and the generation of cytotoxic lymphocytes (cell-mediated lympholysis: CML) are two such methods used for the detection of cell-surface antigens. Antigens detected by these assays are known as lymphocyte-defined (LD) antigens.

#### III.3.1 *Mixed Lymphocyte Reaction (MLR)*

The proliferative response in mixed lymphocyte culture was for a long time thought to be due to the same determinants as the SD major histocompatibility antigens, but cells from SD identical un-related individuals stimulate each other in culture, as do some SD identical sibling pairs. This led to the suggestion that the response in the MLR is governed by a locus apart from the SD antigen genes, and subsequent discovery of recombinant human families supported this concept (Eisvoogel *et al.*, 1972).

One of the cell populations in the MLR is frequently inhibited from division by prior treatment with mitomycin or irradiation. This is called a one-way MLR.

#### III.3.2 *Cell-mediated Lympholysis (CML)*

In the CML test, the effector cells are derived from a mixed lym-phocyte culture several days after the start. The $^{51}$Cr-labelled target cells carry histocompatibility antigens and are either trans-formed cells or tumour cells. In the presence of effector cells, the target cells are lysed and the released isotope is assayed.

As described in Chapter 17, neither the MLR nor the CML re-actions really provide good *in vitro* models for grafting reactions, nor do they accurately predict allograft survival.

### III.3.3 The distinction between SD and LD antigens

Antisera are now being found which recognize determinants involved in the cell-mediated reactions, including some which inhibit the MLR. Consequently, the distinction between the two classes of antigens is breaking down and, although it provides a convenient shorthand notation, this should not be permitted to interfere with a clear understanding that the distinctions are of little or no real significance.

# Chapter 15
# The Major Histocompatibility System

# S. Bright and A. Munro

## 15.1 Introduction

Both mice and men have one genetic region which has a pre-dominant influence on the survival of grafts. These major histocompatibility systems (MHS), *H-2* in mice and HLA in man, have many features in common. The work with mice has made much use of inbred strains and recombinants constructed between these strains. On the other hand, the human population is essentially outbred and consequently the methods used and type of data obtained differs with the two species. This has led to differences in the descriptions of the two systems.

## 15.2 The *H-2* Complex

The major mouse histocompatibility gene complex is called *H-2*. It is a complex of closely linked genes responsible for the rapid rejection of skin grafts, graft versus host reactions and other immunological phenomena. The presence of differences in the *H-2* region between strains of mice can be demonstrated serologically both by the use of alloantibody to agglutinate red cells and to cause the complement-mediated lysis of lymphocytes. The *H-2* complex is in the 9th linkage group (17th chromosome). The genes of the *H-2* complex carried on an individual chromosome form an *H-2* haplotype.

At least 26 other loci involved in histocompatibility have been reported, and there are probably considerably more. These non-*H-2* genes are called *H-1*, *H-3*, *H-4* and so on. If two strains differ by only a single locus other than *H-2*, the mean survival time for skin grafts is longer, often considerably longer, than that seen for an *H-2* difference. On the other hand, it would be wrong to think that these minor mouse histocompatibility loci are not important in a transplantation situation, as an accumulation of differences in several minor *H* loci will lead to rejection of skin as rapidly as a difference at the major *H-2* complex (Graff & Bailey, 1973).

228

## 15.2.1 The H-2 Map

The structure of the *H-2* complex has been unravelled by serological analysis using alloantibody raised between different inbred strains and tested on cells from a panel of mouse strains, including recombinants between strains of known alloantigenic status. Although each *H-2* haplotype contains a large number of different antigenic determinants, for simplicity, each haplotype is designated by a letter or combination of letters, for example: $H$-$2^a$, $H$-$2^b$, etc. It is now generally accepted that each *H-2* haplotype consists of four regions (K, I, Ss-Slp and D). The basic gene map is shown in Fig. 15.1, with the centromere to the left.

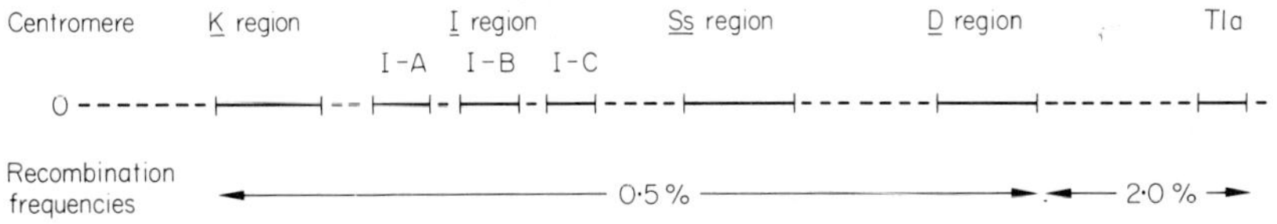

Fig. 15.1. Basic gene map of major histocompatibility complex in mice (*H-2*). Further I subregions are being defined.

## 15.3 K and D regions

The gene products of the K and D regions are detected serologically and are found on most cell types including lymphocytes, although their concentration may vary on different cell types (e.g. red blood cells have less *H-2* antigen than other tissues). Some alloantibodies react with cells other than the cells carrying the same haplotype as the cells used for immunization. Analysis of anti-*H-2* antisera by absorption tests using strains with different *H-2* haplotypes led to the definition of an *H-2* antigenic specificity as a pattern of reaction with a standard panel of inbred strains. In each case an antiserum behaves monospecifically when tested on the standard panel. This definition of an antigenic specificity is purely serological and the correlation to an antigenic determinant need not be straightforward. For example, the D region product of $H$-$2^d$ reacts with at least ten different antisera. This may present ten different antigenic determinants or, at the other extreme, a single reactive site capable of evoking an antibody response and of reacting with a variety of different antisera. The antigenic determinants defined in this way were given a number and Table 15.1 shows the distribution of the antigenic determinants found on the K and D regions of *H-2* haplotypes of different origin. Other haplotypes are known or thought to have been derived by recombination.

From Table 15.1, it will be seen that the antigenic determinants fall into three classes:

1. Those which are unique for a particular haplotype. These are known as the Private antigens.

**Table 15.1.** *H-2* Antigenic specificities amongst the *H-2* Haplotypes in mice

| H-2 haplotype | Public (H-2K Region) | | | | | | | | | | | | | | | | | | | | | Private | | | | | | | | | | |
|---|---|---|---|---|---|---|---|---|---|---|---|---|---|---|---|---|---|---|---|---|---|---|---|---|---|---|---|---|---|---|---|---|
| | Shared with D | | | | | | | Unique for K | | | | | | | | | | | | | | | | | | | | | | | | |
| | 1 | 3 | 5 | 28 | 35 | 36 | 42 | 7 | 8 | 11 | 25 | 34 | 37 | 38 | 39 | 46 | 47 | 51 | 52 | 53 | 54 | 9 | 15 | 16 | 17 | 18 | 19 | 20 | 21 | 23 | 31 | 33 |
| b | - | - | 5 | 28 | 35 | 36 | - | - | - | - | - | - | - | - | 39 | 46 | - | - | - | 53 | 54 | - | - | - | - | - | - | - | - | - | - | 33 |
| d | - | 3 | - | 28 | 35 | 36 | 42 | - | 8 | - | - | 34 | - | - | - | 46 | 47 | - | - | - | - | - | - | - | - | - | - | - | - | - | 31 | - |
| f | - | - | - | 28 | - | - | - | 7 | 8 | - | - | - | 37 | - | 39 | 46 | - | - | - | 53 | - | 9 | - | - | - | - | - | - | - | - | - | - |
| j | - | - | - | 28 | - | - | - | - | 8 | 11 | 25 | - | - | 38 | - | 46 | 47 | 51 | - | - | - | - | 15 | - | - | - | - | - | - | - | - | - |
| k | 1 | 3 | 5 | - | - | - | - | - | 8 | 11 | 25 | 34 | 37 | - | - | 46 | 47 | - | 52 | - | - | - | - | - | - | - | - | - | - | 23 | - | - |
| p | 1 | 3 | 5 | - | 35 | - | - | 7 | 8 | 11 | - | 34 | 37 | 38 | - | 46 | - | - | - | - | - | - | - | 16 | - | - | - | - | - | - | - | - |
| q | 1 | 3 | 5 | 28 | - | - | - | - | - | - | - | 34 | - | - | - | - | - | - | 52 | - | 54 | - | - | - | 17 | - | - | - | - | - | - | - |
| r | 1 | 3 | 5 | - | - | - | - | 7 | 8 | 11 | 25 | - | - | - | - | - | 47 | - | 52 | - | 54 | - | - | - | - | 18 | - | - | - | - | - | - |
| s | 1 | 3 | 5 | 28 | - | 36 | 42 | 7 | - | - | - | - | - | - | - | - | 47 | 51 | - | - | - | - | - | - | - | - | 19 | - | - | - | - | - |
| v | 1 | 3 | 5 | 28 | - | - | - | - | - | - | - | - | - | - | - | - | - | - | - | - | - | - | - | - | - | - | - | - | 21 | - | - | - |

**Table 15.1** (*cont.*)

| H-2 haplotype | Public | | | | | | | | | | | | | | Private | | | | | Unassigned | | | | |
|---|---|---|---|---|---|---|---|---|---|---|---|---|---|---|---|---|---|---|---|---|---|---|---|---|
| | Shared with K | | | | | | | Unique for D | | | | | | | | | | | | | | | | |
| | 1, | 3, | 5, | 28, | 35, | 36, | 42 | 6, | 13, | 41, | 43, | 44, | 55, | 56 | 2, | 4, | 12, | 30, | 32 | 10, | 14, | 40, | 45, | 49 |
| b | - | - | 5, | 28, | 35, | 36 | - | 6, | - | - | - | - | - | 56 | 2 | - | - | - | - | - | 14 | - | - | - |
| d | - | 3 | - | 28, | 35, | 36, | 42 | 6, | 13 | 41, | 43, | 44 | - | - | - | 4 | - | - | - | 10, | 14, | 40 | - | 49 |
| f | - | - | - | 28 | . | . | . | 6 | - | - | . | - | - | - | - | - | - | - | - | - | - | - | - | - |
| j | - | - | - | 28 | . | . | . | 6 | - | . | . | 44 | - | 56 | 2 | - | - | - | 32 | - | - | - | 45 | 49 |
| k | 1, | 3, | 5 | - | - | - | - | - | - | - | . | - | - | - | - | - | - | - | - | - | - | - | 45, | 49 |
| p | 1, | 3, | 5 | - | 35 | - | - | 6 | - | 41 | - | - | - | - | - | - | - | - | - | 10? | - | - | - | 49 |
| q | 1, | 3, | 5, | 28 | - | - | - | 6, | 13 | - | - | - | 55, | 56 | - | - | - | 30 | - | - | - | - | 45, | 49 |
| r | 1, | 3, | 5 | - | - | - | - | 6 | - | - | - | - | - | - | - | - | 12 | - | - | - | - | - | 45, | 49 |
| s | 1, | 3, | 5, | 28 | - | 36, | 42 | 6 | - | - | - | - | - | - | - | - | 12 | - | - | - | - | - | 45, | 49 |
| v | 1, | 3, | 5, | 28 | - | - | - | . | - | - | 43 | . | 55 | - | - | - | - | 30 | - | . | . | . | 45? | . |

- = not present

. = not tested

Data from Snell *et al.* (1973), Demant (1973), and Klein (1975).

2. Public antigens which are shared between different haplotypes but are still unique for K or D regions (e.g. 39, 46, 44, 56).

3. Public antigens which are shared between the K and D regions. These are the determinants 1, 3, 5, 28, 36 and 42.

4. There are also a number of specificities which are, as yet unassigned to either the K or D regions.

## 15.4 The *I* region

### 15.4.1 The Ia antigens

The *I* region has been divided into three subregions: *I–A*, *I–B* and *I–C*. Each region is associated with particular antigenic determin-

Table 15.2.

Ia Map

| *I–A* | *I–B* | *I–C* |
|---|---|---|
| 1    9 | | 6 |
| 2    11 | | 7 |
| 8    W20 | | W21 |

| | | |
|---|---|---|
| 3    13 | | |
| 4    15 | | |
| 5    17 | | |
| 12    18 | | |

| | | |
|---|---|---|
| | 10    16 | |
| | 14    19 | |

Ia specificities in independent haplotypes

| Strain | H-2 type | 1 | 2 | 3 | 4 | 5 | 6 | 7 | 8 | 9 | 10 | 11 | 12 | 13 | 14 | 15 | 16 | 17 | 18 | 19 | W20 | W21 |
|---|---|---|---|---|---|---|---|---|---|---|---|---|---|---|---|---|---|---|---|---|---|---|
| C57B1/10 | b | – | – | 3 | – | – | – | – | 8 | 9 | – | – | – | – | – | 15 | – | – | – | – | W20 | – |
| B10.D2 | d | – | – | – | – | – | 6 | 7 | 8 | – | – | 11 | – | – | – | 15 | 16 | – | – | – | – | – |
| B10.M | f | 1 | – | – | – | 5 | – | – | – | – | – | – | – | – | 14 | – | – | 17 | 18 | – | – | – |
| B10.K | k | 1 | 2 | 3 | – | – | – | 7 | – | – | – | – | – | – | – | 15 | – | 17 | 18 | 19 | – | – |
| B10.P | p | – | – | – | – | 5 | 6 | 7 | – | – | – | – | – | 13 | – | – | – | – | – | – | – | W21 |
| B10.G | q | – | – | 3 | – | 5 | – | – | – | 9 | 10 | – | – | 13 | – | – | 16 | – | – | – | – | – |
| B10.R111 | r | 1 | – | 3 | – | 5 | – | 7 | – | – | – | – | 12 | – | – | – | – | 17 | – | 19 | – | – |
| B10.S | s | – | – | – | 4 | 5 | – | – | – | 9 | – | – | 12 | – | – | – | – | 17 | 18 | – | – | – |

Distribution and gene map of *Ia* antigen specificities in the *I* region of various independent *H-2* haplotypes. (Data from Shreffler *et al.*, 1976.)

ants found predominantly on B rather than T lymphocytes. They are known as the Ia antigens, and are also found on certain other cells, notably epidermal cells, macrophages and sperm but not on red cells. The discovery and characterization of the Ia antigens is very recent and has been made possible by the construction of strains which are recombinant in this region of the *H-2* complex (McDevitt *et al.*, 1974). Table 15.2 shows the distribution of the Ia

*Section III: Immunogenetics*

antigens amongst the different *H-2* haplotypes and their assignment to the different subregions of the *I* region. It seems likely that more Ia antigens will be discovered and that certain public specificities in the *H-2K* region may turn out to be Ia antigens. It is already known that Ia7 is identical with 47 in the *K* region.

### 15.4.2 *Immune response genes*

Genes controlling the response to specific antigens are known as the *Ir* genes and are located in the *I-A* and *I-B* subregions and, recently, in the *I-C* subregion. The *Ir* genes are discussed in greater detail in Chapter 16. Although the *Ir* genes map in the same subregions as the *Ia* specificities, there is no correlation between the *Ia* specificity and immune responsiveness. This suggests that the *Ia* determinants are either on different molecules to the *Ir* gene products, or if on the same molecules, then not a part involved in the specificity of the *Ir* gene-controlled responses.

## 15.5 The Ss-Slp region

This region controls the level and probably allotypic determinants on a serum $\beta$-globulin which is thought to be involved in the complement system (Demant *et al.*, 1973). Since C2 and factor B seem to be linked to HLA it is possible that some complement components are coded within the Ss region. There is now evidence that Ss is C4 (Lachmann *et al.*, 1975).

## 16. The Tla region

This region lies outside the *H-2* complex and will not be discussed here. It codes for the TL antigen found only on cells in the thymus and leukaemic T cells (see Chapter 7).

## 15.7 The human major histocompatibility system

In man, one genetic region located on chromosome 6 is thought to control the major histocompatibility determinants. Siblings identical for this region can exchange and accept grafts much more readily than non-identical siblings. Fig. 15.2 shows the arrangement of some of the genes in this region. As in the mouse there are minor loci which can have an influence on histocompatibility.

## 15.8 HLA system

The HLA antigens were first discovered by the use of antisera

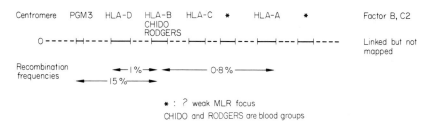

Centromere    PGM3    HLA-D    HLA-B    HLA-C    *    HLA-A    *         Factor B, C2
                                CHIDO
                                RODGERS

O ----H---- |---- |-- |--- |-- |--- |--- |---- |----    Linked but not
                                                                          mapped

Recombination                   ◄─1%─►  ◄────── 0·8% ──────►
frequencies         ◄──── 15% ────►

* :  ? weak MLR focus
CHIDO and RODGERS are blood groups

**Fig. 15.2.** Basic gene map of major histocompatibility in man (HLA).

**Table 15.3.** HLA antigens: their cross reactions and gene frequencies

| HLA-A | Gene frequency | | HLA-B | Gene frequency | | HLA-C | Gene frequency | HLA-D | Gene frequency |
|---|---|---|---|---|---|---|---|---|---|
| Antigen | a | b | Antigen | a | b | Antigen | | Antigen | |
| A1 | 0·18 | 0·19 | B5 | 0·04 | 0·03 | CW1 | 0·034 | DW1 | 0·102 |
| A3 | 0·14 | 0·19 | BW35 | 0·03 | 0·08 | CW2 | 0·065 | DW2 | 0·078 |
| A11 | 0·07 | 0·05 | BW15 | 0·05 | 0·07 | CW3 | 0·193 | DW3 | 0·085 |
| A2 | 0·29 | 0·23 | BW21 | 0·02 | 0·01 | (Scandinavians) | | DW4 | 0·082 |
| A28 | 0·05 | 0·05 | B7 | 0·17 | 0·16 | CW4 | 0·137 | DW5 | 0·075 |
| AW23 }A9 | 0·01 | 0·03 | BW22 | 0·03 | 0·03 | CW5 | 0·057 | DW6 | 0·054 |
| AW24 } | 0·07 | 0·05 | B27 | 0·04 | 0·01 | | | | |
| AW25 }A10 | 0·02 | 0·01 | B8 | 0·13 | 0·16 | | | | |
| AW26 } | 0·01 | 0·05 | B14 | 0·05 | 0·03 | | | | |
| A29 | 0·06 | 0·02 | B12 | 0·18 | 0·15 | | | | |
| AW30 | 0 | 0·02 | B13 | 0·01 | 0·02 | | | | |
| AW31 | 0 | 0·03 | BW40 | 0·08 | 0·09 | | | | |
| AW32 | 0·02 | 0·03 | BW17 | 0·05 | 0·04 | | | | |
| AW33 | 0·04 | 0·02 | B18 | 0·01 | 0·05 | | | | |
| Blank | 0·04 | 0·03 | BW37 | 0·02 | | | | | |
| AW34 | Malays | | BW38 }BW16 | 0·04 | 0·05 | | | | |
| AW36 } | { African | | BW39 } | | | | | | |
| AW43 } | { Blacks | | BW41 | (very low in | | | | | |
| | | | | Caucasians) | | | | | |
| | | | BW42 | African Blacks | | | | | |

a and b refer to gene frequencies reported at the 1972 Histocompatibility Workshop for two independent English populations. Data also from Histocompatability Testing, 1975.

[ = Serological cross reactivity.

W designation indicates fairly well characterized antigen which awaits confirmation. The columns of the table are independent and do *not* indicate common haplotypes.

See Appendix C for former nomenclature.

*Section III: Immunogenetics*

produced in multigravid women, polytransfused patients, and transplant recipients, and tested in agglutination and cytotoxicity assays on white blood cells. When the antisera were grouped according to their reaction patterns, it was found that certain groups seemed to detect alleles. They were, therefore, said to define the HLA antigens which were subsequently given numbers. At first, only two segregant series of antigens were discovered, HLA-A and HLA-B (see Appendix C), but the discovery of antisera with discordant reaction patterns suggests the existence of a third locus (HLA-C).

Fig. 15.2 shows the position of these three HLA (SD) loci. As they are closely linked loci, alleles are usually inherited 'en bloc' as haplotypes, but in family studies, rare recombinants between the loci have been observed.

### 15.8.1 HLA antigens

The HLA antigens currently recognized in a Caucasian population are shown in Table 15.3. Studies on determining the alleles at the third locus have only recently begun, and few have been described. It is probable that the lists of alleles at the first and second loci are not yet complete.

It should be emphasized that many antisera occur which do not precisely define an allele and although these may be mixtures of specificities they may also be antisera cross-reacting with more than one allele. Many antisera show that there is extensive cross-reactivity within, but probably not between the HLA-A and HLA-B locus antigens. Some major cross-reacting groups are shown in Table 15.3 and recent studies have indicated that cross-reactivity between antigens can be much more extensive than this (Mittal & Terasaki, 1974).

Some of this cross-reactivity in the HLA system suggests that antigens may have common antigenic determinants analogous to the public specificities of the mouse *H-2* system. If this is the case, it would be better to describe the HLA antigens as a series of numbered determinants like the *H-2* antigens, rather than as 'one name alleles'.

## 15.9 Special features of HLA genetics

### 15.9.1 Extent of polymorphism

A feature of the HLA system is the large number of alleles at each locus, most with low gene frequencies (Table 15.3). Bodmer (1972) has emphasized that this balanced polymorphism must be due to some selective pressure acting now, or which has acted in the past, on the HLA or closely-linked genes, to discourage homozygosity.

### 15.9.2 Linkage disequilibrium

In a random breeding population which has reached equilibrium, the frequency with which a particular pair of alleles at different loci segregate together will be the product of the frequencies of the two alleles. Thus, if allele A occurs with a frequency of 0·05 and allele B with a frequency of 0·2, then A and B will occur together with a frequency $(0·05 \times 0·2) = 0·01$. This holds true for the population irrespective of whether the loci for A and B are linked or unlinked. In a population which has reached true equilibrium, linked alleles will be randomly distributed through the populations as a result of past recombinations.

When the actual frequency of a pair of alleles at linked loci is larger or smaller than the product of the frequencies of the two individual alleles, then the alleles are said to be in linkage disequilibrium. This may reflect a system which has not yet come to equilibrium as insufficient time has elapsed since the origin of the alleles to ensure random mixing of linked genes. Alternatively, in a system which has reached equilibrium, natural selection may be acting in favour of or against particular combinations of alleles.

Human populations seem to be approximately in genetic equilibrium for HLA genes but a few pairs of HLA alleles show linkage disequilibrium. In Caucasian populations, the combinations A1 with B8, A3 with B7 and A2 with B12 occur more frequently as pairs than would be expected from the frequency of the individual alleles. It may also be relevant that these are the three commonest haplotypes in these populations. It has been suggested that individuals carrying one of these pairs of antigenic specificities have, or have had, some selective advantage. Linkage disequilibrium has not only been observed between alleles of HLA-A and HLA-B, but also between alleles of HLA-B and HLA-C and between the SD loci and other loci in the MHS. The existence of linkage disequilibrium is important in understanding the association of HLA antigens and disease, as discussed in Chapter 18.

## 15.10 The MHS gene products

### 15.10.1 The biochemistry of the H-2 and HLA gene products

The biochemistry of the $K$ and $D$ region products of $H-2$ has been approached by labelling cells with radioactive amino acids or fucose. Membrane extracts are then prepared, and the $K$ and $D$ region products isolated by the addition of appropriate alloantisera, followed by anti-mouse immunoglobulin to precipitate the complexes. A similar process has been used in the isolation of the HLA gene products.

The precipitates are dissolved and analysed on SDS polyacrylamide gel, following reduction. In this way it has been shown that the $D$ region product has an apparent molecular weight of 43,000, while that of the $K$ region product is 47,000 (Schwarz et al., 1973). In humans, the HLA determinants are carried on a glycopeptide of about 44,000 molecular weight (Springer et al., 1974). Sequence studies on N-terminal fragments of HLA and $H$-$2$ antigens show that the HLA-A and B locus products are closely related. Similarly, the $H$-$2D$ and $K$ region antigens are closely related to each other. They are also related to HLA-A and B, but the homology between the different human and murine antigens is greater within a species than between species. For speculation on the significance of this finding, see Silver and Hood, 1976.

Both the $H$-$2$ and HLA gene products are associated with a 12,000 m.w. glycoprotein, which in man is $\beta_2$ microglobulin (Silver & Hood, 1974; Springer et al., 1974) a protein showing some homology to the immunoglobulin domains.

There is some evidence that the HLA determinants are due to differences in the amino acid composition of the large glycoprotein, and not to some more trivial component such as carbohydrate.

### 15.10.2 The biochemistry of the Ia gene product

The product of the $Ia$ genes is isolated as a glycoprotein composed of two polypeptide chains of 33,000 and 28,000 molecular weight. The products of the three $I$ subregions may be a structurally related family of molecules.

### 15.10.3 Arrangement of MHS products on the cell surface

It is of some interest to know if the 45,000 m.w. and 12,000 m.w. glycoproteins which are associated in the isolated material from cells are also associated in the membranes of the living cell. Similarly, it is interesting to know if the different surface structures coded by the MHS gene complex are also associated or separate. These possibilities are readily studied by 'capping' experiments using labelled specific antisera, and these clearly show that $\beta_2$ microglobulin is associated in the membrane with the large glycoprotein carrying the HLA alloantigens. However, the $K$ region and $D$ region or first, second and third locus HLA gene products move independently (Neuport-Sautes et al., 1973, 1974).

### References

BACH F.H., BACH M.L., SONDEL P.M. & SUNDHARADAS G. (1972) Genetic control of mixed lymphocyte culture. Transplant. Rev. 12, 30.

BODMER W.F. (1972) Evolutionary significance of the HL-A system. Nature (Lond.) 237, 139.

CULLEN S.E., DAVID D.C., SHREFFLER D.C. & NATHENSON S.G. (1974)

Membrane molecules determined by the H-2 associated immune response region: Isolation and some properties. *Proc. Nat. Acad. Sci. (Wash.)* **71**, 648.

DÉMANT P. (1973) H-2 gene complex and its role in alloimmune reactions. *Transplant. Rev.* **15**, 162.

DÉMANT P., CAPKOVÁ J., HINZOVÁ E. & VORÁCOVÁ B. (1973) The role of the histocompatibility-2-linked Ss-Slp region in the control of mouse complement. *Proc. Nat. Acad. Sci. (Wash.)* **70**, 863.

GRAFF R.J. & BAILEY D.W. (1973) The Non-H-2 Histocompatibility Loci and their Antigens. *Transplant. Rev.* **15**, 26.

KLEIN J. (1975) *Biology of the mouse histocompatibility-2 complex.* Spinger-Verlag, Berlin.

LACHMANN P.J., GRENNAN D., MARTIN A.M. & DEMANT P. (1975)·Identification of Ss protein as murine C4. *Nature, Lond.* **258**, 242.

MITTAL K.M. & TERASAKI P.I. (1974) Serological cross reactivity in the HL-A system. *Tissue antigens* **4**, 146.

NEAUPORT-SAUTES C., LILLEY F., SILVESTRE D. & KORILISKY F.M. (1973) Independence of H-2K and H-2D antigenic determinants on the surface of mouse lymphocytes. *J. exp. Med.* **137**, 511.

NEAUPORT-SAUTES C., BESMUTH A., KOURILSKY F.M. & MANUEL Y. (1974) Relationship between HL-A antigens and $\beta_2$-microglobulin as studied in immunofluorescence on the lymphocyte membrane. *J. exp. Med.* **139**, 957.

SCHWARTZ B., KATO K., CULLEN S. & NATHENSON S. (1973) H-2 histocompatibility alloantigens. Some biochemical properties of the molecules. *Biochemistry* **12**, 2157.

SHREFFLER D.C., MEO T. & DAVID C.S. (1976) Genetic resolution of the products and functions of the *I* & *S* region genes of the mouse *H-2* complex. In KATZ & BENACERRAF: *The role of the products of the major histocompatibility complex in immune responses.* Academic Press, New York. p. 3.

SILVER J. & HOOD L. (1974) Detergent-solubilised H-2 alloantigen is associated with a small molecular weight polypeptide. *Nature (Lond.)* **249**, 764.

SILVER J. & HOOD L. (1976) Preliminary amino acid sequences of transplantation antigens: genetic and evolutionary implications. *Cont. Tropics Molec. Immunol.* in press.

SNELL G.D., CHERRY M. & DÉMANT P. (1973) H-2: Its structure and similarity to HL-A. *Transplant. Rev.* **15**, 3.

SPRINGER T.A., STROMINGER J.L. & MANN D. (1974) Partial purification of detergent soluble HL-A antigen and its cleavage by papain. *Proc. Natl. Acad. Sci. (Wash.)* **71**, 139.

*Section III: Immunogenetics*

# Chapter 16
# The Genetic Control of Immune Responses

# A. J. Munro

## 16.1 Introduction

There are a variety of genes which are responsible for the control of the quantity and specificity of immune responses. They are known as immune response or Ir genes and act in various ways. For example, there are genes which control the mechanisms of antigen handling and affect the overall level of responses in a non-specific way. Genes which effect the response to specific antigens fall into two groups: those linked to the Ig constant region genes and those associated with the major histocompatibility system. The former are probably V-genes, and represent inheritable idiotypes, showing great antigen specificity, while the latter, H-linked *Ir* genes, are the principal subject of the chapter.

## 16.2 Genes controlling the overall level of antibody responses

Genetic control of the overall level of the response has been shown to occur in mice. Biozzi *et al.* (1972) immunized outbred mice with sheep erythrocytes and selected those which responded well and those which responded poorly. By selective mating, but not inbreeding, within each of the two groups for about twenty generations, two lines of mice were eventually developed: a 'high responder' line whose agglutinin titres were of the order of 1:10,000 to a standard antigen dose, and a 'low responder' line whose titres were about 1:40 (Fig. 16.1). This difference in responsiveness is not antigen-specific and the two lines respond well or poorly to a variety of antigens. Analysis of the distribution of responsiveness in interstrain $F_1$ hybrids and their backcrosses has indicated that the differences in antibody responses are under the control of about 8 to 10 different loci whose cumulative effect gives rise to the character being selected for. There is now data to suggest that one or more of the loci control antigen handling by macrophages (Wiener & Bandieri, 1974). The macrophages of the low-responder strain have been shown to be more active and to degrade antigen more readily than those of the high-responder strain (Table 16.1). It is probable that antigen is more readily rendered non-immunogenic in the low-responder line, compared to the high-responder line, giving rise to a larger antibody response. It is not known whether the hyper-reactivity of the macrophages of the low-responder line is related to increased release of macrophage-activating lymphokines by T lymphocytes (see Chapter 12).

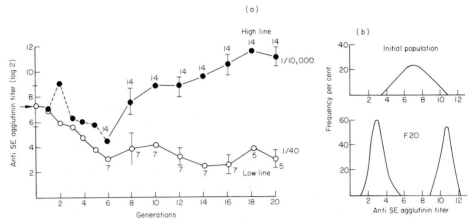

**Fig. 16.1.** (A) Separation of 'high'- and 'low'-responder mice in the course of selective breeding. The day of maximum agglutinin titre is shown for each generation. (B) Frequency distribution of agglutinin titres in mice of the initial population and in $F_{20}$ mice of the high- and low-responder lines.

SE = Sheep erythrocytes

(From Biozzi *et al.*, 1972.)

**Table 16.1.**

| Macrophage function | Ab/L | Ab/H |
|---|---|---|
| 1. Antigen uptake | +++ | + |
| 2. Lysosomal enzyme activity | +++ | + |
| 3. Intracellular degradation of antigen | +++ | + |
| 4. Surface persistence of antigen | + | +++ |

Antigen handling by peritoneal macrophages in Biozzi high (Ab/H) and low (Ab/L) responder mice. (Weiner & Bandieri, 1974.)

## 16.3 Immunoglobulin-linked immune response genes

A number of systems have been described in which the capacity of mice or rabbits to respond to antigens is related to their inheritance of genes in the clusters coding for the immunoglobulins. These response differences are peculiar in a number of respects:

(a) the antigens used are those which give rise to antibodies of

240

restricted heterogeneity or to a monoclonal response (Type C streptococcal polysaccharide, etc.).

(b) in the high responder animals, the antibodies are of restricted heterogeneity, many of them having the character of inheritable idiotypes (see Chapter 2).

(c) with varying degrees of certainty, both the capacity for response and the inheritable idiotypic markers can be shown to be genetically linked to the immunoglobulin allotypes.

The most reasonable hypothesis is that the capacity for response is associated with, if not identical to, the inheritance of V-region germ-line genes which code for the antibody.

## 16.4 The histocompatibility-linked immune response genes

Specific responses to some antigens have been shown to be under the control of autosomal dominant genes which are inherited in a strict Mendelian fashion and are linked to the major histocompatibility loci (McDevitt & Benacerraf, 1969).

### 16.4.1 Antigens to which the response is controlled

Specific *Ir* genes have been predominantly defined by measuring the immune response to a restricted antigenic challenge. To do this the antigens used are those with limited structural heterogeneity, for example, the synthetic polypeptides (T,G)-A--L, (Phe,G)-A--L, Poly-L-lysine (PLL), allogeneic antigens such as the immunoglobulin allotypes and low doses of heterologous protein antigens like bovine serum albumin, ovomucoid and lactate dehydrogenase.

The genetic control of the response to these antigens is seen in several species. Strain 2 guinea-pigs are responders to PLL and GA, whereas strain 13 animals are not. The reverse is true for GT. The response to a variety of synthetic polymers shows marked strain differences in mice (Table 16.2). The genetic control of immune responses is also now established in monkeys, rats and chickens.

### 16.4.2 Inheritance and arrangement of Ir genes

Ir genes are autosomal dominant or pseudo-dominant genes since the $F_1$ cross between high- and low-responder mice have the high-responder characteristic. Linkage of these genes to the *H-2* locus is clearly shown by backcross analysis of $F_1$ to parent, where the high- or low-responder characteristic segregates with the appropriate *H-2* type.

This was first recognized by McDevitt and Chinitz (1969) who showed that the response of mice to (T,G)-A--L, (Phe,G)-A--L and

**Table 16.2.** Strain distribution of response to antigens under *Ir* gene control in mice

| Antigen | *H-2* haplotype | | | | | |
|---|---|---|---|---|---|---|
| | $H\text{-}2^a$ | $H\text{-}2^d$ | $H\text{-}2^k$ | $H\text{-}2^q$ | $H\text{-}2^b$ | $H\text{-}2^n$ |
| (a) Synthetic polypeptides | | | | | | |
| (T,G)-A--L | − | − | − | − | + | − |
| (Phe,G)-A--L | + | + | + | + | + | − |
| (H,G)-A--L | + | − | + | − | − | − |
| (b) Allotypic antigens | | | | | | |
| IgA | + | − | + | − | − | + |
| IgG | − | − | − | − | + | + |

+ : high responder
− : low responder

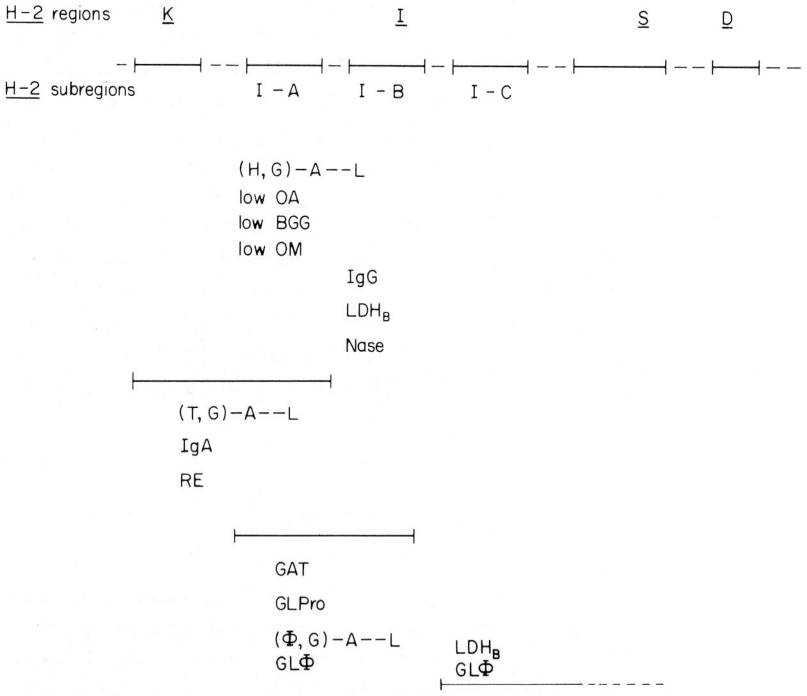


**Fig. 16.2.** Genetic mapping of the *Ir* genes within the *H-2* complex of the mouse. (From Benacerraf & Katz, 1976 adapted.)

(H,G)-A--L was strictly related to *H-2* status. This region was designated *Ir-1* and, as described in Chapter 15, we now recognize that it is part of a larger genetic region, located between the *K* end and the *Ss* region of the *H-2* complex. The *I* region is subdivided into the *I-A*, *I-B* and *I-C* subregions and, to date, most of the *Ir* genes have been found in the *I-A* and *I-B* subregions. Fig. 16.2 shows the present status of the *Ir* gene map within the *H-2* complex.

### 16.4.3 The number of Ir genes

It is important to know whether the *I* region is a single locus with multiple alleles or whether it contains several distinct loci. The clearest data on this is available for mice, where there are a large number of recombinant strains.

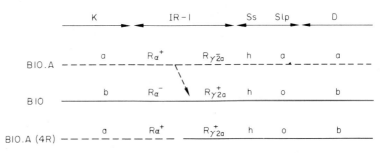

**Fig. 16.3.** Schematic representation of the *H-2* region of chromosomes from congenic mouse strains B10.A (*H-2$^a$*), B10(*H-2$^b$*) and B10.A(4R) (*H-2$^a$/H-2$^b$* crossover). K and D refer to the K and D regions of *H-2*, R$\alpha$ and R$\gamma$2a refer to the IR1 genes which control the response to IgA and IgG2a myeloma proteins from BALB/C mice. The pattern of response to IgA and IgG2a shows that the crossover in B10.A(4R) occurs between two IR-1 genes. (From Lieberman & Humphrey, 1972.)

Studies by Lieberman and Humphrey (1972) were the first to show that a recombinational event could take place within the *I* region, indicating that there are at least two *Ir* loci in the region. As shown in Fig. 16.3, B10 mice were low responders to the IgA allotype (*R$\alpha$*−) but high responders to the IgG2a allotype (*R$\gamma$2a*+). B10A mice, on the other hand, are high responders to the IgA allotype (*R$\alpha$*+) but low responders to IgG2a (*R$\gamma$2a*−). Strains of mice derived from these two parent strains which were recombinant in the *H-2* region were tested for their response to these two antigens. The B10A(4R) were found to be high responders for both. Thus, in the 4R strain, the recombinational event has taken place within the *I* region, showing that there are at least two immune response loci there. B10A(4R) is the strain of mouse which defines the distinction between *I-A* and *I-B*.

*Chapter 16: The Genetic Control of Immune Responses*

## 16.5 The significance of H-linked *Ir* genes

The failure to respond to an antigen does not necessarily mean the absence of a structural gene coding for the specificity. For example, a DNP-specific B cell will only respond to the hapten if it is properly presented, and failure to produce such a response does not necessarily mean absence of receptors specific for DNP. It would thus be unwise at this stage to say that mice which are unresponsive to certain antigens lack structural genes for that specificity. In fact, there is some evidence that there is no difference in the numbers of specific antigen-binding cells in unprimed high- and low-responder mice, indicating that the defect is not due to a specific failure to bind antigen.

The fact that *Ir* genes which control specific immune responses are linked to genes which determine the main histocompatibility antigens is of considerable significance because, in both mice and man, the genes coding for the kappa and heavy immunoglobulin chains are not linked to the major histocompatibility loci. This formally shows that the H-linked *Ir* genes are not the same as the genes coding for the immunoglobulins. They are distinct from the allotype-linked *Ir* genes, which are not linked to the MHS. H-linked genes either code for structures which constitute a new antigen recognition system or, alternatively, they code for cell-surface structures which interfere with the 'established' recognition system, which is antibody. If they do code for a new type of specific recognition system, it is important to define the cellular level of its expression.

## 16.6 The cellular level of expression of *Ir* genes

This is at present a controversial area where there is no general agreement, probably because the various experimental systems used to investigate the problem are not directly comparable. Since no definitive view can be presented at this moment, some background data will be briefly mentioned, but the bulk of the discussion will be devoted to the response of mice to (T,G)-A--L.

### 16.6.1 The response to PLL in guinea-pigs: evidence for expression of Ir genes by T-cells

The response to PLL in guinea-pigs seems to be controlled among the T cell population. Strain 2 (responder) animals give delayed hypersensitivity reactions and show helper activity to PLL, producing good titres of anti-DNP when challenged with DNP-PLL. Strain 13 (non-responder) animals do not show these responses, but will make anti-DNP in response to challenge with DNP-PLL-BSA conjugates (McDevitt & Benacerraf, 1969), see Table 16.3. In this case, BSA acts as an indirect carrier for DNP.

### 16.6.2 *The response to (T,G)-A--L: evidence for expression of* Ir *by T cells*

Studies in mice have shown that the response to (T,G)-A--L is T-dependent. As shown in Fig. 16.4, both responder and non-responder mice make similar amounts of IgM antibody to certain batches of (T,G)-A--L, but only responders make appreciable amounts of IgG

**Table 16.3.** Responses to PLL in guinea-pigs

| Response | Delayed hypersensitivity to PLL | | Anti-DNP | |
|---|---|---|---|---|
| | Strain 2 | Strain 13 | Strain 2 | Strain 13 |
| Antigen | | | | |
| PLL | + | − | | |
| DNP-PLL | + | − | + | − |
| DNP-PLL-BSA | + | − | + | + |
| DNP-PLL-BSA (G. pigs tolerant to BSA) | + | − | + | − |

Delayed hypersensitivity responses to PLL and anti-DNP responses to DNP-PLL in responder (strain 2) and non-responder (strain 13) guinea-pigs.

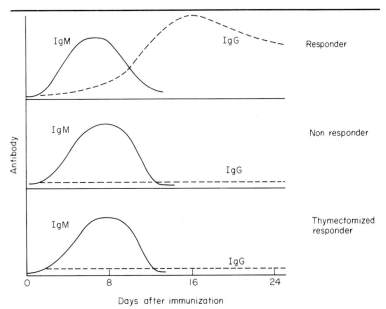

Fig. 16.4. Antibody production to (T,G)-A--L in responder, non-responder and thymectomized responder mice. (Data from Grumet *et al.*, 1971, and Mitchell *et al.*, 1972.)

*Chapter 16: The Genetic Control of Immune Responses*

antibody to this antigen. Thymectomized responders behave like non-responders, making no IgG antibody to (T,G)-A--L. This implies that the *Ir* gene is expressed on the T cell (Grumet *et al.*, 1971; Mitchell *et al.*, 1972). A further experiment which leads to similar conclusions, and which is in many ways very elegant, is the investigation of the responsiveness of tetraparental mice. These are constructed by the fusion of blastocysts from different mice, followed by transfer to pseudopregnant females. The mice which are eventually born carry the cells of both embryos (four parents). McDevitt *et al.* (1974) have constructed tetraparental mice from (T,G)-A--L high- and low-responder mice which also differed with respect to their immunoglobulin allotype. Different tetraparental mice differ in proportion of 'mix' in different tissues. However, after challenge with (T,G)-A--L the proportion of the two allotypes is the same in the anti-(T,G)-A--L antibody as in the rest of the mouse's serum, indicating that not only high- but also low-responder B cells can synthesize antibody to (T,G)-A--L. Thus, the defect in the low responders is not at the B cell level and it is suggested that it may be at the T cell level.

### 16.6.3 *The response to (T,G)-A--L: evidence for expression of* Ir *by B cells*

An obvious way to test whether (T,G)-A--L low responders lack T cells capable of recognizing (T,G)-A--L would be to assay the response of a mixture of low-responder T cells and high-responder B cells in the adoptive transfer system. This cannot be done, since high and low responders are not syngeneic and in a mixed cell transfer system the non-responder T cells will give a GVH reaction in the recipient mouse which non-specifically obviates the T cell requirement for B cell triggering (the allogeneic effect—see Chapter 9). This makes interpretation of the experiment impossible. The problem was overcome by the limiting dilution assay which measures the frequency of antigen-sensitive units in cell suspensions (Shearer *et al.*, 1972). The experiment is done by transferring graded or limiting numbers of spleen cells into syngeneic irradiated recipients which are then challenged with antigen. By plotting the number of cells transferred against the percentage of mice giving a positive response, an estimate of the number of antigen-sensitive units per inoculum can be derived (Fig. 16.5). If spleen is used as a source of cells, it is not possible to separately detect the frequency of antigen-sensitive T and B cells, since the spleen is a mixed population of these cells, and so separate populations have to be used. By transferring graded numbers of bone-marrow cells together with a constant excess of thymus cells, the number of antigen-sensitive bone-marrow cells can be counted, since in this case the B cells are limiting. Conversely, by transferring graded numbers of thymus cells with a constant excess of bone-marrow cells, the number of thymic antigen-sensitive cells can be assayed. This type

*Section III: Immunogenetics*

of approach was used to see if the defect in low-responder mice was at the T cell level. It was found that there was no difference in the dilution patterns between high- or low-responder T cells, but there was a difference for B cells. This indicates that the genetic defect in response to (T,G)-A--L is not entirely at the T cell level and is perhaps at the B-cell level. This data obviously conflicts with the earlier studies which claimed that the *Ir* gene controlled T cell recognition.

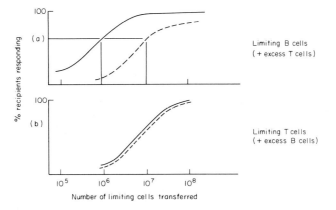

**Fig. 16.5.** Adoptive transfer of the response to (T,G)-Pro--L using limiting dilutions of thymus (T) and bone-marrow (B) cells from high (——) and low (– – –) responder mice. This experiment assays for (T,G)-Pro--L specific precursors in bone marrow (a) and thymus (b). Based on data from Sheare *et al.*, 1972.)

An alternative approach to the use of cell populations is to assay specific soluble T-cell factor produced by cells from high- and low-responder mice. Taussig *et al.* (1974) have shown that (T,G)-A--L educated spleen cells release an antigen-specific factor after *in vitro* challenge with antigen. This factor substitutes for specific T cells and is not an immunoglobulin (Chapter 9). However, (T,G)-A--L high- and low-responder mice produce equal amounts of this factor, an unexpected result if the defect is at the T cell level. *In vivo* the factor cooperates with high-responder B cells, but fails to cooperate with low-responder B cells. This suggests that the defect is at the B cell level.

There is now good evidence that the *Ir* genes contribute to two molecular systems: the specific antigen receptor on T cells and an acceptor molecule on B cells (or macrophages) for T cell cooperating factor. A low responder mouse can lack either or both classes of gene. Some low responder strains make T cell factor but not B cell acceptor. Others have the B cell acceptor, but cannot make factor (Munro and Taussig, 1975). This could explain the fact that $F_1$s between some non-responder strains are responders, which is the case for a number of antigens where the response is *Ir* gene controlled.

## 16.7 Conclusion

There are other possible explanations for the action of *Ir* genes and it is not clear whether the failure to respond is due, in some cases, to tolerance or to the presence of suppressor T cells. In at least one *Ir*-gene controlled response, the latter has been shown to operate.

## References

BENACERRAF B. & KATZ D.H. (1975) The histocompatability-linked immune response genes. *Adv. Cancer Res.* **21**, 121.

BIOZZI G., STIFFEL C., MOUTON D., BOUTHILLIER Y. & DECREUSFOND C. (1972) Cytodynamics of the immune response in two lines of mice genetically selected for 'high' and 'low' antibody synthesis. *J. exp. Med.* **135**, 1071.

GASSER P.L. & SILVERS W.K. (1974) Genetic determinants of immunological responsiveness. *Adv. Immunol.* **18**, 1.

GRUMET F.C., MITCHELL G.F. & McDEVITT H.O. (1971) Genetic control of specific immune responses in inbred mice. *Ann. N.Y. Acad. Sci.* **190**, 170.

LIEBERMAN R. & HUMPHREY W. (1972) Association of *H-2* types with genetic control of immune responsiveness to IgG (γ2a) allotypes in the mouse. *J. exp. Med.* **136**, 1222.

McDEVITT H.O. & BENACERRAF B. (1969) Genetic control of specific immune responses. *Adv. Immunol.* **11**, 31.

McDEVITT H.O. & CHINITZ A. (1969) Genetic control of the antibody responses: relationship between immune response and histocompatibility (H-2) type. *Science* **163**, 1207.

MILSTEIN C. & MUNRO A.J. (1973) Genetics of Immunoglobulins and of the Immune Response. In PORTER R.R. *Defence and Recognition.* M.T.P. & Butterworths, London.

MITCHELL G.F., GRUMET F.C. & McDEVITT H.O. (1972) Genetic control of the immune response. The effect of thymectomy on the primary and secondary antibody responses of mice to Poly-L (Tyr,Glu)-, poly-D, L-Ala-, -poly-L-Lys. *J. exp. Med.* **135**, 126.

MUNRO A.J., TAUSSIG M.J., CAMPBELL R., WILLIAMS H. & LAWSON Y. (1974) Antigen-specific T-cell factor in cell cooperation: physical properties and mapping in the left hand (*K*) half of *H-2*. *J. exp. Med.* **140**, 1579.

MUNRO A.J. & TAUSSIG M.J. (1975) Two genes in the major histocompatibility complex control immune response. *Nature (Lond.)* **256**, 103.

SHEARER G.M., MOZES E. & SELA M. (1972) Contribution of different cell types to the genetic control of immune responses as a function of the chemical nature of the polymeric side chains (poly-L-prolyl and poly-D, L-alanyl) of synthetic immunogens. *J. exp. Med.* **135**, 1009.

TAUSSIG M.J., MOZES E. & ISAC R. (1974) Antigen-specific thymus cell factors in the genetic control of the immune response to poly-(tyrosyl, glutamyl)-poly-D,L-alynyl--poly-lysyl. *J. exp. Med.* **140**, 301.

WEINER E. & BANDIERI A. (1974) Differences in antigen handling by peritoneal macrophages from the Biozzi high and low responder lines of mice. *Eur. J. Immunol.* **4**, 457.

*Section III: Immunogenetics*

# Chapter 17
# The Genetic Basis of Cell-mediated Reactions

## H. Festenstein and P. Démant

### 17.1 Introduction

Cell-mediated immune reactions are characterized by a series of *in vivo* and *in vitro* phenomena such as graft-rejection, graft-versus-host reactions and mixed lymphocyte reactions. This chapter will describe the genetic basis of some of these phenomena.

It is important to remember that most of the arguments in this chapter derive from genetic experiments involving recombinant analysis and do not speak to the molecular nature of the gene product. In most cases, it will be assumed that responses are due to gene products behaving as antigens, but it is important to bear in mind that in some cases the gene could equally well be an *Ir* gene which controls responses.

### 17.2 Genes controlling lymphocyte activating determinants (Lads)

The determinants now classified operationally as lymphocyte activating determinants (Lads), were previously known as LD determinants. They are detected by the proliferation of lymphocytes in a one-way MLR.

#### 17.2.1 Lads in man

In man there are two loci within the major histocompatibility system (MHS) which code for the lymphocyte activating determinants. The strong Lad locus maps outside HLA-B while the weaker one maps near to HLA-A on the sixth chromosome (Fig. 17.1).

#### 17.2.2 Lads in mice

In the mouse, in contrast, there are two genetic systems which make lymphocyte activating determinants—the major histocompatibility system as in man, and M locus system which is not linked to them and is on chromosome 1 (Festenstein and Taylor,

249

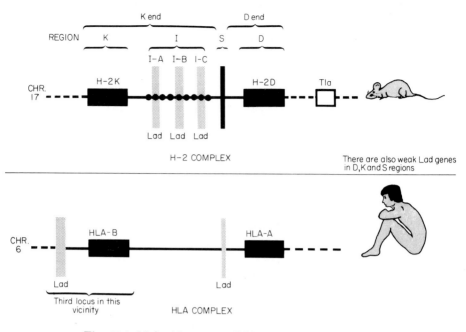

**Fig. 17.1.** Major histocompatibility systems of mouse and man.
● ● = Ia specificity genes
(Festenstein and Demant, 1974.)

1975, unpublished data). Within the *H-2* complex there are several genes coding for lymphocyte activating determinants, and the strong ones, in contrast to those in man, map between the *H-2 D* and *H-2 K* regions (HLA-A and HLA-B locus homologues). There are also probably weaker Lad genes in the *K, D* and *S* regions of the complex. A simplified map of the *Lads*, and the *H-2 K* and *H-2 D* determinants of the MHS of mouse and man is shown in Fig. 17.1.

### 17.3 Relationship of the Lads antigens to other products of the *H-2* region of mice

By the use of recombinant strains it is possible to test which differences in each region can produce an MLR. Differences in the *K* and *D* regions alone lead to only small MLR. When the differences include the *I* region, the stimulation is marked. Since the discovery of the *Ia* antigens which are controlled by genes within the *I* region, a crucial question has been to see if these antigens are responsible for MLR stimulation. It is certainly true that both *Ia* antigens, the strong Lads and the *Ir* genes all map in the *I* region, but the mapping of two different genes into the same chromosome segment by no means indicates identity, as there is enough room in each *I* subregion for at least 500 genes.

### 17.3.1 Molecular identity of the Lads gene products

A proposed approach to comparing the molecular identity of the *Ia* gene products and the Lads products is to examine their distribution on different cells. It has been shown (McDevitt *et al.*, 1974) that purified populations of T cells will function both as stimulators and responders in MLR. Few of them were shown to express serologically detectable *Ia* antigens. However, since mixed lymphocyte reactions have different biological characteristics from serological tests, these experiments should be cautiously interpreted. The failure to detect an antigen by one test does not imply that it is not present: other tests may be more sensitive in detecting it. Indeed, there are non-lytic serological tests which show *Ia* antigen on T cells, and certain anti-*Ia* antisera directed against the stimulating cells will block an MLR. It is possible that some Lads may be serologically detectable and identical with some *Ia* antigens.

## 17.4 The M locus

In the mouse there is a well-defined system which makes lymphocyte activating determinants and which is known as the M locus (Mls). So far, four alleles have been found distributed among the twenty mouse strains which have been tested. The determinants are not yet serologically detectable, activate T lymphocytes in MLR, are present on B cells and macrophages but not on T cells. M locus differences initiate graft rejection poorly, either because they are not represented, or are poorly represented on the test tissue, are intrinsically weak or generate suppressor cells.

The first indication of the existence of the M locus came from observing that lymphocytes from *H-2$^d$* identical BALB/c and DBA/2 mice produced marked MLR. Similar results were subsequently obtained with several other *H-2* identical combinations, for instance, C3H and CBA/J, (both *H-2$^k$*) and others, which are *H-2* identical but differ at an unknown number of non-*H-2* loci. Several workers postulated therefore that non-*H-2* MLR stimulation was the effect of their gene products acting in concert, but this was shown not to be the case, and that the difference was due to a single gene or gene complex (Festenstein, 1966; 1970, Festenstein *et al.*, 1972). Table 17.1 shows the distribution of the M-locus determinants among the twenty mouse strains tested to date.

The different determinants vary in their stimulating capacity. Mls$^a$ and Mls$^d$ were found to be most strongly stimulatory, followed by Mls$^c$. Mls$^b$ was found to be very weak or non-stimulatory (Festenstein, 1973).

### 17.4.1 Comparison of M-locus with MHS Lads

Table 17.2 shows the differences and similarities between the two systems.

The two points which principally require expansion from the above table are the 'one way' reactions, and the discrepancy between grafting and GVH reactions.

'One-way' reactions have been observed in all three of the experimental systems described in this chapter (MHS Lads, M-locus, and *ECS* locus). In the MLR, it is found that B10A.4R cells are stimulated by B10A.2R and Mls$^b$ cells by Mls$^a$, but in neither

**Table 17.1.** M locus alleles of various mouse strains

| M locus allele | Strain | *H-2* allele |
|---|---|---|
| Mls$^a$ | VM/Dk | b |
| | DBA/2, NZB | d |
| | AKR, BRVR/Dk, RNC-nu/nu | k |
| | DBA/1 | q |
| | SM/Skc/Dk | |
| Mls$^b$ | C57BL/6, C57BL/10, SnPh, C57/L | b |
| | BALB/c | d |
| | CBA/H, CBA/H. T6T6 | k |
| Mls$^c$ | Ajax | a |
| | C3H/J, C3H/He | k |
| | SJL | s |
| Mls$^d$ | CBAJ | k |
| Mls$^a$ or Mls$^b$ | C58 | k |

**Table 17.2.** Comparison of M locus and MHS Lads

| Feature | M locus | MHS Lads |
|---|---|---|
| Cellular expression (mainly) | B lymphocytes | B lymphocytes |
| One way reactions | yes | yes |
| Initiation of rejection | no | not alone |
| Initiation of GVH | weak | yes |

case is the reverse true. Possible explanations for this type of event are given in 17.5.2.

The principal operational differences between the M-locus and MHS Lads are in their *in vivo* reactions. As determined by spleno-megaly assay, differences largely restricted to the *I-B*, *I-C* and *S* regions of the MHS (B10.2R/B10A.4R) will evoke GVH but not initiate the rejection of heart (40 days+survival) or skin (240 days+) grafts. M-locus does not alone give rise to either graft rejection or GVH. The relationship of *in vitro* incompatibilities is covered in 17.7 and 17.8.

## 17.5 Genetic determinants involved in CML

After 5 or 6 days in mixed lymphocyte culture, specific CML killer cells develop, whose activity is tested on PHA or LPS transformed lymphoblasts. The suggestion that a separate effector cell stimulating (*ECS*) locus incompatibility is required for the generation of killer cells came from the observation that *H-2 D* and *H-2 K* determinant incompatibility alone was insufficient for CML to occur. The generation of the CML killer cells is stimulated by non-*H-2 D* or *H-2 K* incompatibility, but they recognize and kill via the *H-2 D* and *H-2 K* or closely linked determinants. Since incompatibility is required, it seems reasonable to imagine that there are recognition units (antigens or receptors) on the responding and the stimulating cell surfaces different from those involved in the *H-2 D* and *H-2 K* systems. It seems simplest to assume that the incompatibility is due to polymorphism at a single locus coding for a particular antigenic determinant.

### 17.5.1 The effector cell stimulating locus (ECS)

The genes controlling the generation of effector capacity are found in the *I* region of the *H-2* gene complex close to the Lad genes. Mapping of the area concerned was carried out using 20 congenic and recombinant mouse strains. The incompatible regions tested are shown in Fig. 17.2. According to this, the major *ECS* genes probably map in the *I-B/I-C* junction region of the *H-2* complex between the major Lads and the *S* regions.

By both mapping and other criteria, the determinants for MLR and CML seem to be distinct:

(a) There are mixed lymphocyte cultures which show strong MLR and no CML.

(b) There are mixed lymphocyte cultures which show weak MLR and good CML.

These distinctions do not rule out the possibility that the *ECS* genes are special Lads genes which control the proliferation of the CML precursor cells specifically (assuming that there are any such precomitted cells!).

### 17.5.2 One way situations

An interesting feature of the *ECS* locus is that in some tests involving the B10A.5R recombinant, the reactions only work one way. B10A.5R fails to produce effector cells when cultured with $F_1$ cells carrying the B10 or D2 haplotypes (see Fig. 17.2), but both B10 and D2 cells produce effectors when cultured with $F_1$ cells carrying the B10A.5R haplotype.

The effect is not due to any intrinsic inability to respond, since B10A.5R responds to B10.HTT. There are a number of possible explanations for this phenomenon, in which the B10A.5R behaves as an $F_1$ between B10 and D2.

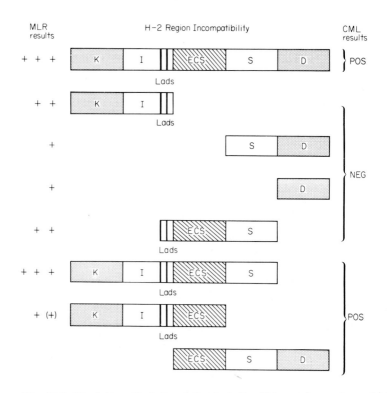

**Fig. 17.2.** The letters $K$, $I$, $S$ and $D$ refer to the $H$-$2$ complex regions which were incompatible for the selected combinations. The MLR results show the strength of the mixed lymphocyte reactions and the CML results indicate whether cell-mediated lympholysis occurred. Lads = strong lymphocyte activating determinants in the $I$ regions (vertical bars). Other Lads are coded for by the other regions. ECS = locus, probably in IR-IB/I-C subregion, responsible for the generation of effectors in CML. The congenic resistant mouse strains used in these experiments were all on the B10 background and the combinations used have been published elsewhere.

For CML to occur there must be D and/or K region incompatibility plus ECS incompatibility.

Perhaps the most attractive is that the 5R recombinational event involved an unequal crossover, so that both alleles ($ECS^b$ and $ECS^b$) are present on the recombinants, which are consequently tolerant in the same way as an $F_1$ (Fig. 17.3).

Alternatively, the $ECS$ 'locus' may be occupied by a number of tandem duplicated genes with identical or closely similar function,

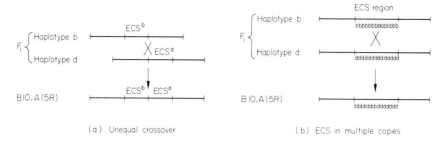

**Fig. 17.3.** Possible nature and origins of B10.A(5R).

and the recombination event occurred within this duplicated region (Fig. 17.3).

## 17.6 *In vivo* significance of Lads

It is important to bear in mind that in addition to the predictable difference between *in vitro* models and *in vivo* models, there are also differences between the *in vivo* models themselves. Not all the antigens which might be involved in stimulating responses are represented on all the tissues. Therefore, the transplantation of an organ may not present as many antigenic systems to the responding cells as a graft-versus-host reaction, in which the responding cells circulate, encountering (potentially) all the host's antigens.

### 17.6.1 Experimental

Should Lads be transplantation antigens in themselves, as suggested by Bach and others, then it would be surprising if the Lad incompatible combinations failed to reject; yet they do. In several MHS congenic and M locus different combinations, heart and skin grafts were not rejected. It is not known whether Lads are present in the test tissues, but if absent, a strong *in vitro* response would be irrelevant to this discussion. In those cases, where graft rejection occurs, the mapping of a Lad gene and a graft-rejecting gene (*H-2 I*) in the same region by no means indicates identity.

Graft-versus-host reactions must also represent a situation where Lads are detectable, though it is difficult to be certain whether the sensitized lymphocytes are reacting against Lad-containing tissue, or some other determinants, e.g. through an *ECS*-type reaction.

The M locus does not accelerate graft rejection *in vivo*, nor does it evoke or help to produce effector cell responses *in vitro*, but there are interesting associations between Mls types and diseases.

## 17.6.2 Clinical

In man it is difficult to accurately predict the fact of grafted non-lymphoid tissues on the results of compatibility testing on lymphocytes. HLA homozygous cells (from children of first cousin marriages) are now being used to define the polymorphism of human Lads at the dominant locus (Festenstein & Peña-Martinez, 1975).

In the rare instances where two unrelated individuals have identical HLA specifications, there is, on average, a small mixed lymphocyte reaction. A fair proportion of these test pairs were non-stimulatory or weakly stimulatory, and a few strongly stimulatory. Some of the grafts between pairs which stimulated strongly survived well, and some between weakly stimulating pairs survived for short periods (Sachs et al., 1974). While the number of test cases involved were small, one would expect that if the Lads were first-line transplantation antigens, that all those displaying strong stimulation would be rejected. Neither in this series nor in experimental series in animals was this found. Conversely, there are many instances of no MLR or weak MLR and poor allograft survival (Huber et al., 1973; Salaman et al., 1971; Festenstein et al., 1971). These findings speak strongly against the theory put forward by some authors (see Lancet Editorial June 1974) that the lymphocyte activation determinants are the transplantation antigens, and that the HLA specificities are in linkage disequilibrium with them.

## 17.7 Genetic control of magnitude reaction

### 17.7.1 Mixed lymphocyte reactions

The intensity of mixed lymphocyte reactions is under genetic control in both man and mouse.

Yunis and Amos (1971) first postulated a mixed lymphocyte culture response gene in Man which they called MLR-R. This gene regulates the HL-A linked Lads.

In the mouse there are genes which influence the degree of response in MLR. The response to $D$ and $K$ end $Lads$ is controlled by gene not linked to $H$-$2$ while those which control the response to M locus differences map within the $H$-$2$ region. As shown in Table 17.3 the MLR between congenic strains of mice of identical $H$-$2$ haplotype but incompatible at $Mls^b$ and $Mls^c$ is strongest in mice of $H$-$2^k$ and $H$-$2^a$ haplotype and weaker with the $H$-$2^b$ haplotype. The differences cannot be due to $Lad$ differences which in each pair are identical, but must be due to other genes controlling the degree of MLR.

The simplest speculation is that in some cases in the mouse, the M and MHS Lads act additively. The human results, by analogy if the MLR maps outside HLA could be used to argue the existence

**Table 17.3.** *H-2* dependent MLR of *H-2* identical and M locus different combinations

| Strain combination | H–2 type | Mls type | Transformation index |
|---|---|---|---|
| B10.A + A | a + a | b + c | 2·6 |
| B10 + A.BY | b + b | b + c | 1·04 |
| B10.M + A.CA | f + f | b + c | 1·3 |
| B10.BR + C3H | k + k | b + c | 2·87 |
| B10 + C3H.SW | b + b | b + c | 0·98 |
| B10.Y + C3H.NB | p + p | b + c | 1·2 |

(Data from Rychlíková, Démant & Ivanyi 1973.)

of an 'M locus equivalent'. Formal proof of this is hindered by the lack of congenic strains of humans!

### 17.7.2 CML reactions and the rejection of grafts

Fig. 17.4 shows the graft survival times of the pairs which were used earlier in the mapping of the *ECS* locus. It seems that there is a good correlation between *ECS* compatibility and graft survival in several strains. The potential significance of this result is obviously very great, though it should be remembered that in a large number of the cases of graft survival the B10A.5R strain is involved, with its apparent functional deletion of part of the MHS complex incompatibilities. The subject is more fully discussed in the next section (17.8.3).

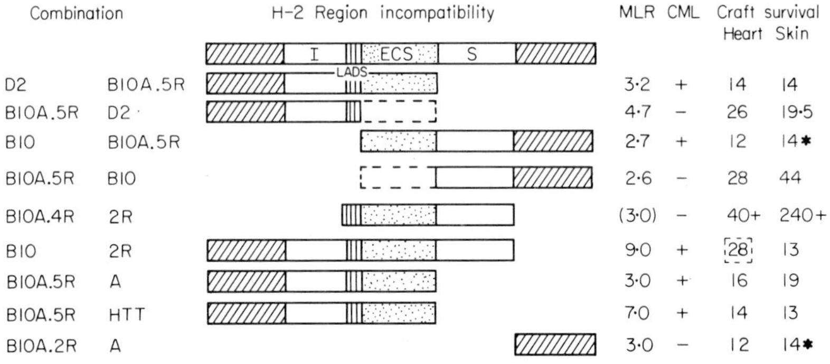

| Combination | | H-2 Region incompatibility | MLR | CML | Craft survival Heart | Skin |
|---|---|---|---|---|---|---|
| D2 | B10A.5R | | 3·2 | + | 14 | 14 |
| B10A.5R | D2 | | 4·7 | − | 26 | 19·5 |
| B10 | B10A.5R | | 2·7 | + | 12 | 14* |
| B10A.5R | B10 | | 2·6 | − | 28 | 44 |
| B10A.4R | 2R | | (3·0) | − | 40+ | 240+ |
| B10 | 2R | | 9·0 | + | [28] | 13 |
| B10A.5R | A | | 3·0 | + | 16 | 19 |
| B10A.5R | HTT | | 7·0 | + | 14 | 13 |
| B10A.2R | A | | 3·0 | − | 12 | 14* |

**Fig. 17.4.** The relationship of ECS to graft survival. Graft survival correlates well with ECS compatibility except where *H-2.13* or *H-2.19* antigens are present (*). One case of heart graft survival seems aberrant (⌐⌐).

## 17.8 Tissue typing and graft survival

HLA serological determinant typing is successful in predicting graft survival between siblings, but less successful in predicting the survival of grafts between unrelated individuals. Nevertheless, there are very real differences in the success of grafts matched for four alleles rather than three or fewer. Some mismatched grafts survive well (see Fig. 17.5).

In 1965, Simonsen postulated that the genes which are important for graft rejection are a small number of alleles (perhaps 3) at a single locus, and that chance would be sufficient to explain the 30 per cent survival of the unmatched pairs. The discovery of the highly polymorphic nature of the HLA specificities shows that they are not the same as the important graft rejection genes, and it must now be held that these are not currently identifiable by any phenomenon other than that of graft rejection *in vivo*.

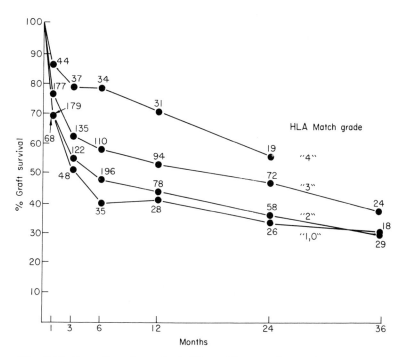

**Fig. 17.5.** Overall graft survival. (From Oliver *et al.*, 1970.)

## 17.8.1 *The role of linkage*

The differential between the sibling matched grafts and unrelated matched grafts is explained by the assumption that the important graft rejecting genes (undetectable except by grafting) are linked to the HLA system. In matched siblings, there is a very small possibility of the important graft rejecting genes having recombined, so that the inheritance of identical HLA-A and HLA-B locus haplotypes implies the inheritance of identical important graft rejecting genes.

258

### 17.8.2 The role of linkage disequilibrium

The differences in graft survival between unrelated individuals can be explained by the existence of linkage disequilibrium between the important graft rejection alleles and the HLA-A and HLA-B locus alleles (Oliver *et al.*, 1972; Dausett *et al.*, 1974; van Hooff *et al.*, 1972). Thus, a 'four antigen match' is more likely to carry the same important graft rejection alleles than a poorer match. There is some evidence that the HLA-B locus is more important to match. Furthermore some HLA-B locus alleles seem to be in linkage disequilibrium with certain Lad alleles, and also with some genes which predispose to disease (see Chapter 18).

### 17.8.3 The role of summative effects and 'controlling' loci

An alternative explanation for the diversity of results of grafts between unrelated individuals is that the differences are due to summation of numerous incompatibilities. Incompatibility at some loci might be more important than at others, and some of these incompatibilities might take on the character of 'controlling' incompatibilities, amplifying the effect of other incompatibilities. Such 'controlling' incompatibilities might have no obvious *in vitro* correlate, and would be difficult to identify in any specific sense. They would operationally fit the description of 'important graft rejection loci' described above.

A current exciting speculation is that the *ECS* locus of mouse is one of these 'controlling' loci. It requires for its manifestation an *H-2 D* region or *H-2 K* incompatibility although the *ECS* locus incompatibility is not necessary for graft rejection: the presence of *H-2.13* at the *H-2 D* locus or *H-2.19* at the *H-2 K* locus is sufficient for graft rejection to occur. It should be understood that the *H-2.13* and *H-2.19* genes themselves may not be the important genes, but that they may be markers for important closely linked genes.

The correlation of *ECS* compatibility with prolonged graft survival is otherwise good in the tested examples.

### 17.8.4 The role of multi-locus typing

The more HLA loci are matched, the greater the possibility that the relevant loci for graft rejection will be matched, irrespective of whether the linkage disequilibrium theory or the summative theory is true. In the first case, the more loci are matched, the greater the chance that the important genes, in linkage disequilibrium, will also prove to be matched. Alternatively the more detectable loci are matched, the less the summative effect they will have, and even a strong 'controlling' incompatibility would have little to work on.

On either theory, the case for multiple locus matching seems to be solid, and its results may lead to the discovery of the relative roles of linkage disequilibrium and summation, and to a better and more selective basis for future typing schemes.

## References

DAUSET J., FESTENSTEIN H., HORS J., OLIVER R.T.D., PARIS A.M.I. & SACHS J.A. (1974) Serologically defined HL-A antigens and long-term survival of cadaver kidney transplants. *New England J. Med.* **290**, 979.

FESTENSTEIN H. (1966) Antigenic strength investigated by mixed cultures of allogenic mouse spleen cells. *Ann. N.Y. Acad. Sci.* **129**, 567.

FESTENSTEIN H. (1970) Strong and weak histocompatability antigens: General Discussion. *Transpl. Rev.* **3**, 74.

FESTENSTEIN H. (1973) Immunogenic and biological aspects of *in vitro* lymphocyte allotransformation (MLR) in the mouse. *Transpl. Rev.* **15**, 62.

FESTENSTEIN H. & DEMANT P. (1975) Antigenic recognition in cell mediated immune reactions. In BRENT L. & HOLBOROUGH J. *Progress in Immunology II* **2**, 45 North-Holland, Amsterdam.

FESTENSTEIN H., LUBLING N., CALNE R. & BINNS R. (1971) *4th Symposium Charles Salt Research Centre, Oswestry*, Immunological Tolerance to tissue antigens, 215.

FESTENSTEIN H. & PENA-MARTINEZ J. (1975) Mixed lymphocyte reaction stimulating antigens, their detection, their relation to disease and the other markers of the major histocompatibility system. *Ann. rheum. Dis.* **34**, suppl. 1, p. 7.

FESTENSTEIN H., SACHS J.A., ABBASI K. & OLIVER R.T.D. (1972) Serologically undetectable immune responses in transplantation. *Transpl. Proc.* **4**, 219.

VAN HOOFF J.P., SCHIPPERS H.M.A., VAN DER STEEN G.J. & VAN ROOD J.J. (1972) Efficacy of HL-A matching in Eurotransplant. *Lancet* **ii**, 1385.

HUBER B., DEMANT P. & FESTENSTEIN H. (1973) Influence of M-Locus (Mon H-2) and K-end and D-end (H-2 region) incompatibility on heart muscle allograft survival time. *Transpl. Proc.* **5**, 1377.

McDEVITT H.O., BECHTOL K.B., HAMMERLING G.J., LONAI P. & DELOVICH T.L. (1974) Ig genes and antigen recognition. In SERCARZ E., WILLIAMSON A. & FOX C.F. *The Immune System: Genes, Receptors, Signals*, p. 597, 70.

OLIVER R.T.D., SACHS J.A. & FESTENSTEIN H. (1970) A collaborative scheme for tissue typing and matching in renal transplantation. VI. Clinical relevance of HL-A matching in 349 cadaver renal transplants. *Tranplant. Proc.* **5**, 245.

OLIVER R.T.D., SACHS J.A., FESTENSTEIN H., PEGRUM G.D. & MOORHEAD J.F. (1972) Influence of HL-A matching antigenic strength and immune responsiveness on outcome of 349 cadaver renal grafts. *Lancet* 1381.

RYCHLIKOVÁ M., DÉMANT P. & IVANYI P. (1973) The mixed lymphocyte reactions in H-2K, H-2D and non H-2 histocompatibility. *Biomedicine* **18**, 401.

SACHS J.A., FESTENSTEIN H. & OLIVER R.T.D. (1974) *Abstracts of Vth International Congress of the Transplantation Society, Jerusalem*, p. 13 and *Transpl. Proc.* (in press).

SALAMAN J., ELVES M. & FESTENSTEIN H. (1971) Factors contributing to survival of rats transplanted with kidneys mismatched at major locus. *Transpl. Proc.* **3**, 577.

SIMONSEN M. (1965) Strong transplantation antigens in man. *Lancet* **i**, 415.

# Chapter 18
# HLA and Disease

# R. Harris

## 18.1 Introduction

Of the topics discussed in the preceding chapters, the phenomenon
of linkage disequilibrium is, perhaps, the most important to understanding the relationship of HLA types to disease.

### 18.1.1 Linkage disequilibrium

The formal genetics of the HLA system have been described in
Chapter 15 and it should be re-emphasized that certain genes in
the HLA system tend to occur together in the same individuals in
Caucasian populations. The best examples are HLA-A1 and HLA-B8
at the first and second loci respectively, which are found together
on the same chromosome very much more frequently than would be
predicted by the product of their gene frequencies. Unless HLA-A1
and HLA-B8 have been introduced into European populations very
recently, it seems probable that natural selection is operating to
favour individuals who inherit the A1,B8 haplotype (HLA-A1 and
HLA-B8 on the same chromosome; linkage in coupling).

### 18.1.2 Disease associations

Some of the many reported HLA disease associations are shown in
Table 18.1. Historically, Hodgkin's disease and acute lymphatic
leukaemia (ALL) were the first diseases in which it appeared that
certain HLA types occurred more frequently in patients with these
diseases than in normal controls. Independent support for these
assertions was forthcoming but the differences between patients
and controls were small. Technical problems occurred and differences between the HLA antigens involved were reported. There
were also statistical problems and it was not always appreciated
that differences significant at the $P = 0.05$ level will arise by chance
on average once in every 20 antigen comparisons made (for a
review of the statistical problems, see Svejgaard et al., 1974).

However, diseases with much stronger HLA associations have
now been identified and confirmed by independent groups of
workers. Four of these, ankylosing spondylitis, ragweed hay fever,

**Table 18.1.** Some of the positive associations between HLA and disease

| Disease | Associated antigens | References |
|---|---|---|
| Hodgkin's disease | BW35 | Amiel, 1967 |
| | A1,B8 | Morris *et al.*, 1973 |
| Acute lymphatic leukaemia | A2,B12 | Walford *et al.*, 1970 |
| Ankylosing spondylitis | B27 | Brewerton *et al.*, 1973 |
| | | Schlosstein *et al.*, 1973 |
| Associated diseases: | | |
| Acute anterior uveitis | B27 | Russel *et al.*, 1972 |
| Reiter's syndrome | B27 | Brewerton *et al.*, 1973 |
| Psoriasis | B27 | White *et al.*, 1972 |
| Grave's disease | B8 | Grumet *et al.*, 1973 |
| Coeliac disease | B8 | Stokes *et al.*, 1972 |
| | | Falchuk *et al.*, 1972 |
| Dermatitis herpetiformis occurring with coeliac disease | B8 | Katz *et al.*, 1972 |
| Myesthenia gravis | B8 | Fritze *et al.*, 1974 |
| Chronic active hepatitis | B8 | Mackay & Morris, 1972 |
| Systemic lupus erythematosis | BW15 | McDevitt & Bodmer, 1972 |
| | | Waters *et al.*, 1971 |
| Multiple sclerosis | A3 | Naito *et al.*, 1972 |
| | B7 | Jersild *et al.*, 1973 |
| | DW2 | Bertrams *et al.*, 1972 |
| Paralytic poliomyelitis | A3,B7 | Morris & Pietsch, 1973 |
| Ragweed allergy (antigen E sensitivity) | Multiple | Levine *et al.*, 1973 |

coeliac disease and multiple sclerosis are of particular interest because they provide clues to the ways in which HLA linked genes may determine differential susceptibility to disease.

## 18.2 Ankylosing spondylitis

Several groups of workers have reported from different parts of the world a strikingly high incidence of the HLA antigen B27 in patients with ankylosing spondylitis (Table 18.2). Other forms of arthritis have been investigated, notably rheumatoid arthritis and gout, and no excess incidence of B27 positive individuals has been found. However, amongst patients with diseases often associated with ankylosing spondylitis there is an increased frequency of B27 positive individuals. This observation applies to acute anterior uveitis, psoriasis and Reiter's disease when accompanied by bilateral sacro-iliitis and spondylitis.

It may be said that the raised frequency of B27 in Reiter's disease provides the clue to the meaning of the association since this disease is probably infective. Other forms of infective sacroiliitis and spondylitis, notably Yersinia, gonococcal and salmonella arthritis, also appear to be associated with an excess of B27.

**Table 18.2.** Evidence for association of HLA-B27 with ankylosing spondylitis

| % Patients B27 | Number of patients | % Controls B27 | Number of controls | Reference |
|---|---|---|---|---|
| 96 | 75 | 4 | 75 (Age and sex matched) | Brewerton *et al.* (1973) |
| 88 | 40 | 8 | 906 | Schlosstein *et al.* (1973) |

*18.2.1 Inheritance of ankylosing spondylitis*

It has been suggested that the disease is carried by an autosomal dominant with 70 per cent penetrance in males and only 10 per cent in females, although Emery & Laurence (1967) concluded that ankylosing spondylitis was a multifactorial condition. It now appears that B27 is associated with one of the inherited factors since 90 per cent or more of cases are positive for this antigen, although only about 8 per cent of males and 1 per cent of females with B27 develop ankylosing spondylitis. Clearly other factors must be operating as well. Being male lowers the threshold for the disease while the association with acute anterior uveitis, Reiter's disease, ulcerative colitis, regional iliitis, Yersinia, gonococcal and salmonella arthritis suggests that other, perhaps infective, environmental co-factors exist. Indeed it seems likely that a B27 positive male has a very high probability of developing ankylosing spondylitis if he contracts any of these other diseases.

In certain races the correlation of incidence of B27 and ankylosing spondylitis is good. The Pima Amerindians have a high population frequency of B27 (10 per cent) and ankylosing spondylitis (5 per cent) while in African blacks B27 is rare (0–1 per cent) and ankylosing spondylitis is likewise rare. In the Japanese, however, the incidence of ankylosing spondylitis is said to be similar to that amongst Caucasians although B27 is present in only about 1 per cent of normal Japanese. It is interesting to speculate that the selective pressures which keep B27 and the gene predisposing to ankylosing spondylitis in linkage disequilibrium in other populations may be different in the Japanese, permitting a higher recombination frequency.

Dick and her colleagues (1974) described an interesting family in which it was likely that genetic recombination had occurred separating the gene for B27 from that responsible for increased susceptibility to ankylosing spondylitis. It was concluded that it is not the possession of the antigen B27 alone which determines the disease pattern. It is suggested that a disease susceptibility gene, perhaps an *Ir* gene, is adjacent to the gene for B27.

## 18.3 Ragweed hay fever and HLA

Levine *et al.* (1972) reported what appears to be the first example in man of an HLA linked *Ir* gene. Seven families were investigated in which there were at least two patients suffering from ragweed hay fever. Skin tests using Antigen-E extracted from ragweed produced an intense wheal and flare reaction in these patients. Weak positive skin test reactions with this antigen were also obtained with relatives who did not suffer from clinical allergy. The majority of family members without allergy had negative skin tests to the antigen. In each family, clinical hay fever occurred only in individuals who shared one of the two HLA haplotypes of the index case (or propositus). Thus, 77 per cent (20/26) of individuals in the families who shared the hay fever associated haplotype had developed clinical hay fever. No cases of hay fever occurred in relatives who share the other haplotypes of the index cases or in those who had neither of the haplotypes of the index cases. However, four relations out of a total of 31 had weak positive skin reactions to antigen-E although they lacked the hay fever associated haplotypes of the index cases and of course did not have hay fever. In some of these individuals weakly positive skin test reactivity appeared to have been inherited independently through spouses. It was suggested that an HLA linked *Ir* gene is responsible for the control of specific antibody production (responsible for hypersensitivity). It was also suggested that a separate unlinked gene is responsible for the class of immunoglobulin produced (presumably a gene concerned with ε or γ heavy chain constant region production). Inheritance of both the *Ir* gene and the 'IgE' gene predisposes to hay fever. Further investigations in these families tended to confirm that the allergy was specific for antigen-E although patients with hay fever were more likely to have allergies to other allergens than were the normal individuals.

Since in the 7 families specific response to antigen-E was associated with 7 different haplotypes, this type of response was not associated with any particular HLA antigen, unlike the other disease associations discussed.

## 18.4 Coeliac disease and HLA-A1,B8

At least four independent groups of workers have demonstrated an excess incidence of B8 in patients with coeliac disease. 66–88 per cent of patients with coeliac disease have B8 compared with only 16–30 per cent in normal Caucasians. Since A1 and B8 are commonly found together in Caucasians as a result of linkage disequilibrium, an increased frequency of A1 is also found in some series of coeliacs.

Patients with coeliac diseases have small intestinal villous atrophy and commonly have serum antibodies to gluten, milk and other dietary proteins. It is unknown whether these antibodies are formed as a result of the passage of dietary macromolecules through a mucosa whose integrity has failed for unknown reasons, or if the normal passage of minute amounts of these antigens gives rise to an immunologically-based pathology as a result of abnormal sensitivity to the minor challenge. In either case, the damaged mucosa and immune responses are likely to be self-perpetuating once established. Scott *et al.* (1974) have recently reported an association between gluten antibody titre and the HLA phenotype whether in patients with coeliac disease, those with other diseases or in normals, perhaps due to an *Ir* gene. This is an attractive hypothesis, although the data is at present inconclusive with regard to the disease independent association of B8 and high antigluten antibody titres. Quantitative specific antibody studies on coeliacs and their normal relatives may help to clarify this problem.

### 18.5 Multiple sclerosis (MS) and HLA

Several groups of workers have confirmed an association between B7 (and perhaps A3) with multiple sclerosis. Recently, Jersild *et al.* (1973) have demonstrated an even closer association with an MLC allele, called DW2 in linkage disequilibrium with B7 Amongst 28 randomly selected patients with MS, 19 (70 per cent) were DW2 positive compared with only 16 per cent in healthy individuals. Family studies have confirmed that DW2 is inherited and not acquired by patients with MS, i.e. DW2 is not viral antigen. Disease progression appeared to have been more rapid in those patients who were DW2 positive and it was suggested that possession of the DW2 antigen not only decreases the threshold for developing multiple sclerosis but also increased the rate of progression of this disease.

When normal leucocytes are exposed to measles virus, leucocyte migration inhibitory factor (MIF) is released. In contrast, leucocyte obtained from patients with MS do not release MIF when exposed to measles and other myxoviruses *in vitro*, suggesting an impairment in the T cell response. However, high levels of humoral antibody are found in patients with MS. It has been suggested that the DW2 antigen or a closely linked *Ir* gene is associated with a deficiency of the T cell response, rendering patients with MS incapable of eradicating persistent virus infections although capable of producing abundant antibody.

The studies of Morris and Pietsch (1973) have found evidence which further suggests that A3 and B7 can be associated with other viral diseases of the CNS. They showed an excess incidence of A3 and B7 in people who had developed paralytic polio during the 1950s. They also suggested that it would be worthwhile to compare the HLA types of patients who had developed paralytic polio with their normal siblings, since polio virus infection would certainly have occurred in both groups.

Petranyi *et al.* (1974) investigated the immunological status of normal people who had high responses to bacterial antigens and blood group antigens. Those who were A3,B7 had poor T cell activity *in vitro* for heterologous target cells. Thus, it may be that the A3,B7 haplotype is associated with some defect which permits antigen to persist (? macrophage), which in turn leads to increased antibody levels which interfere with or block CMI reactions to certain viruses.

## 18.6 Possible explanations for HLA associations

Disease associations may imply that either increased susceptibility or increased resistance to particular diseases is conferred by HLA type. In general, positive associations suggest increased susceptibility but an excess of patients with a particular HLA type amongst the survivors of a disease with a high mortality suggests increased resistance.

Also, a reduced frequency of a particular HLA antigen might indicate that the missing antigen conferred some type of resistance to non-lethal disease.

### 18.6.1 Ir *genes and hypersensitivity*

HLA linked *Ir* genes are probably involved in certain clinical hypersensitivities. This is particularly clear in the case of ragweed hay fever, in which the disease is directly caused by IgE antibodies against the antigen E of ragweed. Although the disease seems to require the action of two genes, one concerned with the class of antibody produced, there is clear evidence for the need for an HLA linked *Ir* gene for antigen E. In coeliac disease, the association of the disease with B8 may be due to the presence of a linked *Ir* gene for gluten. Nevertheless, it has not been clearly demonstrated that antibody is implicated in the pathogenesis of the disease. In multiple sclerosis, HLA linked *Ir* genes which either lead to impaired T cell response or to enhanced B cell response to measles virus may be important pathogenetic factors. In the latter case, excessive antibody formation is not necessarily paradoxical, since serum blocking factors (?immune complexes) often impair cell-mediated responses.

### 18.6.2 Direct participation of the HLA macromolecules in disease

There are two essentially different possibilities here: 'Molecular mimicry' and what might be termed 'functional'. Pathogens may share a cross-reacting antigen with HLA and be to some extent protected by the host's tolerance to these HLA antigens—'molecular mimicry'. Although there is some evidence for HLA type specificities amongst bacteria, no evidence has yet been found for this phenomenon amongst viruses, which would be much better candidates. 'Molecular mimicry' provides at least a speculative explanation for the existence of large numbers of different HLA SD antigens. The polymorphism would help to ensure that there were some individuals within human populations with HLA antigens unlike those of epidemic pathogens or oncogenic viruses. The second ('functional') possibility is that the HLA SD determinants are incidental parts of macromolecules with important functions in the cell's economy, e.g. they might control membrane permeability, cell–cell interactions or they might be receptors for viruses or in some way make the cell more susceptible to invasion. While the molecules carrying the HLA antigens are reasonably well characterized chemically (see Chapter 15) the functions of the HLA molecule remain unknown and attempts to attribute disease associations directly to HLA antigens are purely speculative.

### 18.6.3 Which of these explanations most plausibly explains the associations between HLA antigens and various diseases?

Since 90 per cent or more patients with ankylosing spondylitis have the B27 specificity, the B27 gene could be directly involved in the causation of the disease. If one accepts this, it is necessary to account for the 5–10 per cent of patients with this disease who are B27 negative. The simplest explanation might be that there is more than one aetiological variety of the disease. Probably B27 is only one of several genetic factors, albeit an important one, in a multifactorial genetic and environmental interaction. Thus, an unusually heavy concentration of other genetic and environmental factors allows the threshold of liability to be exceeded, even without B27.

For most HLA disease associations, including ankylosing spondylitis, the HLA SD gene product may be a convenient marker, the 'real disease gene' being linked to the SD genes. The strength of the HLA disease association is determined by the degree of linkage disequilibrium between the relevant gene and the appropriate SD locus (usually the second). This explanation is certainly consistent with Ragweed hay fever referred to earlier and with what is known of genetic recombination within the HLA chromosomal region. For example, multiple sclerosis is more strongly associated with the HLA-D allele DW2 than with the closely linked HLA SD second locus and the family reported by Dick, referred to earlier, appears to illustrate the existence of separate B27 and ankylosing spondylitis loci.

Thus, most HLA disease associations can probably be explained most convincingly by reference to genes in the HLA chromosome region. They are currently identifiable only in the presence of the diseases with which they are associated and by the frequency with which they co-exist with particular HLA SD antigens. In the case of ankylosing spondylitis, linkage disequilibrium would be so strong that B27 and the gene conferring susceptibility to ankylosing spondylitis occur together in the same individual in 90 per cent or more of gases. In contrast, although located in the HLA region, the *Ir* gene thought to be responsible for specific responsiveness to Ragweed antigen-E does not appear to occur preferentially with any particular HLA antigen probably because the *Ir* gene and the SD genes have been separated by genetic recombination and are distributed in the populations nearly at random to each other. Consequently the association of Ragweed allergy with HLA can at present be detected only by family studies.

Since it is believed that the strength of linkage disequilibrium determines the ease with which associations can be detected in population studies, it is not surprising that a number of associations have been somewhat difficult to substantiate, e.g. acute lymphatic leukaemia with A2,B12 and Hodgkin's disease with BW35 and other specificities. Assuming that true associations exist between HLA and these diseases, linkage disequilibrium is presumably weak. Multiple cases of these diseases occur rarely in families and when they do, the index case may be the only patient alive and available for HLA typing so that family studies are currently of limited value. Only when some means of directly recognizing the true disease genes is available will it be possible positively to associate HLA with many diseases.

We have no means of knowing yet how many genes in the HLA system are involved in differential susceptibility to disease or how many of these are *Ir* genes. Although the total number of genes in the HLA region is not known, it is likely to be large with little linkage disequilibrium. It may be, as in the case of Ragweed hay fever, that linkage with the HLA system can only be recognized in family studies. The ragweed hay fever *Ir* gene is therefore, an exciting example of the potential importance to immunology of HLA.

## 18.7 Practical applications of HLA disease associations

### 18.7.1 At risk individuals

The most obvious application of associations is to identify individuals at risk of developing particular diseases. Since HLA antigens are detectable (with difficulty) in the early fetus, the identification of such individuals is theoretically possible as a preliminary to therapeutic abortion. Thus, a man with ankylosing spondylitis who was B27 positive would have an equal chance of fathering a B27 positive or negative fetus. Following early aminocentesis and HLA typing it would be possible to abort a B27 positive fetus. This procedure would of course be open to criticism since only a minority of B27 positive individuals actually develop ankylosing spondylitis and it is probable that effective preventative or therapeutic treatment will become available. The strongest argument for the identification post-natally of individuals at risk is that this would facilitate the systematic search for removable environmental co-factors.

### 18.7.2 Diagnosis

HLA typing is now in fairly widespread use in the diagnosis of sacro-spinal arthritis, those cases which are HLA B27 being considered to have ankylosing spondylitis. Similar trends are evident in the diagnosis of inflammatory bowel disease, psoriasis and acute anterior uveitis.

There are a number of potential hazards in these trends. First, in no human disease is the mechanism of disease association with HLA type fully understood. It remains to be seen whether the associations are based on a common aetiology or simply a final common pathological pathway irrespective of aetiology. To the geneticist, a more worrying problem is that the ascertainment of disease associations with HLA types will be greatly disturbed by the shift of diagnostic criteria from conventional methods to HLA typing methods. This will make it more difficult for the epidemiological geneticist to investigate the nature of these associations.

### 18.7.3 Prognosis

It has been suggested that A1,B8 positive patients with myasthenia gravis are more likely to have non-malignant pathology (thymic germinal centres), while those that are B12 are more likely to have thymomas. These observations have implications for the choice of treatment and ultimate prognosis (Fritze et al., 1974). In acute lymphatic leukaemia there appears to be an excess of A9 positive children amongst the long-term survivors (Lawler

*Chapter 18: HLA and Disease*

*et al.*, 1974). In multiple sclerosis DW2 positive patients may have a more rapidly progressive course (Jersild *et al.*, 1973).

### 18.7.4 Epidemiology

The HLA disease association provide great scope for epidemiological research especially in the study of different ethnic groups since widely different frequencies of HLA antigens and disease occur in different parts of the world.

### 18.7.5 Genetics

The HLA system is a complex linkage system conveniently marked by three series of highly polymorphic serologically detected antigens. In the majority of families, parents will be HLA heterozygotes and different from each other, thus greatly facilitating formal linkage studies. The HLA disease association already known exceed in strength and in number anything previously reported, except perhaps the protection afforded by sickle-cell haemoglobin against falciparum malaria. There are many unanswered questions relating to HLA disease associations. What is the nature of these associations, are they related to the extraordinary polymorphism of the SD antigens and what are the functions of the HLA antigenic determinants? Is this polymorphism fortuitous and unimportant or does it have important implications in the fields of cellular differentiation, materno-fetal interaction and cancer immuno-surveillance?

Linked genes should be encountered in coupling and repulsion in a proportion determined by their relative frequency. This is clearly not the case with the HLA SD antigens, e.g. the HLA-A1,8 and HLA-A3,B7 occur with much greater frequency than their individual gene frequencies predict. This also appears to be true for the DW2 antigen and B7. Such combinations must have some selective advantage even though paradoxically, A1,B8 and A3,B7, the two commonest Caucasian haplotypes have been associated with susceptibility to auto-immune disease and multiple sclerosis respectively.

To the geneticist one of the most exciting problems must be the nature of the forces maintaining linkage disequilibrium in outbreeding populations.

### References

AMIEL J.L. (1967) Study of the leucocyte phenotypes in Hodgkin's disease. In CURTONI *et al. Histocompatibility testing*. Munksgaard, Copenhagen.

BERTRAMS J., KUWERT E. & LIEDTKE U. (1972) HL-A antigens and multiple sclerosis. *Tissue Antigens* **2**, 405.

*Section III: Immunogenetics*

BREWERTON D.A., CAFFREY M., HART F.D., JAMES D.C.O., NICHOLLS A. & STURROCK R.D. (1973) Ankylosing spondylitis and HL-A 27. *Lancet* i, 904.

DICK H.M., STURROCK R.D., CARSON DICK W. & BUCHANAN W.W. (1974) Inheritance of ankylosing spondylitis and HL-A antigen W27. *Lancet* ii, 24.

EMERY A.E.H. & LAWRENCE J.S. (1967) Genetics of ankylosing spondylitis. *J. Med. Genetics* 4, 239.

FALCHUK Z.M., ROGENTINE G.N. & STROBER W. (1972) Predominance of histocompatibility antigen HL-A8 in patients with Gluten sensitive enteropathy. *J. Clin. Invest.* 51, 1602.

FRITZE D., HERMANN C., SMITH G.T. & WALFORD R.L. (1974) HL-A antigens in myesthenia gravis: Relation to sex, age and thymic pathology. *Lancet* i, 240.

GRUMET F.C., KONISHI J., PAYNE R.O. & KRISS J.P. (1973) Association of Graves' Disease with HL-A8. *Clin. Res.* 21, 493.

JERSILD C., HANSEN G.S., SVEJGAARD A., FOG T., THOMSON M. & DUPONT B. (1973) Histocompatibility determinants in multiple sclerosis with special reference to clinical course. *Lancet* ii, 240.

KATZ S.I., FALCHUK Z.M., DAHL M.V., ROGENTINE G.N. & STROBER W.J. (1972) HL-A8: Genetic link between dermatitis herpetiformis and gluten-sensitive enteropathy. *J. Clin. Invest.* 51, 2977.

LAWLER S.D., KLOUDA P.J., SMITH P.G., TILL M.M. & HARDISTY R.M. (1974) Survival and HL-A system in acute lymphoblastic leukaemia. *Brit. Med. J.* i, 547.

LEVINE B.B., STEMBER R.H. & FOTINO M. (1973) Association of the HL-A7 Cross-reacting group with a specific reaginic antibody response in allergic man. *Science* 179, 691.

MORRIS P.J., LAWLER S.D. & OLIVER R.T. (1973) HL-A and Hodgkin's disease. In DAUSSET J. & COLOMBIANI J. *Histocompatibility Testing 1972*, p. 669. Munksgaard, Copenhagen.

McDEVITT H.O. & BODMER W.F. (1972) Histocompatibility antigens, immune responsiveness and susceptibility to disease. *Am. J. Med.* 52, 1.

MACKAY I.R. & MORRIS P.J. (1972) Associations of Autoimmune Active Chronic Hepatitis with HL-A 1,8. *Lancet* ii, 793.

MORRIS P.J. & PIETSCH M.C. (1973) A possible association between paralytic poliomyelitis and multiple sclerosis. *Lancet* ii, 847.

NAITO S., NAMEROW N., MICKEY M.R. & TERASAKI P.I. (1972) Multiple sclerosis association with HL-A3. *Tissue Antigens* 2, 1.

PETRANYI G.G., BENCZUR M., ONODY C.E., HOLLAN S.R. & IVANYI P. (1974) HL-A 3.7 and lymphocyte cytotoxic activity. *Lancet* i, 736.

RUSSELL T.J., SCHUKTES L.M. & KUBAN D.J. (1972) Histocompatibility (HL-A) antigens associated with psoriasis. *New Engl. J. Med.* 287, 738.

SCHLOSSTEIN L., TERASAKI P.I., BLUESTONE R. & PEARSON C.M. (1973) High association of an HL-A antigen, W27 with ankylosing spondylitis. *New Engl. J. Med.* 288, 704.

SCOTT B.B., SWINBURNE M.L., RAJAH S.M. & LOSOWSKY M.S. (1974) HL-A8 and the immune response to gluten. *Lancet* ii, 169.

SVEJGAARD A., JERSILD C., STAUB NIELSEN L. & BODMER W.F. (1974) HL-A antigens and disease: Statistical and genetical considerations. *Tissue Antigens* 4, 95.

WATERS H., KONRAD P. & WALFORD R.L. (1971) The distribution of HL-A histocompatibility factors and genes in patients with systemic lupus erythematosis. *Tissue Antigens* **1**, 68.

WALFORD R.L., FINKELSTEIN S., NEERHOUT R., KONRAD P. & SHANBRON E. (1970) Acute childhood leukaemia in relation to the HL-A human transplantation genes. *Nature* **225,** 461.

WHITE S.H., NEWCOMER V.D., MICKEY M.R. & TERSAKI P.I. (1972) Disturbances of HL-A antigen frequency in psoriasis. *New Engl. J. Med.* **287,** 740.

## Further reading

CEPPELLINI R. & VAN ROOD J.J. (1974) The HL-A system. I. Genetics and molecular biology. *Seminars in Haematology* **XI,** No. 3, 233.

DAUSSET J. (1972) Correlation between histocompatibility antigens and susceptibility to illness. In SCHWARTZ R.S. *Progress in Clinical Immunology* **1,** 183.

McDEVITT H.O. & BODMER W.F. (1974) HL-A, immune response genes, and disease. *Lancet* **i,** 1269.

SVEJGAARD A., JERSILD C., STAUB-NIELSEN L. & BODMER W.F. (1974) HL-A antigens and disease statistical and genetical considerations. *Tissue Antigens* **4,** 95.

# SECTION IV
# IMMUNOPATHOLOGY

### Immunity and disease

In these days of economic stress, it is held that science needs to show that it is useful to the community. In this section of the book, the relationship of the immune system to disease is discussed, together with the information which specific diseases, 'experiments of nature' can give to the understanding of the basic biological processes. Chapter 19 covers the topics of humoral effector mechanisms seen in both the combating of disease and the causation of pathology. The damage to the individual which may be associated with the immune response to autoantigens is described in Chapter 20, and the nature and extent of the immunologists response (!) to tumours in Chapter 21. Why babies are not rejected as grafts, and more subtle relationships between the mother and the fetus are described in Chapter 22. The book concludes with an overall view of immunity, in the sense of resistance to disease, and its failure.

# Chapter 19
# Biological Activities of Complement

## D. L. Brown

### 19.1 Introduction

The complement system is the principal humoral effector mechanism responsible for the elimination of foreign antigens. This powerful effector system may also exert its effects on surrounding tissues and cells, leading to extensive secondary damage.

### 19.2 Adherence reactions

Adherence reactions appear to be the most important biological activity of the complement system and are expressed when the foreign particle or complex becomes coated with C3b (active, fixed C3) (Henson, 1972). Particles coated with C3b adhere to the surface of cells of the mononuclear phagocytic system, which include peripheral blood monocytes, fixed and free macrophages (Fig. 19.1). They also adhere to a number of other cell types shown in Table 19.1.

**Table 19.1.** Cells bearing C3 receptors

| Cell | Receptor for | Term formerly used |
|---|---|---|
| B lymphocyte | C3b, C3d | |
| Macrophage | C3b | Opsonic adherence |
| Polymorph | C3b | Opsonic adherence |
| Platelet (non-primate) | C3b | Immune adherence |
| Red cell (primate) | C3b | Immune adherence |

The nature of the cell receptors for C3 is poorly defined and distinctions have been made between opsonic and immune adherence phenomena. These are principally distinguished by the cell types involved: phagocytic in one case and passive in the other. No such distinction will be made in this chapter.

274

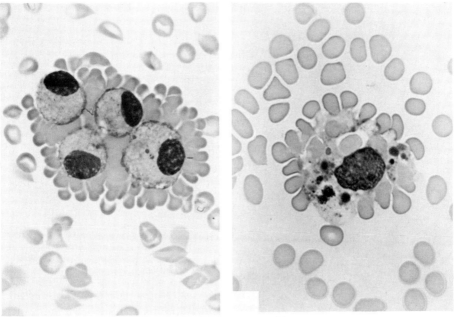

(a)                                    (b)

**Fig. 19.1.** Immune (opsonic) adherence of C3b coated red cells to:
(a) Rabbit alveolar macrophages *in vitro.*
(b) A rabbit Kupffer cell. Interaction between the two cell types occurred *in vivo.* Note the small degree of phagocytosis.

### 19.2.1 *Adherence reactions* in vivo

*In vivo*, adherence reactions result in the rapid clearance of C3b-coated particles by polymorphs or monocytes and sequestration in the reticuloendothelial system, often aided by platelet adherence reactions.

The clearance mechanism critically depends on the functional integrity of the bound C3b which is attacked from the moment of its formation by the C3b inactivator (KAF), present in all extracellular fluids. This destroys the haemolytic and opsonic activity of C3b both *in vivo* and *in vitro.* For example, the half-life of the immune adherence activity of a C3b-coated rabbit red cell is about 30 minutes *in vivo.* C3b finally decays by the cleavage of a major fragment, C3c, from the bound molecule, to leave a comparatively stable inactive fragment, C3d, which remains on the membrane. The activity of the C3b receptor on cells is not competed for or blocked by native C3, and is thus fully active in blood. Although this may be an advantage for the removal of C3b coated particles, it also means that the receptors are highly vulnerable to irreversible blockade by any free C3b produced in the fluid phase. These relationships can be contrasted with the powerful but reversible inhibitory effects of unbound IgG on immune complex-Fc: Fc-receptor interaction in whole serum or plasma.

## 19.3 Peptide fragments

Two peptide fragments, C3a, 8,000 m.w. and C5a, 15,000 m.w., split from C3 and C5 by their respective convertases, are comparatively well characterized. There is more uncertainty about a third 'kinin' peptide derived from the $C\overline{42}$ step, which has a higher molecular weight (approximately 25,000) and may be one of the active substances responsible for increased vascular permeability in angio-oedema. Both C3a and C5a are inactivated in plasma by the high molecular weight (300,000) carboxypeptidase B which cleaves the C-terminal arginine residue. Since the enzyme is highly active in man, the effective *in vivo* half-life of C3a and C5a must be very short.

### 19.3.1 Anaphylatoxins

The term 'anaphylatoxin' was coined by Friedberger in 1910 and the biological activities of both C3a and C5a seem to be embraced by this term. C3a and C5a cause the degranulation of mast cells and basophils, causing the liberation of histamine and, in some species, 5-hydroxytryptamine, both in the tissues and in the circulation. It might be predicted that the activity of C3a and C5a would be greater when they are generated at extravascular sites, where the carboxypeptidase B activity is low. Both peptides increase vascular permeability following intradermal injection, an effect which is blocked by antihistamines. A likely mechanism for their action is that they cause endothelial cell separation in the postcapillary venule via histamine liberation. In bioassay, C3a and C5a show non-cross-reacting tachyphylaxis, suggesting that they either act on different mast cell receptors or on different subpopulations of mast cells.

### 19.3.2 Chemotactic factors

C5a and the trimolecular complex C567, in both its active and inactive forms, are chemotactic *in vitro* for neutrophils, eosinophils, and possibly monocytes. This is based on assaying the migration of the cells through membranes of 3–5 micron pore size. However, their role as chemotactic agents *in vivo* is not clearly understood. If chemotaxis requires the establishment of a concentration gradient, then this cannot occur in circulating blood, though it might conceivably be established across vessel walls or basement membranes.

### 19.3.3 Neutrophil mobilizing factor

A low molecular weight cleavage product of C3, distinct from C3a has been shown to mobilize neutrophils and monocytes when perfused through the femoral bone marrow of mice *in vitro*, though its precise mode of action is obscure. Massive C3 activation *in vivo*, produced by injection of cobra venom factor, causes a sustained neutrophilia and monocytosis, whereas C3 deficient patients consistently fail to generate leucocytosis in response to bacterial infection.

## 19.4 Lytic reactions

### 19.4.1 Complement deficiencies

The lytic, cytocidal and bacteriocidal reactions are the most obvious *in vitro* manifestations of complement action. However, evidence from animals and man with inherited autosomal recessive deficiencies at the C5–9 steps suggests that the absence of these functions *in vivo* is compatible with normal survival (Fig. 19.2). It can only be speculated that possession of an intravascular bacteriocidal capacity might be of survival advantage in certain septicaemias or bacteraemias, though there is no clinical or experimental evidence to support such a suggestion. In contrast, there is rather firm evidence that the lytic phase may be a potentiating factor in Type II and Type III allergic tissue damage (see 19.8 and 19.9 below). Cell membranes may be damaged by indirect lysis following activation of the whole complement sequence.

### 19.4.2 Bystander lysis

Subtle forms of bystander lysis occur if biological membranes are in close proximity to an unrelated complement fixing site. Bystander lysis arises from the contagious transfer of C$\overline{567}$, the active trimolecular complex of C5, C6 and C7 formed in the fluid phase. It may even occur with the larger complex C$\overline{56789}$. The haemolytic half-life of C$\overline{567}$ is very short in the fluid phase, and the effective diffusion radius of damage by attachment to membranes is only a few microns.

The most effective way that transfer of lytic potential can occur is when the complement fixing particle and the target cell are brought together by prior immune adherence. For example, rabbit platelets are lysed by endotoxin in a reaction which requires first a C3-dependent immune adherence step, and second, the C5–9 lytic phase of the complement sequence.

## 19.5 Complement components as auto-antigens

Auto-stimulated antibodies or immunoconglutinins arise to fixed complement components. These are directed primarily against C3b or C4 and may be of the IgM or IgG class. They can be raised ex-

*Chapter 19: Biological Activities of Complement*

perimentally by repeated intravenous injections of heat-killed gram-negative organisms into rabbits and clinically are found at elevated titres in patients with chronic complement-fixing auto-allergic states such as rheumatoid arthritis and chronic cold haemagglutinin disease. In such a setting, they are somewhat analogous to rheumatoid factors. Unusual variants of immuno-

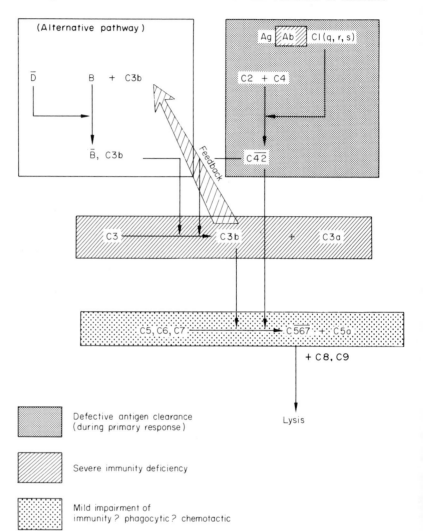

**Fig. 19.2.** Schema demonstrating possible functional disturbances arising from inherited complement deficiencies. Group 1 (fine stippling): deficiencies of the classical pathway at the C142 level predispose to defective antigen clearance (or handling). Group 2 (cross-hatched): primary or secondary deficiency of C3 result in severe immunity deficiency resembling the agammaglobulinaemic type (cross-hatched antibody). Group 3 (coarse stippling): deficiency of C5, C6 or C7 found in healthy individuals, but sometimes associated with immunity impairment, possibly due to phagocytic or chemotactic defects.

*Section IV: Immunopathology*

conglutinins occur in saliva. These are polymers of IgA, whose conglutination (agglutination) reaction with EAC1423 cells can be inhibited by EDTA, indicating a requirement for divalent cations. They also differ from normal immunoconglutinins in showing specificity for native C3 as well as C3b.

Immunoconglutinins agglutinate particles coated with C3b *in vitro*, and by further complement fixation in serum will lyse otherwise unlysable red cell-complement intermediates such as EAC43b. They have no specificity for C3d and so fail to agglutinate EAC43b cells which have undergone prolonged incubation with C3b inactivator.

## 19.6 Role of complement in destruction of microorganisms

### 19.6.1 Bacteria

There is good evidence that opsonization and phagocytosis of bacteria, at least the common pathogens, such as *Staph. spp.*, *Strep. spp.* and *E. coli*, can occur in the absence of complement provided that high titre IgG anti-bacterial antibody of an opsonizing subclass is present. The presence or absence of complement may therefore be of greater relevance when non-opsonizing IgM antibody is being formed very early in the immune response. In the case of gram-negative infection, complement fixation via the alternative (properdin) pathway can occur before any antibody is formed, though there is evidence that activation of alternative pathway components may be less efficient here than if there has been some 'priming' of the system via the classical pathway.

Much of the data supporting the above statements has come from *in vitro* observations on phagocytosis and bacterial killing by neutrophils. *In vivo* evidence has come from the observations of rare individuals with total absence of C3 due to primary or secondary C3 deficiency (see Chapter 5). All these individuals have markedly increased susceptibility to pneumonia, septicaemia or meningitis. During infection they respond to antibiotics normally, though one patient with C3 deficiency is known not to develop a leucocytosis. Their ability to produce opsonizing IgG may well account for their ability to recover normally after antibiotic therapy.

Complement seems to have no role in immunity to facultative intracellular organisms such as *M. tuberculosis*, *M. leprae*, *Listeria spp.* and *Brucella spp.* Here, type IV delayed reactions apparently operate in the absence of complement (see appendix A).

### 19.6.2 Virus neutralization

Antibody and complement may produce lytic lesions on lipid-containing virus envelopes (e.g. *Vaccinia*), or IgG antibody may be formed to viral envelope proteins. The antibody coats the virus and, if present in high titre may prevent cell-to-cell transfer of virus in the absence of complement, limiting the cytopathic effect. Such mechanisms fail if direct cell-to-cell transfer of virus occurs without an extracellular phase, as is found in *herpes simplex* infections.

Complement may, however, have a more subtle role in immunity to viruses. Oldstone *et al.* (1974) showed that in the presence of limiting doses of antibody, neutralization of the cytopathic effect of polyoma virus on mouse cells was critically dependent on classical pathway complement fixation of C3b. It appears that complement aggregates the virus and reduces the number of infective particles. It is not clear what relevance these findings have to virus elimination *in vivo*. Nevertheless, a number of patients have been reported with inherited deficiencies of either C1r, C2 or C4 associated with diseases commonly recognized as having an immune complex pathogenesis. These disorders include classical SLE, SLE-like syndrome without anti-nuclear antibodies, glomerulonephritis and polyarteritis. A common aetiology for such disorders may be immune complex disease arising from failure to eliminate a proliferating antigen (Fig. 19.2). Although viruses have not yet been shown to be the causal agent in these diseases, the evidence suggests that this is the case. An interesting model for the association between a virus disease and glomerulonephritis is the combination of lipodystrophy following measles infection, high levels of C3 nephritic factor, low C3 and subsequent mesangiocapillary glomerulonephritis, a disease in which immune complexes play an important pathogenetic role.

## 19.7 Interrelationships between the complement and co-agulation systems

The two systems may interact at several points during major 'pathological' activation of either system. However, there is little evidence to support the notions that:

(a) complement components are required for normal hemostasis, or

(b) that normal hemostasis *in vivo* leads to secondary activation or conversion of complement components.

### 19.7.1 Platelet reactions

Platelets which are immune adherence positive undergo bystander lysis (see 19.4.2 above) if activation of C5-9 occurs in the vicinity of the C3 fixation sites to which they are attached. The reaction occurs *in vivo* and in platelet-rich plasma *in vitro*. It is well demonstrated by complement activating particles such as endotoxins, crystalline

*Section IV: Immunopathology*

inulin and IgG immune complexes either in antibody excess (4–250×) or in slight antigen excess (2–4×), though poorly at equivalence. Platelet lysis is accompanied by activation of platelet factor 3 (PF3) and release of platelet factor 4 (PF4, anti-heparin factor). There is concomitant total platelet degranulation with release of a major portion of the platelet vasoactive amines, ADP and LDH. PF3 is a phospholipid derived from the platelet membrane. As defined, PF3 cannot initiate coagulation, but rather accelerates the coagulation cascade at the point where activated factor X (Xa) in the presence of factor V, converts prothrombin to thrombin.

In the absence of complement-mediated lysis, mere aggregation of platelets may be sufficient to trigger mediator release. (Becker & Henson, 1974). It is well recognized that primate platelets, including those of man, aggregate in the presence of immune complexes containing IgG, presumably due to the platelet's possession of an IgG receptor. Recent evidence suggests that the aggregation and release of human platelets by immune complexes or zymosan may be complex and that the intensity of aggregation is reinforced by a complement-dependent step which may require C3.

### 19.7.2 Hageman Factor Activation and Hereditary Angio-oedema (HAE)

Activated Hageman factor (XIIa) and its fragments initiate the intrinsic coagulation, the kinin and the fibrinolytic pathways (Magoon et al., 1974; Revak et al., 1974; Colman, 1974). Fig. 19.3 shows a schema for the interrelationship of these pathways derived mainly from in vitro studies with purified components. During activation of these three systems, several serine-histidine esterases are generated, including plasmin, kallikrein and factor XIa, in addition to XIIa itself. Plasmin and thrombin cleave C3 directly and plasmin will also convert C1 to active C1-esterase.

It is uncertain to what extent major activation of the plasmin and kinin systems leads to secondary complement consumption in vivo. This problem might be approached by further investigation of the trigger mechanisms for attacks of oedema in HAE. The disease is due to inherited partial deficiency of the C1̄-inhibitor and is characterized by intermittent attacks of deep non-pitting 'brawny' oedema.

C1̄-inhibitor acts by irreversible stoichiometric combination with the enzymes on which it acts, consuming both enzyme and inhibitor. In addition to C1̄, the inhibitor acts on plasmin, kallikrein, thrombin and factors XIa and XIIa (Fig. 19.3), though it may not be the preferred inhibitor for all these enzymes.

Patients with partial deficiency of C1̄ inhibitor are in a 'knife-edge' situation. Normally, the low levels are sufficient for homeostasis, but events which lead to its rapid depletion may result in the uncontrolled action of C1. This autocatalyses the conversion of

C1 to C1-esterase, which appears free in the fluid phase, and then acts on C4 and C2 without producing an effective $C\overline{42}$ complex, but nevertheless releasing the permeability-producing 'kinin' fragment.

The trigger for attacks of angio-oedema is unknown, but it seems possible that activation of Hageman factor at localized tissue sites, leading to the formation of plasmin and kallikrein, perhaps amplified by a feedback mechanism, may lead to the local consumption of the $C\overline{1}$-inhibitor and release of C1 from homeostatic control.

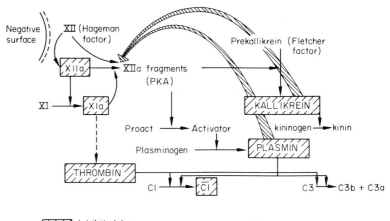

**Fig. 19.3.** Interrelationships between activated Hageman factor (XIIa) and the fibrinolytic, kinin and complement systems.

XIIa (or lower molecular weight fragments of XIIa) activates plasminogen proactivator to activator and prekallikrein to kallikrein. Intrinsic coagulation is also activated via XIa (activated plasma thromboplastin antecedent). The active forms of enzymes (shaded), i.e. XIIa, kallikrein, etc., are stoichiometrically inhibited by irreversible binding to C1-esterase inhibitor ($\alpha_2$-neuraminoglycoprotein).

The active enzymes, principally thought to be kallikrein and plasmin, activate more Hageman factor, so producing a positive feedback in the system. One or more of the enzymes may be activated during an attack of angio-oedema, leading to total depletion of the limited amount of available C1-esterase inhibitor. The complement system may then activate by an autocatalytic mechanism or via a protease such as plasmin.

## COMPLEMENT AND ALLERGIC INFLAMMATION

It should already be clear from the preceding sections of the chapter that complement may amplify the intensity of allergic reactions, but may not always be essential for their expression. The *in vivo* activities of the complement system may not always be beneficial.

*Section IV: Immunopathology*

## 19.8 Type II allergic reactions

These are defined as cytotoxic reactions in which antibody sensitizes target-cell membranes, including vascular basement membranes (Gell & Coombs, 1963, see Appendix A). Cell destruction can occur by two complement-independent mechanisms:

(a) Reticuloendothelial sequestration and phagocytosis of circulating cells following sensitization with opsonizing IgG.

(b) Destruction by cytotoxic K cells.

Red cells or platelets 'lightly' opsonized with IgG antibodies (e.g. anti-Rh antibodies, 'warm' red-cell autoantibodies, antibodies in 'idiopathic' thrombocytopenic purpura) are sequestered by trapping in the Bilroth cords of the spleen. These reside in the red pulp and are thought to act as a macrophage filter bed. Complement fixation by antibody alters the sequestration pattern of red cells. Cells with complement fixed adhere to macrophages, monocytes, and neutrophils as a result of interaction between C3b and the corresponding C3b receptors on these cells. The liver then becomes the dominant sequestration site since it is the largest reticuloendothelial organ with the greatest blood flow, and by pre-emption sequesters C3b-coated cells.

If the complement-fixing antibody is non-opsonizing IgM, then sequestration is often only temporary. For example, red cells in the form EA (IgM) C1423 or EC43 attach by immune adherence to the surface of liver Kupffer cells and are poorly phagocytosed, presumably because they lack a good opsonic coat. The adhering red cells undergo surface microfragmentation while in contact with the macrophage membrane, losing both surface and volume, After 1–3 hours the adhering red cells break away from the sequestration site and return to the circulation. Such a cycle of sequestration and release is seen in chronic cold haemagglutinin disease and is explained by the progressive action of C3b inactivator destroying immune adherence. The red cells finally circulating in patients with chronic cold haemagglutinin disease are in the form EC(4)3d, the C3 being fully degraded.

### 19.8.1 Forssman shock

IgM anti-Forssman antibody injected intravenously into guinea-pigs is bound to endothelial cells in the alveolar capillaries and fixes complement. Platelets and neutrophils adhere and aggregate at the site of C3b fixation and destruction of the endothelial cells results. The animal succumbs from acute pulmonary obstruction, pulmonary oedema and haemorrhage. The reaction is entirely dependent on complement fixation via the classical pathway and is abrogated in C4-deficient guinea-pigs or animals depleted of C3–9 by cobra venom factor.

### 19.8.2 Anti-glomerular basement membrane (GBM)

Glomerular damage is caused by the injection of heterologous anti-GBM antibody. Complement fixation on the GBM may occur and be followed quickly by a mild neutrophil infiltration. It can be shown that the proteinuria which develops during this heterologous phase of anti-GBM nephritis is not dependent on complement or neutrophils. The reaction takes place with equal severity in C4-deficient and C3–9 depleted guinea-pigs and can be elicited by avian anti-GBM antibody, which does not fix mammalian complement. Mammalian antibodies which do not activate the classical complement pathway (e.g. sheep IgG2 and F(ab')$_2$) will also cause the reaction, and it seems that a mechanism independent of the numbered complement components is the principal means of producing proteinuria in guinea-pigs.

## 19.9 Type III allergic reactions

These reactions are caused by either circulating or tissue-fixed immune complexes.

### 19.9.1 The Arthus reaction

The Arthus reaction develops when IgG antibody and antigen combine at a vessel wall after one is initially presented at an extravascular site. For example, the direct active Arthus reaction occurs when antigen is injected subcutaneously into a recipient carrying high titre circulating antibody to that antigen from previous immunization. The same reaction can be elicited in reversed and passive form by injecting antibody subcutaneously and shortly afterwards injecting the antigen intravenously. Antigen and antibody combine in the walls of small vessels and fix complement. Neutrophils infiltrate the area, platelets aggregate, haemorrhage and stasis follow. The end result is a focal haemorrhagic vasculitis which may progress to necrosis.

The lesion is not totally complement-dependent. It develops in an attenuated form in animals depleted of C3–9 by CVF and with normal intensity in C4-deficient guinea-pigs and C6-deficient rabbits, implying that full expression of the lesion can be mediated via the alternative pathway without requirement for the C5–9 step. However, the reaction is highly dependent on the presence of neutrophils and it would appear that these can be recruited to the lesion by the action of IgG antibody alone.

### 19.9.2 Serum sickness

In serum sickness, intravenously injected antigen is removed as an immune complex. During this self-limiting disease, a mild proliferative glomerulonephritis develops, a few polymorphs are present in the glomerulus and there is an associated arteritis. Prior decomplementation abrogates the arteritis and polymorph infiltrate, but has little or no effect on the intensity of the proteinuria. It would therefore appear that complement does not play an essential role in the development of the glomerular lesion. It is, for technical reasons, more difficult to evaluate the role of complement in the pathogenesis of chronic serum sickness, though it would be feasible to produce prolonged decomplementation by injecting CVF into animals which have been made tolerant to it.

### 19.9.3 Aggregate anaphylaxis and acute endotoxaemia

An acute shock state develops when antigen combines in the circulation with high titre complement-fixing antibody. Complement fixation results in platelet aggregation with immune complex by the immune adherence reaction. This is followed by bystander lysis of platelets and release of vaso-active amines and PF3 (see 19.7). Neutrophils and aggregated platelets accumulate in the pulmonary capillaries and the animal may die acutely from pulmonary obstruction and right heart failure. This acute shock state has been called aggregate anaphylaxis.

A more progressive shock state develops when soluble immune complexes or endotoxin, both microparticulate complement fixing substances, are injected intravenously. The initial aggregate shock is less prominent and soluble complex or endotoxin may be trapped by a mechanism involving the vascular endothelium. It is known that immune complexes deposit in vessel walls at subendothelial sites if histamine or 5-HT are injected or released at the same time. Vasoactive amines of this type cause contraction and separation of endothelial cells, allowing leakage and trapping of colloidal particles at the gaps between cells (Manjo & Palade, 1961). When the particle fixes complement with great efficiency, as in the case of endotoxin, vasoactive amines are released from platelets and possibly from other circulating cells such as basophils. This action of vaso-active amines aids the deposition of complement-fixing particles at subendothelial sites. The end result of this process is a vasculitis which, if sufficiently intense and widespread may lead to disseminated intravascular coagulation (DIC).

In man, platelets aggregate and release vasoactive amines via a reaction between a platelet Fc receptor and the Fc sites in IgG-containing immune complexes. Dengue haemorrhagic shock may be an example of such a reaction in its severe form. It occurs in patients who have previously made an uncomplicated recovery from a primary attack of Dengue caused by one strain of Dengue virus. IgG antibody is formed but is not protective against other cross-reacting Dengue strains. Subsequently, an attack of a second serotypically different virus strain may occur. During the phase of viraemia an acute haemorrhagic shock state develops associated with severe thrombocytopaenia, complement consumption and DIC. It appears that the virus and hyperimmune antibody combine in the circulation during the shock phase. The reaction therefore appears to qualify as an acute immune complex disease with an associated haemorrhagic vasculitis and shock.

## References

BECKER L.E. & HENSON P.M. (1973) *In vitro* studies of immunologically induced secretion of mediators from cells and related phenomena. *Adv. Immunol.* **17,** 94.

COLMAN R.W. (1974) Formation of human plasma kinin. *New Engl. J. Med.* **291,** 509.

HENSON P.M. (1972) Complement-dependent adherence of cells to antigen and antibody: Mechanisms and consequences. In INGRAM D.G. *Biological Activities of Complement*, p. 173. Karger, Basel.

MAGOON E.H., SPRAGG J. & AUSTEN K.F. (1974) Human Hageman factor dependent pathways. In RASPE G. *Advances in the Biosciences*, **12,** p. 225. Pergamon Press, Oxford.

MANJO G. & PALADE G.E. (1961) Studies on inflammation (i) The effect of histamine and serotonin on vascular permeability; an electron microscope study. *J. cell. Biol.* **11,** 571.

OLDSTONE M.B.A., COOPER N.R. & LARSON D.L. (1974) Formation and Biologic role of polyoma virus-antibody complexes. A critical role for complement. *J. exp. Med.* **140,** 549.

REVAK S.D., COCHRANE C.G., JOHNSTON A.R. & HUGLI T.E. (1974) Structural changes accompanying enzymatic activation of human Hageman factor. *J. clin. Invest.* **54,** 619.

## Further reading

Relevant sections of the Proceedings of the Second International Immunology Congress, 1974:

*Symposium on Complement: Progress in Immunology II*, **1,** 171 ff.

*Symposium on Immune Complexes and Disease: Progress in Immunology II*, **5,** 49ff.

*Workshop reports*: **1,** 305, 309; **4,** 359, **5,** 329, 333.

PETERS D.K.P. (1975) The Kidney in Allergic Disease. In GELL, P.G.H., COOMBS R.R.A. & LACHMANN P.J. *Clinical Aspects of Immunology*, Chap. 43. Blackwell Scientific Publications, Oxford.

# Chapter 20
# Autoallergic Diseases

# C. J. F. Spry

## 20.1 Introduction

Under normal circumstances allergic reactions are not mounted against autoantigens. This specific failure of an animal to respond to its own tissue antigens is as intriguing a phenomenon as its ability to react to foreign ones. However, there are both clinical and experimental situations where autoallergic reactions do occur and recent advances in understanding T cell reactivity have contributed much to our knowledge of the basic mechanisms involved.

## 20.2 Concepts of autoallergic disease

There is considerable experimental support for the view that lymphocytes capable of reacting to autologous transplantation antigens do not exist in adult animals (Brent *et al.* 1972 and Chapter 10). Two main explanations have been put forward to account for this observation: first, that 'self' reactive clones are never developed and second, that they are produced at an early stage in fetal life and then eliminated after contact with autoantigens, ('clonal elimination', Burnet, 1959). Studies by Medawar and his colleagues on the induction of tolerance to histocompatibility antigens following neo-natal injection of allogeneic cells support the latter concept. However, autoallergic reactions can be readily induced in normal animals when they are injected with other types of autoantigens especially if they are emulsified in complete Freund's adjuvant. Furthermore, lymphocytes of normal individuals have been shown to possess specific receptors for several autologous antigens (*Lancet*, Leading article, 1973). Therefore some autoreactive cells do persist into adult life despite the predictions of the 'clonal elimination' hypothesis. It thus becomes necessary to explain why these cells fail to respond to autoantigens in normal individuals. Recent studies on the induction and regulation of allergic reactions goes some way towards explaining this dilemma.

### 20.2.1 T lymphocyte unresponsiveness to autoantigens

Antibody formation to many antigens requires the cooperative interaction of T and B lymphocytes (Chapter 9). In 1971 it was suggested by two groups that T lymphocytes were required for antibody formation to autoantigens (Allison, 1971; Allison *et al.*, 1973; Chiller *et al.*, 1971).

One suggestion made was that in normal individuals the amount of autoantigen was too small to stimulate T lymphocytes. In this case, one would expect that immunization with high doses of autoantigen would induce an autoallergic state. This has been shown to be the case for thyroglobulin in guinea-pigs where immunization with this antigen induces autoallergic thyroiditis.

An alternative suggestion is that a state of low-zone or T cell tolerance exists to autoantigens. In this case it was postulated that autoreactive B lymphocytes could be stimulated by immunizing with heterologous antigens which bypassed tolerance at the T cell level thus stimulating B cells (see Fig. 10.4). This hypothesis derives considerable experimental support from the studies of Weigle and his colleagues who have shown that autoallergic thyroiditis can be induced in rabbits following immunization with heterologous thyroglobulin. Furthermore, in mice this autoallergic state can be transferred to normal recipients by T lymphocytes (Clagett & Weigle, 1974).

This concept applies to several types of drug-induced autoallergic disorders. It may also apply to systemic lupus erythematosus (SLE) for example, where viral material could be incorporated into the cell membrane or genome, and act as a carrier for 'self' membrane antigens or DNA.

*20.2.2 The role of suppressor T lymphocytes*

Studies on cell interactions in the allergic response have shown that T lymphocytes both enhance and suppress B lymphocyte differentiation (Chapters 9 and 10) (Gershon, 1974). If suppression were lacking, it is possible that B lymphocytes might respond to antigenic stimulation by uncontrolled clonal proliferation leading to an overproduction of monoclonal antibody. It might be interesting to see if the monoclonal autoantibody in autoallergic states such as chronic cold haemagglutinin disease is due to such a phenomenon. However, in thyroid diseases, and probably in the majority of other autoallergic diseases, antibodies are not monoclonal. Also, if autoallergic reactions are due to loss of suppressor T lymphocytes it should be possible to inhibit autoallergic responses by injecting these suppressor cells. Initial experiments which support this hypothesis have been done in NZB/NZW mice which develop spontaneous autoallergic disease and where multiple thymus grafts have prolonged their survival (Kysela & Steinberg, 1973).

## 20.3 Autoallergic disease in man

There is a large, and ever growing, list of diseases in man which are associated with the presence of autoantibodies and other auto-allergic phenomena (Table 20.1). These autoantibodies are generally held to be involved in tissue destruction. However, it is important to realize that these reactions may be the consequence

**Table 20.1.** Human diseases in which autoallergic reactions occur

| | |
|---|---|
| *Endocrine diseases* | *Renal and lung diseases* |
| Hashimoto's thyroiditis | Glomerulonephritis |
| Graves' disease | Goodpasture's syndrome |
| Myxoedema | |
| Diabetes mellitus | |
| | *Eye diseases* |
| | Uveitis |
| *Skin diseases* | |
| Pemphigus vulgaris | |
| Pemphigoid | *Muscle and skin diseases* |
| | Myasthenia gravis |
| *Liver diseases* | Dermatomyositis |
| Primary biliary cirrhosis | Scleroderma |
| Chronic active hepatitis | |
| Cryptogenic cirrhosis | |
| Lupoid hepatitis | *Blood diseases* |
| | Haemolytic anaemia |
| | Idiopathic thrombocytopenic |
| *Gastrointestinal diseases* | purpura |
| Coeliac disease | |
| Ulcerative colitis | |
| Pernicious anaemia | *'Rheumatic' diseases* |
| | Rheumatic fever |
| | Rheumatoid arthritis |
| *Lymphoid tumours* | Ankylosing spondylitis |
| Thymoma | Polymalgia rheumatica |
| Hodgkin's disease | Sjögren's syndrome |
| | Systemic lupus erythematosus |
| *Neurological diseases* | |
| Encephalitis | |
| Multiple sclerosis | |

rather than the cause of tissue damage and, at present, there is no way to distinguish these two possibilities. Non-cytotoxic antibodies are found, for example, in Graves' disease where 50 per cent of patients have an IgG antibody known as Long Acting Thyroid Stimulator (LATS). This autoantibody stimulates thyroid cells to secrete thyroid hormones by combining with the receptor for thyroid stimulating hormone.

*Chapter 20: Autoallergic Disease*

Recently Grabar (1974) has made the provocative suggestions that autoantibody levels are simply a measure of the extent of tissue damage due to any cause, and that autoantibodies act as opsonins for autoantigens released from damaged tissues. They could therefore promote the phagocytosis and destruction of autoantigens which would be poorly dealt with by the reticuloendothelial system. However tissue destruction is not invariably accompanied by autoantibody formation, so other factors must be involved.

### 20.3.1 Types of autoallergic diseases in man

Clinically there is a very wide spectrum of autoallergic diseases. They may be considered to be 'organ specific' or 'non-organ specific'. 'Organ specific' diseases include the autoallergic endocrine diseases and autoallergic haemolytic anaemias. In 'non-organ specific' diseases, the disease process is normally widespread, and examples include SLE, rheumatoid arthritis, Sjögren's syndrome and rheumatic fever. At one time it was considered that these reactions involved abnormal collagen, and so were called 'Collagen Diseases'. In the absence of evidence that collagen is defective, it is best not to use this term. The extent of the autoallergic diseases among different tissues is probably an indication both as to the sites of the autoantigens involved and their accessibility to allergic effector mechanisms.

### 20.3.2 Autoantibodies in man

Autoantibodies with many different specificities may be detected in the blood of patients with autoallergic diseases. Indeed, it is unusual to find only one type of antibody in a patient. In SLE antibodies to a wide range of autoantigens such as DNA, RNA, cytoplasmic organelles, erythrocytes, platelets and clotting factors have all been described.

A number of autoantibodies have been shown to be of clinical diagnostic value. These are listed in Table 20.2. As these autoantibodies and their antigens are better characterized it is to be hoped that their value in clinical work will increase.

### 20.3.3 Antibody to lymphocytes

In view of the evidence that T lymphocytes are somehow involved in autoallergic diseases, it is not surprising that considerable interest has been taken in the detection of autoantibody to different lymphocyte populations. In man, about half of those with SLE have antibodies to their own T lymphocytes (Lies *et al.*, 1973). Detection of cytotoxic antibodies to lymphocytes may be of clinical value, since they appear to correlate with the presence of immune-complex renal disease, which could be initiated by the release of antigens from these damaged lymphocytes (Ooi *et al.*, 1974).

Autoantibodies to T lymphocytes are also found in NZB mice which develop a disease analogous to SLE. By one month of age, 50 per cent of NZB mice have the antibody and the incidence continues to rise with age. These autoantibodies react with the T lymphocytes of both normal and diseased mice (Shirai *et al.*, 1973) and may contain anti-$\theta$ specificity (Parker *et al.*, 1974). The relationship of this autoantibody to the universal infection of these mice with 'C' type murine leukaemia virus remains to be explored.

The finding of antibodies to lymphocytes in autoallergic disease has two important consequences. The first is a practical one: lymphocytes bearing immunoglobulin on their surfaces may be T

Table 20.2. Some autoantibodies of clinical diagnostic value

| Autoantibody to | Disease |
| --- | --- |
| Thyroglobulin, mitochondria | Thyroid diseases |
| Nucleii and DNA | SLE, Sjögren's syndrome and chronic active hepatitis |
| Immunoglobulin | Rheumatoid arthritis |
| C3 | Chronic infections |
| Erythrocytes | Haemolytic anaemias |
| Parietal cells, intrinsic factor | Pernicious anaemia |
| Basement membrane | Nephritis, Goodpasture's syndrome |
| Skin | Pemphigus, pemphigoid |
| Mitochondria | Primary biliary cirrhosis |
| Smooth muscle microsomes | Chronic active hepatitis |
| Reticulin | Coeliac disease |

lymphocytes coated with antibody and would be $Ig^+$ in T/B lymphocyte evaluation. They would thus be mistaken for B cells. Secondly, these autoantibodies may be cytotoxic for T lymphocytes and induce a secondary immunity deficiency state.

### 20.3.4 Type IV reactions to autoantigens

Most immunological studies on autoallergic disease have centred on autoantibodies, but in many instances, Type IV reactions may be more important. In man, the main evidence for Type IV reactions is histological, but *in vitro* tests are being developed which show some promise. In the most widely studied *in vitro* test, patients' lymphocytes are incubated with autoantigens to see whether they will produce migration inhibition factor (MIF). Positive MIF tests have been detected in a number of diseases, and these are shown in

Table 20.3. As can be seen, mitochondrial antigens appear to play a special role in this type of reaction. Autoantibodies to mitochondria are also found in these diseases but their significance is unknown.

In animals there is more convincing evidence for the role of Type IV reactions in autoallergic disease. Rats immunized with a low molecular weight 'encephalitogenic protein' which is extracted from brain tissue, develop an experimental autoallergic encephalomyelitis. On histological examination of the brain there is a typical Type IV reaction and the disease can be transferred to other animals with washed living lymphocytes, but not with serum.

**Table 20.3.** Cell-mediated reactions to 'self' antigen in autoallergic diseases

| Disease | Antigen inducing MIF production |
|---|---|
| Hashimoto's thyroiditis | |
| Pernicious anaemia | Rat liver mitochondria |
| Primary biliary cirrhosis | |
| Primary biliary cirrhosis | Liver extracts |
| Hashimoto's thyroiditis | Human mitochondria, thyroid, kidney, liver |
| Pernicious anaemia | Human mitochondria liver and stomach |
| Addison's disease | Human adrenal |
| Diabetes mellitus | Rat liver mitochondria Nuclear antigens |

## 20.4 Experimental models of autoallergic diseases

Much of the experimental work on autoallergic diseases in animals has centred on diseases induced by injecting autoantigens in complete Freund's adjuvant. These studies suffer from the disadvantages that the process of immunization is designed to overcome normal homeostatic mechanisms, and unless it is postulated that autoallergic diseases are initiated in a similar way, including environmental exposure to adjuvant, they could prove to be misleading. Recently a number of spontaneous autoallergic diseases in animals have been discovered which appear to be the counterpart of similar diseases in man.

### 20.4.1 NZB/NZW mice and SLE

NZB/NZW mice develop an autoallergic disease spontaneously which has close analogies to SLE. This is now one of the best studied animal models of an autoallergic disease in man. Both disorders are associated with the occurrence of antibodies to nuclear antigens, positive LE cell tests and haemolytic anaemia. The animals eventually die from anaemia, or renal failure due to antigen–antibody complexes. The haemolytic component of the disorders is particularly marked in the NZB parent strain. As described in 20.3.3 they show antibodies to T lymphocytes, which eventually lead to gross deficiency in both T lymphocyte numbers and function.

### 20.4.2 Thyroiditis in obese chickens

The discovery that spontaneous autoallergic thyroiditis occurs in obese White Leghorn chickens has been particularly important as it has provided an experimental model in which B lymphocyte responses to autoantigens can be studied. Autoantibodies to thyroid tissue normally appear in the blood of these chickens within two weeks of hatching and after several months they become lethargic, with poor feather formation and obesity. Finally the complete picture of hypothyroidism occurs. Neonatal bursectomy results in a diminution of the thyroiditis (Wick, 1970) and autoantibody titres are correspondingly reduced. Here, therefore, it is difficult to avoid the conclusion that the autoantibodies cause the thyroid damage. This disorder is analogous to Hashimoto's thyroiditis in man where progressively thyroid failure can also be correlated with high levels of anti-thyroid antibodies.

## 20.5 Genetic aspects of autoallergic diseases

Genetic factors have been recognized in autoallergic diseases for many years, particularly in family studies on patients with auto-allergic thyroid diseases, pernicious anaemia, and myasthenia gravis. In addition, it has been known for some years that there is a link between histocompatibility genes and allergic responses (Demant, 1973). More recently, support for the genetic basis for some of the autoallergic diseases in man has been developed from studies of histocompatibility markers (HLA antigens) and an increasing number of autoallergic diseases in man have been found to be associated with particular HLA haplotypes (McDevitt & Bodmer, 1974), see Chapter 18.

It is of interest that the majority of associations are with second locus genes, and these may be close to the immune response genes in man. This could mean that these disease susceptibilities are linked to genes regulating immune responsiveness. It is thus possible that T lymphocytes from patients with autoallergic diseases may have a lower 'threshold' to stimulation by auto-antigens. Clinical experience of SLE would support this concept,

*Chapter 20: Autoallergic Disease*

as these patients are notoriously easy to sensitize with drugs, especially antibiotics.

The association with HLA antigens has been found to be marked in the case of ankylosing spondylitis in which patients are found to possess the HLA-B27 antigen in as many as 90 per cent of cases. However, it should be noted that the association does not imply that the disease is 'caused' in some way by possession of the HLA-B27 antigen. As previously discussed (see Chapter 18) there may be other factors involved in the induction of these diseases. The rational management of this group of important chronic diseases will depend on elucidation of these factors and an understanding of the way in which they interact in susceptible individuals.

## References

ALLISON A.C. (1971). Unresponsiveness to self antigens. *Lancet* ii, 1401.

ALLISON A.C., DENMAN A.M. & BARNES R.D. (1971) Cooperating and controlling functions of thymus-derived lymphocytes in relation to autoimmunity. *Lancet* ii, 135.

BRENT L., BROOKS C., LUBLING N. & THOMAS A.V. (1972). Attempts to demonstrate an *in vivo* role for serum blocking factors in tolerant mice. *Transplantation* 14, 382.

BURNET F.M. (1959) *The clonal selection of acquired immunity*. Cambridge University Press.

CHILLER J.M., HABICHT G.S. & WEIGLE W.O. (1971) Kinetic differences in unresponsiveness of thymus and bone marrow cells. *Science* 171, 813.

CLAGETT J.A. & WEIGLE W.O. (1974) Roles of T and B lymphocytes in the termination of unresponsiveness to autologous thyroglobulin in mice. *J. exp. Med.* 139, 643.

DÉMANT P. (1973) H-2 gene complex and its role in alloimmune reactions. *Transpl. Revs.* 15, 162.

GERSHON R.K. (1974) T cell control of antibody production. In COOPER M.D. & WARNER N.L. *Contemporary Topics in Immunobiology, Vol. III*, p. 1. New York.

GRABER P. (1974) 'Self' and 'Not-Self' in immunology. *Lancet* i, 1320.

KYSELA S. & STEINBERG A.D. (1974) Increased survival of NZB/W mice given multiple syngeneic young thymus grafts. *Clin. Immunol. Immunopath.* 2, 133.

Leading article (1973) Lymphocytes reactive to autoantigens. *Lancet* ii, 949.

LIES R.B., MESSNER R.P. & WILLIAMS R.C. (1973) Relative T-cell specificity of lymphocytotoxins from patients with systemic lupus erythematosus. *Rheum.* 16, 369.

McDEVITT H.O. & BODMER W.F. (1974) HL-A, Immune response genes, and disease. *Lancet* i, 1269.

OOI B.S., ORLINA A.R., PESCE A.J., MENDOZA N., MASAITIS L. & POLLAK V.E. (1974) Lymphocytotoxic antibodies in patients with systemic lupus erythematosus. *Clin. exp. Immunol.* 17, 237.

SHIRAI T., YOSHIKI T. & MELLORS R.C. (1973) Effects of natural thymocytotoxic autoantibody of NZB mice and of specifically prepared anti-

*Section IV: Immunopathology*

lymphocyte serum on the tissue distribution of $^{51}$Cr-labelled lymphocytes. *J. Immunol.* **110,** 517.

PARKER L.M., CHUSED T.M. & STEINBERG A.D. (1974) Immunofluorescence studies on thymocytotoxic antibody from New Zealand Black Mice. *J. Immunol.* **112,** 285.

WICK G. (1970) The effect of bursectomy, thymectomy, and X-irradiation on the incidence of precipitating liver and kindey auto-antibodies in chickens of the obese strain (OS). *Clin. exp. Immunol.* **7,** 187.

**Further reading**

GLYNN L.E. & HOLBOROW E.J. (1974). *Autoimmunity and disease.* 2nd ed. Blackwell, Oxford.

# Chapter 21
# Tumour Immunology

## P. Alexander

### 21.1 Introduction

Until relatively recently, many experimentalists regarded the host–tumour relationship as passive on the part of the host and active on the part of the tumour. The host was thought to supply only essential nutriments and oxygen, these being the only factors by which the host exercised tumour restraint. The clinical history of tumours lent a little support to this view, since cancers, at least in the early stages, were not found to progress relentlessly. In melanoma, for example, individual nodules frequently remain static and often partially regress although total spontaneous regression is rare. Furthermore, the reappearance of metastases years after the removal of a primary tumour cannot be reconciled with the autonomous tumour cell hypothesis, since this would demand a prodigiously long cell cycle time. The finding within tumours of numerous normal host cells such as macrophages, polymorphs and lymphocytes is clear evidence for an active involvement of the host in tumour growth. Host cells frequently constitute half the tumour mass (Evans, 1972).

That the host might exert some form of specific immunological control was first observed twenty years ago. Foley (1953) demonstrated weak homograft-like reactions when experimentally induced murine sarcomas were transplanted into sensitized recipients. At the time, this type of host response to tumour antigens was widely believed to be a special case and not to apply generally to all malignancies.

### 21.2 The nature of tumour-specific transplantation antigens (TSTAs)

In recent years, the existence of specific antigens on tumours induced by chemical, physical and viral agents has been found to be the rule rather than the exception, although their role in malignant transformation remains unclear.

The term 'tumour antigen' has been used to describe two entirely different classes of macromolecules; those present on or in tumour cells which elicit an immunological reaction in the host, and those which are associated with the tumour, but are only antigenic in species other than the host. Carcino-embryogenic antigen and α-fetal protein are examples of the latter class, but being non-antigenic in the host cannot constitute a point of attack for its allergic mechanisms.

### 21.2.1 Detection of TSTAs

In experimental animals, the detection of TSTAs principally rests on resistance to challenge, but in man this is clearly not a useable method.

In man evidence for the existence of TSTAs comes mainly from cell-mediated cytotoxic reactions wherein it can be shown that the blood mononuclear cells of patients are cytotoxic for their own tumour cells *in vitro*. However, there are people who have killer mononuclear cells, but who do not have cancer, and there are even 'universal killers', whose cells will, in favourable circumstances, kill all cancer cells. The nature of these cytotoxic cells is unclear, and they are an embarrassment to this type of *in vitro* approach to human TSTAs. Antibodies against tumour cells have also been described, but are difficult to distinguish from the more general autoantibodies common in cancer patients (Whitehouse & Holborrow, 1971).

### 21.2.2 Classification of TSTAs

(a) *Oncogenic viral antigens.* Expression of these antigens does not require the persistence of intact virus, since in some cases the viral genome may be incorporated into the host cell genome. These antigens are identical irrespective of the species in which they are expressed.

(b) *Embryogenic antigens.* These macromolecules are normally present during early embryogenic life, but since they are suppressed before the development of the immune system, immunological tolerance to them is consequently not induced. Malignant cells may begin to translate these otherwise silent genes. The antigens cross-react widely within different tumours within a species and occasionally even between species (Coggin, 1970).

(c) *Unique tumour antigens.* These macromolecules are novel not only to the species but also to individual tumours induced within the same strain of animals by the same carcinogen. They are not found in embryos, and often occur after the induction of tumours by chemical, physical and even viral agents, although in the latter case they are distinct from those described in (a). The origin of the genes coding for these antigens is unknown, but a number of hypotheses can be offered:

1. The inducing agent causes mutation of the transformed cell.
2. That they are the products of genes which are usually wholly

*Chapter 21: Tumour Immunology*

suppressed even during embryogenesis. The principal difficulty of this hypothesis is that the antigens are very heterogeneous: each of ten sarcomas induced in the same strain of mice by a chemical carcinogen have individual, non-cross-reacting TSTAs. Even different tumours induced at two sites in a single animal have different, non-cross-reacting antigens.

In general, chemically induced tumours contain TSTAs of types (b) and (c). On the other hand, virally induced tumours express TSTAs of types (a) and (b) and sometimes (c).

The TSTAs of humans have a feature not seen hitherto in experimental animals: the antigens are characteristic of the histogenic origin of the tumour but are not specific to individual tumours as in (c). Thus, all melanomas have melanoma-specific antigens which are shared by all melanomas, but not by carcinomas of the bladder, which in turn all have their own characteristic antigens. In this sense there is a formal similarity between human cancers and virally induced tumours, though to sustain the analogy, it would be necessary to postulate that all human tumours of the bladder are due to a specific oncogenic virus, different from that which might be causing all melanomas—a nearly absurd concept. It seems much more tenable that the human TSTAs are specialized embryogenic antigens.

### 21.3 Immune surveillance

It has been postulated first by Ehrlich (1909) and more recently by Burnet (1970) that the immune system constantly surveys the tissue cells of individuals, eliminating any mutant cells which have become neoplastic. If this were true, it should be expected that patients on immunosuppressive therapy, e.g. transplant cases should have a higher incidence of tumours than usual. Claims to this effect have been made, though for the common tumours such as carcinomas, they have not been properly validated by the use of appropriate control population statistics. The only class of tumour which has a genuinely higher incidence in transplant recipients are lymphoreticular, in particular, reticulum cell sarcoma, whose oncogenesis may be related to the co-existence of immunosuppressives and strong antigenic stimuli in transplant patients. In intensively immunosuppressed mice (e.g. thymectomized and ALS treated) there is an increased incidence of neoplastic disease due to viruses such as polyoma which normally only act in newborn and not in adults, but there is no increase in spontaneous or chemically induced tumours. (See also Alexander (1976)).

### 21.4 Resistance to tumours

TSTAs of types (a) and (c) constitute effective targets for allergic destruction of target cells, since immunization with these antigens promotes host resistance. It is surprising and disappointing that neither of these types of antigen seem to be common in human tumours. It may be that tumours bearing these antigens do arise in humans, but that they are efficiently destroyed by our immune system. The widely cross-reactive TSTAs of embryonic origin (b) do not constitute suitable targets for allergic destruction in mice and rats, though they may in hamsters (Coggin, 1970).

Large established tumour masses, often clinically detectable and containing perhaps $10^{10}$ rapidly dividing cells are probably an overwhelming problem as far as the immune system is concerned. It seems more rational that the main thrust of immunological control will be directed at the eradication of small tumour masses or isolated groups of metastases. Whilst the large tumour masses may be controlled by surgery and radiotherapy, it is the prevention of the growth of small secondary tumour deposits that is the clinical problem. In experimental situations, immunized animals can eradicate small tumour masses.

### 21.4.1 Tumour escape from allergic destruction

A number of mechanisms (see Table 21.1) have been postulated for the escape of small tumour masses from immunological control:

(a) *Central failure of the allergic response.* Specific immunological tolerance had at one time been claimed to occur in mice bearing virally-induced mammary tumours or leukaemias, but the evidence has now been refuted. In human cases, evidence for reactivity against TSTA would also argue against tolerance. Immunological paralysis has also been postulated as a mechanism, but in man the anergy of advanced cancer patients is general, rather than tumour-specific and is a consequence, rather than a cause, of advanced cancer.

**Table 21.1.** Biological mechanisms which have been considered to be relevant to the escape of antigenic tumours

---

A: *Not of general importance:*
    (a) Specific tolerance to tumour-specific antigen.
    (b) Generalized immune defect (genetic: ageing; drug induced).

B: *Of general importance:*
    (a) Interference by immunologically specific humoral factors which 'inhibit' cytotoxic cells or 'block' target cells.
    (b) Anatomical (unequal distribution of various effector processes).

C: *Role remains to be established:*
    (a) Membrane antigen does not constitute target for cytotoxic attack.

---

                   *Chapter 21: Tumour Immunology*

(b) *Failure of the effector limb of the allergic response.*

(i) Anatomical reasons: all sites in the body are not equally access-ible to the effector limb of the allergic response, and there are sites wherein bacteria or tumour cells 'seek immunological sanctuary'. Although this is a recognized phenomenon in bacterial infection (e.g. tubercle bacilli in macrophages), it is undocumented for tumours although there is powerful circumstantial evidence. There is also evidence that certain types of cytotoxic cells are unevenly distributed (Alexander & Hall, 1970). Some cells which promote cell-mediated cytotoxicity are present for long periods in the blood but appear only transiently in the lymph (Grant *et al.*, 1974).

(ii) Interference with the effector limb: A failure of cell-mediated cytotoxic reactions on account of blocking factors has been put forward as a serious candidate for an escape mechanism. The ex-perimental observation is that cells from tumour bearing animals or humans can kill the tumour cells *in vitro*, but that the specific cytotoxic killing is interfered with by factors present in the serum of the tumour bearer whose sites of action are classified in Table 21.2.

**Table 21.2.** Definitions of interference by serum factors in *in vitro* cytotoxicity tests

| Agent binds to | Definition |
| --- | --- |
| Aggressor cells (macrophages or lymphocytes) | Inhibition |
| Target cells | Blocking |
| Either (experiment does not distinguish) | Interference |

Hellstrom & Hellstrom (1969) originally proposed that these factors were antibody which coated the target cells. They have recently suggested that they are immune complexes which speci-fically 'block' the target cells and thereby prevent interaction between cytotoxic cells and tumour cells leading to killing (Hell-strom & Hellstrom, 1974). The evidence that antibody plays a significant role in the interference by antigen-antibody complexes is not wholly immunochemically acceptable and the role of anti-body has been called into question by the recent experiments of Linna *et al.* (1974). These showed that bursectomized birds which are totally agammaglobulinaemic and incapable of making anti-body, nonetheless develop potent blocking factors to tumour antigens. The facts to date would appear to support the hypothesis that the interfering factors are soluble tumour antigens, and al-though immune complexes can prevent the reaction, the active component in this is antigen.

(c) *Soluble antigens and inhibition of cell-mediated reactions.* Soluble tumour antigens have been shown to inhibit both antibody

*Section IV: Immunopathology*

and cell-mediated limbs of the allergic response (Table 21.3) (Currie & Basham, 1972). Excess soluble antigens in serum could come either from the autolysis of tumour cells, or by spontaneous release from the tumour. A high rate of spontaneous shedding of tumour antigens can be measured *in vitro*, and this has been shown to correlate well with the ability of such tumours to metastasize (Currie & Alexander, 1974). The ability of small tumour masses to grow in the immediate environment of a pre-existing primary is probably due to a zone of shed antigen which prevents allergic destruction. Finally, the role of antigen in altering lymphocyte traffic, and hence proper immune surveillance, is obviously yet another mechanism whereby antigen can promote tumour escape (Alexander & Hall, 1970).

**Table 21.3.**

A. *Properties of serum inhibitor (circulating tumour-specific antigen)*
1. Inhibits cytotoxicity to tumour of mononuclear cells from sera of patients and rats with tumours.
2. Combines with cytotoxic cells but not with tumour cells in the *in vitro* test system.
3. Molecular weight less than 100,000.
4. Substances with similar properties can be isolated from tumour membranes (man and rats).
5. In rats immunization with the soluble antigen (with adjuvant) does not induce immunity.

B. *Experimental evidence for the presence of circulating TSTAs in serum*
1. Inhibition of cytotoxicity of mononuclear cells from blood or lymph nodes of tumour bearers.
2. Serological
   (i) Neutralization of syngeneic antiserum obtained from rats after excision of tumour.
   (ii) Radioimmunoassay using $I^{125}$ labelled TSTA isolated from tumour by affinity chromatography.

## 21.5 Immunotherapy of cancer (see Table 21.4)

The aim of immunotherapy should be to overcome the escape mechanisms of the tumour, though in practice most attempts at immunotherapy have borne little relation to the reasons why a particular tumour has, in fact, escaped. It is for this reason that an understanding of the mechanisms involved in tumour growth are crucial if immunotherapy is to have a rational basis.

### 21.5.1 Passive immunotherapy

The administration of cells or antibody from a suitably immunized

**Table 21.4.** Procedures shown to have an anti-tumour action in experimental tumours and classified as 'immunotherapy'

---

*Passive:*

Antibodies
Allergized lymphocytes $\Big\}$ obtained from suitably immunized donors.

Products isolated from allergized lymphocytes (RNA:transfer factor (?)).

*Active:*

Specific—inject tumour antigens in an immunogenic form.

Non-specific—treat with microbial products that simulate the reticulo-endothelial system.

Inflammation—non-specific destruction of tumour cells by products of inflammatory exudate (activated macrophages).

---

donor against TSTA has been used in experimental animal systems, though with success only when the tumour burden is small (Alexander, 1968). It is clearly futile to attempt to bolster the effector limb if the animal is already making a response which is rendered ineffective by a vast excess of free antigen which inhibits.

At present, passive forms of immunotherapy cannot be considered suitable for clinical application either in terms of effectiveness or safety since, quite apart from the fact that the injection of large amounts of foreign protein is hazardous, there is no suitable potential source of immune cells for human use. The possibility has been explored of injecting RNA from immune lymphoid cells instead of the cells themselves. The mechanism by which such RNA exerts an anti-tumour action is not understood, and it has been proposed that this RNA transferred immunological information to the host lymphocytes. In spite of the fact that some years ago we were ourselves experimenting with this procedure, I cannot demonstrate any enthusiasm for it. Even more problematical is the injection of transfer factor. Here, of course, no animal experiments can be done, and the procedure can only be tested in man. Claims have been made for the therapeutic effect of a low molecular weight substance extracted from the lymphocytes of suitable donors, suitability being defined as having cells that are cytotoxic to the types of tumour to be treated. As yet, however, I know of no convincing data to show that this procedure has any effect.

### 21.5.2 Active immunotherapy

*Specific immunotherapy* by the injection of tumour vaccines has a venerable history dating from 1909. An effect can be demonstrated in carefully controlled experiments in rats (Haddow & Alexander, 1964) where immunization with lethally irradiated biopsy fragments removed from the tumours provided an efficient anti-tumour action in the host. This prevented the local recurrence of partially treated primary sarcomas.

*Non-specific immunotherapy* also has a long history dating from 1924 when Murphy showed that the cure rate following surgical excision of mouse mammary tumours was higher if the reticuloendothelial system had been stimulated by injections of oleic acid. More recently BCG and C. parvum have been in vogue as nonspecific reticuloendothelial stimulants following the demonstration by Dubos (1957) that BCG vaccination improved resistance to certain types of bacterial infection. It is known that BCG potentiates the effect of specific immunotherapeutic efforts, though since the BCG is often given at a different site, or at a different time from the irradiated tumour cells, it is not clear whether the effect is that of an RES stimulant or an adjuvant (see Table 21.5).

**Table 21.5.** Mechanisms that contribute to the anti-tumour activity of BCG

1. When injected into the tumour—intense local inflammatory response.
2. Systemic—stimulation of RE system—macrophage proliferation.
3. Given with tumour cells—adjuvant for potentiating specific active immunotherapy.
4. Following sensitization to BCG a suitable antigen (e.g. PPD) will cause macrophages to become 'activated' and thus cytotoxic to tumour cells.

The term immunotherapy has been applied to the injection of live BCG into cutaneous tumours, notably isolated melanoma deposits, which frequently disappear. The method produces intense local reaction frequently with unpleasant ulceration, a process which I have termed 'floating the tumour away on a sea of pus'. I find it difficult to justify the treatment of skin melanomas by local injection of BCG since there is little evidence of tumours remote from the site of injection regressing. Such regression of uninjected tumours as has been reported is usually close to the injected nodule, and may be a result of cross-infection or of spread of local reaction. Tumours do not grow well at the sites of delayed hypersensitivity reactions, and basal cell carcinomas can be destroyed by inducing local hypersensitivity reactions at the site of the tumour. However, the local skin response and systemic effects of such treatment can be severe. In general, surgery or regional chemotherapy are to be preferred as methods of treatment.

### 21.6 Attempts to establish the role of immunotherapy in the management of malignant disease

The only way to establish whether immunological manoeuvres are of clinical benefit to cancer patients is by carefully controlled

*Chapter 21: Tumour Immunology*

clinical trials. For nearly 100 years there have been haphazard adventures from which no conclusions can be drawn. Occasional responses were claimed, but these were rarely reproduced by other investigators who used apparently similar techniques of immunotherapy. We must guard against producing a similar set of uninterpretable data in this new era of enthusiasm for tumour immunology. In my opinion, the use of immunotherapy in malignant disease is unethical unless it is carried out as part of a controlled clinical trial. Not only may we fail to gain any information from isolated treatment of patients, but since such treatment may be harmful, we shall not find out if harm has, in fact, been done.

### 21.6.1 Conduct of trials

It is important that trials should be carried out in a manner which will yield information. An example of an inadequate trial was one in which patients with melanoma were first treated conventionally until in clinical remission, and then given BCG therapy. The control patients (given no BCG) were a group treated ten years earlier, who did worse than the BCG treated group. This whole study has to be repeated before it can be taken as established because of the inadequacy of the control data.

### 21.6.2 Trials of non-specific immunotherapy

Mathé (1970) reported the first controlled immunotherapy trial on acute lymphoblastic leukaemia. Two groups of children in whom complete remission had been established for 18 months by chemotherapy were divided into four groups, of whom three received immunotherapy according to one of three protocols, which were BCG only, killed tumour cells only and both BCG and tumour cells. While it is clear that, as a group, those who received BCG immunotherapy did better than those who were not treated, the numbers were insufficient to establish the nature of the improved performance. An MRC trial of the effect of BCG treatment as a maintenance regime in childhood leukaemia showed that the treated children did no better than those who were not treated, and worse than those who received maintenance chemotherapy. These findings do not negate those of Mathé, since the method of application and source of BCG were different. A finding similar to that of the MRC trial has been reported from the USA in which a protocol more closely resembling that of Mathé was used in the treatment of childhood leukaemia.

BCG therapy for Burkitt's lymphoma following rigorously the Mathé regime in children who had attained complete remission failed to show any difference between treated and control groups. However, very recently, BCG only was found to prolong remission induced by chemotherapy in adults with acute leukaemia.

### 21.6.3 Trials of specific immunotherapy

Immediately following the demonstration in 1964 that rats benefited from therapy with irradiated tumour cells, we started a trial on patients with anaplastic gliomas (Bloom *et al.*, 1973). Conventional surgery and radiotherapy was followed in half of the cases by autografts of tumour which had been isolated with their own tumour and irradiated *in vitro*. This first carefully controlled human trial proved decisively negative. The principal conclusion to be drawn was that immunotherapy protocols must be designed carefully in the light of measurements of the patient's immune responses. Investigation of melanoma patients indicated that in order to produce a measurable change in the patient's immune status a regime of $10^8$–$10^9$ irradiated tumour cells weekly is needed: quite different from the single dose given in the glioma trial (Ikonopisov *et al.*, 1970).

The problem of the supply of such massive numbers of tumour cells has been solved in the case of acute adult (myeloblastic) leukaemia by the use of the IBM continuous-flow cell separation centrifuge, together with modern cryostorage techniques (Powles *et al.*, 1973). Patients in chemotherapeutically induced clinical remission are given either chemotherapy alone or chemotherapy and immunotherapy as maintenance regimes. The immunotherapy protocol is the administration of $10^9$ irradiated allogeneic leukaemia cells irradiated and BCG at a different site. The patients on immunotherapy are currently doing better than those on chemotherapy alone, though most still relapse and die. It is possible that a more intensive maintenance chemotherapy would be more effective than immunotherapy/chemotherapy. It is not justified to take these preliminary hopeful results as a proof that immunotherapy has a real role in the treatment of human malignant disease.


## 21.7 Conclusion

It has been suggested that the use of intensive chemotherapy of tumours may have a harmful effect on the ability of the host to deal with them by immunological means, since the agents used have a potent immunosuppressive effect. That such a view is manifest nonsense is shown not only by the poor results of no therapy, but by consideration of the tumour 'dose' phenomenon (21.4 above). Chemotherapy and surgical removal of lymph nodes are certainly justified procedures in the fight to reduce the tumour burden, particularly when chemotherapy is used in controlled pulses, a regime which spares immune function, rather than continuously.

There is no conclusive evidence in humans for those kinds of TSTAs which exist in chemically induced experimental tumours, namely those which might be involved in immune rejection mechanisms. Such experiments as there are which show that in humans

*Chapter 21: Tumour Immunology*

there are such antigens comes exclusively from *in vitro* work. They should be taken seriously since they show parallels with established animal models. This opens up the possibility of new approaches to treatment and diagnosis. I believe this is the right attitude but we should remember that the great effort which is being put into clinical tumour immunology does not rest on foundations which are as firm as one might wish.

## References

ALEXANDER P. (1968) Immunotherapy of cancer: experiments with primary tumours and syngeneic tumour grafts. *Progr. Exptl. Tumor Res.* **10**, 22.

ALEXANDER P. (1976) Surveillance against neoplastic cells—is it mediated by macrophages? *Brit. J. Cancer* **33**, 344.

ALEXANDER P. & HALL J.G. (1970) The role of immunoblasts in host resistance and immunotherapy of primary sarcomata. *Advances in Cancer Res.* **13**, 1.

BLOOM H.J.G., PECKHAM M.J., RICHARDSON A.E., ALEXANDER P. & PAYNE P.M. (1973) Glioblastoma multiforme: a controlled trial to assess the value of specific active immunotherapy in patients treated to radical surgery and radiotherapy. *Brit. J. Cancer* **27**, 253.

BURNET M. (1970) *Immunological Surveillance.* Pergamon Press, Oxford.

COGGIN J.H., AMBROSE K.R. & ANDERSON N.G. (1970) Fetal antigen capable of inducing transplantation immunity against SV40 Hamster tumour cells. *J. Immunol.* **105**, 524.

CURRIE G.A. & ALEXANDER P.A. (1974) Spontaneous shedding of TSTA by viable sarcoma cells: its possible role in facilitating metastatic spread. *Brit. J. Cancer* **29**, 72.

CURRIE G.A. & BASHAM C. (1972) Serum-mediated inhibition of the immunological reactions of the patient to his own tumour: A possible role for circulating antigen. *Brit. J. Cancer* **26**, 427.

DUBOS R.J. & SCHAEDLER R.W. (1957) Effects of cellular constituents of mycobacteria on the resistance of mice to heterologous infections. I. Protective effects. *J. exp. Med.* **106**, 703.

EHRLICH P. (1909) See reprint in DALE H. *The collected papers of Paul Ehrlich, Vol. 2*, 561. Pergamon Press, London 1957.

EVANS R. (1972) Macrophages in syngeneic animal tumours. *Transplantation* **14**, 468.

FOLEY E.J. (1953) Attempts to induce immunity against mammary adenocarcinoma in inbred mice. *Cancer Res.* **13**, 578.

GRANT C.K., GLOVER D.J., HALL J.G. & ALEXANDER P. (1974) The nature of blood-borne cytotoxic cells. 1. Co-operation between the white cells of the blood and lymph of sheep in the destruction of xenogeneic tumour cells *in vitro*. *Transplantation* **17**, 254.

HADDOW A. & ALEXANDER P. (1964) An immunological method of increasing the sensitivity of primary sarcomas to local irradiation with x-rays. *Lancet* **i**, 452.

HELLSTROM I. & HELLSTROM K.E. (1969) Studies on cellular immunity and its serum-mediated inhibition on Moloney-virus-induced monkey sarcomas. *Int. J. Cancer Res.* **4**, 587.

IKONOPISOV R.L., LEWIS M.G., HUNTER-CRAIG I.D., BODENHAM D.C., PHILLIPS T.M., COOLING C.I., PROCTOR J., HAMILTON-FAIRLEY G. & ALEXANDER P. (1970) Auto-immunization with irradiated tumour cells in human malignant melanoma. *Brit. Med. J.* **2**, 752.

LINNA T.J., HU C. & THOMPSON K.D. (1974) Development of systemic and local tumours induced by avian reticuloendotheliosis virus after thymectomy or bursectomy. *J. Nat. Cancer Institute.* **53**, 847.

MATHÉ G. (1970) Immunological treatment of leukaemias. *Brit. Med. J.* **4**, 487.

POWLES R.L., CROWTHER D., BATEMAN C.J.T., BEARD M.E.J., McELWAIN T.J., RUSSELL J., LISTER T.A., WHITEHOUSE J.M.A., WRIGLEY P.F.M., PIKE M., ALEXANDER P. & HAMILTON FAIRLEY G. (1973) Immunotherapy for acute myelogenous leukaemia. *Brit. J. Cancer* **28**, 365.

WHITEHOUSE J.M.A. & HOLBORROW E.J. (1971) Smooth muscle antibody in malignant disease. *Brit. Med. J.* **4**, 511.

## Further reading

ALEXANDER P. (1976) The functions of the macrophage in malignant disease. *Ann. Rev. Med.* **27**, 207.

BALDWIN R.W., BOWEN J.G., EMBLETON M.J., PRICE M.R. & ROBINS R.A. (1974) Cellular and humoral immune responses to neoantigens associated with chemically induced tumours. In BRENT L. & HOLBOROUGH J. *Progress in Immunology II*, **3**, p. 239. North-Holland, Amsterdam.

HELLSTROM K.E. & HELLSTROM I. (1974) Lymphocyte-mediated cytotoxicity and blocking serum activity to tumour antigens. *Advanc. Immunol.* **18**, 209.

*Chapter 21: Tumour Immunology*

# Chapter 22
# Feto-maternal Relationships

## C. M. Stern

## 22.1 Introduction

Pregnancy involves the development of one or more members of a species in intimate physiological contact with another member of the species which, in outbred populations, is usually histo-incompatible. In the absence of any modification of normal allergic responsiveness, the recognition of and reaction to antigenic differences, either by the fetus or its mother, might be expected to lead to the termination of the pregnancy. Since this does not usually happen, either there is no allergic response or, it is modified to neutral, or possibly beneficial ends.

This chapter attempts to cover the evidence for mutual allergic responses on the part of both the mother and the fetus and the mechanisms which control them.

## 22.2 Mutual exposure to antigen

### 22.2.1 Maternal exposure to antigen

The fetus differs antigenically from its mother only with respect to paternal antigens and exposure to these antigens takes place before pregnancy.

(a) Spermatozoa carry histocompatibility antigens and, despite the local infusion of these antigens which follows sexual intercourse, sensitization seems to occur rarely, probably because too few spermatozoa pass the cervix to be immunogenic.

(b) Embryonic antigens, although expressed by the embryo before implantation, are hidden at this stage by the zona pellucida, which does not carry histocompatibility antigens. In the mouse embryo, non *H-2* antigens are expressed before *H-2* antigens and maternal *H-2* determinants before paternal *H-2* determinants (Johnson & Billington, 1974).

(c) Exposure of the maternal lymphon to fetal antigens follows transfer of fetal cells to the maternal circulation. Haemorrhages of fetal blood into the maternal bloodstream occur more frequently and more extensively as the pregnancy progresses and may be detected either by the discovery of fetal red blood cells, or of white cells of male karyotype in women subsequently shown to be carrying a male fetus (Walkanowska *et al.*, 1969). Despite the frequent dissemination of islands of trophoblast, which carry significant amounts of histocompatibility antigen, into the maternal circulation, they are cleared from their resting places in the lungs without any inflammatory response.

### 22.2.2 Fetal exposure to antigen

The establishment of persistent chimerism following *in utero* blood transfusion for Rhesus iso-immunization has provoked a search for transferred maternal cells by examining male fetuses for female cells. Such examinations have proved singularly unrewarding in that no female cells have been found. However, since it seems that fetal cells may inhibit the division of allogeneic cells in MLC (see 22.4.3 below) and that these cells may be sequestered in the fetal lymphon, such negative evidence cannot be considered conclusive. There are occasional reports of malignant maternal cells becoming established in the fetus.

Tuffrey *et al.* (1969) transplanted CWF (non-T6) blastocysts into pseudopregnant female mice of an inbred CBA.T6T6 strain. Examination of the lymphatic tissues of the offspring suggested that considerable numbers of maternal cells were colonizing fetal tissue.

## 22.3 Maternal responses to fetal antigen

### 22.3.1 Humoral responses

A wide range of maternal antibodies are produced against fetal antigens.

In humans, anti-HLA antibody is often produced by multiparous women and up to 40 per cent of all women show evidence of priming with successive pregnancies. Titres of antibody rise during pregnancy and fall off slightly after delivery. In contrast, non-anti-HLA cytotoxic antibodies can also be found and show different kinetics from the anti-HLA antibodies. These cytotoxic antibodies disappear during the last third of pregnancy, reappearing after delivery. It is interesting to speculate that the disappearance of these antibodies may be due to the shedding of large amounts of fetal antigen into the maternal bloodstream, mopping up cytotoxic antibody as immune complexes. This may then have a profound specific effect in interfering with the effector limb of the mother's allergic response against the fetus.

The production of anti-Rh antibody by Rhdd women carrying RhD fetuses is another well-known example of maternal anti-fetal

*Chapter 22: Feto-maternal Relationships*

antibody formation. In addition, mothers lacking the A or B red-cell antigen who carry a fetus possessing the antigen, usually show a rise in either their anti-A or anti-B titre.

Syncytiotrophoblast carries a coating of maternal IgG by eight to twelve weeks' gestation and this can be eluted and shown to bind back to fetal tissue.

In mice, non-anti-*H-2*, antibody of unknown specificity, produced as a result of pregnancy may be responsible for several phenomena. These are: the prolonged survival of male skin grafts on multigravid females (these grafts are usually rejected by virtue of the Y antigen); the accelerated rejection of leukaemia transplanted from the male to the female (a cytotoxicity effect); and the prolonged survival of sarcomata transplanted from the same source (an enhancement phenomenon). This antibody shows the same kinetics as the human cytotoxic antibody mentioned earlier, probably also because of fetal antigen being shed into the maternal circulation.

### 22.3.2 Cell-mediated responses

*In vitro* studies on the responses of maternal lymphocytes in a variety of cell-mediated reactions have thrown up some surprising results. As shown in Table 22.1 maternal lymphocytes have a lower

Table 22.1. *In vivo* CML, MLR and mitogenic responses of fetal and maternal lymphocytes

| Stimulus or target | Maternal cell mitogenic response | Spontaneous killing by maternal cells | Fetal cell mitogenic response |
|---|---|---|---|
| PHA | + + | — | + |
| Maternal lymphocytes[1] | — | — | + + + + |
| Paternal lymphocytes[1] | + + | + | + + |
| Fetal lymphocytes[1] | 0 | + + + + | — |
| Third-party lymphocytes[1] | + + | — | + + + |
| Trophoblast from own fetus | — | + + + + | — |
| Trophoblast from unrelated fetus | — | + + | — |

+ + + = a normal mitogenic response. No CML responses would normally be expected in this system.

— = irrelevant.

[1] = PHA transformed targets.

than normal mitogenic and MLR response, as compared with the lymphocytes of non-pregnant females. Cells which are *directly* cytotoxic against fetal cells, and to a lesser extent paternal cells (but not third party cells), are also found in the maternal circulation. CML-reactive lymphocytes are not usually found circulating as such in the bloodstream of normal individuals and are usually generated in an MLC reaction *in vitro*. The presence of these cells in the blood of pregnant women indicates an active maternal response to fetal HLA antigens *in vivo*. Cytotoxicity is also shown by maternal cells for trophoblast from their own fetuses and, to a lesser extent, for trophoblast from unrelated fetuses. Because trophoblast cells may carry large amounts of bound IgG, even after vigorous washing and growth *in vitro*, this phenomenon may be K cell mediated.

Despite this positive CML against fetal lymphocytes, there is no MLR in response to mitomycin-treated fetal lymphocytes, although a weak response to paternal cells and a stronger reaction to third-party cells can be detected. This surprising result may be associated with the observation that fetal lymphocytes inhibit responding cells in the bi-directional MLR (see 22.4.3).

Further evidence of cell-mediated priming on the part of maternal cells against fetal antigens is demonstrated by the production of MIF by the lymphocytes of multigravid women in MLC with fetal lymphocytes (Rocklin *et al.*, 1973).

## 22.4 Fetal responses to antigen

### 22.4.1 Fetal immunocompetence

Any consideration of fetal anti-maternal allergic responses must take into account the fact that fetal immunocompetence develops as the fetal lymphon matures. It is therefore appropriate to review briefly the evidence for the capacity of the fetus to respond to different antigens.

Small laboratory animals, such as the mouse, are relatively immuno-incompetent during gestation and acquire adult responsiveness to antigens in postnatal life. The ability to produce an antibody response depends not only upon postnatal age, but also upon the antigen used. For example, the ability of newborn mice to respond to rat, rabbit and sheep erythrocytes, and the age at which these responses can be induced, varies from strain to strain. By contrast, cell-mediated responses in the neonatal mouse are comparable with those of adult animals, since neonatal mice can reject allogeneic skin grafts and be primed for subsequent second set graft rejection as effectively as adult animals. The classic acquisition of tolerance by day-old mice is largely dose-dependent. There are no reliable studies on the ability of fetal mice to mount allergic responses *in utero*.

On the other hand, Silverstein and his colleagues have made detailed studies of the cell-mediated and humoral responses of the fetal lamb. Antibody responses to $\Phi$X174 can be elicited by 40 days gestation, horse ferritin by 56 days gestation, and so on, through a range of antigens showing the development of positive responses at different gestational ages. The responses to diphtheria toxoid, *Salmonella typhosa* and BCG were never detected until postnatal life. The response to allografts and autografts of fetal sheep was also investigated, showing that allografts of skin placed orthotopically were always rejected after the 77th day of gestation. This reaction was as rapid as that seen in adult sheep and no plasma cells were ever observed to take part in the response (Silverstein & Prendergast, 1970). If the differences in the time of onset of these responses to different antigens are not a reflection of the sensitivity of the antibody assay or of antigen handling mechanisms, then they suggest that different variable region genes may be expressed at different times during gestation and are not suddenly transcribed together at a given point in gestation. This contrasts with the sudden acquisition of the ability to reject allografted skin.

In humans, antibody to rubella virus has been detected in infected fetuses as early as 112 days' of gestation and other 'immunizations' by intrauterine infections show that antibody responses can be mounted. Experimental priming with ΦX174 bacteriophage has shown that premature infants (birth weight 1320–1900 g) can produce good primary and secondary responses. Other antigens, such as tetanus toxoid, provoke rather weak antibody responses when given neonatally, but powerful reactions when injected at seven months of age. However, it is difficult to draw conclusions concerning these differences in response to varying antigens at changing gestational ages because of the presence of maternal IgG antibody, transferred to the fetus in the last trimester. This problem does not arise in sheep, because maternal antibody transfer occurs only postnatally, in the colostrum.

Cell-mediated responses in humans show that both full-term and premature normal infants are capable of rejecting skin allografts and will also show priming to a secondary challenge. Studies with BCG, poison ivy and 2:4 dinitrofluorobenzene sensitivity demonstrate both the generation of a positive skin reaction and the maintenance of a sensitive state. It is likely that the immunological capacity of the human fetus *in utero* is at least as good as that of the fetal lamb.

The ability of the fetus to respond to challenge by maternal antigen will vary from species to species, with the stage of gestation and with the type of antigen.

### 22.4.2 Humoral responses

Some human infants receive donations of maternal IgG *in utero* where a maternal Gm marker may differ from those inherited by the child. Investigation has shown that these children may be producing anti-Gm antibody by six months of age. This does not mean that these particular immune responses were induced antenatally.

Anti-I IgM and anti-A or anti-B agglutinins have been found in a percentage of cord sera However, strong evidence for significant antimaternal antibody production by the fetus is lacking.

### 22.4.3 Cell-mediated responses

*In vitro* tests on fetal lymphocytes have revealed several very interesting characteristics. Cord blood lymphocytes have a high spontaneous transformation rate in the first few hours of culture and this early response can be potentiated by the addition of PHA or maternal cells, but not third-party cells. Transformation to all but the lowest doses of PHA is reduced when measured after three days of culture, but this may simply reflect the large population of dividing cells in the initial culture. In addition, although mito-mycin-treated maternal cells are poor stimulators of paternal and third-party cells in MLC, fetal cells respond quite well. It is intriguing to speculate that the spontaneous transforming cells may be responding to maternal antigen.

There is now persuasive evidence that fetal lymphocytes in bi-directional MLR suppress the division of allogeneic cells, both maternal and third party (Olding & Oldstone, 1974). This is not a cytotoxic effect, as the cells, although unable to divide, still produce MIF in MLC with fetal cells (see 22.3.2).

Earlier work, using skin graft rejection as a criterion of specific sensitization, gave much more complex results. Human infants, given fresh heparinized blood transfusions for Rhesus iso-immuni-zation, tolerate subsequent skin grafts from these donors indefi-nitely, whereas skin grafts from unrelated donors are rejected normally. In the same babies, maternal skin grafts survived twice as long as third-party grafts. On the other hand, when Lewis/Bn female rats, whose ovaries have been replaced by homozygous Lewis ovaries, were crossed with Lewis males, the homozygous Lewis offspring rejected BN skin grafts in an accelerated fashion.

## 22.5 Factors which may suppress allergic reactivity

There is good evidence for transfer of fetal antigen to the mother and for her response. This has induced a number of workers to search for factors which might block the immune response of the mother, and some of these are worth mentioning.

A number of hormones have the effect of reducing lymphocyte responsiveness to mitogens, antigens and in MLR. The strongest candidate for an important role in fetal protection is human chori-onic gonadotrophin (HCG). The amount of HCG needed to suppress mitogen responsiveness is supraphysiological, although it has been pointed out that HCG is produced by the trophoblast and binds to it, which may enhance its effect *in vivo*. A complex of at least seven mucoproteins have been described with a similar effect. It is possible that these substances are involved in the effect of fetal lymphocytes on allogeneic cells in MLC, mentioned earlier (see 22.4.3). Other workers have described various placental extracts which have similar non-specific effects on allergic responses.

Perhaps of more interest is the potentially specific effect of blocking factors responsible for immunological enhancement. For example, lymphocytes from CBA female mice multigravid by C57Bl males kill male target cells in the absence of their own serum but not in its presence. It has been suggested that this substance is of fundamental importance for fetal survival, but there is not enough evidence to support this view.

## 22.6 The effect of histo-incompatibility

One of the more remarkable biological effects, seen in different ways in plants and animals, is that of hybrid vigour. When two inbred strains are crossed, the offspring are larger, more numerous and sometimes more fruitful in themselves than either original strain. It has been attractive to explain this phenomenon in terms of a greater variety in the genome, with less possibility for the expression of recessive characteristics. Since one function of the allergic system is concerned with the recognition of and reaction to differences between cells, some workers have suggested an immunological basis for hybrid vigour. They have proposed that, among viviparous animals, the greater histocompatibility difference between mother and fetus in allogeneic matings, when compared with syngeneic matings, might lead to a greater ability on the part of the mother to react against fetal antigen, and that such a reaction might generate heterozygote selection.

Clarke & Kirby (1966) made calculations based upon the *assumption* that the mother was able to mount a beneficial immune response against her fetus. By applying Fisher's formula under a Hardy-Weinberg equilibrium, they were able to show that such an assumption could explain some of the examples of heterozygote selection reported in viviparous animals.

Experimental evidence directly relating to this point is sparse but sound. James (1970) manipulated the immune response of C57Bl female mice to paternal histocompatibility antigens and showed that tolerant females produce offspring smaller than normal while immune females produce offspring larger than normal. Blastocyst transfer experiments made it unlikely that this was simply a heterozygote effect.

Palm (1970) crossed and backcrossed two populations of DA and BN rats, showing a selective advantage for DA/BN heterozygotes in backcrosses of DA females with DA/BN males. She felt that this selection could be explained if AgB differences protected against lethal attack by maternal lymphocytes (which must have crossed to the fetus during pregnancy), directed against non-AgB differences, since the background DA homozygotes should differ at their non-AgB loci as much as heterozygotes. The phenomenon was found to increase with parity, which might argue the priming of maternal effector lymphocytes.

Recently, Beer *et al.* (1975) have shown that the larger fetoplacental units observed in interstrain matings in rats, hamsters and mice correlate with maternal allergic responses to fetal alloantigens. The changes are not observed in mothers tolerant to fetal antigens and can be induced by passive antibody. Blastocyst transfer studies in mice rule out the possibility that the phenomenon is due to heterosis.

From these studies it would seem that it may be advantageous, in terms of fetal survival, for the mother to be able to mount an antifetal response, but at present it can be said only to apply to certain species under certain circumstances.

### 22.7 Conclusion

The following points emerge from this chapter:

1. Fetal cells cross the placenta and can be found in the maternal circulation quite early in pregnancy.

2. Mothers show specific, anti-fetal, humoral and cell-mediated priming as a result of pregnancy.

3. Fetal lymphocytes can inhibit the mitogenic response of allogeneic lymphocytes in mixed lymphocyte culture.

4. Although the evidence for the existence of humoral immunosuppressive mechanisms may appear impressive, there is nothing to suggest that they play any part in the maintenance of fetal health during pregnancy.

To attempt to pull together the evidence presented here would be foolhardy. Much of the work has been done by people in different disciplines and cannot be forced into any overall pattern. The evidence is strongly in favour of an immune response of pregnancy, at least on the part of the mother and possibly also on the part of the fetus.

In trying to analyse the immunological interactions which occur during pregnancy in terms of a modern understanding of immunological mechanisms, it seems to me that there are a number of questions which we might hope to be able to answer in the near future. Do fetal antigen and immune complexes circulate in pregnancy? What are the localizations of subpopulations of sensitized maternal lymphocytes and are they effective or blocked in some way? How do fetal cells protect themselves from maternal attack? What are the effect of small differences in the histocompatibility gene complex upon fertility and does maternal sensitization against these differences affect fetal survival? What are the differences between pregnancies involving inbred and outbred populations of animals? What is the explanation of the dissociation of the maternal lymphocyte response shown by positive CML reaction and negative MLR against cells from their own fetuses? With this sort of information we should be able to build up a clearer picture of the immune response of pregnancy.

## References

CLARKE B. & KIRBY D.R.S. (1966) Maintenance of histocompatibility polymorphisms. *Nature (Lond.)* **211**, 999.

BEER A.E., SCOTT J.R. & BILLINGHAM R.E. (1975) Histocompatability and maternal immunological status as determinants of fetoplacental weight and litter size in rodents. *J. exp. Med.* **142**, 180.

JAMES D.A. (1965) Effect of antigenic dissimilarity between mother and fetus on placental size in the mouse. *Nature (Lond.)* **205**, 613.

JOHNSON R.E. & BILLINGTON W.D. (1974) Personal communication.

OLDING L.B. & OLDSTONE M.B.A. (1974) Lymphocytes from human newborns abrogate mitosis of their mother's lymphocytes. *Nature (Lond.)* **249**, 161.

PALM J. (1971) Immunogenetic analysis of Ag-B histocompatibility antigens in rats. *Transplantation* **11**, 175.

ROCKLIN R.E., ZUCKERMAN J.E., ALPORT E. & DAVID J.R. (1973) Effect of multiparity on human maternal sensitivity to foetal antigen. *Nature (Lond.)* **241**, 130.

SILVERSTEIN A.M. & PRENDERGAST R.A. (1970) In STERZL J. & RIHA I. *Developmental Aspects of Antibody Formation and Structure*, pp. 69–77. Academia, Prague.

TUFFREY M., BISHUN N.P. & BARNES R.D. (1969) Porosity of the mouse placenta to maternal cells. *Nature (Lond.)* **221**, 1029.

WALKANOWSKA J., CONTE F.A. & GRUMBACH M.M. (1969) Practical and theoretical implications of fetal/maternal lymphocyte transfer. *Lancet* **i**, 1119.

## Further reading

BILLINGHAM R.E. (1971) The transplantation biology of mammalian gestation. *Amer. J. Obstet. Gynaec.* **111**, 469.

BEER A.E. & BILLINGHAM R.E. (1971) Immunobiology of mammalian reproduction. *Adv. Immunol.* **14**, 1.

EDWARDS R.G. & COOMBS R.R.A. (1974) Immunological interactions between mother and fetus. In GELL, P.G.H., COOMBS R.R.A. & LACHMANN P.J. *Clinical Aspects of Immunology*, 3rd edition. Blackwell, Oxford.

*Section IV: Immunopathology*

# Chapter 23
# Immunity and Immunity Deficiency

## H. Valdimarsson

### 23.1 Introduction

In its broadest sense, the term immunity applies to all the mechanisms whereby animals are protected from infection. These include physical barriers, non-specific humoral factors and effector cells, as well as the specific immune components. Immunity deficiency occurs when any biological deviation renders an individual more susceptible to infections than most other members of the same species. Such deviation can be genetically transmitted or brought about by environmental factors.

Major constitutional defects in the defence mechanisms are usually manifested shortly after birth. In affluent and hygenic environments, minor defects may be compatible with satisfactory health and only be exposed late in life or not at all. Conversely, in communities where malnutrition is combined with heavy and frequent pathogen contact, minor immunity disadvantages may prove fatal early in life.

The main aim of this chapter will be to discuss some general aspects of host–parasite relationships and the mechanisms whereby self-defence is accomplished. An attempt will also be made to relate some of the major immunity deficiency syndromes to blocks at various levels in the maturation of the cells which participate in defence reactions.

### 23.2 Protective mechanisms

The immune system consists of two main components: the non-specific and the specific mechanisms. The non-specific mechanisms constitute the first line of defence and are largely responsible for the natural (innate) immunity which animals possess to the vast majority of environmental micro-organisms. The specific mechanisms deal primarily with those organisms which are capable of passing the non-specific barriers.

Specific immunity is always acquired. Its cardinal features are the ability to recognize and memorize antigenic experience, thus leading to an enhanced capacity to resist infections. It is not an

317

absolute phenomenon, however, and the outcome of an infection may depend on the amount of the infectious agent, its virulence and its mode of entry. Table 23.1 illustrates the range of relationships which can exist between host and parasite. The host may successfully eliminate the pathogen or vice versa because these defence mechanisms fail. Between these two extremes there is a spectrum of possible compromises. The relationship between humans and herpes viruses is an example of a generally peaceful co-existence. In chronic infections such as leprosy or tuberculosis the compromise can be uneasy or disastrous for the host.

**Table 23.1.** Range of host–parasite (pathogen) relationship

1. Host eliminates the pathogen.
2. An easy compromise.
   Host–parasite symbiosis (LCM in mice, herpes virus in humans).
3. An uneasy compromise.
   Compromised host–parasite relationship (chronic infections).
4. Parasite eliminates the host.

### 23.2.1 Evolution of protective mechanisms

A schematic outline of the evolution of protective mechanisms is shown in Fig. 23.1. Phagocytosis and hydrolytic enzymes are the most primitive mechanisms of self-defence. Many unicellular organisms are phagocytic but in primitive multicellular organisms there are specialized phagocytic cells within the mesoderm that remove irritants which penetrate the surface barriers. In the lower vertebrates a specific recognition system evolves, capable of producing factors which amplify and direct the phagocytic process. In the higher vertebrates these recognition systems have reached a high degree of complexity.

This type of evolution is additive with the primitive mechanisms being preserved in the higher animals. It is important to realize that, in spite of the complexity of the immune system in mammals, the bulwark of their bodily defences is still largely dependent on surface barriers and phagocytic mechanisms. Complete absence of T or B lymphocytes or a major defect in the complement system is not as immediately life-endangering as complete absence of phagocytic function. Loss of surface barriers through extensive burns frequently leads to fatal invasion by micro-organisms which are normally non-pathogenic.

### 23.2.2 Non-specific surface factors

Apart from acting as physical barriers, skin and mucous membranes can actively suppress or kill micro-organisms by poorly understood mechanisms. It has been suggested that humidity, lactic acid

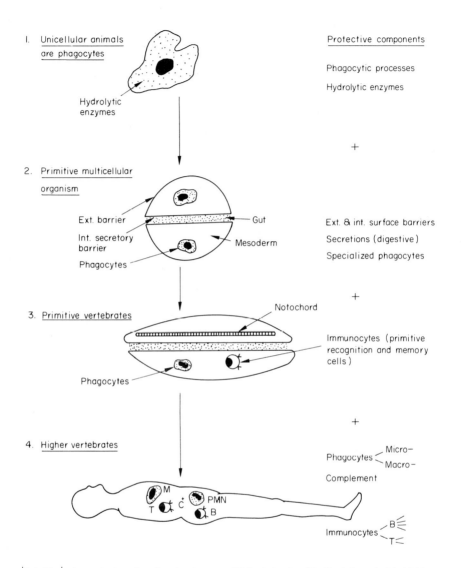

I. Unicellular animals are phagocytes

Hydrolytic enzymes

2. Primitive multicellular organism

Ext. barrier
Int. secretory barrier
Phagocytes
Gut
Mesoderm

3. Primitive vertebrates

Notochord
Phagocytes

4. Higher vertebrates

M
T    C    PMN
B

Protective components

Phagocytic processes
Hydrolytic enzymes

+

Ext. & int. surface barriers
Secretions (digestive)
Specialized phagocytes

+

Immunocytes (primitive recognition and memory cells)

+

Phagocytes — Micro−
          — Macro−
Complement

Immunocytes — B
            — T

'Primitive' phagocytosis and surface barriers are still the bulwarks of bodily defence in this highly developed animal

**Fig. 23.1.** The evolution of protective mechanisms.
M: Mononuclear phagocytes
PMN: Polymorphonuclear phagocytes
C: Complement
T: T lymphocytes
B: B lymphocytes.

and unsaturated fatty acids all play a role on skin. The acid production in the stomach is a powerful sterilizing device for the gastrointestinal tract. Mucous secretions contain proteins which block virus attachment to susceptible cells and many enzymes including lysozyme. The normal microbial flora of the body surfaces probably also constitutes an important defence by itself and major insults to these ecosystems via broad-spectrum antibiotics may have disastrous effects.

### 23.2.3 Non-specific humoral (tissue) factors

Many soluble non-specific tissue factors suppress or kill microbes *in vitro* and a few of these are mentioned here.

Lysozyme is present in most tissues and properdin, in the presence of complement, is also capable of killing some bacteria.

In addition to proteins blocking virus attachment, tissues can also produce interferons that suppress virus replication.

The concentration of lactic acid in inflammatory foci can exceed the level which kills some bacterial pathogens *in vitro*. Lactic acid production is decreased in diabetic subjects and this may contribute to the diminished ability of these patients to localize infections.

Availability of iron can be a limiting factor in microbe replication. Bacteria such as *Pasturella septica*, *Clostridium welchii* and *E. coli* require for their growth free iron at concentrations higher than are normally present in serum and tissue fluids. These pathogens can nevertheless multiply in animals and there is some evidence that they are capable of acquiring enough iron *in vivo* by releasing it from transferrin. The increased resistance of animals immunized against these bacteria seems, at least partly, to be due to inactivation by antibody and complement of the iron-releasing bacterial component. Immune animals, challenged with these bacteria and given iron at the same time, no longer show resistance above non-immune controls (Bullen *et al.*, 1971).

The physiological importance of this bacteriostatic mechanism is not obvious, however, and there is certainly no evidence that oral administration of iron in modest quantities is detrimental for patients with infections. On the contrary, iron deficiency may be associated with increased susceptibility to chronic infections, notably candidiasis, which is often improved by a prolonged iron treatment (Higgs & Wells, 1972).

### 23.2.4 Non-specific cellular mechanisms

There are two principal classes of phagocytic cells in mammals: macrophages and polymorphonuclear (PMN) leucocytes. Table 23.2 shows the differences in their maturation and regulation of their phagocytic function. Macrophages have been discussed in

**Table 23.2.** Regulation of phagocytic function

| Cell | Maturation and life-span | Factors directing activity | | | |
|---|---|---|---|---|---|
| | | | | Sensitizing | |
| | | Chemotactic | Target (opsonization) | Effector cell (arming) | |
| Neutrophils | Released fully mature | 2 days | Complement derived | IgG, C3 | — |
| Macrophages | Released immature Environmental differentiation activated by lymphokines | Months or years | T-lymphocyte derived lymphokines? | IgG, C3, ? T cell factors | Lymphokines (e.g. SMAF) |

detail in Chapter 12. The principal points to note are that their *intrinsic* bactericidal capacity can be enhanced by lymphokines and that they differentiate after release from the bone marrow. They are also characteristic for the tissues in which they reside.

PMN leucocytes are produced in the bone marrow of healthy individuals at a rate of approximately $8 \times 10^7$ cells per minute. They are fully mature cells on leaving the bone marrow and their *intrinsic* bactericidal capacity cannot be enhanced by mediators of cellular immunity. On average they stay in the circulation for only 6–7 hours and probably survive only one or two days in the tissues after leaving the blood.

Although phagocytic cells are not equipped with any *intrinsic* immunological specificity, their function is controlled by specific mediators (antibodies and lymphokines) and other factors acting in concert with antibodies (notably complement). This control occurs both at a distance from the target organisms, by means of chemotactic factors, and at the surface of the target in the form of opsonization. Macrophages, but not PMN leucocytes, can passively acquire specific molecules which help them to recognize foreign antigens (e.g. SMAF, Chapter 12).

### 23.2.5 Phagocytosis and intracellular killing mechanisms

Once an infection is established, phagocytic killing is the principal mechanism whereby infectious agents are removed. The mechanisms are not fully understood, but the sequence of events is attachment (see Chapter 19), ingestion, killing and digestion. Microbes which adhere to the phagocyte plasma membrane are rapidly engulfed by invaginations of the membrane, which are interiorized as vacuoles (phagosomes) and surrounded by lysosomes. These discharge their hydrolases into the phagosomes (phago-lysosomes). If organisms survive this, they may establish themselves (in macrophages) as intracellular parasites.

There are undoubtedly a number of killing mechanisms operating in the phagolysosomes, four of which are:

1. Low pH and lactic acid.

2. Phagocytins, a group of basic proteins lethal for some bacteria *in vitro*.

3. Lysozyme, a major lysosomal enzyme which can lyse some gram-positive organisms.

4. The endocytic process activates glucose oxidation through the hexose monophosphate shunt, a reaction which results in the generation of hydrogen peroxide ($H_2O_2$). This is an important mechanism for phagocytic killing of many bacteria and fungi. Klebanoff & White (1969) elegantly demonstrated that it depends on the interaction of peroxidase with $H_2O_2$ and a halide cofactor. Bactericidal activity was associated with iodination of the bacterial wall.

*Section IV: Immunopathology*

The relative importance of these mechanisms depends on the species of organisms under attack and there is evidence that the killing mechanisms induced can differ depending on the characteristics of the pathogen. Abnormal phagocytic cells which fail to produce $H_2O_2$ have greatly reduced capacity to kill micro-organisms unless the latter produce $H_2O_2$. Hitherto uncharacterized lysosmal abnormalities may be responsible for decreased resistance to infections in a number of patients who suffer from chronic infections.

## 23.3 Specific defence mechanisms

Specific recognition evolved as an ancillary mechanism to phagocytic defence. Antigen binding by antibody alone is insufficient for pathogen elimination and the presence of antibody only indicates antigenic experience. It is not to be equated with immunity. The latter depends on the integrated function of both the specific recognition molecules and the phagocytic mechanisms leading to pathogen elimination. This functional integration occurs through the different parts of a single molecule, for instance the variable and constant regions of immunoglobulin. The evolutionary pressures favouring this link are clear and the possible mechanisms are described in Chapter 6.

Two distinct types of recognition-elimination mechanisms emerged: cell-mediated immunity evolving around mononuclear phagocytes on the one hand and humoral immunity with PMN leucocytes as the principal combatants on the other. The evolutionary sequence in the latter case is unclear.

### 23.3.1 The functional dichotomy of specific immunity

The *cellular axis* of specific immunity comprises T lymphocytes, lymphokines and macrophages (Table 23.2). The system is activated by antigen recognition by T lymphocytes leading to lymphokine release and characteristic activation of macrophages (Chapter 12). If specific factors produced by T lymphocytes become attached to activated macrophages, the destructive propensity of the latter is preferentially directed towards a specific target.

The *humoral axis* comprises B lymphocytes, antibodies, complement and PMN leucocytes (Chapters 1–9, 19).

Experimental animals and patients with selective deficiency in cellular immunity show decreased resistance to infections with Mycobacteria and other facultative intracellular bacteria. They are also unduly susceptible to fungal infections and their capacity to contain certain viral infections, notably pox, herpes and myxoviruses is severely reduced. In contrast their ability to cope with encapsulated pyogenic bacteria appears normal. Congenital deficiency of this axis is more immediately life-endangering than that of the humoral immune axis.

Selective antibody deficiency is associated with infections by Meningococci, Staphylococci, Pneumococci, Streptocci and Haemophilus influenzae, whereas the resistance to common viral diseases and fungi is normal. Combined deficiencies of both axes leads to lack of resistance to all types of infectious agents.

This functional dichotomy is illustrated in Fig. 23.2 and Table 23.3.

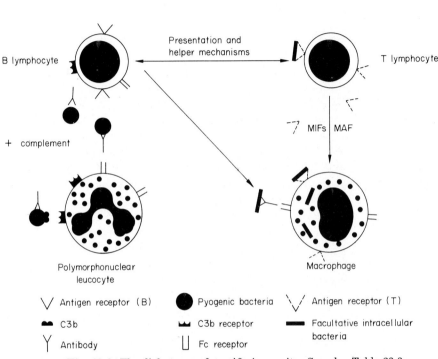

**Fig. 23.2.** The dichotomy of specific immunity. See also Table 23.3.

**Table 23.3.** The dichotomy of specific immunity

| Component | | Humoral axis | Cellular axis |
|---|---|---|---|
| Specific cell | | B lymphocyte | T lymphocyte |
| Specific molecule | | Antibody | Lymphokine ? |
| Effector cell | | PMN leucocyte | Macrophage |
| Amplifying mechanism | | Complement | Lymphokine ? |
| Targets | Bacteria | Prevention and recovery | Prevention and recovery (especially facultative intracellular bacteria) |
| | Viruses | Prevention (some) | Prevention and recovery |
| | Fungi | Recovery from ? systemic infections | Prevention and recovery |
| | Tumours | Enhancement ? | Prevention ? |

## 23.4 Anergy

The absence of an expected immunological reactivity in sensitized individuals is often referred to as anergy. It includes both the failure to express delayed hypersensitivity (its most common usage) as well as other types of immunological hyporeactivity. Anergy can be primary or result from diseases affecting the immune system. It may be generalized (immune paralysis) or restricted to one or a few related antigens (specific unresponsiveness). In the context of resistance to infection, anergy can be defined as any immunological hyporeactivity which leads to defective immunity.

### 23.4.1 Cellular anergy

Fig. 23.3 shows some of the blocks which theoretically can prevent the expression of cellular immunity.

BLOCKS AFFECTING SPECIFIC CELLS

*Block 1*: Both specific and non-specific blocking factors may interfere with interactions between T lymphocytes and antigen. These have been described in patients with cancer and some chronic infections and may be partly responsible for their anergy.

*Block 2*: Occurs when the lymphocytes are absent, either specifically (central tolerance) or due to severe combined immunity deficiency or thymic aplastia.

*Block 3*: Defective lymphokine production. This has so far only been observed in some patients with chronic mucocutaneous candidiasis who fail to make MIF.

*Block 4*: Defective lymphocyte proliferation is seen in some patients with chronic infections whose lymphocytes can produce lymphokines *in vitro* but fail to undergo blastoid transformation or mitosis.

BLOCKS AFFECTING NON-SPECIFIC CELLS

*Block 5*: Proliferation of promonocytes can be experimentally inhibited by mild irradiation (400R). This leads to the disappearance of monocytes from the blood and simultaneous failure to express delayed hypersensitivity, even though the circulating lymphocytes are apparently unaffected. Spontaneous reversion occurs as monocytes gradually reappear in the blood, or immediately following transfusion of syngeneic bone marrow but not lymphocytes.

In clinical situations, defective expression of CMI may be due to lack of circulating monocytes, maturation defects or damage to macrophages. These could give rise to problems somewhat similar to T lymphocyte deficiency.

*Block 6*: Hypothetical maturation defect which has not yet been identified.

*Block 7*: Defects in the lysosomal enzyme system either as a result of acute viral infection or stabilization of lysosomal membranes by drugs (steroids, chloroquinone and phenothiazines) can all lead to suppressed delayed hypersensitivity and failure to kill.

Anergy is rarely due to a single block. For example, steroids suppress CMI partly by decreasing the release of monocytes from bone marrow (Block 5), by directly affecting T lymphocytes (Block 2) and partly by stabilizing lysosomal membranes (Block 7).

Anergy is a secondary feature of many diseases, some of which are not necessarily associated with a major increase in susceptibility to infection.

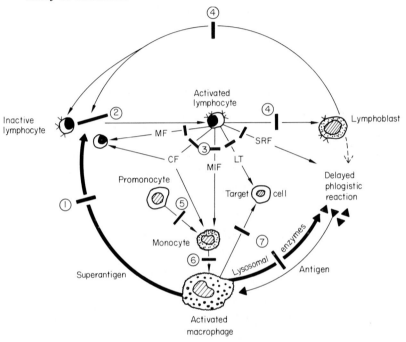

**Fig. 23.3.** Blocks along the axis of specific-cell mediated immunity.
MF: Mitogenic factors
CF: Chemotactic factors
MIF: Migration inhibitory factors
LT: Cytotoxic factors
SRF: Skin reactive factors.

In the clinical application of the model (Fig. 23.3), it is important to realize that the expression of delayed hypersensitivity in the skin is the last step of the process and that a strong skin response depends on all the previous steps being intact. More laborious investigations can, therefore, be avoided if skin tests are strongly positive.

### 23.4.2 Humoral anergy

Any abnormality which seriously affects the sequential interaction

*Section IV: Immunopathology*

of antibodies, complement and PMN leucocytes will cause humoral anergy.

The mechanisms of specific humoral immunity are schematically illustrated in Fig. 23.4, together with some blocks which may occur along this pathway.

BLOCKS AFFECTING SPECIFIC CELLS
*Antibody deficiency* may result from blocks at various stages of B lymphocyte differentiation, and is the most commonly recognized cause of humoral anergy.

*Block 1*: Absence of B lymphocytes is observed in Bruton's sex-linked agammaglobulinaemia (Block 1a), although some of these patients may have lymphoid cells with Fc and C3 receptors but no immunoglobulin. These are perhaps primitive B cells (Block 1b).

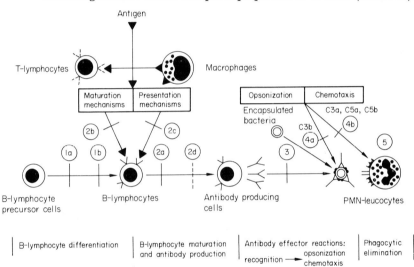

**Fig. 23.4.** Blocks along the axis of specific humoral immunity. Same symbols as in Fig. 23.2.

*Block 2*: B lymphocytes exist but fail to differentiate into plasma cells. The causes are unknown but may be due to either an intrinsic defect in the B lymphocyte (Block 2a) or in the T cell dependent stages of B lymphocyte differentiation (Block 2b) (see Chapter 9). Defective antigen presentation mechanisms by macrophages have been suggested as the primary defect in patients with Wiscott–Aldrich syndrome (Block 2c). They fail to produce antibodies to polysaccharide antigens but respond normally to proteins.

Selective deficiency of an immunoglobulin class or subclass also occurs. The most commonly affected is IgA (relatively benign), but a more interesting type is characterized by absence of IgG and IgA and *raised* IgM. This is an X-linked disorder. Response of peripheral blood lymphocytes to PHA *in vitro* is subnormal, suggesting that the defect is in the T cells, an important point, since IgG and

327                    *Chapter 23: Immunity and Immunity Deficiency*

IgA production are generally more T-dependent than IgM. This syndrome may be a useful model for probing the maturation of B cell responses.

*Block 3*: Failure to give rise to specific *antibody* on challenge despite normal immunoglobulin levels has been noted in some patients.

BLOCKS AFFECTING NON-SPECIFIC COMPONENTS

*Block 4*: Certain complement deficiencies (notably at the C3 stage) seriously interfere with opsonization and chemotaxis and predispose to immunity deficiency.

*Block 5*: Deficiency of PMN leucocytes may be due to either their absence or a functional failure (see below).

Failure of the humoral axis immunity divides functionally into two parts: failure of the antibody response or complement deficiency and failure of the neutrophils. The former is characterized by increased susceptibility to pyogenic infections with encapsulated bacteria which require opsonization before they can be phagocytosed. These infections often occur within the body, manifested for instance as pneumonia, meningitis, and septicaemia. In contrast, failure of the PMN leucocytes predisposes especially to infections of certain external surfaces, notably the mouth, eyes and reproductive tract. Chronic granulomatous disease, due to deficiency of the $H_2O_2$ killing mechanism is a special case (see below), characterized by infections with non-capsulated, catalase positive organisms of low virulence.

## 23.5 Immunity deficiency syndromes

Immunity deficiency syndromes exhibit a variety of genetic and immunological features which have been used in the formulation of a preliminary classification which I believe to be premature (Cooper *et al.*, 1974). Extensive reviews of immunity deficiency are available (Soothill, 1974; Hermans *et al.*, 1973). This chapter will discuss only those conditions which are well enough understood to be used to illustrate the various blocks discussed above.

### 23.5.1 General haemopoetic deficiency

*Reticular dysgenesis* is a familial defect in which all types of leucocytes are completely absent or greatly reduced in number (Block A in Fig. 23.5). Affected infants die of overwhelming infection within a few days of birth.

### 23.5.2 Combined phagocytic defects in patients with normal lymphocyte function

Several functional defects affecting both polymorphs and macrophages have been characterized (Block B, Fig. 23.5), though selective failure in the production of all phagocytic cells is not known.

*Chronic granulomatous disease* is an X-linked recessive disorder in which all phagocytes fail to produce $H_2O_2$. These patients are predominantly infected with catalase-producing bacteria rather than the encapsulated pyogens which are common in other defects in the 'humoral axis'. The disease is characterized by recurrent skin infections, chronic lymphadenopathy with discharging sinuses, osteomyelitis and liver abscesses. Affected boys rarely survive beyond adolescence in spite of antibiotic therapy.

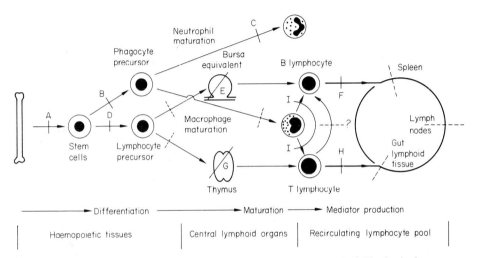

**Fig. 23.5.** Immunity deficiency syndromes related to blocks in leucocyte maturation. Theoretical maturation arrests, not yet identified clinically, as are indicated by broken lines.

*Chediak-Higashi disease* is an autosomal recessive disorder characterized by giant lysosomes in both granulocytes, monocytes and other cells. The patients are moderately neutropaenic and suffer from pyogenic infections which can be fatal. Many develop a lethal lymphoma-like disease before puberty.

*Myeloperoxidase deficiency* of PMN leucocytes and monocytes has been reported to be an autosomal recessive disorder which predisposes to systemic candidiasis (Lehrer & Cline, 1969).

### 23.5.3 Selective defects of PMN leucocytes

Patients with selective neutrophil defects (Block C, Fig. 23.5) suffer predominantly from stomatitis, vaginitis, otitis, mastitis and skin infections which suggest that these cells are particularly important for protection of certain exposed surfaces.

Several varieties of *hereditary neutropaenias* have been described, some of which show a cyclic pattern (periodic neutropaenia). These

329                          *Chapter 23: Immunity and Immunity Deficiency*

patients are capable of monocyte production and some may have monocytosis.

Infections usually appear if blood neutrophils remain below $500/\text{mm}^3$. When there is an associated functional neutrophil abnormality, moderate neutropaenia ($1000$–$1500/\text{mm}^3$) can give rise to severe symptoms.

*The Lazy Leucocyte Syndrome* is characterized by a moderate neutropaenia and a decrease in random mobility and chemotactic responsiveness of PMN leucocytes. These neutrophils have normal phagocytic and bacteriocidal capacity. The underlying biochemical defect is unknown.

Syndromes associated with isolated monocyte defects have not yet been clearly defined (see Wiscott–Aldrich syndrome below). One family with severe acquired monocytopaenia has been reported. The predominant symptoms were chronic fungal infections, recurrent chest infections and giant warts.

### 23.5.4 Combined deficiency of B and T lymphocytes

These diseases have been claimed to be the cause of up to 10 per cent of postnatal mortality. In severe form there is profound depletion of lymphocytes throughout the lymphoid tissues with blood lymphocytes at less than $1000/\text{mm}^3$, but normal phagocytic function (Block D, Fig. 23.5). Less severe variants have considerable numbers of B (but less commonly T) lymphocytes and foci of lymphocytes in the spleen and lymph nodes. Some patients show biochemical abnormalities (deficiency of adenosine deaminase, transcobalamin II). In one case the immunity deficiency was corrected by administration of vitamin $B_{12}$. Both X-linked and autosomal recessive forms have been reported.

Clinically, fungal infections are usually predominant. These children fail to thrive and die before two years of age, T lymphocyte deficiency being more rapidly fatal than B lymphocyte deficiency. Reconstitution with histocompatible bone marrow has successfully corrected the condition in several cases.

### 23.5.5 Failure of B lymphopoesis (Block E, Fig. 23.5)

*Infantile X-linked hypogammaglobulinaemia (Bruton's disease)* was the first immunity deficiency disease to be identified (1952). Serum IgG is less than 100 mg/100 ml and IgA and IgM are virtually absent. Antibody responses are undetectable or very low but cellular immunity is virtually intact. There are no B lymphocytes in the blood or secondary lymphoid tissues of these patients.

### 23.5.6 Antibody deficiency (B lymphocyte maturation defects)

B lymphocyte maturation defects (Block F, Fig. 23.5) are more frequent than X-linked agammaglobulinaemia. These patients have normal blood T and B lymphocyte counts but virtual absence of all or some serum immunoglobulins. The B lymphocytes carry surface immunoglobulin but fail to secrete it. In addition to intrinsic B cell defects, it is possible that the condition is due to T lymphocyte dysfunction, leading to failure of B cell maturation, antigen presentation or cell cooperation. Maternal antibody protects agammaglobulinaemic patients during the early part of life.

### 23.5.7 *Isolated failure of T lymphocyte differentiation* (Fig. 23.5G)

Severe T lymphocyte deficiency is associated with congenital aplasia of the thymus.

*di George syndrome.* Abnormal embryogenesis of the third and fourth pharangeal pouches results in failure of development of the thymus and parathyroid glands as well as severe cardiovascular abnormalities (characteristic facial features are also common). T lymphocyte levels are low and CMI defective. Although the anatomical defect is similar to that of nude or thymectomized mice, the serum IgA level is normal and their ability to produce antibodies is only marginally affected. This suggests that antibody responses may be less thymus dependent in humans than in mice.

The first symptoms are neonatal tetany brought on by the parathyroid defect, usually followed by candidiasis and other infections characteristic of deficiency of the 'cellular axis'. Correction of the immunological defect by thymus grafting has been reported. Variants with minor degrees of T cell deficiency have also occurred, often with spontaneous improvement.

*Nezelof's syndrome* is an autosomal recessive form of thymic hypoplasia with characteristic T cell deficiency. In contrast to di George syndrome, parathyroid function and the cardiovascular system are normal.

In *ataxia telangectasia* there is also thymic hypoplasia with defective T cell function and a selective IgA deficiency.

Finally, certain antibody deficiencies and autoimmune disorders may be due directly or indirectly to selective T lymphocyte deficiency.

### 23.5.8 *Lymphokine deficiency (T lymphocyte maturation defects,* Fig. 23.5H)

Patients with chronic mucocutaneous candidiasis are sometimes incapable of producing MIF *in vitro*. Although this may explain their condition, it is a poorly worked-out area of immunity deficiency whose future development will await the immunochemical characterization of lymphokines.

### 23.5.9 *Combined T and B lymphocyte dysfunction due to putative macrophage defect* (Block I, Fig. 23.5)

The Wiscott–Aldrich syndrome, an X-linked recessive condition, is characterized by eczema, thrombocytopaenia and recurrent infection. Serum immunoglobulin levels are normal but the patients fail to make antibodies to polysaccharide antigens. There is indirect evidence that the defect is at the level of antigen presentation (Blaese *et al.*, 1968). There is progressive loss of CMI and the monocytes of about half of the patients lack the receptor for Fc of IgG. *In vitro*, the lymphocytes of these patients fail to respond to antigens, though their responses to non-specific mitogens are normal.

## References

BLAESE R.M., STROBER W., BROWN R.S. & WALDMANN T.A. (1968) The Wiskott–Aldrich syndrome, a disorder with a possible defect in antigen processing or recognition. *Lancet* i, 1054.

BULLEN J.J., ROGERS H.J. & LEWIN J.E. (1971) The bacteriostatic effect of serum on Pasteurella septica and its abolition by iron compounds. *Immunology* **20,** 391.

COOPER M.D., FAULK W.P., FUDENBERG H.H., GOOD R.A., HITZIG W., KUNKEL H.G., ROITT I.M., ROSEN F.S., SELIGMANN M., SOOTHILL J.F. & WEDGEWOOD R.J. (1974) Primary immunodeficiencies, Meeting report of the 2nd International Workshop on Primary Immunodeficiency Diseases in May. *Clin. Immunol. & Immunopathol.* **2,** 416.

HERMANS P.E., RITTS R.E. & GLEICH G.J. (1973) Immunity deficiency diseases. *Postgrad. Med.* **54,** 66.

HIGGS J.M. & WELLS R.S. (1972) Chronic mucocutaneous candidiasis associated with abnormalities of iron metabolism. *British Journal of Dermatology* **86,** Suppl. 8, 88.

KLEBANOFF S.J. & WHITE L.R. (1969) Iodination defect in the leucocytes of a patient with chronic granulomatous disease of childhood. *New Engl. J. Med.* **280,** 460.

LEHRER R.I. & CLINE M.J. (1969) Leucocyte myeloperoxidase deficiency and disseminated candidiasis. The role of myeloperoxidase in resistance to *Candida* infection. *J. Clin. Invest.* **48,** 1478.

SOOTHILL J.F. (1974) Immunity deficiency states. In COOMBS R.R.A., GELL P.H.G. & LACHMANN P.J. *Clinical Aspects of Immunology*, 3rd edition, Chapter 23. Blackwell, Oxford.

# APPENDICES

# Appendix A
# Classification of Tissue-damaging Allergic Reactions

(Reprinted from Gell P.G.H., Coombs R.R.A. and Lachmann P.J. *Clinical Aspects of Immunology*, 3rd edition, Blackwell Scientific Publications, Oxford.)

### Type I reaction (anaphylactic, reagin-dependent)

Initiated by allergen or antigen reacting with tissue cells (basophils and mast cells) passively sensitized (allergized) by antibody produced elsewhere, leading to the release of pharmacologically active substances (vasoactive amines).

### Type II reaction (cytotoxic or cell stimulating)

Initiated by antibody reacting with either (a) an antigenic component of a cell or tissue element or (b) an antigen or hapten which has become intimately associated with these; damage may then occur in the presence of complement or of certain kinds of mononuclear cells. Stimulation of secretor organs may also occur, e.g. the thyroid.

### Type III reaction (damage by antigen–antibody complexes)

Initiated when antigen reacts in the tissue spaces with potentially precipitating antibody, forming microprecipitates in and around the small vessels causing damage to cells secondarily, or being precipitated in and interfering with the function of membranes, or when antigen in excess reacts in the bloodstream with potentially precipitating antibody, forming soluble circulating complexes which are deposited in the blood-vessel walls or in the basement membrane and cause local inflammation or massive complement activation.

### Type IV reaction (delayed, tuberculin-type, cell-mediated)

Initiated essentially by the reaction of actively allergized lymphocytes, probably of the T (thymus-derived) population responding specifically to allergen by the release of lymphokines, and/or the development of cytotoxicity, without the participation of free antibody. Locally it is manifested by the infiltration of cells, at the site where the antigen is injected.

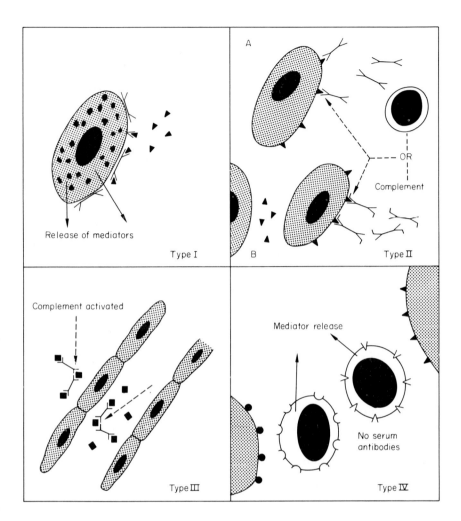

Release of mediators

Type I

A

OR

Complement

B

Type II

Complement activated

Type III

Mediator release

No serum
antibodies

Type IV

Key:

● ▲ ◆    Antigens

⟶    Liberation of histamine and other
     pharmacologically active substances

>< >< ><  Antibody

----▶    Sites of involvement of complement or
         non-allergized lymphocytes

⊃ <    Specific antigen-combining receptors on
       membrane of specifically allergized lymphocytes

# Appendix B
# Gentle Genetics

Some of the concepts in this book require a slight knowledge of genetics for their understanding. This appendix attempts to provide this painlessly, though it would horrify 'proper' geneticists.

## Representation of genes

Since the sequence of the DNA codes EXACTLY for the amino acid sequence of a polypeptide, the two can be regarded as informationally almost equivalent and colinear. Thus, the representation of an amino acid sequence stands adequately for the DNA sequence which codes for it, other than for the 'punctuation' elements in the DNA sequence. In this book, both genes and polypeptides are frequently represented as lines: they are almost equivalent.

## Arrangements of genes

The genes are arranged in a linear fashion on the chromosomes. In a large number of cases examined by immunogeneticists, there is more than one copy of a gene on a single chromosome. Such genes are said to be arranged in tandem and are the result of *tandem duplication** (see Chapters 1, 2 and 6). Tandem copies of genes serve similar functions, but because they persist for significantly long periods in evolutionary terms the copies tend to accumulate a large number of *mutations*, more especially as there is always a 'spare' gene to carry on the essential work.

The position of a gene on a chromosome is called a *locus*. Where two loci are close together on a chromosome, they are said to be linked, a term which refers ONLY to their relative positions. Tandem duplications are linked.

Mammals are diploid animals: we have paired chromosomes. Except in the case of loci on the X (the sex) chromosome, we have two copies of the genes at each locus. Probably most genes exist in

* Glossarized words italicized.

336

a number of variants which contribute to the heterogeneity of the population. All the variants at a particular locus are called *alleles*, and are inherited as alternatives, since only one chromosome from each pair is included in the *gametes*.

During meiosis, there is an exchange of material between the paired chromosomes by the process of *crossing over*. This leads to the *recombination* of alleles at linked loci: characters which were separately received from parents are passed to offspring together. Because the position of crossovers is (usually) random, the frequency with which alleles at linked loci recombine is related to the distance between the loci, loci close together seldom having a crossover between them. In turn, this allows us to measure the distance between loci in terms of recombination frequency, even in total ignorance of which chromosome they lie on.

A set of alleles at a number of closely linked loci will usually be transmitted together. This kind of 'array' of alleles is called a *haplotype*, and is said to be in *coupling* linkage.


### Association and linkage

While linkage refers only to the relative positions of two loci, association is the term applied to the FREQUENT CONCUR-RENCE OF PHENOTYPIC CHARACTERS. Possession of Haemoglobin S is associated with bad anaesthetic risk. This is a causal relationship: HbS distorts erythrocytes under conditions of low oxygen-tension and causes haemolytic anaemia. However, the origin of an association may be very far from obvious. A Martian geneticist might observe that the possession of genes conferring black skin coloration in humans is associated with low income. The causal relationships would be far from obvious to him, unless he had a keen appreciation of the workings of human societies, greed, prejudice and history.

Sometimes situations arise where there is both linkage and association. An example of this is the case of the alleles at the two most commonly typed loci of the HLA system (see Chapter 15). An unexpectedly high proportion of English people who are A1 are also B8, alleles which are coded at different loci. These loci are close together but there is a significant rate of recombination (0·8 per cent) between them. Nevertheless, inheritance of one allele at one locus is frequently associated with inheritance of a particular allele at the other locus. In other words, some haplo-types are much more common than would be expected if free recombination had been permitted to redistribute the alleles at random. This phenomenon is called *linkage disequilibrium* and can be explained as being due to:

1. Lack of free mixing of the gene pools during the time required for recombination to take place (stratification). In this case, it is

*Appendices*

estimated that about 5,000 years of random breeding would be required.

2. Selective advantage for particular haplotypes, leading to reproductive success, and hence a high population incidence.

## Genetic analysis

The principal aim of genetic analysis is the enumeration of the genes which are responsible for the transmission of a character. There are two common methods, whose use depends on whether the genes are in a single linkage group or on different chromosomes.

*Backcross analysis* is used to determine the number of linkage groups involved. In the simplest case, a trait is identified as present in one inbred strain and absent from another. The $F_1$ cross between the strains shows the character, i.e. it is inherited as a dominant. The $F_1$ is 'backcrossed' onto the parental strain which does not show the character. If a single gene is involved, half of the offspring will have the character and half will not. All those which carry the character will give rise to further 1:1 ratios of offspring on re-backcrossing to the recessive parental strain. If two or more genes add their effects then the backcross progeny will give heterogeneous results. However, if two genes which depend on each other are responsible for the inheritance of the character, then only a quarter of the backcross offspring will show the character. Further backcrosses will give more heterogeneous results or small ratios. An estimate of the number of genes involved can be made from the size of the ratio in backcross experiments or in attempts to 'reconstitute' the $F_1$ by intercrossing $F_2$s (see Fig. B.1).

Linkage between loci for genes controlling two characters is established by showing that they are 'invariably' inherited together in every generation of backcross, while most of the other characters are lost. It is useful to find SOME recombinants, however, lest the two characters turn out to be determined by a single gene!

Backcross analysis does not easily distinguish between single genes and closely linked genes determining a single character. The specialized form of *recombinant analysis* must be used. $F_1$s are backcrossed onto the parental strain *ad nauseam*. Depending on the closeness of linkage of the genes under consideration, a fraction of the offspring produced will receive chromosomes in which crossing over has led to the transmission of only some of the linked genes. By painstakingly identifying and characterizing the recombinant individuals, an estimate can be made of the number of genes which are involved in determining the character.

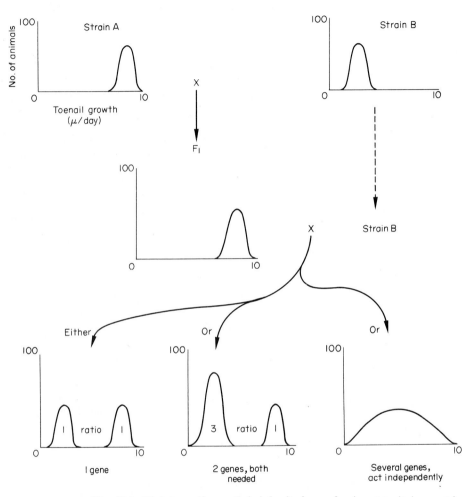

**Fig. B.1.** High toenail-growth is inherited as a dominant trait (present in the $F_1$). When the $F_1$ is backcrossed onto the low toenail-growth strain the offspring may have one of three patterns:

(a) Equal numbers of high and low toenail-growth animals: 1 gene.

(b) 3 low growth to 1 high growth: 2 genes, both needed.

(c) A spread of growth rates: several genes, acting independently and controlling, for instance, eating habits, walking habits, scratching habits, biochemistry of nailbed cells.

339

# Appendix C
# W.H.O. Nomenclature for the HLA System, July 1975

The region is now called HLA (the hyphen is dropped).
The loci are renamed:

| Old | MLC | SD2 FOUR | SD3 AJ | SD1 LA |
|---|---|---|---|---|
| O———‖——————————‖——————————‖——————————‖ — — | | | | |
| New | HLA-D | HLA-B | HLA-C | HLA-A |

The antigens are renamed: (new nomenclature in left columns).

| LOCUS | HLA-A | First (LA) | HLA-B | Second (FOUR) | HLA-C | Third (AJ) |
|---|---|---|---|---|---|---|
| ANTIGENS | HLA-A1 | HL-A1 | HLA-B5 | HL-A5 | HLA-CW1 | T1 AJ |
| | HLA-A2 | HL-A2 | HLA-B7 | HL-A7 | HLA-CW2 | T2 170 |
| | HLA-A3 | HL-A3 | HLA-B8 | HL-A8 | HLA-CW3 | T3UPS |
| | HLA-A9 | HL-A9 | HLA-B12 | HL-A12 | HLA-CW4 | TA 315 |
| | HLA-A10 | HL-A10 | HLA-B13 | HL-A13 | HLA-CW5 | T5 |
| | HLA-A11 | HL-A11 | HLA-B14 | W14 | | |
| | HLA-A28 | W28 | HLA-B18 | W18 | | |
| | HLA-A29 | W29 | HLA-B27 | W27 | | |
| | HLA-AW23 | W23 | HLA-BW35 | W5 | ——— | |
| | HLA-AW24 | W24 | HLA-BW40 | W10 | HLA-D | MLC |
| | HLA-AW25 | W25 | HLA-BW15 | W15 | | LD1 |
| | HLA-AW26 | W26 | HLA-BW16 | W16 | ——— | |
| | HLA-AW30 | W30 | HLA-BW17 | W17 | HLA-DW1 | |
| | HLA-AW31 | W31 | HLA-BW21 | W21 | HLA-DW2 | LD7a |
| | HLA-AW32 | W32 | HLA-BW22 | W22 | HLA-DW3 | LD8a |
| | HLA-AW33 | W19.6, Mal 1, Fe55 | HLA-BW37 | TY | HLA-DW4 | |
| | | | HLA-BW38 | W16.1 (DA31) | HLA-DW5 | |
| | HLA-AW34 | Malay 2, 10.35 etc. | HLA-BW39 | W16.2 | HLA-DW6 | |
| | | | HLA-BW41 | Sabell, LK | | |
| | HLA-AW36 | MO*, LT | | | | |
| | HLA-AW43 | BK | HLA-BW42 | MWA | | |

Antigens not included in the above list will continue to be referred to by their locally assigned names.

The prefix HLA can be dropped in referring to antigens where the context is clear. When an antigen has intermediate 'W' status, it will be referred to, for example, as HLA-BW15 or briefly as BW15. This indicates intermediate status at the second or B locus.

## Reference

KISSMEYER-NIELSEN F. (1975) (Editor) *Histocompatibility Testing 1975.* Munksgaard, Copenhagen.

# Glossary

*adjuvant*: a substance which can increase specific antibody formation to an antigen (see also Freund's adjuvant).

*affinity*: intrinsic binding power of a single (antibody) combining site with a single (antigenic) substrate binding site (i.e. *epitope*).

*affinity chromatography*: method of purification of molecules or cells by attaching substances for which they have affinity to an insoluble support medium, and then using this as a chromatography medium. Not easy to elute antibodies from such media as their affinities are often too high.

*allele*: inherited variant at a locus.

*allergic*: pertaining to a state of altered reactivity. Commonly used to describe a state of susceptibility to exposure to environmental agents, but used in its original sense in this book (see Appendix A).

*allo-*: between members of a species with different genetic constitution.

*allogeneic*: different genetic constitution. Usually used to describe *intra*species antigenic differences (cf. xenogeneic).

*allophenic*: having more than one genetic constitution: usually applied to animals 'made' by fusing two blastocysts. Such animals are therefore tetraparental. The cells making them up are virtually inextricably mixed.

*allotype*: genetic marker at an individual *locus*. Inherited as alternatives.

*anergy*: absence of immunological reactivity.

*antibody*: molecule produced by animals in response to exposure to antigen (q.v.) which has the property of combining specifically with the antigen.

*antigen*: molecule or particle which combines with antibody (q.v.) (see also II).

*antigen suicide*: method of specifically destroying cells carrying receptors for antigens by exposing them to antigen of very high specific radioactivity. The local irradiation effects lead to the death of the cells.

*antiparallel*: same as parallel but with directions opposite:

Parallel                     Antiparallel

$\longrightarrow$              $\longrightarrow$
$\longrightarrow$              $\longleftarrow$

*ascertainment*: the extent to which all relevant data is collected and its lack of bias. Selection of material for study on the basis of any characteristic which is functionally related to the subject of the study will produce a disturbance of ascertainment.

*association*: the phenomenon of two phenotypic markers being frequently found together. The association may be due to a causal relationship between the observed phenomena (e.g. HAE is due to $C\bar{1}$ inh. deficiency (see Chapters 5, 6, 17), or to linkage disequilibrium between the genes which code for the phenotypic events (see Chapters 15 and 18).

*autoradiography*: see *radioautography*.

*autosomal*: not on the X or Y chromosomes.

*avidity*: net combining power of an antibody molecule with its antigen: related to both the affinity and the valencies of the antibody and the antigen.

*BCG*: Bacille Calmette-Guerin, an attenuated strain of Mycobacterium tuberculosis, in general use as a prophylactic vaccine, but also used as a stimulant to the immune system in, for instance, 'immunotherapy' of cancer.

*Bence-Jones proteins*—'free' light chains found in the urine of people (or mice) with myelomatosis. Characteristically they precipitate on heating the urine to $60°C$ and redissolve at higher temperatures.

$\beta_2$ *microglobulin*: small polypeptide component of HLA molecules. Abundant in urine from tubular nephrotic syndromes. Has structural similarities with immunoglobulin domains and has been reported to activate the complement system.

*bursa of Fabricius*: lymphoepithelial organ unique to birds, located at the junction of the hind gut and cloaca.

*capping*: process of redistribution of cell-surface determinants to one small part of the cell surface. Usually accomplished by antibody (often labelled with fluorescein or radioactivity), which MUST be at least divalent (see Chapter 7).

*carrier*: immunogenic molecule to which a hapten (q.v.) is coupled.

*cell cycle*: stages from one cell division to the next.

*chimerism*: a situation in which cells from two genetically different individuals coexist in one body. Classically shown by most cattle twins, which share circulations *in utero* and are mutually tolerant (see Chapters 10 and 16).

*cis*: using genetic material from only one chromosome.

*clone*: a family of cells (or organisms) of identical genetical constitutions derived asexually from a single cell by repeated division. Plasma cells of one clone have fixed the *idiotype* of their product.

*CMI*: cell-mediated immunity. Includes phenomena of graft rejection, delayed hypersensitivity (tuberculin type), etc. (see Chapters 12, 17 and 23).

*congenic*: animals which differ from a base syngeneic strain at a single locus. Produced by backcrossing of an $F_1$ to the parent

343

*Glossary*

strain, followed by selection of offspring for heterozygosity at the specified locus and further repeated backcrossing to the parent, ending by intercrossing the 'last' generation and selection of homozygotes to found the congenic line.

*coupling*: alleles at different loci on the *same* chromosome.

*crossing over*: the breakage and repair of homologous DNA strands during meiosis, such that part of the one derived from one parent is passed on to the gamete with the remainder from the other parent. The mechanism for recombination between genes on a chromosome.

*CVF*: Cobra Venom Factor, a C3b analogue isolated from the venom of cobras. It has the property of activating the 'alternative pathway' of complement activation so as to activate and destroy C3-9. The active complex which is formed with the factor B of the blood has a very long half-life both *in vitro* and *in vivo*. Pure CVF lacks both neurotoxic and phospholipase activity, and is suitable for experimental use *in vivo* in animals.

*cyclic AMP*: an intracellular mediator, having an especially important effect on the activity of the microtubules and other contractile elements of the cell. A rise in C-AMP levels leads to a decrease in the mobility of the cell.

*cyanogen bromide*: useful and simple reagent for 'activating' poly-saccharides so that they will covalently bind to proteins, thus making an affinity chromatography medium. Also used to split polypeptide chains at methyonyl residues.

*cytophilic*: having affinity for cells. Usually applied to antibodies which bind to macrophages.

*cytotoxicity*: the killing of cells by cells, antibody and complement or other agents.

*D*: the diffusion constant of a molecule, a measure of its intrinsic thermal diffusability, dependent on its size and shape. The molecular weight of a molecule can be calculated from the knowledge of its sedimentation and diffusion constants: m.w. $=f\frac{s}{D}$. A parameter closely related to D can be measured by gel filtration, though accurate measurements require optical methods, for instance in an ultracentrifuge (running slow!).

*discontinuous gradient*: contradiction in terms used by cellular immunologists to describe tube partially filled with high density medium (e.g. Ficoll/Hypaque) through which cells can be differentially centrifuged.

*dizygotic*: derived from two separate fusions of spermatozoa and ova.

*DNA*: desoxyribose nucleic acid: fundamental genetic material which carries all genetic information passed from generation to generation. Specific sequences of nucleotide bases code in a colinear manner for the sequence of a protein.

*DNP*: Dinitrophenol. A traditional hapten.

*domain*: a single homology region of an immunoglobulin, encompassing about 110 amino acids and held together by a disulphide bridge spanning about the central 60 residues. Folds into a characteristic compact shape (see Chapter 3).

*double diffusion*: a method of immunochemical analysis of antigenic relationships pioneered by Ouchterlony.

*doubling time*: time required for a population to double its numbers. NOT simply related to the interval between divisions unless all the cells are dividing at the same rate.

*E.B. virus*: Epstein-Barr virus, found in association with Burkett's lymphoma. It may be oncogenic in certain circumstances, e.g. when malarial infection is widespread.

*effector cell*: mindless hit-man of the cellular underworld. Has been programmed to do one thing until gunned down or natural death.

*electron microscopy*: ultra-high magnification method of microscopy based on casting electron 'shadows' of the sample. Atoms of high atomic number cast deeper shadows than lighter atoms.

*Endoplasmic reticulum*: intracytoplasmic membranes of cells usually arranged in parallel. The space between the membranes often contains the protein being synthesized. Membranes with ribosomes attached to their outer surface are known as rough endoplasmic reticulum. Plasma cells contain massive amounts of endoplasmic reticulum.

*enhancement*: the surprising event of prolongation of graft survival by antibody to the graft, probably by interfering with the effector limb of the immune response.

*epitope*: single antigenic determinant: the portion of a molecule which will combine with a particular antibody combining site.

*evanescent*: Lachmannesque term for short-lived.

*Flagellin*: protein derived from flagella (usually of Salmonellae).

*Forsmann antigen*: a carbohydrate antigen with wide but non-uniform distribution in mammals. In some species (e.g. sheep) it is present on both tissue and red blood cells, but in others (e.g. guinea-pig) is present on tissue cells alone. Antisera are classically raised by the injection of boiled horse kidney into rabbits (which wholly lack the antigen).

*Freund's adjuvant*: a water–oil emulsion of antigen (usually in aqueous phase) and killed *M. tuberculosis* usually in the oily phase (complete Freund's adjuvant). Incomplete Freund's adjuvant contains no organisms in the oil phase.

*gamete*: specialized cells which combine in sexual reproduction to form the zygote which will develop into the new individual. Ova and sperm in vertebrates.

*GBM*: Glomerular Basement Membrane: seems to have partially distinct antigenic structure from other basement membranes. Antibodies to it can be found in natural glomerulonephritis and can be raised for experimental studies.

*genome*: the total complement of genetic material within a cell.

*genotype*: genetic characteristics inherited from parents, but not necessarily observable in the phenotype.

*germ line*: genetic information which is passed from generation to generation in the conventional Mendelian way.

*gluten*: protein from wheat. Dietary component involved in the pathogenesis of coeliac disease.

*H-2*: genetic region concerned with histocompatibility in mice.

*haplotype*: set of genetic determinants located on a single chromosome.

*hapten*: small molecule which will combine with antibody but which is not capable of evoking an antibody response when injected alone (see Preamble II, Chapters 4, 7, 8 and 9).

*heterologous*: foreign: usually used to denote inter-species antigenic differences.

*histocompatibility*: compatibility as determined by transplantation.

*histogenic*: pertaining to tissue of origin.

*HLA*: genetic region concerned with histocompatibility in man.

*humoral*: pertaining to the extracellular fluids.

*hydrodynamic:* pertaining to movement in fluids: used here to include all methods of molecular analysis which depend on such movement. e.g. sedimentation analysis (see *S*), diffusion (see *D*), *gel filtration*, etc.

*idioepitope*: see Idiotope.

*idiotope: epitope* (i.e. antigenic determinant) characteristic of an *idiotype*.

*idiotype*: antigenic marker for the antibody combining site. The antigen is found in the variable region of the antibody secreted by a single *clone* of lymphoid cells. Antibodies of *different* specificities have different *idiotypes*.

*immunoconglutinins*: antibodies (often autoantibodies) formed to complement components or their breakdown products (abbreviated as IK).

*immunofluorescence*: method involving the use of fluorochrome-labelled antibody to cellular determinants.

*immunogenic*: capable of provoking an animal to make an *allergic* response.

*iso*: same, of identical genetic constitution—isologous, isogeneic (synonym for syngeneic).

*isoantibody*: antibody which reacts with an antigen present in another member of the *same* species but not in the animal itself— e.g. blood group antibodies (term now in the literature but not strictly correct—q.v. iso-).

*isoantigen*: antigen which can elicit antibody formation in another member of same species not genetically identical (e.g. isotype).

*isoelectric focusing*: high resolution electrophoretic separation method in which molecules migrate to their isoelectric points in a self-generating pH gradient.

*isotopes*: a number of radioisotopes are commonly used by immunologists: see table:

346

| Isotope | Use | Emission | Half-Life |
|---|---|---|---|
| $^{125}I$ | External protein label | Soft $\gamma$ | 60 days |
| $^{131}I$ | External protein label | Hard $\gamma$ | 8 days |
| $^{51}Cr$ | Releasable cell label (escapes on death) | Hard $\gamma$ | 26 days |
| $^{3}H$ | In nucleic acid or protein precursors | Soft $\beta$ | 12·5 years |
| $^{14}C$ | In nucleic acid or protein precursors | Hard $\beta$ | 5700 years |

Generally used to trace label molecules or cells for their subsequent detection.

*karyotype*: chromosomal pattern, characteristic for male and female, and for some abnormal chromosome markers (e.g. T6T6—see Chapter 9).

*Kupffer cells*: liver macrophages.

*LCM*: Lymphocytic Chorio-meningitis. Viral disease of mice, characterized in many cases by the production of immune complexes. It is a classical model for diseases mediated in this manner.

*linkage*: the coexistence of two genes in reasonably close proximity on a chromosome. Not to be confused with association.

*linkage disequilibrium*: concurrence of two alleles at different loci on a chromosome in coupling linkage more commonly than would be expected from the product of their individual frequencies. See also Chapters 15, 16, 17 and 18, Appendix B, and Chapter 6.

*locus*: position on a chromosome at which a gene is to be found. Defined as the smallest discovered unit of recombination. See also Chapters 2, 6, 15, 16 and 17.

*lymphokine*: generic term for non-antibody molecules produced by or with the aid of lymphocytes and having various biological activities (see Chapter 12).

*lymphocyte*: little round lymphoid cell without much cytoplasm which is what immunology is really all about (see Chapter 7).

*lymphon*: collective term for cells and their environment which constitute the immune system.

*mediator*: conveniently vague term for molecule which mediates a biological phenomenon. Often the same as lymphokine (q.v.).

*MIF*: Macrophage Inhibition Factor: a generic name for any factor or complex of factors which are derived from lymphocytes and which inhibit the migration of macrophages from capillary tubes *in vitro*.

*mitogen*: substance which causes lymphocytes to undergo cell division, e.g. PHA (q.v.), endotoxin.

*mitomycin*: a cell poison of plant origin which disrupts the formation of the microtubules of the mitotic spindles, thus preventing cell division.

*MLR*: Mixed Lymphocyte Reaction: *in vitro* assay for cell-mediated reactivity to cellular antigens. The assay attempts to measure the degree of proliferation of the stimulated cell population, usually by the incorporation of tritiated thymidine into their DNA.

*monoclonal*: derived from a single-cell clone: usually of immunoglobulin, to denote unusual homogeneity.

*multigravid*: having had numerous pregnancies.

*mutation*: single specific alteration in the genetic constitution of a cell (notably a germ cell) which was not present in its parent.

*m.w.*: molecular weight. Despite the fact that an exact definition has been available since Avogadro, immunologists have a habit of making a single measurement of a physical parameter of a protein, and announcing a molecular weight (sic) on the basis of this. Accurate molecular weights ($\pm 2$ per cent) can be derived by painstaking experiments on highly purified material in the ultra-centrifuge, or by *gel filtration* of fully denatured chains in 6M Guanidine hydrochloride. *SDS* gel electrophoresis gives good measurements of the weight of fully denatured, carbohydrate free, polypeptide chains. For proteins, the only fully accurate method is the summation of the residue molecular weights determined by sequence.

*myeloma*: see *plasmacytoma*.

*neotonization*: the evolution of sexual maturity in a larval form.

*NIP*: 4-hydroxy-3-Iodo-5-nitrophenacetyl—an iodine-containing hapten, in which the iodine atom can be radioactive.

*non-covalent forces*: chemical bonding forces weaker than covalent bonds, for example hydrogen bonds, non-polar (hydrophobic) and electrostatic bonds. These forces are of immense importance in the maintenance of configuration in protein molecules, and are disrupted by classical denaturing agents, e.g. detergents, urea, guanidine HCl, etc.

*nude mouse*: genetically athymic hairless mouse (see Chapter 9).

*nuclepore*: commercial name for cell impermeable, molecule permeable membrane.

*Oocyte*: precursor cell in the ovary which is richly supplied with protein biosynthetic apparatus, and which can be enucleated and injected with heterologous messenger *RNA*.

*Opsonization*: process of coating an antigen which facilitates the phagocytosis of the antigen.

*Parbiosis*: surgical creation of 'Siamese' twin arrangement by fusing the circulations.

*PHA*: PhytoHaemAgglutinin: plant lectin which stimulates T lymphocytes to divide promiscuously.

*phagocytosis*: the process of ingestion of solid or semisolid material into a cell by closing off an invagination of the protoplasm. This process requires the activity of contractile elements of the cell and aerobic respiration. Following ingestion, the contents of the phagosome are usually digested by the discharge of cathepsins and other enzymes into the phagosome.

*phenotype*: individual characteristics as observed (cf. genotype).

*phytomitogen*: Mitogen (q.v.) of plant origin, e.g. PHA, PWM (poke weed mitogen).

*pinocytosis*: the process of ingestion of liquids or very small particles into the cell. This process is not dependent on aerobic respiration.

*plasma cell*: terminally differentiated antibody forming cell with short half life.

*plasmacytoma*: tumour of immunoglobulin secreting cells, almost always secreting a homogeneous product. Syn: *Myeloma* (though should not be applied to IgM secretors.)

*PPD*: Purified Protein Derivative, a fraction of the supernate of culture of *M. tuberculosis*, now in general use as a test antigen in tuberculin skin tests rather than old tuberculin.

*prostaglandins*: a highly potent series of extracellular mediators of cellular reactivity.

*prime*: to give first exposure to antigen.

Φ*X174*: a bacteriophage.

*radioautography*: method of detection of radioactivity by allowing the radiation to blacken a photographic emulsion juxtaposed to the source. Thus the object 'takes its own photograph'.

*reagin*: antique term for IgE antibody.

*recombinant*: offspring in which two characters present separately in the grandparents are transmitted together.

*recombination*: the passing on of a genetic character inherited from one parent with a character inherited from the other parent.

*recombination analysis*: see Appendix B.

*repulsion*: alleles at different loci on opposite chromosomes.

*reticuloendothelial system*: a diffuse 'organ' containing macrophages as the characteristic cell and distributed through the liver, spleen, lymph nodes, serous cavities, lungs, etc.

*ribosome*: organelle concerned with protein synthesis: coordinates the assembly of polypeptide chain according to the instructions in the messenger *RNA*.

*RNA*: ribonucleic acid: the 'extranuclear' nucleic acid, probably principally involved in the control of protein synthesis. Some *RNA* serves structural functions in the *ribosomes*, some as specific transport molecules for amino-acids, and some (messenger RNA) as the copy of the gene coded in the *DNA* which carries the information for a protein sequence.

*S*: Svedberg unit, a measure of the velocity of sedimentation of a molecule or particle in a gravitational field. Accurate measurements are referred to the behaviour of molecules at zero concentration (by extrapolation) in water at $20°C$: $s°_{20w}$. A series of molecules of the same density and the same shape will have higher sedimentation rates as they increase in size, but highly asymmetric molecules (e.g. rods or branched structures) will have very much slower sedimentation characteristics than spherical molecules of the same weight. *S* values can ONLY be derived from experiments in the ultracentrifuge. *Gel filtration* and *SDS* gel methods cannot yield *S* values, nor can *S* values alone give an estimate of molecular weight.

*sarcoma*: malignant connective tissue tumour.

*segregation*: distribution of genes among gametes. Two alleles *must* segregate. Segregation with another allele more often than would be expected is known as linkage.

*SIII*: Type III pneumococcal polysaccharide.

*somatic*: pertaining to a single individual: *Somatic mutation* involves the alteration of the genetic potential of some of the cells in an individual without altering the potential of its germ cells, so that the new potential is not passed from generation to generation, but must be derived anew in the offspring.

*splenomegaly*: increase in spleen size. Used as an assay for graft-versus host reactions.

*synergism*: cooperative action.

*Syngeneic*: animals which have been produced by repeated brother–sisten mating until homozygous at all measurable loci. All animals of a particular strain are thus almost identical in genetic constitution. Particularly important in experiments where cells are transferred from one animal to another.

*stoichiometric*: occurring in a quantitatively fixed relationship, for instance the ability of one inhibitor molecule to react with one, and only one enzyme molecule.

*T6*: morphological chromosome marker in mice.

*tachyphylaxis*: the phenomenon of increasing unreactivity when, for instance, a piece of jejunum is repeatedly challenged with a pharmacologically active peptide. If another stimulus is capable of eliciting a reaction when the first is not, they are said to exhibit non-cross-reacting tachyphylaxis.

*tandem duplicate*: copies of genes lying in a linear array on a chromosome. See also Chapters 2 and 6.

*thymoma*: tumour of the thymus.

*tolerance*: state of specific immunological unresponsiveness induced by exposure to antigen. See Chapter 10.

*trans*: using genetic material from both chromosomes.

*transformation*: morphological change in a cell at about the time of division: the cell, and especially the nucleus, enlarge greatly and the nucleus becomes pale staining.

*uropod*: tail of a lymphocyte.

*xeno*: between species.

*X-ray diffraction*: method for investigating the arrangement of atoms in a crystal. An averaging method which requires a large number of molecules to be oriented in the same way for high resolution. Results *must* be interpreted by mathematical analysis of diffractograms which do not reveal much information by inspection, even to crystallographers, unlike electron or conventional microscopy. Results are analyzed into three-dimensional structure.

# Index

Accurate sample hypothesis **122**
Acetyl tyrosine ethyl ester  61
Acute anterior uveitis  262
Acute lymphatic leukaemia
  HL-A association  261
Adherence reactions
  complement dependant  **274**
  immune  274
  opsonic  274
Adoptive transfer  20, **130,** 206
Affinity labelling  51
  measurement  44
  of antibodies  42
Agammaglobulinaemia
  B lymphocytes in  203
  Bruton's X-linked  327, 330
Alexin  56
Alleles  77, 84, 6
  distinction from tandem genes  16
Allelic exclusion  14, 111
Allergic inflammation
  role of complement  **282,** 192
Allergic reaction
  Type II  **283,** 334
  Type III  **284,** 334
  Type IV  291, 334
Alloantigens
  differentiation  107
  *H-2*  108
  in GVH reactions  131
  Ly  99
  lymphocyte  98
  PC.1  108
  theta  98
  TL  99
$\alpha$ chain  6
$\alpha$-fetal protein  297
$\alpha_2$-neuraminoglycoprotein  61
Allogeneic effect  146
Allotype
  *a* locus (rabbit)  7, 18
  *b* locus (rabbit)  7
  complement  88
  *d* locus (rabbit)  18
  *f* locus (rabbit)  18
  Gm  81
  immunoglobulin  **6,** 81
  Inv  7
  suppression  157

Alternative pathway  **61,** 89, 192, 279
  in cytotoxicity  000
Amniocentesis  269
Anaphylatoxin  67, 276
Anaphylaxis, aggregate  285
Anergy  **325**
  humoral  326
Ankylosing spondylitis
  HL-A association  **262**
Annealing
  of nucleic acids  21
Antibody
  affinity  **42**
  combining site  *see* Combining
    site
  diversity  **124**
  cytotoxic  188
  formation *in vitro*  **134**
  repertoire  125
Antigen  **91**
  coated column  109
  embryonic  308
  localization  217
  modulation  113
  properties for tolerance induction
    **153**
  receptor, T lymphocyte  114
  suicide  109
  thymus dependancy  147
  thymus independant  202
  transplantation  188
  valency  91
Antigenic competition  **165**
  intermolecular  **169**
  intramolecular  **169**
  mechanisms  165
  models  **173**
  sequential  167
Antigenic determinant  91
Arthus reaction  284
Ataxia telangectasia  331
Autoallergic disease  **287**
  thyroiditis  288
Autoantibodies  **290**
  to T cells  106
Avidity  47

Backcross analysis  19

Bacteria
  complement and killing  **279**
Bacteriocide
  mechanisms  181
Bacteriolysis
  immune  56
BCG  303
β₂ microglobulin  79
'Biozzi' mice  239
Blocking factors  **161,** 300
  *in vivo*  **161**
Bone marrow  97
Bruton's agammaglobulinaemia
  327, 330
Burkitt's lymphoma  304
Bursa of Fabricius  93, 198, 208
Bursectomy  198, 293

C3b-inactivator  67, 275  *see also*
  KAF *and* Complement
Cancer immunotherapy  301
  non-specific  304
Candidiasis  193
  chronic  329
  chronic mucocutaneous  325
Capping  112
Carboxypeptidase B  276
Carcinoembryonic antigen  297
Carrier effect  **139**
Cell-mediated immunity
  effector mechanisms  **179**
  genetic control  **249**
  histology  193
  model  193
Cell-mediated Lympholysis (CML)
  253
Cell triggering
  affinity considerations  43
Cellular immunity  323
Chediak-Higashi disease  329
Chemotactic factors  67, 276
Chemotaxis  276
Chimerism
  erythrocyte  199
Chromosome markers  137
Chronic granulomatous disease
  328, 329
Clonal
  development  197
  elimination  152, 287
  selection hypothesis  122
Clone  95
(CML) Cell-mediated lympholysis
  226
Coagulation
  interaction with complement
  **280**
  system  56
Cobra venom factor  61, **65,** 284
Coeliac disease
  HL-A association  **264**
Cold agglutinins  106
Cold haemagglutinin disease
  chronic  283, 288

Collagen diseases  290
Colostrum  13
Combined immunodeficiency  330
Combining site  3
  size  48
  specificity  48
Competition
  antigenic  **165**  *see also*
    Antigenic competition
Complement  56
  C1 activation  **59**
  C1 inhibitor  61
  C1-inhibitor deficiency  281
  C1q  11
  C2  61
  C3 activation  **67**
  C3b  275
  C3b feedback cycle  64
  C3b inactivator  65
  C3 biosynthesis  68
  C3 catabolism  69
  C3 convertases  59
  C3 inactivation  67
  C3 proactivator  62, 66
  C3 receptors on lymphocytes
    103
  C4  61
  C5  70
  C6  70
  C7  70
  C8  70
  C9  70
  activation  **57**
  activation by IgG and IgM  28
  adherence reactions  **274**
  allergic inflammation  **282**
  allotypes  88
  alternative pathway  **61**
  anaphylatoxin  67
  biological activities  **274**
  bystander lysis  277
  cell cytotoxicity  188
  chemotactic factors  67
  'classical' pathway triggering
    11, 28
  conglutinin  67
  deficiencies  87, 277
  destruction of microorganisms
    **279**
  evolution and genetics  **87**
  factor B  62, 65, 66, 192
  factor B genetics  88
  factor D  62
  fixation by antibody  3, 11, 28
  fixation, immunoglobulin
    flexability  24
  GBG (glycine rich beta glyco-
    protein)  62
  homeostasis  56
  immune adherence  67
  immunoconglutinins  277
  kinetics  73
  lesions  70, 71
  lysis  70, 277

Complement (*cont.*):
  opsonic adherence  67, 274
  proenzymes  57
  properdin  62, 66
  reactive lysis  70
  relationship to coagulation  280
  terminal sequence  **70**
Conglutinin  67
Cooperation
  cellular  95
  *in vivo* significance  **147**
  non-specific  **143**
  specific  **141**
  T-B cell  130, **136**
  T-B *in vivo*  220
  T-T  148
*Corynebacterium parvum*  303
Crossing over  16
  unequal  78
Cytotoxicity  188
  allograft  188
  antibody mediated  191
  K cell  182, 191
  mitogen induced  191
  tumour  189

Delayed hypersensitivity  93, 179
Delta chain or δ chain  6, 111, 201
Dengue  285
Diabetes  320
Differentiation
  B lymphocyte  **197**
di George syndrome  331
Diversity
  of antibodies  **124**
DNA  14, 16, 19, 21, 78, 121, 123,
    206, 288, 290, 336
DNA annealing  21
DNP  46, 53, 92, 120, 125, 140, 142,
    159, 160, 166
Domain  3, 31  *see also* Immuno-
    globulins
Domain
  evolution  79
  pairing  31

Effector cells  95
  CMI  179
Effector cell stimulating locus (ECS)
    253
Effector mechanisms
  cellular  **179**
EGTA  64
Elasmobranch fishes  76
Electron microscopy
  of immunoglobulins  24
Embryos
  antigens  308
Encephalomyelitis
  autoallergic  292
Endotoxaemia, acute  285
Endotoxin  61
Eiptope  91
  density, in tolerance  159

Epsilon chain  6
Equilibrium
  antigen–antibody  42
  dialysis  44
Evolution
  Adaptive immunity  76
  conserved structures in Igs  35
  protective mechanisms  318

Factor B  *see* Complement
Factor D  62
FDNB  217
Ferritin
  electron microscopy of immune
    complexes  24
Fetus
  exposure to maternal antigen
    309
  immunocompetence  311
Fibrinolytic system  56
Fluorescence quenching  46
Forssman shock  283

GALT *see* Gut associated lymphoid
    tissue
Gametes  16
Gamma chain  6
GBG (glycine rich beta glyco-
    protein)  62
Gene duplication  77
Generation of diversity  **125**
Germinal centre  211, 220
Germ-line hypothesis  **20**
Glioma  305
Glomerulonephritis  280
Glomerulus
  Antibody-mediated damage  284
Gluten  265
Gm types  84
Graft
  rejection  93, 226
  survival, tissue typing  **257**
Graft versus host reaction (GVH)
    130
Granuloma  181
Granulomatous  disease,  chronic
    328, 329
Graves' disease  289
Gut  associated  lymphoid  tissue
    (GALT)  97, 212

H-2  108, **228**
  Biochemistry of antigens  236
  gene map  229
  Ia antigens  232
  in cell cooperation  149
  I region and Lads  250
  *K* and *D* regions  **229**
  Public and private antigens  232
  Ss-S1p  233
Hageman factor  61, 281

Hapten 92
  bifunctional, for E.M. 25
Hapten-carrier response 139
Haptoglobin 78
Hashimoto's disease 293
Heavy chain
  classes **6**
  evolution 81
Haemoglobin
  lepore 78
Haemolysis
  immune 56
Hereditory Angio-oedema (HAE) 61, 281
Hereditory neutropaenia 329
Heterogeneity index 46
Hexose monophosphate pathway 181, 322
Histamine
  Release: by anaphylatoxins 276
  initiation by antibody 3
Histocompatibility
  antigens on spermatozoa 308
  cell cooperation 149
  cytotoxicity 188
  Major system **225**
  HL-A 228, **233**
    antigens 233
    autoallergic disease 293
    biochemistry of antigens 236
    disease associations **261**
    disease diagnosis 269
    extent of polymorphism 235
    linkage disequilibrium 236
  Nomenclature 340
Hodgkin's disease 261
Humoral immunity 323
Hydrocortisone 132
Hydrogen peroxide 322
Hypersensitivity
  delayed 93, 179
Hypervariable regions 11, 125

Ia antigens 232
Idiotype **8**
  marker for V region gene 18
  paradox 127
Immune adherence 67, 274
Immune complex 275
  as blocking factors 161
  role in disease 280
Immune response
  effector phase 95
  genetic control **239**
  homeostasis 96
  initial phase 94
Immune response genes
  cellular expression 244
  Ig-linked 240
  map 241
  number 243
  T cell products 116
Immune surveillance 298

Immunity
  cell-mediated *see* Cell-mediated immunity
  protective mechanisms 317
Immunity deficiency 317
  combined 325
  secondary 291
  syndromes **328**
Immunoconglutinins 277
Immunodominant group 49
Immunofluorescence
  anti-idiotype 20
Immunoglobulin
  IgA
    local secretion 13
    secretory component 9
  IgE 13
  IgM
    7S subunits 34
    central disc 25
    cross-linking antibody 25
    dissociation 34
    electron microscopic appearance 25
    papain digestion 35
  allelic exclusion 14
  allotypes **6**
  antibody affinity **42**
  antibody repertoire 19
  arrangement of genes 17
  assembly of polymers 15
  biosynthesis 13, **14**
  carbohydrate 15, 34
  cell-binding 13
  chains 3, 6
  colostrum 13
  combining site 3
  complement fixation 3, **11**, 28
  constant region genes 201
  electron microscopy **24**
  evolution 79
  flexibility 31
  fragments 3
  genetic relationship of variable and constant regions 18
  Gm types 84
  heavy chain classes **6**
  Hinge region 3
  histamine release 3
  hydrodynamic studies 24
  idiotypes **8**
  inherited idiotypes 19, 21
  integration 13, **14**
  Inv allotypes 7
  J chain 9, 15, 35
  Kern markers 6
  light chain types **3**
  lymphocyte surface 103, 112
  membrane transfer 12
  messenger RNA 14
  monoclonal antibodies 19
  non covalent interactions 31
  Oz markers 6
  placental transfer 13

*Index*

Immunoglobin (*cont.*):
  plasmacytoma  3
  'rules' for building models  **35**
  secretory component  9
  'switch' region  3
  variable region  **9**
  X-ray crystallography  **31**
Immunosuppression  298
Immunotherapy
  of cancer  301
Inflammation  179, 194
Integration
  *trans* of immunoglobulin genes
    18
Inv allotypes  7
Ir gene  *see* Immune response gene
Iron  320
Irradiation
  as immunosuppressive  136
Isoelectric focusing  20

J chain  9, 15, 35
Jerne plaque assay  135

K
  affinity constant  **42**
K cells  182
KAF  65, 275
Kappa chains  **3**
Kern markers  6
Killing mechanisms  181
Kinin
  system  56
Kininogenase  61

Lads  249
  *in vivo*  255
Lambda chains  **3**
LATS  289
Lazy leucocyte syndrome  330
Lectin  105
Lepore
  haemoglobin  78
  immunoglobulins  84, 86
Light chains  3
  types  **3**
Limiting dilution assay  246
Linkage  16
Linkage disequilibrium  236, 261
Lipopolysaccharide (LPS)  105
Liposomes  71
Liver
  fetal  208
Long acting thyroid stimulator
    (LATS)  289
LPS  105
Ly alloantigens  99
Lymphatics  **214**
Lymph node  97, 209
Lymphocyte
  absence  325
  activation  182
  activating determinants (Lads)
    246

affinity chromatography  109
alloantigens  98
antigen receptors of T lympho-
    cytes  114
antigen recognition  **108**
antigen suicide  109
bone marrow  131, 133
C3 receptors  103
capping  112
cytotoxic T  188
differentiation, B  **197**
expression of class and subclass
    110
extravasation  214
markers  98
mitogen responsiveness  105
patching  112
physiology  203, **206**
population analysis  105
proliferative defects  325
'purified' T and B cells  **131**
recirculation  **206, 214**
recruitment  219
spleen  131, 133
surface immunoglobulin  103
surface receptors  **99**
T and B  **98**
thoracic duct  131, 133, 207
thymus  131, 132
traffic  **206, 219**
trapping  219
Lymphoid organs
  primary  97, 197, 213
  secondary  97
Lymphoid tissue
  gut associated  97, 199, 212
Lymphokine  179, 322
  classification  183
  cytotoxic  191
  defective production  325
  *in vivo*  192
Lymphon  125, **206**
  tolerance induction  **153**
Lyon phenomenon  14
Lysosome  181, 322
  enzymes  181
Lysozyme  320
Lytic reactions
  biological effects of  **277**

Macrophage  94, 96, 130, 135, 142,
    176, **179**, 180, 211, **274**, 317
  activation  181
  'angry'  181
Marbrook culture  135
Meiosis  16, 77
Memory
  cells  202
    cells T  214
  immunological  76, 93, 317
Metastases  296
Metmyoglobin  50
MHS (major compatibility system)
    **225**

Microbicidal mechanisms   181
MIF   183, 265, 291
Mishell and Dutton culture   135
Mitogen
    induction of cytotoxicity   191
    responsiveness   105
Mixed lymphocyte reaction   226, 249, 251
M locus   **251**
MLR   *see* mixed lymphocyte reaction
MON   153
Mononuclear phagocytes   180
Multiple sclerosis   **265**
Myasthenia gravis   293
Myeloblastic leukaemia   305
Myelomas
    with antibody activity   19
Myeloperoxidase deficiency   329

NAP   53
Negative staining   24
Network theory   127
Neutrophil mobilizing factor   276
Nezelof's syndrome   331
NIP   20, 92, 120, 125
Nucleolar organizer   79
'Nude mice'   134, 191
NZB mice   291
NZB/NZW   288, 292

'One way' reactions
    CML   253
    MLR   252
Ontogeny   198
Opsonic adherence   67, 274
Opsonization
    bacteria   279
Oz markers   6

PALS (periarteriolar lymphoid sheaths)   216
Panhypogammaglobulinaemia   202
Papain   3, 35
Parabiosis   152
Patch formation   112
Pathogens
    killing   179
PC.1   108
Pepsin   3
Pernicious anaemia   293
PGA   126
PHA   105
Phagocytes   **320**
    mononuclear   180
Phagocytins   322
Phagocytosis   322
    of bacteria   279
Phytohaemagglutinin (PHA)   105
Placenta
    immunoglobulin transfer   13
Plaque assay, Jerne   135
Plasma cells   95
    half life   202

Plasmacytoma   3
Plasmin   59, 61
Platelets   **280**
Pokeweed mitogen (PWM)   105
POL   153
Poliomyelitis   266
Polymorphs   182
Polyploid gene duplication   77
Pregnancy   308
Promonocytes
    proliferative defects   325
Properdin   62, 66
Psoriasis   262
PWM   105

Radioimmunoassay   20
Ragweed hayfever   **264**
RAT   126
Reactive lysis   70
Receptors
    lymphocyte surface   **99**
Recombination   17
Recruitment of lymphocytes   219
Reiter's disease   262
Reticular dysgenesis   328
Reticuloendothelial system   94
    antigen presentation   **217**
    antigen uptake   **217**
Reverse transcriptase   22
Rhesus iso-immunization   309
Rheumatic fever   290
Rheumatoid arthritis   290
RNA   14, 22, 121, 123, 206, 290, 302
Rosette   **99**

Scatchard plot   44
Second signal hypothesis   147
Secretory component   9
Segregation of genes   16
Serine/histidine esterases   59
Serum sickness   284
Shutdown of cell traffic in nodes   218
Sips plot   46
Sjögren's syndrome   290
SLE   290, 292
SMAF   191
Somatic mutation hypothesis   **20**
Spermatozoa   308
Spleen   97, 211
Ss-Slp   233
Stem cells   197
Suppression
    allotype   157
    T cell mediated   148, **157**, 288
'Switch' region   3
Synthetic polypeptides in antigenic competition   171
Systemic lupus erythematosus (SLE)   288

T6 chromosome marker   137
Tachyphylaxis   276
Tandem gene duplication   78

Tandem genes
distinction from alleles   16
(T,G)-A--L   49, **244**
Theta antigen   98
Thoracic duct   206
lymphocytes (TDL)   182, 207
Thrombin in complement activation
59
Thy. 1   98
Thymectomy   133, 136
Thymocyte   208
Thymus   97, 208
aplasia   325
Thymus dependancy of antigens
147
Thymus-independant antigens   202
Thyroiditis
autoallergic   288
in obese chickens   293
Tissue typing
graft survival   **257**
TL alloantigens   99
TLA
relationship to *H-2*   233
Tolerance   95, **152**
B cell   155
high zone   154
induction, properties of antigen
**153**
low zone   154
T cell   155
Tolerance induction
antigen dose   154
state of lymphon   **153**
Transplantation antigens   188, 228,
257
Trials, conduct   304

Trials of specific immunotherapy
305
Triggered enzyme cascades   56
Trophoblast   309
Tumour antigens (TSTAs)   **296**
classification   297
detection   297
embryonic   297
viral   297
Tumour
'escape'   299
immunology   **296**
Tumour-specific transplantation
antigens   **296**

Unequal crossing over   78
Unresponsiveness   **152**

Variable region   **9**
genes:
number   **19**
hypervariable regions   11
subgroups   9
Virus
antigens, oncogenic   297
neutralization   43, 279

Wiscott-Aldrich syndrome   327,
331

X-ray crystallography of immunoglobulins   **31**

Yolk sac   198, 208

Zona pellucida   308
Zymosan   61